MW01152942

To Jonathan,
All the best! I hope you
enjoy the book.

Kevin Eeh

SHUT OUT

SHUT OUT

How a Housing Shortage Caused the Great Recession and Crippled Our Economy

KEVIN ERDMANN

ROWMAN & LITTLEFIELD

Lanham • Boulder • New York • London

Published in partnership with the Mercatus Center at
George Mason University

Published by Rowman & Littlefield
A wholly owned subsidiary of The Rowman & Littlefield
Publishing Group, Inc.
4501 Forbes Boulevard, Suite 200, Lanham, Maryland 20706
www.rowman.com

Unit A, Whitacre Mews, 26-34 Stannary Street, London SE11 4AB

British Library Cataloguing in Publication Information Available

978-1-5381-2211-2 cloth
978-1-5381-2212-9 paperback
978-1-5381-2213-6 ebook

Library of Congress Cataloging-in-Publication Data has been requested.

♾™ The paper used in this publication meets the minimum requirements
of American National Standard for Information Sciences—Permanence of
Paper for Printed Library Materials, ANSI/NISO Z39.48-1992.

Printed in the United States of America

[Ludwig Wittgenstein] once greeted me with the question: "Why do people say that it was natural to think that the sun went round the earth rather than that the earth turned on its axis?" I replied: "I suppose, because it looked as if the sun went round the earth." "Well," he asked, "what would it have looked like if it had looked as if the earth turned on its axis?"

—G. E. M. Anscombe, *An Introduction to Wittgenstein's* Tractatus, 2nd edition

CONTENTS

LIST OF FIGURES AND TABLES

FIGURES

TABLE

Introduction

This project started as professional curiosity about the following question: What were the root causes of the housing bubble? The data I checked to confirm the story for myself increasingly shifted my conclusions away from those that were popular at the time. Like everyone else, I once believed that the period before the Great Recession should be characterized as a time of excess—an excess of houses, of money, of federal subsidies, and of activism.

Most of the debates about the bubble accept this characterization as given, and the debates revolve around the causes of the excess. One might blame federal influence—the government-sponsored enterprises such as Fannie Mae and Freddie Mac, the community activists that pressed for more universal home-ownership in the 1990s, or the Federal Reserve that seemingly kept interest rates too low, pumped up asset bubbles, and lined pockets on Wall Street. Or one might blame private financiers—homebuyers caught up in the frenzy of a bubble, bankers grasping for higher fees and high yields on the backs of borrowers who were increasingly in over their heads, securitization that introduced moral hazard into the mortgage market, CEOs ignoring the long term in order to pad their fat bonus checks.

Yet my studies led, to my surprise, to the conclusion that these debates are framed around false premises. The evidence does not support all of those causes—it fact, it often contradicts them. The overriding challenge of the 21st-century economy has not been too much money, too much credit, or too many homes. To the contrary, at the heart of the housing "bubble," the sense of stagnation, and the sense of inequity is a distressing lack of homes.

How could this be? So much ink has been spilled over this topic. So many intelligent minds have toiled over these problems. I have been led to this conclusion because, time and again, as I have looked for ways to confirm the facts, I have found that they contradict the premises of the debate. On a topic that has developed upon such a strong consensus about the premises, it is easy to dismiss an oddball fact that doesn't fit the conventional wisdom. For instance, we don't question gravity when we see a helium balloon rising into the sky or a magician levitating. Gravity is a premise we hold with certainty, so these observations require other explanations. Reasonable people don't spend time second-guessing gravity every time something seems to contradict it. Gravity is canonical.

The concurrence of rising debt levels and various factors that could plausibly cause home prices to rise led to a consensus that some form of excess must have caused home prices to run up. Excess—from one source or another—became canonical as a cause of high home prices. But the canon is wrong. For a decade, explanations of the crisis have been constructed on a Ptolemaic platform where excess money, lending, or federal housing subsidies populate various epicycles meant to explain the housing market and the broader economy. But it is rising rent from a shortage of well-placed housing that is the giant gravitational force around which all else orbits.

We shouldn't ignore an entire body of evidence because of a single outlier. But what if we find one outlier, then another, and another? To understand this book's conclusion you will need to set aside the story that you think you know. This is exceedingly difficult, because there is so much of the story that we have seen with our own eyes, and that has filled us with anger, frustration, and a feeling that scores need to be settled.

Yet I think you will be frequently surprised by the evidence I present. You may come to the end realizing that there is little middle ground in which the conflicting stories can be reconciled.

WHY IS THERE NO MIDDLE GROUND?

The economist Scott Sumner often refers to the problem of "reasoning from a price change." Reasoning from a price change is problematic because, for example, if we think about a price increase in a market characterized by supply and demand, we can draw two potential conclusions: We can conclude that demand has increased, or we can conclude that supply has decreased. Yet these two conclusions suggest diametrically opposed causes and consequences.

Rising demand suggests growth while falling supply suggests deprivation. So it is important to understand the causes behind a price change. If the price of rice is skyrocketing because there has been a drought, trying to fix the problem by decreasing demand would be the height of cruelty. Much of the developed world has been in a politically imposed housing drought, and when households frantically tried to access the housing that was available, we reacted by systematically removing their access to housing by restricting their access to mortgage credit.

This is the nub of the problem. It seems undeniable that from about 1998 to 2005, the housing market experienced an unsustainable surge in both prices and quantities. There was too much building, too much credit—too much demand. Were credit markets or monetary policy to blame for rising home prices? Surely they were, in the same way that oxygen in the air is to blame for a forest fire. We don't fight forest fires by fighting oxygen, yet this is how we have fought the housing bubble. The more appropriate way to fight the bubble would have been to build *more* homes instead of restraining the funding for them. I will demonstrate in the following chapters that there were never too many homes. In fact, there were never enough.

In any market, either cutting demand or increasing supply can pull an inflated price back down, regardless of the cause of the original rise. So, if cutting demand does bring prices down, this is emphatically not a confirmation that excess demand was the problem to begin with. With each year of rising rents and rising home prices, even in the face of a hobbled mortgage market, it becomes clearer that we have actually been suffering from a dearth of supply.

In the following pages, I will demonstrate how housing *supply* has defined the American economy of the past 20 years, not just through its effects on home prices, but also through its effects on monetary policy, wages, cost of living, income inequality, even global capital flows. Policies of housing *deprivation* are at the center of the major economic dilemmas of our time.

A BRIEF INTRODUCTION TO THE PROBLEM

To briefly review, from about 1998 to the end of 2005, on average across the US, home prices persistently rose while housing starts also continued to rise. This is the period I will refer to as the "boom" years or the "bubble" years. The market peaked around the end of 2005, when housing starts began to fall. After that point, home prices generally remained flat until the summer of 2007. Then a series of panics, a financial crisis, and a recession followed. I will refer to this period as the "bust" or the "crisis" period.

An important clue for understanding the housing market during the boom is to view housing markets more locally. National averages cannot convey the fundamental drivers of the market during that time. When we look at the housing market locally, the apparent concurrence of both high home prices and active homebuilding breaks down. There were American cities with strong construction markets and moderate prices. There were also cities with the exact opposite, severely constricted construction markets and very high prices. And there were a few cities where these two regimes briefly collided. At the local level, *constricted* supply is what pushed prices up, and, just as oxygen is drawn into the burning forest by the rising flames, mortgage credit was drawn into those housing markets.

A narrow focus on credit and money has distorted our perception of what happened. We have failed to note many facts that contradict the standard story:

- Housing construction has been constricted in our most prosperous cities. The cities that have historically been sources of opportunity and landing points for immigrants are now so expensive that there are high levels of net domestic migration out of those cities, especially among households with lower incomes. To the extent that housing starts were elevated, they were elevated in cities in the country's interior, where incomes are moderate. In a reversal of the American ideal, families with lower incomes are fleeing prosperous, thriving cities because those cities have sharply curtailed new housing growth. The evidence belies the notion that a housing bubble was built on unsustainable mortgages to buyers with low incomes: in the cities with the most extreme home prices, few households with incomes below the median have mortgages, and families with incomes below the median have been moving away from those housing markets by the millions.

- Home prices in many developed countries rose at least as sharply as in the US. And most of those other countries, such as Canada, did not experience the subsequent sharp drop in home prices that the US did. It is the bust that makes us unusual, not the boom.

- Except during the most dire part of the financial crisis, when households were reducing their housing expenditures involuntarily (via foreclosure), rent inflation has been persistently high for 20 years. Rent for the average home has been rising faster than prices for other goods and services. Housing bubbles are supposed to collapse because home values collapse after overbuilding causes rents to fall. But in 2006 and 2007 (and today), rent inflation was still relatively high. It is difficult to argue that there has ever been an oversupply of housing, even at the national level, when rent inflation has been persistently above core inflation. Wouldn't an oversupply cause rents to decline?[1]

- Growth in real rent expenditures generally had been declining throughout the supposed boom period. In other words, even though we are spending a stable portion of our incomes on rent, this rental expense is buying less house over time. This is because the increase in rents in the expensive cities is inflationary. (The same housing units keep fetching higher rents.) And we can only build large numbers of homes in the places where prices and rents are moderate.

- During the boom, the relative income of the typical homebuyer did not decline.

- During the boom, on average, households that were homeowners did not increase their housing expenditures. (In other words, the rental value of their homes was not increasing, relative to their incomes. They were not "buying up.")

- Homeownership rates, even at their peak levels in 2004, among age groups under 65 years old, were no higher than homeownership rates had been in the late 1970s and early 1980s—this despite the fact that mortgage interest rates at that time had been well above 10%.

- As figure 0-1 demonstrates, when taking account of all types of housing, the number of new housing units never even rose very far above the long-term average. The truly important deviation from the long-term average has been the deep decline in housing starts since 2005.

These findings suggest that we did not have a housing bubble. We had a housing supply bust—first in the places where people want to live, in places where there is more economic opportunity. That supply bust caused prices to rise to extreme levels in those cities—most notably in New York City, Los Angeles, Boston, and San Francisco—metropolitan areas I call the Closed Access cities. After the turn of the century, millions of households flooded out of those cities because of the shortage of housing—so many that they overwhelmed cities in the main destinations for those households, such as inland California, Arizona, and Florida. Then we imposed a credit and monetary bust on the entire country in a misplaced attempt to alleviate the problem.

Because aggregate national housing starts were rising at the same time that prices in the supply-constrained areas were exploding, we assumed, reasonably but incorrectly, that this was excess demand—too much money and credit. We

Figure 0-1. US Housing Starts Plus Manufactured Home Shipments

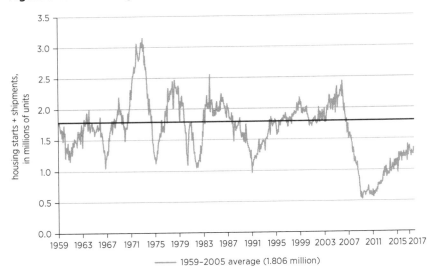

Note: The annual rates of housing starts and manufactured home shipments are seasonally adjusted.
Source: US Census Bureau, Manufactured Housing Survey, "Shipments of New Manufactured Homes: 1959–2017" data available at "MHS Latest Data," https://www.census.gov/data/tables/time-series /econ/mhs/latest-data.html, and data for new housing units started available at "Historical Data," https://www.census.gov/construction/nrc/historical_data/index.html.

experienced a moral panic about these false premises, and—as moral panics tend to do—this led us to create even larger problems while failing to address the root problems that triggered the panic in the first place. Now the supply problem has spread nationwide, and millions of American homeowners and potential homeowners have been needlessly harmed.

How could we have concluded that there was a housing bubble just because of that little blip of activity above the long-term average in 2004 and 2005? Figure 0-2 shows housing starts and shipments, disaggregated by type. Single-unit housing starts did look very strong during the boom period, and this is the measure we most often talk about, because this is where most homeownership happens. But multi-unit housing starts and manufactured home production were both at half the levels normally experienced during expansions.[2]

Housing construction appears even more inflated if we only look at new single-family homes built for sale. This is because homebuilding has become increasingly consolidated among tract homebuilders. This was the only type of homebuilding that was expanding, while the other housing conduits—multi-unit housing, manufactured home shipments, and single-family units built by owners or by contractors—were stagnant or falling. In other words,

Figure 0-2. US Housing Starts and Shipments by Type

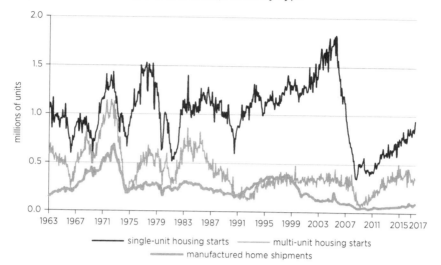

single-unit housing starts ———— multi-unit housing starts
———— manufactured home shipments

Note: The annual rates of housing starts and manufactured home shipments are seasonally adjusted.
Source: US Census Bureau, Manufactured Housing Survey, "Shipments of New Manufactured Homes:
1959–2017" data available at "MHS Latest Data," https://www.census.gov/data/tables/time-series
/econ/mhs/latest-data.html, and data for new housing units started available at "Historical Data,"
https://www.census.gov/construction/nrc/historical_data/index.html.

the perception of an oversupply of houses was enforced by a selective observer
bias. All of that growth (relative to the 1970s and 1980s) was simply a shift of
market share away from the other conduits for new housing units, which
have increasingly been impeded by new regulatory barriers—especially multi-
unit housing in the Closed Access cities.[3]

What's more, the extra new homes were built in cities where home prices were
moderate. This isn't the picture of a speculative bubble. This is the picture of a
distorted migration pattern, driven by limited access to urban opportunity.

We tried to solve that supply problem by imposing a demand bust. The
demand bust succeeded so well that a decade later we are still mired in the
most depressed period of homebuilding since the Great Depression. Since the
demand bust didn't solve the supply problem—in fact, it made it worse—
the problems we associate with the bubble are now worse. This has led to
rising housing costs, income stagnation and inequality, and labor markets
that have been slow to recover. We have put a lid on mortgage credit markets,
spreading the supply bust to the entire country—and now families in coastal
California and the Northeast, who are under economic stress *because of the
housing shortage*, have even fewer options than they did before. We need stable

and growth-sustaining monetary policy and credit markets. Instead, for a decade, monetary and credit policies have been managed explicitly to reduce real investment, as if our problem were having too much—as if the investments we *were* making had been fake or unsustainable.

This book is not a defense of economic recklessness. It is not a defense of financial activities that are systemically destabilizing. And it is certainly not a defense of fraud or misrepresentation. But the existence of those factors when home prices were at their peak is not proof that those factors are the root cause of the high prices. Million-dollar bungalows in places like coastal California have not arrived at those prices because of unscrupulous lenders or speculators. Those high prices are tolls on opportunity. Families who would like nothing more than to live in a house worth a quarter as much must pay the toll for access to jobs and economic opportunities that are located near those houses. They must pay this toll because a handful of cities that are capturing the gains of the new postindustrial economy have virtual walls around them, creating a national divide between haves and have-nots. Americans have not, by and large, been taking out mortgages to fund unsustainable consumption. We have been taking out mortgages in a bid to go where the jobs are.

CHAPTER SUMMARIES

The chapters that follow are divided among three parts.

Part I: The Things We Didn't Know and the Things We Knew That Just Weren't So

Chapter 1 demonstrates that there was never an oversupply of homes. To the contrary, in a handful of cities where economic opportunities are numerous, there has been a severe shortage of homes. Among metro areas, high prices and high rents correlate strongly with the lack of housing supply. This was the cause of high home prices before the financial crisis.

Chapter 2 shows that, before the financial crisis, US housing prices were not particularly unusual compared to prices in similar countries, so there is no reason to look to domestic credit markets, monetary policy, or American federal housing policies to explain price behavior at that time. Sharply rising prices were not particularly related to rising homeownership rates, and where homeownership did increase, it was among professionals with college educations and high incomes. Furthermore, homeowners, on average, were not buying "up," but were buying "down," frequently by migrating to less expensive cities.

Chapter 3 further outlines how, to understand the housing bubble, we must focus on the differences between cities. Research that seemed to point to credit supply for marginal homeowners as the root cause of rising prices ignored the differences between cities and focused narrowly on how rising home prices differed within cities between low-end and high-end housing markets. But the difference in price changes between low-end LA and high-end LA was a small fraction of the difference in price changes between, say, any area in LA and any area in Chicago. It is a lack of supply that makes LA different from Chicago. This is further confirmed by the realization that (1) first-time home-ownership rates were declining at the height of the credit boom, and (2) prices in neighborhoods that seemed to have credit booms have remained high relative to those in other cities, even though mortgage markets have since become very tight.

Part II: What Really Happened

Chapter 4 shows that, in almost every city, before 2008 there was little difference in price appreciation between low-end markets that might have been stimulated by loose lending and high-end markets that would have been less dependent on lending standards. Viewed carefully, different rates of home price changes within cities actually confirm that limited supply was the cause of rising prices, and it was only after 2008, when public policy imposed extremely tight credit markets, that low-end prices collapsed compared to high-end prices. Low-end housing was not propped up by loose lending, and its collapse was not inevitable. In fact, the collapse was publicly imposed.

Chapter 5 shows that the housing bubble was an acceleration of the long-term segregation by income that American households are engaging in as a result of the deprivation of housing in coastal urban centers. Households with high incomes move into those cities, and they bid up both the rent and the price of the limited housing stock until a household with less financial means is forced to move away to the more welcoming cities in the country's interior. By 2005, this segregation had accelerated so much that migrants seeking more affordable cities overwhelmed places like Arizona and Florida. The housing bubble in those places was a bubble in compromised economic opportunity and exclusion. We had something more than a credit boom—we had a refugee crisis.

Part III: Symptoms of the Urban Housing Shortage

Chapter 6 explores the perverse reversal of the traditional pattern of free people moving toward economic opportunity, and how this is leading to a geographically segregated nation of haves and have-nots.

Chapter 7 explains how concerns about the economic power of firms are misplaced. The monopoly power that is claiming the income of workers is the monopoly power of real estate owners in housing-deprived cities, who exclude potential new housing and charge ever-rising rents. This situation means that workers are prevented from transitioning to new service-sector jobs that are available in these cities—and workers who are in these cities must fork over much of their income to the real estate owners.

Chapter 8 explores the international effects of the urban housing shortage. The effects of Closed Access may be at the root of the rising trade deficit and the inflow of global capital.

Chapter 9 provides a brief summary of perhaps the worst outcome of the housing shortage, which was the moral panic that ensued when high prices were blamed on speculation and lending. The US succeeded in bringing prices down with contractionary monetary and credit policies that did nothing to remedy the foundational cause of high prices. Contrary to conventional wisdom, the trigger of the financial crisis was not a surge of mortgage defaults among working-class homeowners. Losses among middle-class and working-class homeowners came late in the crisis, as a result of the recession and the disastrous monetary and credit policy decisions.

The epilogue uses notions of "open access orders" and "limited access orders," which were developed by the economists Douglass C. North, John Joseph Wallis, and Barry R. Weingast, as a conceptual framework for considering the difficult path ahead for cities that have lost the presumption of universal access and free entry for labor and capital.

PART I

THE THINGS WE DIDN'T KNOW AND THE THINGS WE KNEW THAT JUST WEREN'T SO

CHAPTER 1
High Home Prices Are Caused
by Limited Supply

The central challenge facing postindustrial economies lies in the fact that key urban centers have become more important than they used to be. They are the gateways to new sources of abundance, innovation, and growth. At one time 40 acres and a mule opened a path to tolerable self-sufficiency. Today, the same pathway begins with 400 square feet and a subway pass. Anyone wishing to participate in the new economy, however, faces a roadblock: the millions of residents who already live in the key cities. The political system has been blocking the expansion of housing where housing can provide broad opportunity.

Exploding housing costs were a symptom of the housing shortage, but experts blamed high costs on money and credit, convincing themselves that there was *too much* housing. In fact, housing *deprivation* is the challenge of our era.

The low level of new housing starts depicted in the introduction appears even more severe if housing units are viewed in proportion to population growth. As shown in figure 1-1, the number of new housing units per new resident was lower during the past 30 years than it had been for the previous 30 years.

The stagnation in new construction is also confirmed by data on the housing stock. Figure 1-2 shows that the housing stock, adjusted for population,[1] leveled off in the early 1990s and then *declined*. The slight rise in the number of units per adult during the boom after the turn of the century was not an aberration from past levels or growth rates. How could this be? And how did experts arrive at the conclusion that the problem with the economy at this time was an oversupply of homes?

Figure 1-1. New US Housing Units Relative to Population Growth

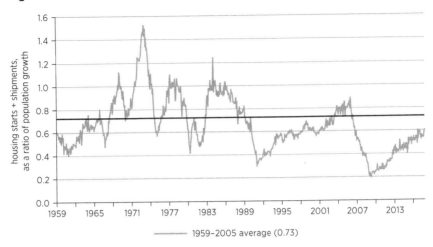

——— 1959–2005 average (0.73)

Note: The annual rates of housing starts and manufactured home shipments are seasonally adjusted.
Sources: US Census Bureau, Manufactured Housing Survey, "Shipments of New Manufactured Homes: 1959–2017" data available at "MHS Latest Data," https://www.census.gov/data/tables/time-series/econ /mhs/latest-data.html, and data for new housing units started available at "Historical Data," https://www .census.gov/construction/nrc/historical_data/index.html; US Census Bureau, "Total Population: All Ages Including Armed Forces Overseas" (POP), retrieved from FRED, Federal Reserve Bank of St. Louis.

Figure 1-2. US Housing Stock, Adjusted for Population

Note: For the purposes of this graph, *adult* means over age 16. Also, an adjustment after the 2000 census in the estimated number of housing units creates a discontinuity in this graph at the end of 2001. This may mean that the number of units became overstated during the 1990s, so that the trend shift to flat or falling numbers of units dates more firmly to the early 1990s. That would better match the housing starts data.
Sources: Table 8 (Quarterly Estimates of the Housing Inventory: 1965 to Present) and table 8a (Estimates of the Housing Inventory) in US Census Bureau, "Housing Vacancies and Homeownership (CPS/HVS): Historical Tables," last modified April 26, 2016, http://www.census.gov/housing/hvs/data/histtabs .html; Bureau of Labor Statistics, "Civilian Noninstitutional Population" (CNP16OV), retrieved from FRED, Federal Reserve Bank of St. Louis.

Housing starts, especially for single-family homes built for sale, were strong before 2006. This reflected a change in housing expansion, from a focus on multi-unit, owner-built, and manufactured home types to a focus on homes built for sale. One reason for the shift away from multi-unit buildings was the development of what I call Closed Access cities. Cities that have long been emblems of opportunity—cities that once were filled with tenements teeming with ambitious immigrants—have swung to the opposite extreme. Now they are mega-sized gated communities, unwilling or unable to allow significant new housing of any kind. The United States has split into distinctly different areas, characterized by local restrictions on housing expansion. The Closed Access areas—generally coastal California and the urban Northeast—have developed strong local economies and potentially lucrative labor markets, but they are unable, or unwilling, to accommodate the inflow of labor with new housing. Most of the rest of the country has not developed such tight legal constraints on housing expansion.

Since the Closed Access cities have become so defined by the exclusivity created through limited housing expansion, the difference between metropolitan areas has become an increasingly important factor influencing the price of homes. When I refer to specific metropolitan areas, I generally mean specific metropolitan statistical area (MSA) designations defined by the Census Bureau and used by many information sources, such as Zillow. (Metropolitan statistical areas typically include all the urbanized counties around a major city.) While many local factors can affect housing markets in individual neighborhoods in various idiosyncratic ways, the markets across individual MSAs do exhibit systematic behavior. This is similar to analysis that is common in the stock market. The stock of an individual firm has a strong statistical relationship with factors on at least three distinct levels: with the stock market in general, with other firms in its sector, and with its own unique constraints and opportunities. Likewise, home prices can be influenced at the national level (by interest rates, for instance), at the MSA level (by local income trends and supply constraints), and at the local level (by very local shifts in neighborhood character and patterns of development).

At times, I refer to MSAs more casually as "cities." Unless I specify that I am referring to a city as a political area, I am generally referring to the metropolitan area, since the metropolitan area is the scale at which housing market substitutions tend to create systematic behaviors across all households in a common, interconnected commuting zone.

I divide the 20 largest metropolitan areas into four general groups: Closed Access cities, Contagion cities, Open Access cities, and Uncategorized cities.[2]

- *Closed Access cities.* The Closed Access cities are New York City, Los Angeles, Boston, San Francisco (with San Jose), and San Diego. These cities have a distinct signature—very low housing starts (even during expansions), high incomes, high rents (even relative to those high incomes), high rent inflation, high prices (even relative to rents), and large rates of out-migration of households with low incomes, especially during the housing boom.

- *Contagion cities.* The Contagion cities are Miami;[3] Riverside, California; Phoenix; and Tampa, Florida. These cities experienced a brief period of sharply rising home prices, but they differ from Closed Access cities in the other respects. Their housing bubbles were caused by massive in-migration from the Closed Access cities. These cities had a refugee crisis of sorts. In this way, they are the mirror image of the Closed Access cities.

- *Open Access cities.* The Open Access cities are Dallas–Fort Worth,[4] Houston, and Atlanta. These growing cities are able to build enough new homes to meet demand. They did not experience the massive migration inflows from Closed Access cities that overwhelmed the Contagion cities, so home prices remained moderate throughout the housing boom. Housing price trends in these cities tend to look much like housing price trends in most of the smaller regional metropolitan areas and rural areas.

- *Uncategorized cities.* The cities of Chicago; Philadelphia; Washington, DC; Detroit; Seattle; Minneapolis; St. Louis; and Baltimore don't fit easily into the other groups. Some of these cities, like Washington, Seattle, and Chicago, are dealing with the same pressures that the Closed Access cities are, and housing costs there have increased. But at the metropolitan area level, housing starts in these cities tend to be much more generous than in the Closed Access cities, housing costs as a proportion of incomes are near national norms, and domestic migration out of the cities isn't as extreme as for the Closed Access cities. Some of these cities have been dealing with struggling economies, so there isn't as much pressure on housing supply. Yet before the recession, even Detroit and St. Louis, with their struggling economies, issued permits at a higher rate than the major Closed Access cities did.

It should be pointed out that this housing crisis is an international phenomenon—especially in the Anglosphere—from Sydney to London to

Vancouver, although it appears that the international cities where home prices have risen have generally expanded their housing stock more generously than the US Closed Access cities have. The international examples might be more comparable to Seattle than to our Closed Access cities.

TWO VERY DIFFERENT HOUSING MARKETS

Housing statistics in the decade after 2000 indicated that we were living in an economy that was simultaneously characterized by rising mortgage credit, rising housing construction, and rising home prices. But if the country is divided between the Closed Access cities and the more open areas, it turns out that relatively few places fit this description in its entirety. Some places experienced moderate home prices and high levels of housing construction, and others had high home prices and low levels of housing construction. In a few places these two markets collided briefly—namely, cities in Arizona, Nevada, inland California, and Florida, which are the areas we most clearly associate with a bubble. But these areas were an anomaly. That's why I call these the Contagion cities. They have little in common with the Closed Access cities that are responsible for the bulk of the problem.

When the country was viewed as a whole, it appeared that irresponsible credit expansion had allowed new homebuyers to engage in wild speculation, causing home prices to veer wildly from long-standing norms relative to rents and to incomes. Viewed on an individual basis, however, few places in fact met this description. In some cities, rents were stable and so were prices. In others, rents were relentlessly rising and so were prices—and, it happens, so were local incomes. Credit markets have little to do with these differing housing markets. Limited access to opportunity does.

Figure 1-3 compares the levels of housing permits issued in several metropolitan areas. Los Angeles has peak levels of housing permits issued that are well below the national norm. Rates of housing starts in all the Closed Access cities are similar to those in Los Angeles. And there is little response to cyclical demand in those cities. High prices do not trigger a significant rise in housing construction in Closed Access cities. The binding constraint is political, and it kicks in well below any sort of healthy rate of expansion.

There are several points to ponder while considering figure 1-3. First, compare Seattle and Los Angeles. Note that before the 1990 recession, both cities permitted more new units than the national average. Then the rate of new units plummeted in both. Seattle remains above average, however, while Los Angeles, like the other Closed Access cities, is persistently well below average.

Figure 1-3. Housing Expansion, by Metro Area

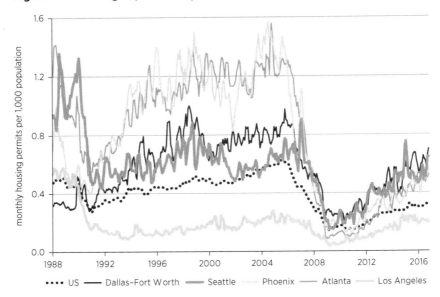

Note: Data are smoothed with a three-month moving average.
Sources: US Census Bureau, "Building Permits Survey," http://www.census.gov/construction/bps/; table CA1 (Personal Income, Population, Per Capita Personal Income) from Bureau of Economic Analysis, available at https://apps.bea.gov/iTable/index_regional.cfm; US Census Bureau, "Total Population: All Ages Including Armed Forces Overseas" (POP), retrieved from FRED, Federal Reserve Bank of St. Louis.

In some ways, one might wonder what Seattle gains by allowing that extra building. Rent inflation has been high in Seattle. Home prices are nearly at the same levels in Seattle as they are in the Closed Access cities.

Seattle is at a crossroads. If the city had building rates closer to those of Phoenix or Atlanta, this extra supply would likely bring local rents and prices down. As it is, Seattle attracts many highly skilled workers who earn high incomes, and—to an extent—they bid local housing costs up to reflect their high incomes. But there are enough new units in Seattle that residents with lower incomes can generally make adjustments and find housing within the metropolitan area that can fit in their budget. The extremely low rate of housing permits in Los Angeles does cause prices there to be somewhat higher than in Seattle. But, once costs hit a certain range where they are uncomfortable for the typical household, rising rents cause households to move away from the city. So the most significant difference between the Closed Access cities and Seattle is that thousands of households with low incomes are forced to move away from the Closed Access cities every year.

Supply moderates rents and prices. In the cities with above-average housing permits, that supply comes from new units. In the Closed Access cities, that supply must come from emptying existing units when families finally become discouraged enough to stop trying to keep up with the rising cost of living, and they move away.

Second, look at the other cities shown in figure 1-3—Phoenix, Atlanta, and Dallas—and notice the large amount of variation among cities. Supply in those cities comes online in response to population growth. All of those cities were building new units at roughly the same rate in 2005 as they had been for a decade. Phoenix and Atlanta were building about 1.3 units per 1,000 residents per month. Most of those units were claimed by households moving into these cities. Populations were rising along with the housing stock. For Phoenix or Atlanta to develop an oversupply of units strong enough to shut down the builders' market for even one year, the builders would need to build at a rate of more than 2 units per 1,000 residents per month for an extended period of time. Oversupply in those cities would have required an extreme aberration in the rate of new units, which simply didn't happen—and in fact could not realistically happen.

When a shock to migration rates or local incomes happens and local housing markets contract in response to the shock, in a city like Atlanta or Phoenix, this contraction will always look like an oversupply problem. Yet, ironically, the only cities where permanent reductions in prices or rents could be realistically triggered by additional supply are the cities that currently suffer from severe undersupply, because in those cities, rents and prices are far above the natural costs of building new units.

Finally, look at all the cities in 2006. If oversupply was the key issue, it would have been a local phenomenon. But construction was collapsing throughout the country by 2006. Even construction in Los Angeles was declining. The housing collapse was caused by a national phenomenon, it was in effect by 2006, and it had nothing to do with oversupply. Clearly, oversupply did not apply to Los Angeles. And, in fact, it is implausible that a simultaneous drop of this scale in construction activity in cities across the country could have been triggered by oversupply.

There were no growing cities with a disruptive oversupply of housing in 2005, but there were a handful of cities with such an *undersupply* of housing that families with lower incomes had been moving away from them by the hundreds of thousands each year. Suddenly, from 2006 to 2008, that flow ground nearly to a halt—even though housing starts in the undersupplied cities were declining along with housing starts in every other type of city.[5]

Figure 1-4. Housing Permits per Resident, 1996–2005

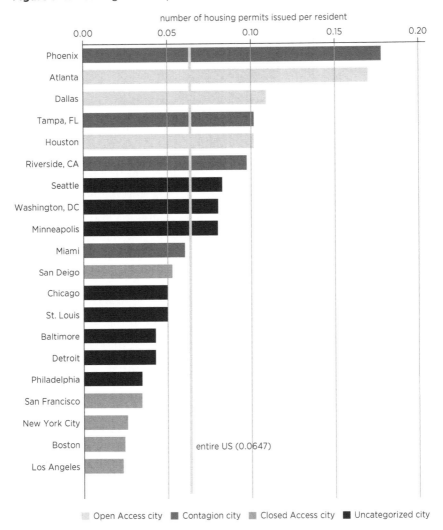

Sources: US Census Bureau, "Building Permits Survey," http://www.census.gov/construction/bps/; table CA1 (Personal Income, Population, Per Capita Personal Income) from Bureau of Economic Analysis, available at https://apps.bea.gov/iTable/index_regional.cfm; US Census Bureau, "Total Population: All Ages Including Armed Forces Overseas" (POP), retrieved from Federal Reserve Bank of St. Louis (FRED), https://fred.stlouisfed.org.

Figure 1-4 compares the rates of housing permit approval across the top 20 metropolitan areas. For most cities, there is a noticeable relationship between supply and demand. Growing cities with strong demand tend to approve more housing to meet demand. The Open Access cities do this very well. The

Figure 1-5. Relative Home Prices, by Metro Area

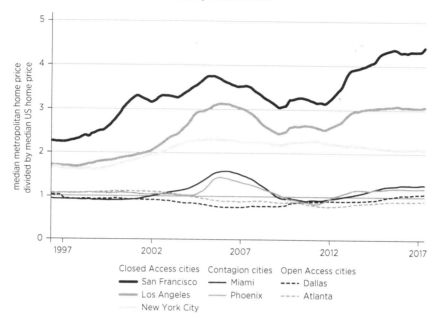

Closed Access cities Contagion cities Open Access cities
San Francisco Miami ---- Dallas
Los Angeles Phoenix ---- Atlanta
New York City

Source: Zillow Home Value Index for metropolitan areas, Zillow data, http://www.zillow.com/research /data/.

Contagion cities tend to do this well but were overwhelmed by too many Closed Access refugees. The other cities respond to demand fairly well, though not as well as the Open Access cities. Oddly, the cities with the lowest rate of housing approvals are either cities dealing with economic decline, such as Detroit, or cities that are the centerpieces of new economic growth, such as San Francisco.

Shifting to the topic of home prices, the Closed Access cities are simply in a different league from other cities. Figure 1-5 compares relative median home prices in several metropolitan areas. Notice that in Phoenix, which was a bubble city where prices briefly shot up at the height of the boom, home prices never even reached the long-term bottom range of prices in the Closed Access cities. Most of the rest of the country had home prices that were moderate.

It has been widely reported that high prices during the housing boom triggered an overinvestment in and an oversupply of homes. A review of the metropolitan areas instead of the national numbers shows, however, that this clearly did not happen. The cities where home prices were double the national average, or more, did not respond to high prices by building more houses. Instead, they have produced a transfer of payments from new renters and owners to the lucky owners who got there first.

The constraint on housing has been a problem in New York City and New England for at least half a century. Population peaked in Manhattan around 1910. Population on the island has fallen by 30% since then, but this is not for lack of demand.

Population in coastal California grew until more recently. Although San Francisco's housing stock began to stagnate decades ago, as late as the 1980s metropolitan coastal California was still growing at a pace above the national average, mostly owing to Los Angeles. This trend shifted in the 1990s.

The constraint is political, not physical. In 1960, the city of Los Angeles was zoned for a population of 10 million, and by 1990, its zoned capacity had shrunk to about 4 million. That is about the population of the city today.[6] This zoning-capacity shrinkage is the case with many of the supply-constrained cities. Much as many Americans have immigrant ancestors who would not have been admitted under today's immigration standards, in many cases Americans live in homes that would not qualify under their cities' current zoning standards. One commonly referenced measure of housing affordability, called the price-to-income ratio (price/income ratio), is the ratio of the price of the median house to median household income. How many years' worth of income would the typical family need to save to buy the typical house? In 1986, before the political constraint from zoning had become binding in Los Angeles, the median price/income ratio for a home was about 3.9×. In Dallas, it was about 3.3×. By the end of 2005, in Dallas it was *down* to 2.8×. In Los Angeles, it was *up* to 11.3×. LA homes have become four times more expensive than Dallas homes, relative to local incomes.[7]

Home prices in the Closed Access cities were somewhat high in the 1980s. This was caused partly by urban density and other geographic factors. Median housing costs might naturally be as much as 50% higher in some metropolitan areas, but the politically created supply problem has pushed those prices to double, triple, or quadruple the national average. This is not the product of geography or natural building costs; it is a political constraint.

Figure 1-6 charts this shift in population growth in the main California metro areas. Growth shifted to below the national average in the early 1990s, then it shifted further down *during the boom*. The combined population of the LA, San Francisco, and San Diego metropolitan areas was *lower* in 2007 than it was in 2004.

This is striking because home prices in these cities were astronomical at the time—in a different league from prices in the rest of the country. The natural

Figure 1-6. Population Growth in Metropolitan Coastal California

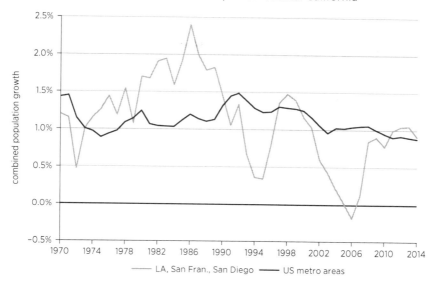

Source: table CA1 (Personal Income, Population, Per Capita Personal Income) from Bureau of Economic Analysis, available at https://www.bea.gov/iTable/index_regional.cfm.

response, to build more housing in a booming local economy, did not occur in these cities. This is especially striking when we consider that incomes in these cities were rising during this same period.

HIGH PRICES STEM FROM HIGH RENTS

It is important for readers to understand the terminology that will be used in this book. Every home has value as shelter; this is called "rent." This value exists whether the home is occupied by a tenant who actually writes a check to a landlord each month or by an owner who does not write a rent check: in either case, the home has rental value to its occupants. Some homeowners have no mortgage at all, and some have mortgages that require large monthly payments. Those mortgage payments are typically part of the family budget, so that is how homeowners think about the cost of housing. But the rental value of each home exists independently of each owner's specific cash financing outlays.

The ownership of a home is a condition separate from tenancy. It is more analogous to owning a financial security, which has future net rental income as its income stream. Its present value is determined by rent growth expectations, long-term interest rates, taxes, and risk premiums.

By comparing home prices and rents over time and across cities, we can get a good idea of the influence of each of these factors, which all have play important roles during the boom and bust. The term "median rent" will refer to the rental value of the median home, regardless of whether it is owned or rented.[8]

Home prices have largely risen because local home rental values have risen. Our most dynamic cities have become especially valuable because of what economists call agglomeration economics. Transportation costs have declined, making the concentration of goods-producing networks less important. But since easier transportation and communication make it easier to spread the value of ideas and knowledge, cities that are knowledge centers attract a dense network of highly skilled information workers who gain important marginal value from being physically close to one another.[9] For example, a janitor in Memphis can clean the floors as well as a janitor in San Francisco. But a tech designer can become immensely more productive by changing locations. In San Francisco, the designer can bounce ideas off coworkers who have also been attracted to the creative hub, evaluate roommates' skunk works and plans, or bump into a young tech entrepreneur at the coffee shop. The designer can also join in many potential new undertakings without moving or disconnecting from this network.

This networking value leads to tremendous demand for residential housing in close proximity to innovative economic centers. The demand for dense, centralized housing has exceeded the willingness of postmodern Western cities to supply it. As a result, when workers move into cities to gain access to prime labor markets, they bid up the price of existing housing until a household with lower income is forced out. The limit to housing expansion that prevents home prices from reverting to normal levels also becomes a limit to labor migration, preventing incomes from reverting to normal levels.

The technology revolution has created a regime shift in the value of these cities, and in recent years they have become extreme outliers in terms of income and housing costs.

Figure 1-7 is a scatterplot of the 100 largest metropolitan areas. The x-axis is the median income of each metropolitan area, relative to the US median income. The y-axis is a measure of rent affordability (i.e., rent as a proportion of income). The plot compares 1991 to 2018. In 1991, rent in most cities claimed about 15% to 25% of the median income, and few cities were far from the norm in either income or rent affordability. This is the natural pattern in a free society.

In other words, if local incomes rise in a booming city, people who are free to move in search of opportunity will migrate to that city, and this will continue until the opportunities in the booming city are no longer superior to those

Figure 1-7. Incomes and Rent Affordability, by Metro Area

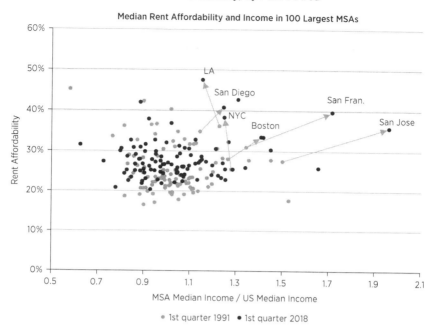

Note: The chart includes the 100 largest US metropolitan statistical areas (MSAs).
Source: Zillow data, http://www.zillow.com/research/data/. Rent affordability is the percentage of the median household income required to rent the median home.

in the potential migrators' cities of origin. Sometimes we can see this in the extreme, such as in California during the Gold Rush. But most of the time this happens incrementally. Residents self-select, and those who are willing to take risks and leave behind the safety of home move to greener pastures, while others stay put. For decades, residents from places like the Deep South moved to northern cities. At the same time, some industries moved their production facilities to areas where incomes were lower. At a certain point, the northern cities presented more opportunities, but over time, this freedom of movement actually helped to equalize incomes between the North and South, and income growth in poorer areas outpaced growth in more prosperous areas.

By the late 1990s, though, an odd pattern emerged. Some of the cities with high incomes started to also develop high housing-rental costs. These were the cities where home prices were extraordinarily high. The prices were a product of this ratcheting up of both local rents and local income levels. These were the cities where homes *weren't* being built. During the housing boom, in the few cities where new housing supply is constrained, incomes and prices began to move away from the norm. Geographically, now, incomes were diverging instead of converging, and the cause was a lack of housing.

High home prices were broadly blamed on an excess of money and credit instead of a dearth of supply, so after 2005, instead of addressing the supply problem, federal policymakers tightened monetary policy and government support of mortgage credit, even while private mortgage markets were collapsing. The misdiagnosis of the housing boom made the supply problem even worse. The severe lack of new construction in the most dynamic US cities has caused both incomes and rents to move even further from the norm since the financial crisis.

This is a striking turn of events. Households in cities with the highest incomes don't just spend more income on housing; they actually spend a higher *proportion* of their incomes on housing. This is a clear sign that housing is operating as a constraint on the dynamics of a free economy.[10]

In the time since the financial crisis, that statement can be made about the entire country. Housing construction has been at very low levels across the country since the financial crisis, so the affordability problem has spread to every city. In 1991, rent in most cities claimed less than 25% of the median income. But by 2018, rent claimed more than 25% of the median income in all but the least expensive cities.

Increasing the supply of houses would have brought both prices and rents down, but limiting demand for home*ownership* through credit regulation has brought prices and supply down, which has only pushed *rents* higher. Attempting to rein in the cost of ownership has been a calamitous error. Rent affordability—the more important measure of housing costs—has become much worse as a result.

NOT THE SUM OF ITS PARTS

One reason that the housing bubble was blamed on credit and demand instead of on a lack of supply is that on a national level it appeared that prices had become unmoored from rents. Estimates of national price-to-rent ratios (price/rent ratios) rose by 40% or more from the mid-1990s to the peak of the boom in 2005. About half of the increase was due to falling real long-term interest rates that affected home values in all cities. This alone would not have moved home prices far from long-term ranges. The other half of the increase was due to rising prices in cities affected by limited supply.

Figure 1-8 shows the development over time of home prices, relative to rents, by metropolitan area. In 1991, there was some relationship between rent and

Figure 1-8. Median Home Prices and Annual Rent, by Metro Area

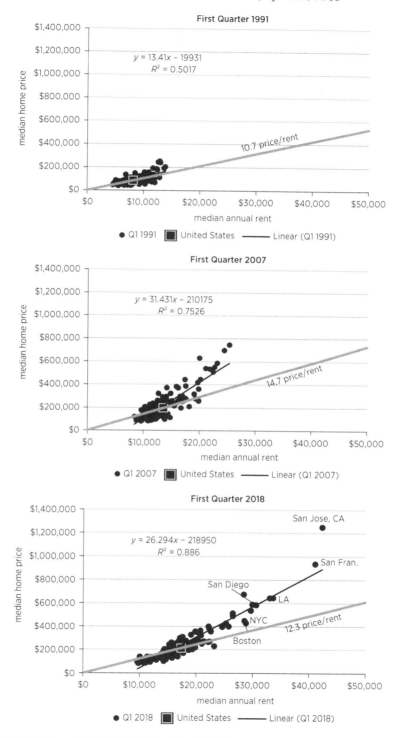

Note: The charts each include 151 US metropolitan statistical areas.
Sources: Data inferred from price-to-income ratio, rent affordability, and median household income measures from Zillow data, http://www.zillow.com/research/data/.

home price. At the time, the median US price/rent ratio was about 10.7×,[11] so the slope of the relationship between price and rent in metropolitan areas of about 13.4× suggests that, on average, households paid more for homes in cities roughly in proportion to the different rents in those cities.

By the end of the housing bubble, in 2007, the median US price/rent ratio had risen from 10.7× to 14.7×, indicating that prices were now somewhat higher, on average, relative to rents. But a few large cities developed very high prices, even relative to the fast-rising rents.

In other words, two things happened between the early 1990s and 2007, and we can see them on these graphs. First, in just a handful of cities, rents shot up far above the national average. (The dots for those cities moved sharply to the right.)

Second, prices in those cities rose even more.[12] The national median price/rent ratio was about 15×, so in a city where annual rent rose from $10,000 to $20,000, we might expect home prices to have risen from $150,000 to $300,000, in proportion. Instead, home prices in cities with rising rents rose at twice the rate that rents did. (The median home cost $15 for each dollar's worth of rental value. Yet the slope of the regression line in the 2007 panel is 31×, which means that for each extra dollar of additional rental value, a homebuyer had to pay an additional $31.) A home in a city with median rent of $20,000 was now selling for about $450,000 instead of $300,000.

Households now had to pay two premiums to gain access to these cities. The first premium was the higher rent. The second premium was the cost of the home, which now reflected both a higher present rental income and a premium for expected future rent inflation.[13] Contrary to the cacophony of reports that home prices became unmoored from rents, the correlation between rent and price strengthened during the housing bubble. On a national scale, it appeared as if rents explained very little, leaving credit expansion as the obvious cause of higher home prices.[14] But this impression is reversed when metro areas are viewed individually, and rent and income effectively explain home price behavior around the country. As rising rent in the Closed Access cities moved further from the national norm, it became a more important factor in the value of homes.

The relationship shown here actually *understates* the rising rents and costs in the Closed Access cities, because the first response of households to rising rents is usually to compensate by reducing their real housing consumption.[15] If households weren't making this adjustment, the median rents and home prices of the Closed Access cities would have moved even further from the norm.[16]

Since the supply problem has only worsened since the collapse in mortgage credit markets, by 2018 rent had shifted even higher among the Closed Access

Figure 1-9. Price-to-Rent Ratios and Annual Rent Levels for 151 Metro Areas

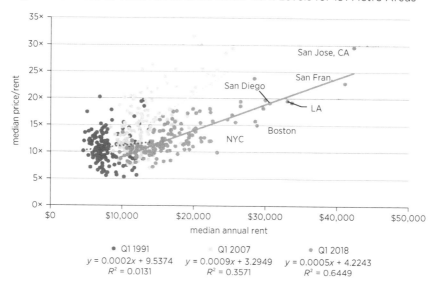

cities, and it became an even more important factor in relative home prices among the metropolitan areas.

The collapse in home prices that has come along with the collapse of the mortgage credit market has pulled down the prices of homes, relative to rents, across the country. Home values have fallen in metropolitan areas, and the median price/rent ratio in the US in 2018 was about 12.3×. The slope of the regression line for the metropolitan areas is 26.3×. So the prices of homes in the housing-constrained cities still rise at about twice the rate (26.3×) of the price/rent level for homes in the median city (12.3×). We have reduced the prices of homes by limiting access to credit, but we have done nothing to fix the cause of the high prices—high rents and expectations that those rents will continue to rise. The relationship between rent and price has remained strong both during the boom, when mortgages were flowing, and during the bust, when mortgage access dried up.

It is helpful to view figure 1-8 in terms of price/rent ratios instead of in terms of prices. I have shown this in figure 1-9. This perspective shows that across metropolitan areas, in 1991, there was really no relationship between rent and the price/rent ratio, because the effect of urban housing constraints was weak in

1991. But increasingly over time, through boom and bust, a systematic relation-ship between rent levels and price/rent levels has developed.[17]

What could be the reason for the relationship between rent levels and price/rent levels? Here are four potential reasons:

1. Where rents are high, it is the result of limited housing in cities where incomes and rents continue to rise as households with high incomes continue to crowd out households with lower incomes. Expected rent infla-tion raises the value of homes. Homeownership is a way to hedge against future rent inflation, and homebuyers are willing to pay some premium for that protection.[18]

2. Where rents are high, housing income is from economic rents[19] that stem from political exclusion, not from capital allocation. The value of hous-ing units accrues to land, not to improvements. Because land does not depreciate, price/rent levels are bid higher because landlords require lower gross returns on their properties. One way to think of this is in terms of upkeep. Think of two identical homes that both cost $200,000 to build. One is worth $500,000 because it is located in a Closed Access city. The other is worth $250,000 because it is located in an Open Access city. Let's say that real estate owners generally demand a 5% return on their investment. So the Closed Access home would fetch $25,000 in rental income, and the Open Access home would fetch $12,500 in rental income. But the homes need to be maintained in order to remain valuable. This maintenance would be the same for both, because the homes are identical. If maintenance and management costs amount to $10,000 a year (in new floors, air-conditioning units, etc.), then the Closed Access home would need to rent for $35,000 while the Open Access home would need to rent for $22,500. That makes the price/rent ratio for the Closed Access home 14.3× while the price/rent ratio for the Open Access home in this hypothetical example is only 11.1×.

3. Where rents are low, housing supply is elastic, which means that low long-term real interest rates might increase the present value of homes, but they also induce new building, which pushes down rents. This makes housing in elastic cities less sensitive to real long-term interest rates. There is little supply response in cities where rents are high. This means that when long-term real interest rates decline, there is no mitigating effect on rents. This causes Closed Access home values to be more sensitive to low long-term real interest rates, as we would expect from a long-lived asset. This may also explain why home prices are relatively high in cities like Seattle, and

why home prices in places like Canada and Australia have continued to rise since the financial crisis. In Seattle, enough new housing is built to accommodate growth and to prevent the migration pattern that has developed in Closed Access cities, but not enough to actually lower rents—so it could be that home prices in Seattle are more sensitive to low real long-term interest rates than home prices in Dallas or Atlanta are. In Dallas and Atlanta, building can be strong enough to lower rents during an expansion.

4. The various income tax subsidies to homeownership—nontaxed imputed rental income, the mortgage interest deduction, and capital gains exemptions—tend to become more effective as home values rise. For instance, the mortgage interest deduction is only valuable for households that itemize deductions. This makes homes more valuable as tax shelters as their value rises.

All of these potential influences on price are caused fundamentally by the rise in rents, so these causes would all correlate highly with one another. This means that even the rise in price/rent ratios, *which is broadly referenced as the reason why rent can be ignored as a factor in the housing boom,* is a *function of rising rents.* If we are to come to any useful conclusions about the causes of the housing "bubble," rent must be the center of the story. Today, it is mostly ignored—literally not mentioned in many articles about the cause of the bubble—in spite of the fact that hundreds of thousands of renters each year choose to migrate out of the high-priced cities *specifically and explicitly because rents are too high.*

It seems obvious that if price/rent ratios have been rising in some places, this is a clear sign of speculative activity that is unrelated to local rental values. But as odd as it sounds, the primary factor causing price/rent ratios to rise in some places is . . . rising rent.

ROBERT SHILLER'S FRIGHTENING HOME PRICE CHART

During the height of the housing boom, a scary chart from Robert Shiller became popular. The chart showed real home prices dating back to 1890.[20] The sharp deviation far outside any previous range seemed to be a clear harbinger of the coming correction. But this highly influential chart suffered from the common problem of conflating two Americas.

Accurate real home prices require an accurate deflator. In the standard version of Shiller's chart, home prices are deflated by the overall consumer price index (CPI).[21] This makes sense, theoretically, as there is good reason to expect the cost of new homes to naturally rise with consumer inflation.

Figure 1-10. Shiller Real Home Price Index—United States

building costs ——— home prices, adjusted with shelter CPI

home prices, adjusted with general CPI

Note: CPI = consumer price index. Home price index adjusted with shelter CPI is set to equal the Shiller real home price index in Jan. 1953 (114.71).
Sources: Robert Shiller, "U.S. Home Price and Related Data," available at http://www.econ.yale .edu/~shiller/data/Fig3-1.xls, for figure 3.1 in Robert Shiller, *Irrational Exuberance*, 3rd ed. (Princeton, NJ: Princeton University Press, 2015); Bureau of Labor Statistics, "CPI—All Urban Consumers" (CUUR0000SA0); Bureau of Labor Statistics, "CPI—All Urban Consumers Shelter" (CUSR0000SAH1).

And over long periods of time, home values have indeed risen roughly in line with general inflation in most places. But indices specifically measuring inflation of rent have been available since at least 1953. By choosing to deflate home prices with the overall CPI, Shiller overlooks the influence of political obstacles to housing expansion that have prevented new supply from moderating rent inflation.

Figure 1-10 adds a new version of the home price index that is deflated with the shelter component of the CPI. Because rents have risen faster than the overall CPI, this pulls down the relative value of homes substantially. If rents have risen at a higher rate than general inflation, then surely this trend should be reflected in home prices.

Since the 1990s, thanks to Shiller, fellow economist Karl Case, and Allan Weiss, city-specific home price indices have been available that can be paired

Figure 1-11. Shiller Real Home Price Index—Cities

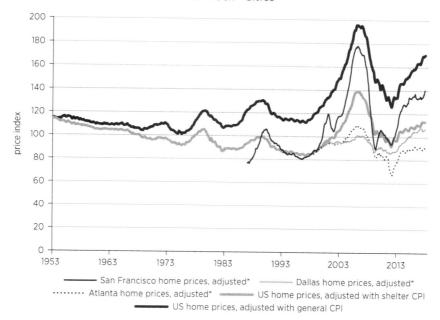

* Each city's home prices are adjusted with the city's specific home price index and CPI owners' equivalent rent.
Note: CPI = consumer price index.
Sources: Robert Shiller, "U.S. Home Price and Related Data," available at http://www.econ.yale.edu/-shiller/data/Fig3-1.xls, for figure 3.1 in Robert Shiller, *Irrational Exuberance*, 3rd ed. (Princeton, NJ: Princeton University Press, 2015); Bureau of Labor Statistics, "CPI—All Urban Consumers Shelter" (CUSR0000SAH1); S&P/Case-Shiller indices and indices for CPI owners' equivalent rent of residences were retrieved from FRED (Federal Reserve Bank of St. Louis) for San Francisco, Atlanta, and Dallas. (The various home price indices referred to as "S&P/Case-Shiller" indices are now maintained and published by CoreLogic*, https://us.spindices.com/index-family/real-estate/sp-corelogic-case-shiller.)

with city-specific rent inflation indices. (These indices are maintained and published today by CoreLogic®.)[22] Figure 1-11 splits the shelter-CPI-adjusted Real Home Price index into three additional indices—a San Francisco index, a Dallas index, and an Atlanta index. There was no bubble in Dallas and Atlanta.

The United States didn't have a bubble in the real valuations of homes. The Closed Access cities did. Most of the country, like Dallas and Atlanta, never left the long-term range of valuations. They were near the high end of the long-term range, which is reasonably explained by low real long-term interest rates. The rest of the rise in the national average real home price, above that level, was from the localized urban housing shortage in cities like San Francisco. The instability was local. It was a Closed Access problem.

REAL VALUE AFFECTS PRICE MORE THAN CHEAP CREDIT

Price/rent ratios were also elevated in the late 1970s and early 1980s. But interest rates on 30-year mortgages were higher than 10% throughout the late 1970s and early 1980s. Plus, there was no developed private securitized mortgage market. The 1970s and 1980s period may have been the antithesis of a period of easy credit. Yet prices were relatively high compared to rents then, also.[23]

Market-based measures of real interest rates only date to the late 1990s, so precise analysis is difficult. But in general, real interest rates (after subtracting inflation) were very low in the late 1970s, much as they have been recently. In 1979, mortgage rates started climbing over 10%, but inflation was also climbing over 10%. Real long-term interest rates were low in the decade after 2000, as they were in the 1970s, but inflation was higher during the 1970s.

Low real interest rates should increase the intrinsic value of homes. And more accessible and affordable credit terms should allow households to purchase homes at higher prices without increasing their cash outflows. Both of these effects should cause home prices to rise as interest rates decline. Low real interest rates mean that a given rental payment in the future is worth more today, because real interest rates reflect the willingness of savers to pay for future income. This willingness to pay more for future income increases the intrinsic value of a home, just as lower interest rates increase the value of existing bonds that were issued at higher rates.[24] Credit access and more affordable mortgage payments mean that homebuyers can afford to bid higher for a given home, regardless of its intrinsic rental value, because they have access to financing.

A comparison of the 1970s and the decade after 2000 shows which of these factors dominates. If housing markets are generally efficient and households that would buy homes do not find mortgage availability to be a significant obstacle, then real interest rates will dominate. If housing markets are not very efficient and households bid up the prices of homes when they have access to credit, with little regard for the present value of future rents, then high nominal interest rates will lead to lower prices.[25] This is because higher nominal interest rates will increase mortgage payments, regardless of whether the high rates are from high real interest rates or from expectations of high inflation.[26]

From the late 1970s to the mid-1990s,

- real long-term interest rates rose, decreasing the intrinsic values of homes; and

- the inflation premium in mortgage interest rates declined steeply, increasing the potential accessibility of credit.

Figure 1-12. Mortgage Affordability, by Metro Area

Note: *Mortgage payment* refers to the payment for a conventional 30-year mortgage on the median home; *income* refers to the median household income.
Source: Mortgage affordability measure from Zillow data, http://www.zillow.com/research/data/.

The net effect of these interest rate changes is shown in figure 1-12. Mortgage payments became much more affordable over this time period, in all cities. This should have allowed households to bid up prices. But instead, those lower rates led to lower mortgage payments because home prices declined relative to rents even while mortgage affordability was improving. It is real long-term interest rates that have the greatest impact on home prices. In other words, credit constraints due to high nominal interest rates don't stop households from bidding home prices higher. Rather, they generally bid prices up to their intrinsic values based on the real interest rate.[27] Moreover, intrinsic values are such a strong influence on price that prices were relatively strong compared to both rents and incomes in the late 1970s in spite of unusually unaffordable mortgage rates.

Then, from the late 1990s to the decade after 2000, nominal rates fell for two reasons:

- Real long-term interest rates fell. The real rate on 30-year Treasury bonds fell from nearly 4% in 1998 to less than 2% by 2005, increasing the intrinsic values of homes.

- Inflation declined slightly, increasing the potential accessibility of credit.

In Open Access cities, mortgage affordability remained stable while home price/income and price/rent levels moved back up to levels similar to those of the late 1970s. This is the outcome we would expect if real long-term interest rates were the dominant influence. Prices reflect intrinsic value in Open Access cities. In these cities, households were not bidding home prices up to high levels because of affordable mortgage terms. Mortgage demand triggered new homebuilding, keeping prices low.

The increased homebuilding boosted supply and pushed rents down, so price/rent levels increased partly because rents were lower. Equilibrium was reached as renting became more affordable. Both renters and owners in Open Access cities had more home at a lower expense. It would be difficult to overbuild in an Open Access city.[28]

Some places didn't follow this pattern. In Closed Access cities where home prices were outrageous relative to incomes, households actually had to reduce their real housing consumption. All of their added costs stemmed from housing cost inflation, because of the bidding war for the limited number of existing homes. In Open Access cities, households were enjoying larger spaces. Open Access cities, *where housing was abundant*, were the *sustainable* cities. In Closed Access cities, *undersupplied* housing markets led to economic disruption.

Note that, in the 1970s and 1980s, mortgage affordability followed a similar pattern in all cities. That's because the primary factor in high mortgage payments was the impact of inflation on mortgage rates. But in the 1990s and in the decade after 2000, mortgage expenses were low in Open Access cities but high in Closed Access cities. That is because high mortgage payments were caused by lack of housing supply, not by interest rates.

In most of the country, when low real long-term interest rates increased the intrinsic value of homes in both the late 1970s and the decade after 2000, this enticed new households into the buyer's market and moderately raised prices. High nominal interest rates didn't prevent prices from rising to their intrinsic value in the late 1970s when real interest rates were low,[29] and low nominal interest rates didn't cause prices to overshoot in the decade after 2000.

This is not to deny that credit was widely available in the decade after 2000, possibly to an extent that was unprecedented. Foreclosure rates in Open Access cities tended to run high when subprime and privately securitized mortgages started to claim a larger portion of the US mortgage market from 2004 until the collapse. This is what a credit boom looks like in a free economy. Marginal households with high default risk did take on mortgages in these cities. Some of these households were defaulting on their mortgages as early as 2003, while the foreclosure crisis didn't hit the Closed Access cities and the Contagion cities until late 2007 and after.

In fact, Texas was a leading center of subprime lending. In 2007, pundits operating on the assumption that poor underwriting was behind the boom expected Texas to take a central place in the bust. At the time, Texas foreclosure rates were relatively high.

In late 2007, the *Texas Observer* reported, "State Sen. Eliot Shapleigh (D–El Paso) calls it an approaching tsunami. In 2008, more than $300 billion worth of volatile subprime home loans will spike to higher interest rates nation-wide, and a torrent of foreclosures will likely follow." Noting that seven of the nation's top ten subprime refinancing markets were in Texas, Shapleigh predicted, "Texas could be the epicenter of this deal because of all the subprime lending."[30]

Since Texas has an elastic housing supply, home prices were relatively moderate there. Since the state had less of a price collapse, there was not a particular spike in delinquencies there after the panics of 2007 and 2008. When Texas escaped the bust in relatively good shape, with fewer foreclosures than most other states, the *Washington Post* was among the outlets where observers expressed surprise. "It's one of the great mysteries of the mortgage crisis: Why did Texas—Texas, of all places!—escape the real estate bust?"[31] Analysts concluded that an important factor was Texas's mortgage regulations, which create some limits to cash-out refinancing.

It should give one pause that it was possible to blame or credit Texas's mortgage credit market whether or not Texas had experienced a sharp foreclosure crisis. In fact, Texas serves as a great example of how credit access is not systematically destabilizing when a market does not have supply constraints.

In an Open Access market, credit availability doesn't lead to significant price increases. High defaults from access to loose credit don't cause the housing market to collapse into a vicious cycle of foreclosures and falling prices.

Causation can apply in both directions here. Loose terms from a deregulated credit market can lead to a supply of risky mortgages. And high prices in supply-constrained cities can lead to demand for risky mortgages. Clearly both of these factors were in effect to some extent during the decade after 2000. Deregulated credit markets have largely been blamed for destabilizing the economy, but it is causation in the other direction, where high costs lead to demand for risky borrowing, that is the more serious source of destabilization.

Rising home prices as a source of cash for marginal households was another factor frequently cited as a cause of excessive home prices in 2004 and 2005.

Homeowners could tap their "housing ATMs" to continue making payments on mortgages on which they would otherwise have defaulted. This supposedly led to a false sense of security among lenders and created a set of borrowers whose credit records were overly rosy.

In fact, in the majority of the country the housing ATM story is a myth. Home prices were rising moderately. Homebuyers who found themselves unable to sustain their mortgage payments were defaulting in those cities. Even Phoenix and Las Vegas, Contagion cities, did not have particularly unusual home price behavior during the years preceding their sudden price bubbles in 2004 and 2005.

In most of the country, government subsidies, loose money, generous banks, and even fraud among borrowers and lenders did not create price bubbles in housing. In the late 1970s, inflation made mortgage expenses high across the country. It was appropriate to address that problem with tighter monetary policy in 1980, and when that happened, mortgage expenses fell in all cities. In the decade after 2000, mortgage expenses were only high in Closed Access cities. The solution to that problem should have applied only to those cities. When policymakers attempted to solve the problem with con-tractionary national banking and monetary policies, mortgage expenses in Open Access cities, which were already at very low levels, shifted downward to even lower levels. In all cities, the cost of buying a home with a mortgage began to decline in 2006. This might have seemed like good news in the Closed Access cities, but this was bad news in the Open Access cities. This was the wrong solution.

Figure 1-13 compares owning versus renting costs for Los Angeles and for the US overall. As previously shown in figure 1-12, mortgage affordability is highly dependent on inflation, since mortgage interest rates rise and fall with expected inflation rates. Here, I have adjusted mortgage affordability so that the portion of the payment that reflects inflation is deducted, then I have added an amount equal to 40% of rental value to account for standard maintenance and upkeep of a home. This produces a mortgage affordability measure that can be compared to rent affordability.

Once the inflation portion of mortgage payments is removed, the mortgage costs in the early 1980s disappear. In fact, for the median US house, real mort-gage affordability after costs and rent affordability remained quite stable until after 2008, when real mortgage affordability moved well below rent affordabil-ity. (After the crisis, the regulators at the Federal Housing Finance Agency and the Consumer Financial Protection Bureau were protecting potential home-buyers from the best buyer's market in a lifetime.)

Figure 1-13. Mortgage Affordability vs. Rent Affordability

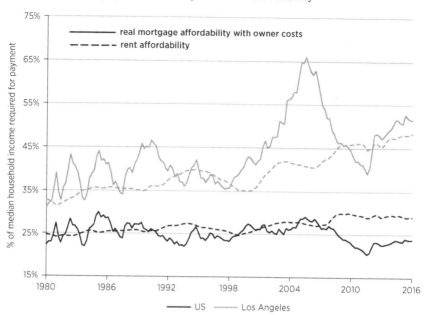

Note: Zillow mortgage affordability and rent affordability data measure the percentage of the median household income required to pay rent or a conventional mortgage payment on the median home. In order to create a comparable metric, "net mortgage affordability with owner costs" does not include the portion of the mortgage payment that accounts for inflation and does include an estimate for home-owner expenses.
Source: Zillow data, http://www.zillow.com/research/data/.

In Los Angeles, real mortgage affordability rose well above rent affordability during the decade after 2000. This was a local phenomenon, not a national phenomenon. It was due to rents that were high and that will continue to rise. Prices reflect those future high rents.

As the depression in housing starts extends to a decade, and rent inflation moves up in all types of cities, it becomes increasingly clear that distortions have been imposed on the housing market. Mortgage expenses to buy homes in Open Access cities are unusually low, yet construction remains sluggish. Given rent levels in 2018, in a normal housing market there should be more home construction across the country today at prices significantly higher than what houses currently sell for. But many families cannot fund new building because they are locked out of credit markets.

The housing-bust economy is an economy of haves and have-nots, depending on access to mortgage credit. This is evident in shifting household sizes. There has been a long-term trend toward smaller households for many years. This trend has continued for homeowners. But, since 2007, the trend has reversed for renters. In all types of cities, household sizes for renters in 2013 were larger than they had been in 2007. Housing costs for owners are low. But, for households that are locked out of ownership in today's tight credit markets, the decade-long depression in homebuilding means ever-rising rents, and these households must retrench and adjust to deal with it.[32]

SPENDING MORE, GETTING LESS, EVEN DURING THE BOOM

Since the financial crisis, the rise in the portion of incomes going to rent has developed during a period with very low rates of homebuilding. The stock of housing has been stagnant, both in terms of units and in terms of real housing expenditures, as shown in figure 1-14. In fact, there has been a long-term

Figure 1-14. Real Housing Expenditures since 1940

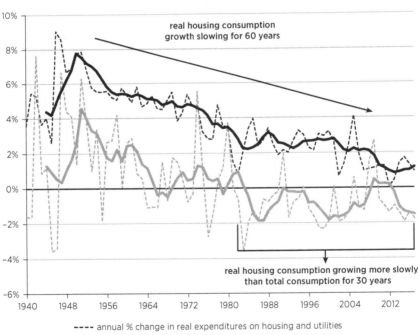

---- annual % change in real expenditures on housing and utilities
---- annual % change in real housing expenditures minus % change in total real personal consumption expenditures

Note: Data represented by the dashed lines are smoothed with five-year moving averages.
Source: Table 1.5.3 (Real Gross Domestic Product, Expanded Detail, Quantity Indexes) from Bureau of Economic Analysis, available at https://apps.bea.gov/iTable/index_nipa.cfm.

decline in the growth rate of real housing expenditures (e.g., rent, adjusted for rent inflation)[33] for decades, both in absolute terms and relative to other expenditures. This was not reversed during the supposed housing boom. For each additional 1% increase in real incomes, households were increasing the real value of their homes (in size, amenities, etc.) by *less* than 1%.[34] They were diverting real consumption, on net, *away* from housing, as they have been for 30 years. Yet inflation caused by a lack of supply has meant that spending on housing has remained stable or risen over that time, even as Americans have been relentlessly downgrading the real value of their homes.

Here is an example of the sort of description that litters the literature on homeownership in the US:

> In the latter part of the twentieth century, homeownership took on added dimensions. Owning a home was now not just about shelter; homes became first nest eggs then trophies.
>
> Of course, homeownership is also synonymous with a sense of making it, of display, and of keeping up with the Joneses.[35]

How can this common characterization be squared with the fact that real spending on housing has been declining compared to total consumption spending for 30 years? Americans are trying to use their homes in a bid to "keep up with the Joneses," but not in the way this phenomenon has generally been described. We are bidding up little condos and bungalows in the metropolitan enclaves of privilege, where high incomes are available but only to a limited number of families. Americans are trying to "keep up with the Joneses" by moving to cities where the Joneses are earning high incomes. Homes haven't become trophies. They have become toll gates barring the way to employment.

Don't we all know people who have moved to the Closed Access cities? When we visit and ask them, "Wait! You paid *how much* for this little unit?" they explain that they had to do it in order to accept a career opportunity. They don't brag about what an amazing unit they bought. They apologize for having so little space for visitors. *These* are the cities that are responsible for the rise in housing expenses, not the cities full of "McMansions."

Of course, every neighborhood has examples of households acting irresponsibly, households that didn't have a history of stable employment and started, say, building a pool in the backyard. This may even have been more common during the bubble, whether because of more lenient sources of credit or because of the wealth effect of growing home equity in some cities.

Yet a growing accumulation of data and some commonsense observations about the shape of the American housing market make it clear that these examples in no way, shape, or fashion added up to the overall American housing bubble.

See the appendix for more details regarding fundamental factors in home prices.

CHAPTER 2
Our Unexceptional Bubble

T he first observation that should cast doubt on the idea that the bubble was caused by Americans' insatiable appetite for trophy homes and reckless borrowing is that the US housing market wasn't particularly unusual in 2005.

The list of proposed causes for the housing bubble presumes a surprising amount of American exceptionalism. American banks, government-sponsored lending organizations, federal tax subsidies, Federal Reserve policies, federal affordable housing programs, private mortgage securitizations, the sharp growth in subprime mortgage originations—it is difficult to find a single proposed cause of the housing bubble, besides the global savings glut hypothesis, that doesn't point to some attribute that is specifically American. Oddly, though, there was nothing exceptional about the US housing market until it collapsed.

Figure 2-1 compares home price/income ratios among selected representative countries and the European average. Until 2007, the US was moving right along with the European average. Home prices rose about 27% above the 1998 levels, relative to incomes—not much more than might be expected from the global decline in long-term real interest rates.

Of the 22 OECD countries with price/income data going back to 1998, 13 have reached price/income levels at least 40% above their 1998 levels. Prices in France and the United Kingdom rose as steeply as prices in US Closed Access cities during the boom, and in those countries prices have remained high. Canada and Australia also have problems with high home prices in key urban

Figure 2-1. International Home Price-to-Income Ratios

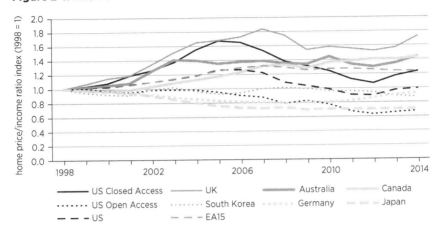

Note: *EA15* includes data for fifteen eurozone countries that are members of the Organisation for Economic Co-operation and Development. *US Closed Access* includes data for New York City, Los Angeles, Boston, San Francisco, San Jose, and San Diego. *US Open Access* includes data for Dallas, Houston, and Atlanta.
Sources: Organisation for Economic Co-operation and Development, "Focus on House Prices," http://www.oecd.org/eco/outlook/focusonhouseprices.htm; Zillow data, http://www.zillow.com/research/data/; table CA1 (Personal Income, Population, Per Capita Personal Income) from Bureau of Economic Analysis, available at https://www.bea.gov/iTable/index_regional.cfm.

centers, and so their national housing trends were at least as strong as housing trends in the US during the decade after 2000, and yet they have continued to remain at these high levels, without a price collapse.[1]

Spain and Ireland are the only other OECD countries that experienced a similar boom and bust cycle to the US.[2] But even in those countries, home prices remain higher than in the US, relative to 1998. Spain and Ireland have relative price/income behavior that looks more like that of the US Closed Access cities than it looks like the general US price trend.

In short, *US housing price changes until 2007 were common; it is the decline since then that was unique.*

In a few OECD countries—Japan, Germany, Switzerland, South Korea, and Finland—home prices were relatively moderate throughout the boom period. Germany and Switzerland have tax policies that don't encourage homeownership and consumption.[3] Germany encouraged building houses after reunification, and the German constitution also has a "right to build" clause. The US encourages ownership and consumption (with tax subsidies, etc.), but some cities discourage supply (with zoning and permitting obstacles). Germany appears to do the opposite: it allows supply but discourages consumption. The US encourages you to *want* to build a home but makes it hard to get permission. Germany discourages you, but isn't as likely to prevent you from building.[4]

Japan famously had its own real estate bubble in the late 1980s, but home prices have remained moderate there during the recent period. One might think that Japan failed to develop a real estate bubble because of its declining population, but it has experienced a trend toward urbanization just like other countries. After the real estate bubble of the 1980s, Japan revamped its housing policy to allow more flexible rules on home construction. In 2014, the city of Tokyo had more housing starts than the entire state of California and more starts than all of England.[5]

South Korea also implemented a series of policies in the 1990s to boost supply and deregulate mortgage markets, which lowered rents. The country lifted price controls, privatized mortgage banking, and allowed more development of agricultural lands near urban areas. In the decade after 2000, South Korea also implemented some demand-side policies aimed at keeping prices low.[6] Although the South Korean liberalization of housing had positive overall results, South Korea shared with many other countries the problem of constrained supply at the local level, where economic opportunity creates housing demand.[7]

In the US, financial liberalization in 2003–2006 boosted demand and allowed Closed Access prices to rise to market levels similar to those of other supply-constrained countries. This was followed by broad-based financial repression to discourage borrowing, which pushed prices back down.

The US Open Access cities experienced price behavior very similar to that of South Korea until 2006. Then financial repression caused home values in the Open Access cities to fall to very low levels. Keep in mind that home prices in 1998 were already near long-term lows, so the current prices are extremely low, especially considering the low level of interest rates.

Despite being home to a single monetary policy and fairly uniform federal mortgage banking policies, US cities followed many different paths during the boom, but both high-priced and low-priced cities suffered a bust after 2006 that was only mirrored in two other small economies. By 2014, US cities were underpriced by 20% to 30% in all contexts: Open Access cities compared to other open-access areas, such as Germany; the overall US average compared to the overall European average; and Closed Access parts of the US compared to expensive, closed-access countries like the United Kingdom.[8]

Theories about the housing boom that rely solely on national US policies fail as explanations. The Federal Reserve didn't cause home prices in Australia to rise. Subprime lending, bank deregulation, Fannie and Freddie, the Community Reinvestment Act, and federal housing subsidies didn't cause home prices in London to skyrocket. It is the differences *between our cities* that explain the boom. Prices skyrocketed in London and New York City, but not in Tokyo and Dallas. The cause of those rising prices must be a cause that is relevant in London but not in Dallas.

After 2007, the US really was different from the rest of the world. Almost every city in the US experienced a bust worse than what any other major country experienced. Most countries did not have much of a bust at all, even if home prices were high. So for the period after 2007, we *should* look to specific, national US policies to explain what happened to US housing prices. We need to ask, "What happened to Fed policy after 2007? What happened to Fannie and Freddie after 2007? What happened to subprime lending markets and bank regulation after 2007?" *These* were major US market and policy shifts that should be able to explain what's exceptional about US housing markets.

Unfortunately, most explanations for the housing bust and the financial crisis come in one form: "X caused the bubble, and once the bubble formed, the bust was inevitable. Therefore, X caused the bust." But if the international evidence suggests that the bubble in the US was not unusual and that the crisis was avoidable, then *any* proposed cause of the bust that takes this form is completely inadequate.

Housing prices appear to be influenced by three main factors, in order of importance: (1) supply constraints, (2) tax benefits, and (3) lending markets. We can see the effect of supply constraints clearly within the US market, where the difference between, say, Texas and California is extreme. And we can see the effect of tax benefits within all cities, where the difference between high-end price/rent ratios and low-end price/rent ratios reflects, in part, the ability to claim tax benefits.

Among different countries, we see a wide variety of mortgage policies. Some include lender recourse and some don't.[9] Some utilize securitization markets and others don't. Some tend to have fixed rates, others adjustable. Some come with long amortization schedules, others with balloon payments. And while some credit regulations certainly can reduce home prices,[10] these characteristics don't map that strongly across bubble and nonbubble markets. Low-priced Germany, for instance, uses securitization while the high-priced United Kingdom depends largely on banks.

There have been many attempts to measure the effects of regulation, and while the effects are certainly not zero, marginal changes in lending standards don't compare to, say, the difference between low-end homes in Open Access cities selling for 6× rent and high-end homes on the West Coast that can reach 30× rent. Those price differences largely reflect supply and tax issues. Even hypotheses that claim an important role for lending must be paired with some sort of supply constraint. No level of reckless lending is going to double price/rent ratios in Texas, for instance. Cheap land and unrestrictive zoning rules keep housing prices close to the cost of construction.

Yet popular culture is filled with polemics about how the lenders supposedly *did this to us*. They describe decades of various American public policy decisions regarding lending that inevitably led to a moment in history when Wall Street conspired to create a housing market that . . . well, basically looked like the housing markets in a dozen other developed countries. According to this story, the market's collapse was fated. This sense of fate is embedded in the heart of practically all discussions of the financial crisis. Whether economists and policymakers argue that the Fed should have tightened monetary policy earlier or that bank regulators should have cracked down earlier or that Fannie Mae and Freddie Mac should have been restrained earlier, all of these conclusions presume that housing markets bloated with credit and money were fated to collapse.

The collapse was not fated.

MORTGAGE MARKETS DURING THE BUBBLE

If car prices suddenly doubled in the next few years, the reason almost certainly wouldn't be slick or corrupt car salesmen, or teenage boys suddenly made ravenous for new sports cars after reading their *Motor Trend* magazines. But, if we were looking for easy answers, those would be the easiest stories to tell. There really are many underhanded car salesmen and impetuous young consumers. Of course we know that in the real world they don't cause car prices to suddenly double or triple.

There might be reasons why the housing market is different from the automobile market. Changing the total stock of supply certainly takes longer in housing. This is why housing supply and trends in rents are frequently ignored in academic debates about the causes of fluctuating home prices. Demand for ownership is more unstable than supply, so demand might cause some short-term price changes. And credit availability is an important factor in the demand for homeownership.

Credit is not an important factor in the demand for housing consumption by tenants. This is why rising rents are the best signal about the overall forces shaping the housing market.[11]

Table 2-1 lists factors that provide clues about the ultimate causes of rising home prices.

Table 2-1. Signs of Whether Limited Supply or Rising Demand Caused Rising Prices

Signs of supply deprivation	Signs of any rising prices	Signs of excess demand
• rising rents from lack of supply • low rates of new building where prices are highest • declining real housing consumption (buying down-market) • migration of marginal households away from hot markets • rising mortgages outstanding from households with high incomes	• high price/rent ratios • high loan-to-value ratios (lower down payments) • rising mortgages outstanding • rising use of home equity loans • rising housing wealth • risky loan terms • increasing defaults and financial stress • growing financial sector • risk of price declines, with associated borrower defaults and lender failures	• falling rents from new supply • high levels of new building where prices are highest • high levels of first-time buyers • low FICO scores for new buyers • rising real housing consumption (buying upmarket) • migration of marginal households to hot markets • rising mortgages outstanding from households with low incomes

In general, among the three broad categories of evidence about the cause of rising prices,

- evidence that points to supply deprivation matches the data, but has been ignored;

- trends that are simply the product of any rising prices, regardless of their cause, have been taken as evidence that loose credit caused high prices; and

- evidence that would specifically point to credit-fueled excess demand as a cause of rising prices doesn't generally match the data when the data are viewed carefully.[12]

The result has been an unwarranted consensus that excessive growth in credit was a primary cause of rising prices, based on evidence that is plausible but not definitive. This consensus has led to the popular view that the housing bubble was part of a long-term system of predation focused on financially marginalized households that were overconsuming housing while also maintaining other forms of consumption that they could not sustain without excessive borrowing. While many of my findings might be considered "bad news," the "good news" is that this predation problem has not been happening in any systematic way. Credit markets have mostly been used by households with high earning potential to buy access to Closed Access labor markets.

THE SUBPRIME BOOM HAD NOTHING TO DO WITH RISING HOMEOWNERSHIP

As I write this, the Wikipedia page titled "Subprime mortgage crisis" contains this paragraph: "The US home ownership rate increased from 64% in 1994 (about where it had been since 1980) to an all-time high of 69.2% in 2004. Subprime lending was a major contributor to this increase in home ownership rates and in the overall demand for housing, which drove prices higher."[13]

The ownership numbers are correct. Everything else in that paragraph— every claim without a citation—is subtly or wholly wrong.

Homeownership rates rose and fell, fairly uniformly, across cities and states during the boom and bust, regardless of local prices or the level of nonconventional lending. If rising home prices and homeownership rates were due to new factors like the Community Reinvestment Act, aggressive activity from Fannie Mae and Freddie Mac, or subprime mortgages, homeownership rates would have correlated with those rising prices. But there does not appear to be much of a relationship, either across time or across geographic areas.

Even at the national level, viewed carefully, the rise in homeownership is not as related to the rise in home prices as cursory impressions imply. Figure 2-2 compares trends in ownership and price. After the homeownership rate began trending higher in 1994 (point 1), real home prices continued to decline for a few years. Homeownership had risen to 66.5% (already halfway to the peak!) by late 1998 (point 2), and real home prices were still about the same as they had been in late 1994. By the end of 2001 (point 3), the homeownership rate had risen from 64% to 68%, just 1% below the peak, yet home prices, relative to rents, were still within the long-term range, similar to levels seen in the late 1970s and late 1980s. Almost all of the rise in homeownership happened before any unusual price movements.

By the second quarter of 2004, homeownership had peaked at just over 69% (point 4). By this time, measured nationally, real home prices were about 19% above their level at the end of 2001. They would rise another 19% *after* homeownership had peaked.

The sharp change in trend in 1994 suggests a policy cause. Stimulus from the federal government that began in the mid-1990s, according to schemes like the Community Reinvestment Act, seems to have led to a sharp rise in homeownership. Some scholars attribute rising demand to deregulated branch banking, which began in 1994.[14]

Figure 2-2. Timeline: US Homeownership and Home Prices

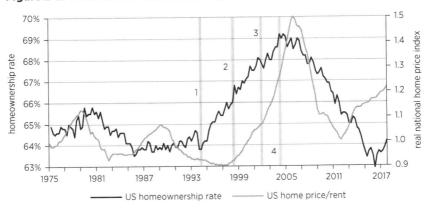

Note: In the index, the 1975–1994 average is set to 1.0. 1 = the point when homeownership rates began trending higher, 2 = the point when homeownership had risen halfway to its peak, 3 = the point when the national average price-to-rent ratio first rose above the peaks of 1979 and 1989, 4 = the point when homeownership peaked.
Sources: S&P/Case-Shiller U.S. National Home Price Index; Bureau of Labor Statistics, "CPI—All Urban Consumers Shelter" (CUSR0000SAH1); table 14 (Quarterly Homeownership Rates for the U.S. and Regions: 1964 to Present) in US Census Bureau, "Housing Vacancies and Homeownership (CPS/HVS): Historical Tables," last modified April 26, 2016, http://www.census.gov/housing/hvs/data/histtabs .html. (The various home price indices referred to as "S&P/Case-Shiller" indices are now maintained and published by CoreLogic®, https://us.spindices.com/index-family/real-estate/sp-corelogic-case-shiller.)

A third factor should be considered as well. In 1994, Fannie Mae engaged in an effort to expand homeownership through its "Showing America a New Way Home" program, which aimed to provide $1 trillion in mortgage funding to households that had been underserved by the industry. This program focused on education, preventing delinquencies from turning into foreclosures, and lowering the cost and difficulty of originations.[15] The high transaction costs of homebuying are a significant barrier to the decision to own, which means that the automation and standardization brought about by new technological developments, credit scores, and Fannie Mae's outreach programs should have broadened ownership. Meanwhile, according to filings submitted to the Securities and Exchange Commission, there didn't appear to be deteriorating standards at Fannie Mae in terms of down payments or borrower FICO scores. By the first decade of the 21st century, the proportion of Fannie Mae mortgages that had been originated with high loan-to-value levels (LTVs) was falling, if anything.[16]

If those programs are judged by home price data, they should be considered striking successes, because most of the marginal new homeowners bought their homes before home prices began to rise. Those households should have seen capital gains.

The use of FICO scores and other forms of automated loan approval have also been widely blamed for the bubble. But such claims imply a strong connection between homeownership and high prices. It's a shame that the rise in homeownership has been conflated with the bubble, because the aforementioned programs were probably helping previously underserved households gain access to ownership, and a careful review suggests that they were benign.

THE ROLE OF AGE DEMOGRAPHICS

Part of the rise in homeownership can be attributed to demographics. Homeownership is strongly tied to life cycles, and it naturally rose as the baby boomer generation moved into the ages associated with high levels of ownership.

Comparing the national homeownership rate in figure 2-3 ("all ages") with the rates for each age group, we can see that, at the peak in 2004, each age group was roughly at the same level it had been in the early 1980s (with the exception

Figure 2-3. US Homeownership, by Age of Household Head

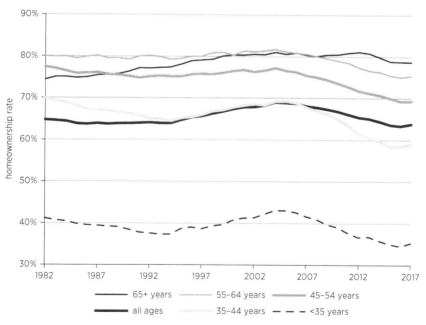

Source: Table 12 (Household Estimates for the United States, by Age of Householder: 1982 to Present) in US Census Bureau, "Housing Vacancies and Homeownership (CPS/HVS): Historical Tables," http://www.census.gov/housing/hvs/data/histtabs.html.

of the 65-and-over group, which had grown steadily over that time along with rising life expectancy, a healthier elderly population, etc.), yet homeownership in 1982 was about 65% compared to a peak of 69% in 2004. Most of this shift was a product of more Americans populating the 45-and-older age groups that tend to have very high ownership rates. The rates among the under-45 groups had fallen from the rates of the late 1970s and early 1980s, then began trending upward again. Relative to the early 1980s, the high level of aggregate ownership in 2004 was entirely an effect of demographics.[17] This graph helps to make clear how much of a chimera the national homeownership rate is.

The difference in ownership rates between 30 years of age and 60 years of age is much greater than the change over time within any age group. Before the mortgage crisis, by the time Americans hit their 60s, about 80% of them owned homes, regardless of the state of the market, and market shifts over time were minor oscillations in that process. Instead of seeing the housing boom as a period when there was a mass of borrowers who shouldn't have been homeowners, it is more accurate to see the boom period as a time when some households were able to proceed through the homeownership process earlier, when an administrator or accountant was able to purchase a first home at 37 years of age instead of at 38. Figure 2-3 belies the extreme images of the shift in the typical borrower that have populated descriptions of the period. Even this minor shift didn't push age-group ownership rates above their historical ranges.

Remember that there are two Americas. In one America home prices are high and few homes are built, and in the other (larger) America many homes are built and prices are moderate. This means that most marginal new homeownership was happening in markets with low home prices. The truth is the opposite of the often-repeated story. The housing market was not characterized by new homebuyers with lower incomes purchasing too-expensive homes. Houses were being bought by relatively younger new homebuyers with stable or high incomes purchasing moderately priced homes.

THE INCOME OF THE AVERAGE HOMEOWNER DID NOT DECLINE

Census Bureau data show no shift in ownership by income. About 39% of homeowners had incomes below the median, and 61% above the median, throughout the boom and bust.[18] The Survey of Consumer Finances confirms this.

Figure 2-4 shows homeownership, both with and without a mortgage, by income quintile. Among all households, homeownership rose from about 65% in 1995 to 69% in 2004, and had fallen back to 64% in 2016. Families in the

Figure 2-4. US Mortgaged and Unmortgaged Homeownership, by Income Quintile

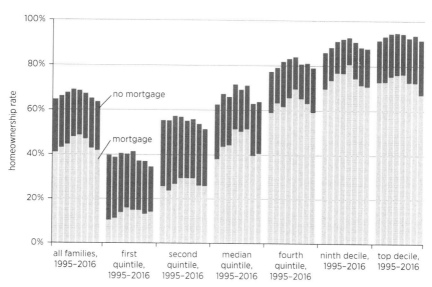

Note: The Survey of Consumer Finances splits the top income quintile into two deciles, and this is reflected in the figure.
Sources: Tables 9 and 13 in Board of Governors of the Federal Reserve System, "Survey of Consumer Finances," last modified November 15, 2017, https://www.federalreserve.gov/econres/scfindex.htm.

bottom 40% of incomes had relatively flat ownership rates during the period up to 2004. The growth in ownership was concentrated among families in the top 60% of income.

Since 2004, ownership has declined in all income groups. For families in the top income quintiles, ownership rates are still above the 1995 levels. For families in the bottom income quintiles, ownership rates are below the 1995 levels. For the bottom 40%, there was never a boom, only a bust. Predatory lending and borrowing among poor families that can't afford a mortgage doesn't show up in these data, but the damage of devastated mortgage and housing markets does.

Roughly one-third of homeowners have no mortgage. They own their homes free and clear. Most owners with incomes below the median have no mortgage. Many of these are older households. During the boom, the proportion of owners with no mortgage declined. There was an increase in mortgaged ownership (about 8% from 1995 to 2007), and it peaked later than total homeownership—2007 instead of 2004. So some of the marginal new

Figure 2-5. US Mortgaged and Unmortgaged Homeownership, by Age of Household Head

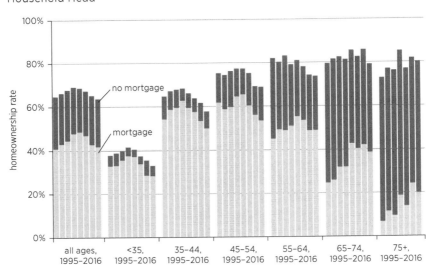

Sources: Tables 9 and 13 in Board of Governors of the Federal Reserve System, "Survey of Consumer Finances," last modified November 15, 2017, https://www.federalreserve.gov/econres/scfindex.htm.

mortgaged ownership was related to increased homeownership, and some of it replaced free-and-clear ownership.

As figure 2-5 shows, the decline in unmortgaged ownership was heavily weighted toward older age groups. Possibly this is related to issues such as medical expenses or a cultural shift toward lengthening labor force participation, longer active lives, and baby boomers' use of debt products like reverse mortgages.[19] In any case, the shift from unmortgaged ownership to mortgaged ownership in older age groups was not likely to involve households with high leverage (mortgages as a high percentage of property values, with little home equity).

There appear to be two broad sources of new mortgages during the boom: new mortgages for first-time homebuyers under 45 years of age, who tended to have higher incomes and would have been highly leveraged at the time of purchase, and mortgages among homeowners older than 55 who tended to have been owners for many years and to have significant equity. Among households with mortgages, across ages and incomes, average mortgages as a percentage of home values were stable or moderately declining during the boom.

THE BOOM FOCUSED ON YOUNG, EDUCATED HOUSEHOLDS

Since homeownership was already nearly universal among the top income quintile before the boom, it would be natural to expect additional new homeowners to be households with lower incomes than the average existing owner. Surprisingly, that wasn't the case. This is because new mortgages targeted the *highest*-income households.

Figure 2-6 is a measure of the number of marginal new homeowners in each income quintile (and the top two deciles), as a percentage of the number of nonowners in 1995. In other words, if 80% of a set of families were homeowners in 1995 and 90% were homeowners in 2004, then the measure of new owners in 2004, as a percentage of 1995 nonowners, would be 50%. Fifty percent of potential homeowners would have become owners during that time:

$$\frac{90\% - 80\%}{100\% - 80\%} = 50\%$$

In the aggregate, between 1995 and 2004, about 12.5% of nonowners became owners. That is a pretty aggressive pace of expansion. Little of this was due to families in the bottom 40% of income, but the chart shows a sharp rise in

Figure 2-6. New US Homeowners as a Percentage of 1995 Nonowners

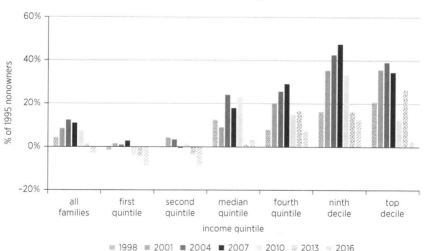

Note: The Survey of Consumer Finances splits the top income quintile into two deciles, and this is reflected in the figure.
Sources: Table 9 in Board of Governors of the Federal Reserve System, "Survey of Consumer Finances," last modified November 15, 2017, https://www.federalreserve.gov/econres/scfindex.htm; author's calculations.

marginal new owners in the top incomes. Among the top quintile, between 1995 and 2004, more than 40% of the beginning number of nonowners became owners! Among the median quintile, more than 20% did. But among the bottom two quintiles there was little change in ownership rates.

In a recent paper, Christopher L. Foote, Lara Loewenstein, and Paul S. Willen, economists with the Federal Reserve Bank of Boston, find strong support for the preceding findings—both with Survey of Consumer Finances data and with data from Equifax and the IRS. New ownership was among young aspirational families with high incomes:

> Overall, there is no evidence of a relative expansion of mortgage borrowing among low-income or marginal borrowers during the boom, particularly after conditioning on age. In fact, income becomes a more-important, not less-important, correlate of homeownership after the mortgage boom begins, especially for young households.[20]

Most recent buyers at the peak of the boom were younger people with above-average incomes and with the high leverage typical of young first-time buyers. These households were the hardest hit by the bust. Homeownership rates among household heads less than 45 years old have plummeted since the peak.

Homeownership among families ages 45–65 has also fallen, even though ownership rates among these age groups had not risen as sharply during the boom. The homeownership rate for all households under 65 years old is *well* below any homeownership rate we have seen for decades. An estimate of homeownership rates, if age group proportions were still the same that they were in 1982, would be around 60%—4% below the stated rate. In other words, baby boomers are moving into age groups that naturally tend to have high rates of ownership, which increases the aggregate homeownership rate. This positive trend is hiding the severity of the bust.

It is interesting how this demographic shift has affected perceptions about what happened. Looking only at the aggregate homeownership rate, it appears that homeownership remained at a very stable level for many years, then jumped far higher for a few years, then moved back to the normal level. On the basis of those data, it is very easy to tell a story of reckless lenders who were selling mortgages to 5% of the population, people who had been reasonably excluded from homeownership before, and surmise that once we came to our senses about prudently regulating the mortgage market, we stopped lending to that additional 5% of households. This has been a salient, but wrong, assertion during the boom and bust.

But, viewing households by age group, it is clear that homeownership rates within age groups have moved within ranges of 3% or less over time, and that homeownership rates were not above that range during the height of the housing boom. Tightening credit markets after the boom have obstructed 4% to 7% of potential homeowners from becoming owners. As with the comparison with international housing markets, here again, it wasn't the 2005 US housing market that was the outlier for being excessive. It is the 2018 US housing market that is the outlier for being exclusive.

The Survey of Consumer Finances also provides a measure of homeownership by education and by occupation. In line with the research cited above, from 1995 to 2004, homeownership among families with a college degree rose by 9%. The other categories of households with less education had homeownership rates that were relatively flat. Managerial or professional workers increased homeownership by just under 6% from 1995 to 2004. Retired owners increased their ownership by about 7%. And the other categories were relatively flat.[21] The newspapers of the time were filled with anecdotes about poor, desperate families being pushed into overpriced homes on extortionary terms. These data don't refute all of those anecdotes, but they do confirm that the scale of that activity was negligible.

I am building a case for a new view, but here it is worth stopping for a moment to consider the shocking distance between the survey data and the consensus view. In a review of the 21st century, on the basis of current perceptions, the decade after 2000 could well be labeled the "anyone with a pulse could get a mortgage" decade. And the following decade has been characterized largely by our anger about the events that seemed to have been set in motion by that lending. Yet, in the 1990s, education and profession were relatively unimportant markers for homeownership. Ownership rates among the various categories of households were not that different. According to the Survey of Consumer Finances, in 1995, the homeownership rate for families with a high school education was 65% and for families with a college degree, 71%—a difference of only 6%. By 2004, the homeownership rate for those with a college degree was 80%. The striking development from the 1990s to the decade after 2000 is how much *more* important education and profession became as gatekeepers to ownership.

Now, after a decade of our self-imposed credit crisis, homeownership among college graduates is still about 3 percentage points higher than it was in 1995. Among less-educated households, the homeownership rate is at least 3 percentage points lower than it was in 1995. As with home prices and homeownership by age and by income, homeownership by education looks normal—even skewed toward more-educated households in 2004—and it is the falling rates of homeownership after 2004 that are the anomaly.

LEVERAGED BUYERS WERE YOUNG, WHICH IS NORMAL

An estimate of leverage, only for families that have a mortgage, is shown in figure 2-7. The data suggest that leverage for those with mortgages is fairly uniform across income quintiles.[22] This should not be surprising. It might seem intuitive that households with low incomes would need to utilize debt more. But leverage is more closely associated with timing than it is with income. Households tend to buy homes with large mortgages, which slowly decline in value over time relative to the homes. There is no indication within any income group of systematic overleverage during the boom. Mortgages outstanding as a percentage of home values only jumped after home prices collapsed.

Atif Mian, an economist at Princeton, and Amir Sufi, an economist at the University of Chicago, have teamed up to produce many important papers describing the causes and consequences of the housing boom and the financial crisis. In their influential book *House of Debt*, they tend to use wealth quintiles,

Figure 2-7. Leverage of US Homeowners with a Mortgage, by Income Quintile

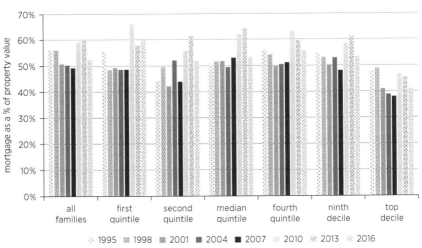

Note: The Survey of Consumer Finances splits the top income quintile into two deciles, and this is reflected in the figure.
Sources: Tables 9 and 13 in Board of Governors of the Federal Reserve System, "Survey of Consumer Finances," last modified November 15, 2017, https://www.federalreserve.gov/econres/scfindex.htm, and author's calculations: mean value of debt secured by primary residence (from table 13) divided by mean value of primary residence (from table 9).

noting that poor households tend to have more debt relative to their net worth. This means that poor households were more likely to suffer from falling home prices and to default. The wealthy, on the other hand, were less leveraged, so they were less affected by falling home prices and less likely to default.[23] This is true, as far as it goes. However, wealth is jointly a product of income and age. Mian and Sufi describe wealth quintiles as "rich" versus "poor," but this could just as well mean "old" versus "young" as it could "high income" versus "low income." There are many "rich" elderly households with low incomes and low debt and "poor" young households with high incomes and high debt.

From 2005 to 2011, households over 55 years old or those with either high incomes or high net worth saw significant gains in net worth. Every other category saw losses in net worth because of the housing bust. Age, wealth, and income are three legs of the stool here, and age is the most important.[24] Mian and Sufi's results may be more accurately interpreted through a generational lens than a poor-versus-rich lens.

With the Survey of Consumer Finances, we can view homeownership and borrowing by age. Leverage is systematically higher among the young (figure 2-8).

Figure 2-8. Leverage of US Homeowners with a Mortgage, by Age of Household Head

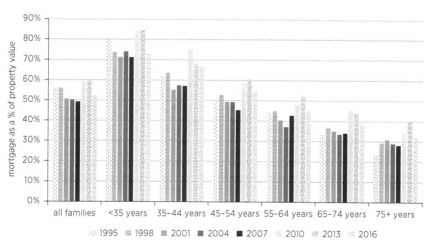

Note: Mean measures in the Survey of Consumer Finances can be sensitive to outliers in subcategories with small sample sizes.

Sources: Tables 9 and 13 in Board of Governors of the Federal Reserve System, "Survey of Consumer Finances," last modified November 15, 2017, https://www.federalreserve.gov/econres/scfindex.htm, and author's calculations: the product of mean value of debt secured by primary residence and percentage of mortgage holders (both from table 13) divided by the product of mean value of primary residence and percentage of primary residence owners (both from table 9).

There was no systematic rise in leverage among any age group during the housing boom. Leverage only rose when home values collapsed.

In a working paper for the National Bureau of Economic Research, Stefania Albanesi, Giacomo De Giorgi, and Jaromir Nosal used a database that identified characteristics of individual borrowers over time in order to further clarify this issue. They found that even in zip codes with high levels of subprime lending, new borrowers tended to have higher credit scores. What debt growth there was among borrowers with lower credit scores tended to be among young borrowers who subsequently maintained rising incomes and rising credit scores. Looking at individual borrowers, there was no shift to high credit risks during the housing boom.[25]

Mian and Sufi conclude, "From 2002 to 2005, there was an expansion in the supply of mortgage credit for home purchase toward marginal households that had previously been unable to obtain a mortgage, and this expansion was unrelated to improved economic circumstances of these individuals."[26] New research, together with the general evidence I have outlined here, suggests that Mian and Sufi were correct that mortgages were available to those who had not been able to borrow as easily before, but that they were incorrect about the economic prospects of those borrowers.[27] It seems, in hindsight, that lenders in the late 1990s and the first few years after 2000 had managed to match new mortgages with households that had positive economic prospects. As Albanesi, De Giorgi, and Nosal report, "Debt growth for young/low credit score borrowers at the start of the boom occurs primarily for individuals who have high income by 2009, and the growth in income is associated in [sic] a growth in credit score."[28]

Albanesi, De Giorgi, and Nosal found that the rise in delinquencies after the bust was largely driven by borrowers with midrange to high credit scores. Many of the delinquencies came from real estate investors who had good credit but utilized nonconventional loans, because such borrowers frequently do not qualify to use conventional mortgage conduits. Given that homeownership and first-time homebuying had been in decline since 2004 and 2005, it is natural—inevitable, really—that more buyers during that period would be investors. And it is true that such buyers may be more likely to use tactical defaults in a market collapse. But this story is much different from the one telling that borrowing by households with bad credit and little means to make mortgage payments led to an inevitable collapse. In this new version of events, it was the collapse in prices that led to increased defaults; the collapse itself wasn't inevitable at all. There weren't millions of hapless new homeowners who were destined to fall behind on their payments. By 2007, the rate of first-time homebuying was exceptionally low, and the investor buyers that took the place of first-time homebuyers were more likely to default tactically when prices declined.

HOMEOWNERS WERE NOT BUYING UP

Figure 2-9 compares the mean and median incomes of homeowners and renters over time. During the housing boom, owner incomes were rising higher while renter incomes were relatively flat.

Combining Bureau of Economic Analysis data and Survey of Consumer Finances data provides an estimate of the relative housing consumption of owners and renters, in terms of the rental values of the homes they inhabited. Rising rents and rising expected future rents were pushing up the prices of homes. The bubble narrative blames this on homeowner speculation, overbuilding, and buyers using credit to purchase homes at prices they couldn't afford. But households were fleeing the high-priced cities, by necessity. The new homes being added to the housing stock were being added in low-cost areas. That is where the marginal new homeownership was concentrated. Rising *rents* in the Closed Access cities, because of the housing supply constraints, were the cause of both the rising prices of homes in the Closed Access cities and the migration to less-expensive cities.

Figure 2-9. Incomes of US Owners and Renters

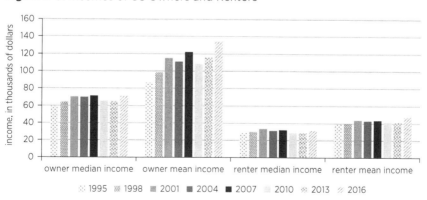

Note: Incomes are in constant 2016 dollars.
Source: Table 1 in Board of Governors of the Federal Reserve System, "Survey of Consumer Finances," last modified November 15, 2017, https://www.federalreserve.gov/econres/scfindex.htm.

Figure 2-10. Rent as a Percentage of Income, for US Owners and Renters

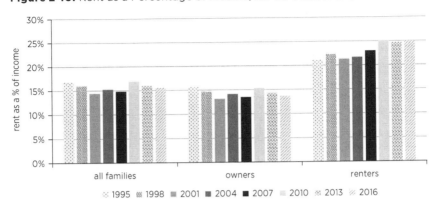

Sources: Tables 1 and 9 in Board of Governors of the Federal Reserve System, "Survey of Consumer Finances," last modified November 15, 2017, https://www.federalreserve.gov/econres/scfindex. htm; table H12-AR from US Census Bureau, https://www2.census.gov/programs-surveys/cps/tables /time-series/historical-income-households/h12ar.xls; table 7.4.5 (Housing Sector Output, Gross Value Added, and Net Value Added) from Bureau of Economic Analysis, accessed September 2018, available at https://apps.bea.gov/iTable/index_nipa.cfm; author's calculations.

Figure 2-10 confirms this. Contrary to vocal complaints about unsustainable consumption enabled by generous credit, homeowners were *downgrading* their housing consumption, in terms of the rental values of their homes. This was mostly accomplished through migration to less-expensive cities. Renters, on the other hand, saw a persistently increasing portion of their income going to rent, especially in the postcrisis years when a lack of new housing across the country has led to high rent inflation.

This situation may be the best example of how confusing homeownership with housing consumption leads to poor judgment. Credit was facilitating housing starts in affordable areas—facilitating a relative *decline* in housing consumption. But because homeownership is so often confused with housing consumption, and housing starts seem as if they must be associated with rising housing consumption, experts mistakenly assumed that rising ownership rates and rising home prices were signs of rising consumption.

Figure 2-11 compares existing home prices (as measured by the Case-Shiller indices published by CoreLogic®) and average new home prices. The Case-Shiller 10 index is an index of 10 leading metropolitan areas that happens to include all five Closed Access cities, and the price spike was centered in those cities. But even the Case-Shiller national price index, which reflects existing home prices across the country, rose more sharply than the average price of new homes.

Figure 2-11. Average Existing and New US Home Prices over Time

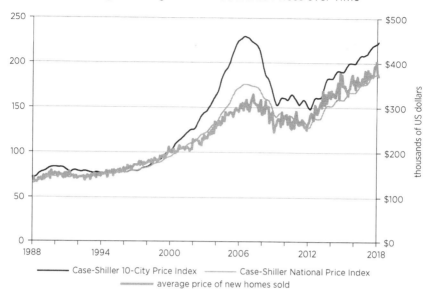

Case-Shiller 10-City Price Index ——— Case-Shiller National Price Index
——— average price of new homes sold

Note: The indices are set to equal the average price of new homes sold in January 1996.
Sources: S&P/Case-Shiller U.S. National Home Price Index and S&P/Case-Shiller 10-City Composite Home Price Index, retrieved from FRED, Federal Reserve Bank of St. Louis; US Census Bureau, "Historical Data," https://www.census.gov/construction/nrc/historical_data/index.html. (The various home price indices referred to as "S&P/Case-Shiller" indices are now maintained and published by CoreLogic®, https://us.spindices.com/index-family/real-estate/sp-corelogic-case-shiller.)

If loose credit had been driving buyers to purchase "too much" housing, new homes would have been expected to rise in price even faster than existing homes.

This chart shows the counterintuitive result of a market with local supply constraints. In this context, consider the following question: If there is a rise in new housing starts, where will those housing starts be located? They must be located where supply is not constrained—the inexpensive areas outside the Closed Access cities. An ironic defining characteristic of the "Two Americas" housing market is that rising housing starts reflect a broad attempt at *reducing* housing expenses. In 2004 and 2005 the strong housing starts were facilitating a mass exodus from Closed Access cities.[29]

Rising housing starts and strong residential investment during the boom were signs of Americans trying to moderate their housing expenses in the face of Closed Access governance—frequently by making compromises concerning career, income, and family in order to move to cities far away where costs were low. In the face of Closed Access, Americans were going to great lengths to find affordable housing.

TROUBLESOME MORTGAGES HELD BY HIGH-INCOME HOUSEHOLDS

In a working paper for the National Bureau of Economic Research, Gene Amromin, an economist with the Federal Reserve Bank of Chicago, and several coauthors, reviewed complex mortgages with creative terms meant to lower early cash payments—mortgages that became very popular during the housing boom. These loans also tended to lack comprehensive documentation, earning them the derisive nickname "liar loans." Amromin and his coauthors concluded,

> Complex mortgages are the contract of choice for high credit quality and high income households, in contrast to the low income population targeted by subprime mortgages.[30] These households use complex mortgages as affordability products to purchase houses that are expensive relative to their incomes, partly due to their expectations of higher future income and house price growth. Complex mortgage borrowers are more likely to provide incomplete documentation for their loans. . . . Overall, both the characteristics of complex mortgage borrowers and their default behavior shed doubt on the popular perception that complex mortgages are pushed by predatory lenders to naive households who do not fully understand the mortgage terms.

They found that these borrowers also tended to default strategically when markets began to collapse.[31]

In other words, troublesome mortgage terms that led to high defaults were due to aspirational, high-income households buying their way into enclaves of privilege—into the cities where spending more than 30% or 40% of your income on rent is just part of the entry fee. In other words, the "liar loans" were going to buyers with *high* incomes. In a Closed Access economy, where real estate is the gatekeeper to opportunity, risky mortgages are taken out by buyers at the top, not those at the bottom.

Amromin and his coauthors' findings are confirmed by the Survey of Consumer Finances.

Figure 2-12. US Households with Debt-to-Income Ratio over 40 Percent

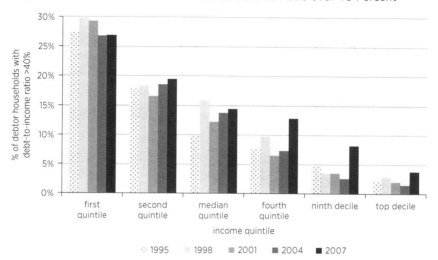

Note: The Survey of Consumer Finances splits the top income quintile into two deciles, and this is reflected in the figure.
Source: Table 17 in in Board of Governors of the Federal Reserve System, "Survey of Consumer Finances," last modified November 15, 2017, https://www.federalreserve.gov/econres/scfindex.htm.

Figure 2-12 shows debtors with debt payments to income over 40%, by income quintile. At the end of the housing boom, there *was* a shift toward mortgages requiring payments of more than 40% of income. From 1995 to 2004, an average of 12.4% of debtors had debt-to-income ratios above 40%. The portion of debtors with payments claiming more than 40% of income increased to 14.8% of debtors in 2007. Yet this shift happened almost entirely among households with high incomes.

Popular opinion wrongly concluded that the housing bubble was built on the backs of marginal households. The situation was quite the opposite. A Closed Access economy means that households will need to segregate by affluence. And we did. Less affluent households were moving to more affordable cities to moderate their cost of living. More affluent households were moving to the enclaves of privilege and paying the fee to enter, in the form of rent or a mortgage.

CHAPTER 3
A Tale of Credit

A common explanation for the financial crisis holds that the middle class was being squeezed, and that families were getting by on unsustainable debt. The thesis presented in this book isn't entirely at odds with this notion. Households are being squeezed by the severe limits to entry into the most prosperous US cities, created by these cities' Closed Access housing policies. But in some ways this narrative of a desperate middle class is at odds with the narrative of a demand-triggered housing bubble. Wouldn't it be very odd if, at the same time that middle-class households were so troubled that they had to utilize debt out of desperation, they also went on an unprecedented buying binge on the single-most-expensive middle-class asset there is? These two stories really don't fit together very well. In the end, the data show that this debt, in the aggregate, was neither a product of desperation nor of lender or borrower excess.[1]

When the rising levels of mortgages are discussed, it is useful to look at mortgages' role in household finances. Mortgages are aspirational. In recent work that carefully reviews data on consumption over time, J. W. Mason, a professor of economics at the City University of New York and a fellow at the Roosevelt Institute, has shown that, since the 1990s, borrowing has generally funded financial assets like housing for high-income households. He further found that consumption and income grew proportionately over time, both for households with high incomes and for those with low incomes.[2] There is no evidence that households with low incomes systematically used debt to fund consumption that exceeded their income growth.

Figure 3-1. US Mortgage Debt, by Income Quintile

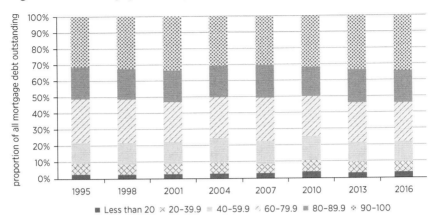

Note: The Survey of Consumer Finances splits the top income quintile into two deciles, and this is reflected in the figure.
Source: Table 13 in in Board of Governors of the Federal Reserve System, "Survey of Consumer Finances," last modified November 15, 2017, https://www.federalreserve.gov/econres/scfindex.htm.

As figure 3-1 shows, *most* mortgage debt across the 20-year period from 1995 to 2016 was held by the *top 20%* of families, by income. Nearly 80% was held by the top 40% of families. More than 90% was held by the top 60%. Less than 10% of mortgages outstanding were held by the *bottom 40%* of families, by income. Any discussion of aggregate mortgages mostly concerns earners with above-average incomes. Further, these proportions in 2007 were nearly identical to the proportions in 1995 and 1998. The only shifts of note were (1) an increase in the proportion of debt held by households in the median income quintile between 1995 and 2004, when homeownership was increasing, from 13% to 15% of the total, and (2) a shift of similar magnitude toward debt held by households with top incomes after the crisis, when homeownership has been declining.

In fact, debt is usually associated with aspirations, not with desperation. Yes, there are cases where someone is laid off and taps a credit card or home equity line for $20,000 or $30,000 of credit in order to bridge a period of distress. But in the vast majority of cases, debt is associated with success and hope. Two-thirds to three-fourths of household debt is mortgage debt. If you have ever been a homeowner, one of the key moments of your life was probably getting the keys and walking into to your first owned home. That joyous and hopeful moment was probably enabled by a tremendous amount of debt.

When debt seems to rise unsustainably above past ranges, it is easy to interpret that rising debt as a sign of distress. And it is true that the sorts of dynamics created by the rising costs of Closed Access cities do impose stress on households. The rising debt that characterized the pre-crisis period was largely due to a bidding war on limited housing, not due to an expansion of homeownership or massive borrowing by households without other decent sources of income.

From the late 1990s to 2008, mortgage debt as a proportion of GDP increased by about two-thirds. But, since most of the rise in homeownership happened in the 1990s, before the rise in prices or in mortgage debt, the expansion of credit to new buyers at the "extensive margin" is an unlikely culprit for the rising prices and debt levels that occurred in the decade after 2000.[3]

THE PASSIVE CREDIT SCHOOL

Debates about the causes of rising home prices in the decade after 2000 have largely coalesced around two schools: the credit supply school, championed most famously by Atif Mian and Amir Sufi, and the passive credit school. Both schools tend to accept the premise that unsustainable pressure from homebuyers created a housing bubble. The credit supply school maintains that it was the supply of credit from increasingly aggressive lenders that induced homebuyers to bid home prices up to unsustainable levels. The passive credit school maintains that the housing bubble was caused by overly optimistic homebuyers of all types, who were seeking credit to fund bids on homes at unsustainably high prices.

It was not unreasonable for researchers to initially assume a bubble had occurred. Before the 1990s, households tended to migrate toward economic opportunity, and cities built homes to accommodate them. With ample new construction, rents largely reflected the cost of building, and these rents tended to equalize between cities. When supply is not being obstructed, real rents are stable in the long run. In that case, changes in home prices tend to be cyclical, and rent is not an important cyclical factor.

The rise in housing prices during the decade after 2000, however, wasn't a typical cyclical event. Rents in Closed Access cities have reached persistently higher levels, far above the norms of other cities. Pundits were confused because a permanent regime shift looks like a cyclical movement when it first begins. It is only when markets don't revert to traditional norms that we can clearly see the difference between a permanent regime shift and the sort of transitory price bubble that was widely assumed to have occurred.

There were several factors influencing home prices between 1997 and 2006. The most important was the impact of supply restrictions in the Closed Access cities. In 2004 and 2005, however, easier access to credit also might have helped to push prices higher, especially in the Contagion cities. The rise in Contagion home prices of more than 50% from the end of 2003 to the 2006 peak is generally viewed as the heart of the housing bubble. When the collapse seemed to pull national average prices back down to near the prices of the late 1990s, this naturally led to broad acceptance of the idea that the entire episode was a cyclical bubble. In fact, a chronic supply problem had triggered a migration event, which may have been briefly accelerated and amplified by more flexible credit access.

There was a close relationship between the housing markets in Closed Access cities and in the Contagion cities. Upwardly mobile young households used mortgage loans to gain entry into Closed Access cities. That triggered heavy out-migration of households priced out of Closed Access cities, which led to a brief housing bubble market in the smaller Contagion cities to which these households fled.

While the Contagion cities did experience a short-lived price jump before prices reverted to levels near where they had been previously, the relative increase in Closed Access house prices has persisted. According to estimates from Zillow, in 1998, real estate in the Closed Access metropolitan statistical areas accounted for about 19% of the national housing stock, by value. At the market top in 2006, it accounted for more than 24%. In 2015, it still accounted for more than 24%. The Contagion MSAs accounted for 6% of national real estate value in 1998; their portion rose to 8% by 2006, then declined back to 6% by 2015.[4] The mass of migrants who were moving from Closed Access cities to Contagion cities, providing fuel for the Contagion bubble, were moving toward cheaper housing.[5] Price data for Contagion cities make it look as if spending on housing was rising, but for many of the individual families moving into those cities, spending on housing was actually declining. In fact, that was the point of the move.

So, in a way, both schools of thought are correct. To the extent that there was a bubble, there was likely a credit supply trigger, but, ironically, even where credit supply appears to have triggered extreme price jumps in cities with more elastic housing supply, the fundamental driver was borrowing by qualified buyers in Closed Access cities, which compelled hundreds of thousands of households to move to *less expensive* housing in other cities.

THE CREDIT SUPPLY SCHOOL

Credit supply proponents have a *self-assured* conclusion that appears to be confirmed by their data.

The early work of Mian and Sufi, originally released in spring 2008, was published before the vast majority of mortgage defaults even occurred, and it was a key element in the development of the excess-credit explanation of the crisis.[6] The country was primed to hear this story, because the rise in private securitizations coincided with the peak period of rising home prices.

The credit supply school builds its case from the following arguments:

- Mortgage lending and home prices increased more in zip codes where incomes were lower, prices were lower, and residents had previously lacked access to credit. Lending at the "extensive margin" to households that previously hadn't been able to borrow pushed prices up.

- These relative price movements happened during the private mortgage securitization boom, suggesting that these new loans were a major source of the new credit supply.

- Incomes in the zip codes where prices were rising the most were not improving relative to incomes in other zip codes, which suggests that the motivation for expanding credit availability was coming from lenders more than from optimistic borrowers.

- Rising home prices led to home equity borrowing, increasing unsustainable credit-fueled consumption at the local level.

- Mortgage fraud was more prevalent in areas with new lending and rising prices.

- Defaults were highest in the areas with the most aggressive lending and price appreciation.

- Prices fell the most in areas where mortgage expansion and price appreciation had been strongest.[7]

These claims require a good deal of analysis. We need to review these claims in light of the alternative Closed Access hypothesis, which says that (1) rising rents in Closed Access cities were the main cause of rising prices and borrowing, (2) those rising prices, potentially facilitated by new mortgages, induced a mass migration event that led to a short-lived bubble in the Contagion cities, and (3) an overreaction in public credit and monetary policies created a housing market collapse and a foreclosure crisis that pulled home prices down across the country without solving the Closed Access problem that is the core cause of high prices.

Much of the evidence that the credit supply hypothesis builds on, such as home equity borrowing, mortgage fraud, and higher defaults where lending was most aggressive, might appear as outcomes in any environment with rising prices, regardless of whether housing supply was scarce or lending was loose.

These outcomes may be associated with credit-fueled price appreciation, but careful analysis is required to confirm that association.

Credit supply researchers have attempted to establish causality between credit availability and various outcomes described above. There is little doubt that, to some degree, frothy markets led to ill-advised or unscrupulous speculating, and vice versa, especially in the smaller Contagion bubble. In contrast, the persistence of high Closed Access real estate values in spite of a crackdown on lending suggests that lenient credit is not a necessary condition for rising prices in Closed Access cities.

Mian and Sufi looked within cities, comparing, for instance, zip codes with low incomes or weak credit within a county to zip codes with high incomes or strong credit in the same county.[8] They didn't pay attention to changes that affected an entire county so that they could focus on the effects of credit supply within the local market. Unfortunately, this focus removed the primary influences on the housing boom from their field of vision. On the other hand, the passive credit researchers have tended to use national data. So, where their conclusions differ from those of the credit supply researchers, it is frequently because the way the passive credit school views the data means they see the differences between households in different metropolitan areas that form the core of the story behind the bubble, while credit supply researchers have tended to remove those differences from the data in order to focus on what they think was the main cause of the bubble.

At a national level, it is true that the places where home prices appreciated the most were places where they had been high to begin with, and naturally the buyers of those homes had relatively high incomes, which is what the passive credit school tends to conclude. Yet lower-priced areas appreciated more than higher-priced areas in select metropolitan areas. And, naturally, within those metro areas, the owners of the homes that appreciated the most were buyers with lower incomes and more credit constraints common for households in those areas. The two schools come to opposite conclusions by focusing on different data. What is the right way to look at the data? Locally or nationally?

It is the national view that is a more accurate guide, because it is the *differences between* metropolitan areas and population shifts between them that have defined the American housing market of the past two decades. Regardless of what caused rising demand, in cities with elastic supply, rising demand tends to lead to more quantity; and in cities with inelastic supply, it leads to higher prices. The fundamental source of demand is the high incomes available in the Closed Access cities, which continue to push up both rents and prices, because these cities have inelastic housing supply. This situation created a secondary source of demand that flowed to other cities, as households were turned away from the Closed Access cities because of a lack of adequate housing and went searching for more affordable places to live.

In order to review the contradictions between these two schools, I will proceed in three sections:

1. In the remainder of this chapter, I will further detail how the Closed Access supply problem is of a scale that dwarfs the differences within any metropolitan areas, and how the evolution of home prices suggests that a lack of housing supply, rather than a surplus of credit, is the cause.

2. In chapter 4, I will detail the peculiar pattern of relative prices within various metropolitan areas. A careful review of that pattern suggests that changing credit access was not the reason low-priced homes within some cities appreciated more than high-priced homes. On the other hand, the late collapse in low-priced home markets *was* caused by tight credit *after* the crisis. The collapse was not the inevitable deflation of a bubble.

3. In chapter 5, I will detail the importance of migration between metropolitan areas, and discuss how migration patterns differed between the Closed Access cities and the Contagion cities. I will highlight how the behavior of homeowners and inter-metro migrants contradicts the notion of a housing boom fueled by unqualified borrowers buying into expensive, low-tier markets. Finally, changes in homeownership during and after the crisis parallel the evidence in home prices, confirming that the early housing bust focused on borrowers with high incomes; and that middle-class homeowners only lost their homes late, after the crisis, when tight credit restrictions had been imposed.

THE BUBBLE WAS ABOUT CITIES, NOT BORROWERS

Figure 3-2 charts about 13,000 zip codes where Zillow tracks median home values from 1996 to 2006. The x-axis measures home values (on a natural log scale), and the y-axis measures the nominal change in median home values from 1996 to 2006. Overlaid on the national scatterplot are those of zip codes in Los Angeles County and in Cook County (Chicago).

Much of the country had moderate home price changes. In more typical places like Chicago, there was little difference between the rate of price changes at the high end of the market and at the low end.

In contrast, in cities affected by the Closed Access problem, (1) prices inside the cities rose much more quickly than in the rest of the country, and (2) prices

Figure 3-2. Home Prices and Price Changes by Zip Code, 1996–2006

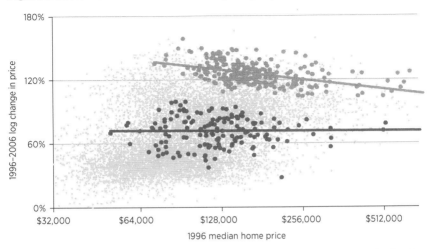

all US zip codes • zip codes in Cook County, Chicago • zip codes in Los Angeles County

Source: Zillow Home Value Index by zip code, Zillow data, https://www.zillow.com/home-values/.

in the low-priced zip codes within the cities rose faster than prices in the high-priced zip codes. Figure 3-2 makes visually clear the question begging to be asked about the housing boom: What was the difference between Chicago and Los Angeles? The question Mian and Sufi asked was about the difference between the different zip codes within Los Angeles or Chicago.

That cloud of small dots clearly tilts up and to the right. Where homes were more expensive to begin with (dots to the right), home prices appreciated more (dots moved up). Where homes were less expensive (dots to the left), home prices appreciated less (dots didn't move up very much). This is what the passive credit proponents see when they look at data at the national scale.

Yet if you look county by county, there are many places that look like Chicago, where there was little difference between the high- and low-tier price changes. And there are a few places where low-tier prices appreciated more than high-tier prices. Mian and Sufi's focus was the difference between the high end and the low end in Los Angeles. If you only look within each county, the question of why prices all across Los Angeles rose by about 50% more than prices all across Chicago remains unaddressed.[9] In general, wherever prices increased more in one part of a county than they did in another, the rising prices happened in lower-priced zip codes where buyers previously had more trouble borrowing. For this reason, it seemed obvious that the cause of those rising prices was

Figure 3-3. Incomes and Income Changes by Zip Code, 1998–2006

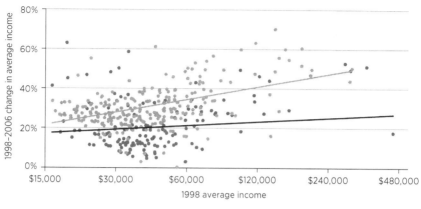

Note: Incomes are estimated by dividing each zip code's total adjusted gross income by its total number of returns. In this chart, for clarity, I have only shown Cook County and Los Angeles County zip codes. *Source:* IRS, "SOI Tax Stats—Individual Income Tax Statistics—Zip Code Data (SOI)," https://www.irs.gov /statistics/soi-tax-stats-individual-income-tax-statistics-zip-code-data-soi.

loose credit. Since all of those differences between counties can be chalked up to fixed effects, using Mian and Sufi's methodology, loose credit appears to be the *primary* explanation for rising home prices.

Ignoring differences between cities also leads to a problematic interpretation of the effect of income on the housing bubble. Figure 3-3 charts income growth much as figure 3-2 charted home price increases. The two counties shown illustrate a widespread pattern among Closed Access and Open Access cities. The Closed Access cities have higher variance in incomes and higher income growth than other cities—*because of* the Closed Access problem. So, compared to Cook County, Los Angeles County has higher income growth across the board, and the difference between income growth at the low end of the spectrum and income growth at the high end of the spectrum is much greater in LA than in Chicago. There has been a small relative increase in income variance in Chicago. High incomes have grown slightly more quickly than low incomes. But incomes in Los Angeles have grown so much faster that the bottom quintile of incomes in Los Angeles has risen as fast as the highest incomes in Chicago.

When passive credit proponents look at data that include both Chicago and Los Angeles, what they see is that home prices are increasing more in Los Angeles, where incomes are also increasing more. This reflects the Closed Access economy. Households are engaged in a bidding war for homes in the economically strong cities where residency is limited. But when Mian and Sufi look at the data within counties, they see slower income growth in low-income areas. Income growth in Los Angeles zip codes where incomes were low was just as strong as income growth anywhere in Chicago, but for Mian and Sufi, the important fact is that incomes in poor areas were growing much more slowly than incomes in rich parts of Los Angeles.[10]

Because the Closed Access cities have much more variation across zip codes in all of these measures—changing home prices, income levels, and income growth—they dominate this analysis. It appears as though everywhere that zip codes had especially low and declining incomes, relative to other zip codes in the same county, lenders were pressing loans onto risky borrowers and pushing prices up far above reasonable values.

The image this paints of the American financial landscape is bleak. It is easy to imagine how one might take this combination of findings to imply that the economy and specifically the housing market were systematically predatory. Mian and Sufi's data make it appear as if the housing market was *broadly characterized* by economically weak, stagnant, and hopeless households being drawn into over-priced houses that were *bound* to collapse in value. This is the dystopian story that has dominated American politics for a generation. And it is simply wrong.

These zip codes were in the middle of the Closed Access migration event. Within Closed Access metropolitan areas, households were moving to less expensive locations, hoping to reduce their housing costs enough to remain in the same metropolitan area. Households from other metropolitan areas were moving in, trying to get a foothold at the rising edge of lucrative postindustrial labor markets. And, every year, hundreds of thousands of the Closed Access households with the lowest incomes were moving away because they couldn't afford to stay. These forces may have been facilitated by credit markets. But this process was not a product of bleak economic conditions in these lower-income areas. Rather, these areas were seen as entry points to exclusivity—the back alleys of the Emerald City.

These stresses are readily visible in the newspaper pages of any Closed Access city—complaints about gentrification, about low-rent tenants being forced out of their homes, and so on. On the ground, the causes of rising prices in these neighborhoods are clear. It is high-income in-migration that those local advocates are fighting.

The complaints at the core of the Closed Access cities, where actual fights about individual new housing developments are waged, don't discuss families being duped into buying overpriced new units that they can't afford. Current occupants complain about highly skilled workers invading legacy neighborhoods. The reason they complain about the new residents is that the newcomers *can* afford more expensive housing units, but those units can't be easily added to the local stock of housing. When high-income residents do move in, they attract more high-income residents, and local activists fear that their *rents* will go up as a result. This is the core battle at the neighborhood level.

In the context of exclusivity and fixed-pie economic wrangling that is created by Closed Access housing, there would be dubious lenders, stretched and stressed buyers, optimistic buyers, speculators, buyers with higher incomes than the average resident of the same zip code, and buyers who lied about their incomes to qualify for a mortgage. All the players that populate the stories of both schools are there. There were hopeful buyers and economically stressed buyers. And credit markets were facilitating their purchases. But credit markets didn't create the context. Rising rents and supply deprivation did.

This activity eventually spilled into the Contagion cities. Contagion cities like Phoenix have long had growing economies in which middle-class families could plug into urban economies where homes were affordable. But increasingly, during the housing bubble, families moving into the Contagion cities were moving as a compromise, away from cities with high costs.[11] Subprime lending claimed above-average market share in the Contagion cities, but at the metropolitan area level, the Closed Access cities had moderate or low rates of subprime lending compared to other cities.[12]

Figure 3-4 shows that these income trends generalize beyond just LA and Chicago. Note the difference between Closed Access income growth and income growth everywhere else. The lowest quintiles in the Closed Access cities were growing as strongly as the highest quintiles in other cities, but from 1998 to 2013, income growth in the top Closed Access quintile outpaced growth in all the other types of cities by about 20%.

Those county-level controls led Mian and Sufi to the wrong conclusion:

> Relative house price growth patterns from 2002 to 2005 are unique in the last eighteen years. This is the only period in which house prices rise by more in ZIP codes with negative relative income growth. This pattern coincides exactly with the expansion of subprime mortgage securitization. Although further research is needed to isolate causality in a more convincing manner, the evidence suggests that the expansion of mortgage originations in subprime ZIP codes, driven by securitization, may itself be responsible for the relative house price growth in subprime areas.[13]

Figure 3-4. Nominal Income Growth, by US Metro Type and Income Quintile, 1998–2013

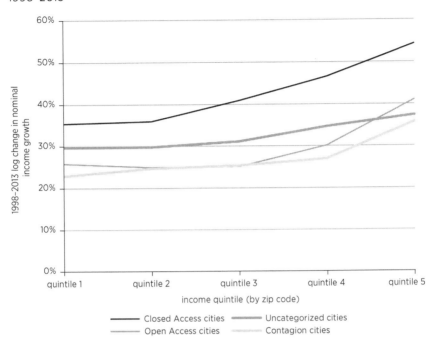

Note: Incomes are estimated by dividing each zip code's total adjusted gross income by its total number of returns. Zip codes are sorted into income quintiles on the basis of the average adjusted gross income reported by tax filers. Zip codes are not weighted by population.
Source: IRS, "SOI Tax Stats—Individual Income Tax Statistics—Zip Code Data (SOI)," https://www.irs.gov/statistics/soi-tax-stats-individual-income-tax-statistics-zip-code-data-soi.

In another paper, Mian and Sufi write,

> House price growth was similar from 1998 to 2002 in high and low credit score zip codes. However, house price growth was much stronger in low credit score zip codes from 2002 to 2006, especially in inelastic housing supply cities. To our knowledge, proponents of the passive credit view have never addressed this pattern. Why did house price growth accelerate so much more dramatically in low credit score zip codes? The credit supply view provides an obvious explanation: mortgage credit for home purchase was expanding rapidly in these neighborhoods, which pushed up housing demand. In inelastic housing supply

cities, house prices rose in response to the demand shock. This is consistent with the evidence . . . showing an expansion of credit to more marginal borrowers.[14]

In this paragraph, we can see how the Closed Access cities (the "inelastic housing supply cities") are a primary source of Mian and Sufi's evidence. And the lack of a comprehensive counternarrative from the passive credit school naturally increases Mian and Sufi's confidence in their own conclusions.

Mian and Sufi conclude, "There is little evidence to suggest that the increased homeowner borrowing that we find in inelastic housing supply MSAs is driven by something other than house prices."[15] That is certainly true. More fundamentally, though, it is driven by house rents. A focus on fast-rising rents in the Closed Access markets can reconcile the empirical findings of these two schools and produces a superior overall explanation of the national housing boom and bust.

FURTHER EVIDENCE THAT LOW-TIER HOME PRICE INCREASES WERE UNRELATED TO CREDIT FOR MARGINAL BUYERS

The idea that credit expansion and private securitizations caused both rising homeownership and rising home prices is contradicted by the fact that the spike in private securitizations lagged homeownership even more than price increases did. As we can see in figure 3-5, when homeownership began to rise (point 1), 6% of residential mortgages were held by private pools, which include subprime and Alt-A loans. Market share had risen to more than 7% by 1998, when half the rise in homeownership had happened and home prices were still near long-term lows (point 2). Privately securitized market share was still only 9% of the total pool of mortgages by the end of 2003. When homeownership peaked in the second quarter of 2004 (point 4), the boom in private securitizations had just begun. By the end of 2006, just 18 months later, private securitizations had ballooned to 21% of outstanding mortgages. The boom in private securitizations came after the rise in homeownership.

The explosion of private mortgage-backed securities and the later development of various versions of collateralized debt obligations (CDOs),[16] which are widely cited as the cause of the price bubble, are clearly lagging indicators here. Strikingly, these securities are also unrelated to new homeownership. Even during the period where privately securitized loan rates were slightly elevated and homeownership was rising, little of the new ownership appears to have come from the net effects of subprime mortgage originations.[17] The sharp jump in

Figure 3-5. Timeline: US Homeownership and Private Mortgage Securitizations

Note: 1 = the point when homeownership began to rise, 2 = the point when half the rise in homeownership had happened and home prices were still near long-term lows, 3 = the point when the national average price-to-rent ratio first rose above the peaks of 1979 and 1989, 4 = the point when homeownership peaked.
Source: Table 14 (Quarterly Homeownership Rates for the U.S. and Regions: 1964 to Present) in US Census Bureau, "Housing Vacancies and Homeownership (CPS/HVS): Historical Tables," http://www.census.gov /housing/hvs/data/histtabs.html; table 1.54 in Board of Governors of the Federal Reserve System, "Mortgage Debt Outstanding," June 2018, https://www.federalreserve.gov/data/mortoutstand/current.htm.

private securitizations and CDOs, if it is an indicator of anything, appears to be an indicator of the beginning of the *bust*.

Figure 3-6 shows the number of first-time homebuyers as a percentage of all households. Starting in the mid-1990s, first-time homeownership picked up by almost 0.5% annually, and total homeownership was also increasing during that period. Then, after rising briefly in 2004, first-time homeownership dropped for the remainder of the private securitization boom.

One could say that the decline in first-time homebuyers after 2004 was a return to the pre-1995 stable trend, but this is a much different claim from saying that private securitizations created a surge of new homeownership that faded as the market was saturated. There was no massive influx of additional buyers when privately securitized mortgages jumped to 21% of the market. If credit expansion had been driving the housing market, we should have expected to see first-time homeownership rising, not dropping to the lowest level of the decade.

THREE CAUSES OF HOME PRICE INCREASES

When home price appreciation is calculated by city and by income, three basic forces on prices are revealed:

1. *Broad-based price increases across all metropolitan areas.* These reflect changes in real interest rates and the general level of inflation. These

Figure 3-6. First-Time Homebuyers as a Percentage of All US Households

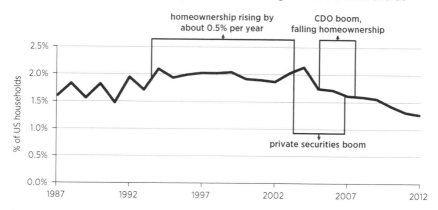

Note: CDO = collateralized debt obligation.
Source: American Housing Survey (US Census Bureau); author's calculations. The survey is biennial.

factors cause prices to increase in the Open Access cities, where ample supply keeps rent inflation low. These cities saw average price appreciation during the period from 1998 to 2006 of about 40%, roughly half from general inflation and half from falling real interest rates that increased the intrinsic value of homes. The rural portions of the country and smaller metropolitan areas tend to look like the Open Access cities.

2. *Metropolitan area–specific changes.* These reflect local rent inflation and expected local rent inflation—the effects of Closed Access. In principle, these increases could reflect either excessive or reasonable expectations for future rent growth.

3. *Prices that differ across income groups within a given metropolitan area.* Since low-income households depend more on lenient credit markets, home prices in low-income areas might rise more sharply than in high-income areas when credit is flowing generously, and they might fall relative to high-income areas when credit is tight. This is the factor that the credit supply school focused on, which I have discussed above.

Figure 3-7 compares home price appreciation from 1998 to 2006. Here, I have placed all zip codes in each MSA into five quintiles, in order of their average income. The Closed Access cities have the pattern that could suggest a credit bubble in the decade after 2000—home price appreciation that was higher in low-income zip codes, even though incomes in those zip codes were not rising as fast as incomes in higher-income zip codes. There is little sign in the

Figure 3-7. US Price Appreciation by Income Quintile and Metro Type, 1998–2006

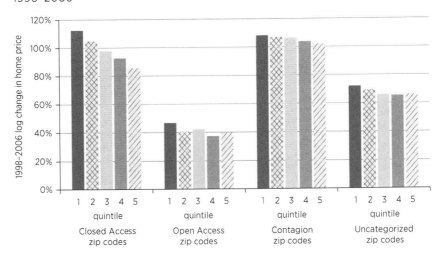

Note: Quintiles were grouped within each metropolitan statistical area.
Sources: IRS, "SOI Tax Stats—Individual Income Tax Statistics—Zip Code Data (SOI)," https://www.irs .gov/statistics/soi-tax-stats-individual-income-tax-statistics-zip-code-data-soi; Zillow Home Value Index by zip code, Zillow data, http://www.zillow.com/research/data/.

other metropolitan areas of unusual increases in home prices among credit-constrained zip codes. Most cities are like Chicago, where prices rose evenly across the metropolitan area. Except in the Closed Access cities, typical price changes across each metro area generally did not vary by more than a few percentage points. Even in the Contagion cities, where home prices shot up rapidly toward the end of the boom, price movements were surprisingly similar across zip codes with different average incomes.

From 1998 to 2006, in the Closed Access cities, home prices in lower-income zip codes rose by about 208%, on average, while home prices in higher-income zip codes rose by about 136%—very different from the pattern in other cities.[18] The only other cities where there was a systematic difference in prices across zip code quintiles are Riverside, California, which has become an exurb of Los Angeles; and, to a lesser extent, Miami and Washington, DC.[19]

Figure 3-8 shows the subsequent price changes among the metropolitan area types after 2006. Here there is definitely a signal that credit access has been tightened across all metropolitan area types. In the Open Access and Contagion cities, since 2006, there has been a credit constraint effect pulling low-end prices down by about 30% compared to high-end prices. In the Open Access cities, home prices were never particularly *high*, and in both Open

Figure 3-8. US Price Appreciation by Income Quintile and Metro Type, 2006–2013

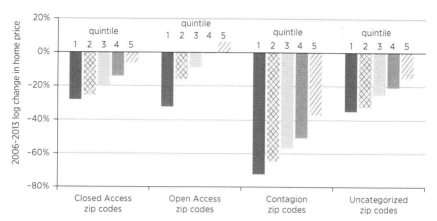

Note: Quintiles were grouped within each metropolitan statistical area.
Sources: IRS, "SOI Tax Stats—Individual Income Tax Statistics—Zip Code Data (SOI)," https://www.irs .gov/statistics/soi-tax-stats-individual-income-tax-statistics-zip-code-data-soi; Zillow Home Value Index by zip code, Zillow data, http://www.zillow.com/research/data/.

Access cities and Contagion cities, home prices in low-income zip codes never rose much higher than in high-income zip codes. But after the bust, home prices in low-income neighborhoods have been knocked back by about 15% to 30% compared to home prices in high-income neighborhoods, in all metropolitan area types, because of suppressed mortgage markets. This is the pattern whether the city is Detroit, Seattle, or Dallas. It doesn't matter whether home prices in a metropolitan area rose by 40% or 100% during the boom.[20]

The preceding evidence has important implications for the "bubble" theory of the housing market. Homeowners in low-income zip codes that never experienced a boom before 2006 still had a bust. What happened to cause that bust? The Open Access cities didn't have sharply rising prices or the spike in foreclosures that the Contagion and Closed Access cities did, yet the divergence between low-end and high-end home prices after 2006 was strong in these cities.

From 2006 to 2013, home prices were relatively flat in higher-income areas in all types of cities except Contagion cities. Where credit constraints are not as important—in zip codes with higher incomes—prices typically recovered (in nominal terms) by 2013.

The difference between the decline of high-tier prices and of low-tier prices after 2006 was smaller in the Closed Access cities and the Uncategorized cities than it was in the Open Access and Contagion cities. If the earlier rise in

Figure 3-9. US Price Appreciation by Income Quintile and Metro Type, 1998–2013

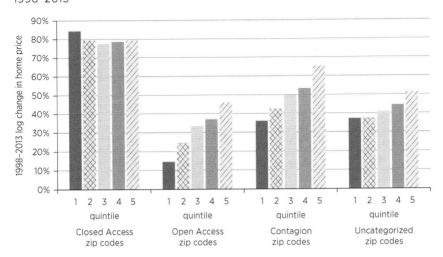

Note: Quintiles were grouped within each metropolitan statistical area.
Sources: IRS, "SOI Tax Stats—Individual Income Tax Statistics—Zip Code Data (SOI)," https://www.irs .gov/statistics/soi-tax-stats-individual-income-tax-statistics-zip-code-data-soi; Zillow Home Value Index by zip code, Zillow data, http://www.zillow.com/research/data/.

low-income Closed Access housing really did reflect a credit boom, wouldn't a shift to a constrained credit market cause the prices of low-income housing in Closed Access cities to fall especially sharply? Yet, from 2006 to 2013, home prices in the bottom quintile fell by less in the Closed Access cities than they did in any other type of city. This suggests that credit availability wasn't actually the primary cause of the boom.

Looking at price appreciation over the entire period from 1998 to 2013 (figure 3-9) reveals a stark difference between the Closed Access cities and the rest of the country. The net effect of the boom and bust has been a sharper decline in prices in low-tier compared to high-tier zip codes in every type of city *except* the Closed Access cities. Even though mortgage markets after the bust have been tighter than they had been for decades, Closed Access home prices remain high in all zip codes. By 2013, credit constraints should have pulled prices at the low end of the market down compared to 1998, yet home prices at the bottom end remain strong in Closed Access cities. These are the markets where price/income multiples are extremely high and credit constraints should be the most binding.

The US did not have a credit-fueled housing bubble that inevitably burst. An endemic supply shortage is pushing prices up in Closed Access cities, and policymakers imposed a credit shock on the entire country that decimated home equity in low-end markets in every city.

The net takeaway from all of this is threefold:

1. There is little evidence that credit-constrained zip codes outside the Closed Access cities exhibited unusual systematic price appreciation during the boom.

2. In Closed Access cities, homes in zip codes with low incomes retain the highest price appreciation over the entire period from 1998 to 2013, even though credit markets have been unusually tight since 2007. Therefore, it seems unlikely that the long-term price upswing of these homes has been caused by loose credit.

3. Outside Closed Access cities, newly adopted credit constraints can certainly be blamed for the relative *decline* in home values in low-income zip codes during the *bust*.

REDUCING MORTGAGE ACCESS CREATED THE BUST

Because most observers, the Federal Reserve, and other policymakers misdiagnosed the problem, their reaction to the housing boom led to a housing bust, and their reaction to the bust was to sharply curtail mortgage credit to all but the most creditworthy households. Some of this might have been a reasonable market reaction. If banks are afraid of more volatility, regardless of its source, they avoid lending to households that would be more sensitive to volatility. Much of the pressure to tighten lending standards has come from policy decisions at the government-sponsored lending organizations and from bank regulators that have created an atmosphere of uncertainty and implicit or explicit liabilities for bankers lending to riskier borrowers.

These misguided reactions to the bust created a lagged reaction in home prices. From 2008 to 2011, the prices of low-priced homes collapsed in all cities, whether the prices of these homes had experienced unusual gains or not. Thus the broad-based and devastating collapse in low-priced housing markets across the country came very late—*after* the recession.

The continued sharp restriction of mortgage credit to low-income and low-FICO-score households has caused housing demand to collapse in zip codes where incomes are lower than average. Across the board, homes in those zip codes are now undervalued.

During the boom, cities were the primary drivers of the housing market. If you knew what city a home was in, you could make a good guess about how

Figure 3-10. Home Prices and Price Changes by Zip Code, 2006–2016

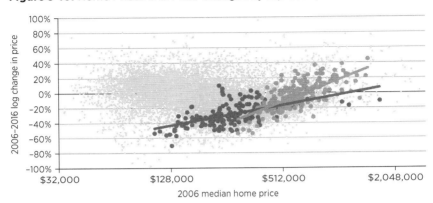

all US zip codes • zip codes in Cook County, Chicago • zip codes in Los Angeles County

Source: Zillow Home Value Index by zip code, Zillow data, https://www.zillow.com/home-values/.

much its price had increased. Since 2006, during the bust, the local differences that the credit supply school was looking for have become dominant. Now you need to know what neighborhood a home is in to have a good idea of how its price has changed. Now, as we see in figure 3-10, Chicago and Los Angeles look more alike. Government policy didn't reverse the trends of the boom—it made new trends. Los Angeles home values continue to outpace those of Chicago. But the overreaction, the moral panic, about the housing boom led to a wholesale desertion of the bottom half of the mortgage market. Instead of having two kinds of cities with two different patterns—Closed Access cities with very high and rising prices (and somewhat stronger price changes at the low end of the market) and other cities with moderate price changes across the market—now all cities look similar. Houses at the top end are just holding on to their value, and home values at the bottom end lag far behind, even in most cities where they never saw unusual gains.

This is how a market characterized by a *negative shock in credit supply* looks. The lack of credit is now a barrier to the owner-occupier market, so low-tier prices reflect the additional costs and the lack of tax benefits available in the landlord market, relative to the owner-occupier market. Policymakers tried to solve a problem that didn't exist, and they have imposed a great cost on the most vulnerable households.[21]

A consensus has developed around the belief that credit access causes price bubbles. The prevailing theory holds that a credit bubble is followed by an inevitable credit bust. That is wrong. Figure 3-2 is a picture of localized exclusion—a bidding war for access. Figure 3-10 is a picture of a national credit collapse. What existed was a localized supply bust, and then a national credit bust was piled on top of it. Predictions that the housing bubble would burst became self-fulfilling prophecies. The bust was taken as proof of its own inevitability, even though a housing bust did not occur in most other countries that experienced similar booms, including Canada, Australia, and the United Kingdom. Policymakers have learned all the wrong lessons. As a result, the credit bust has created an even more fractious divide between the haves and the have-nots.

PART II

WHAT REALLY HAPPENED

CHAPTER 4
How Rising Prices Cause More Rising Prices

M uch of the analysis of home-price behavior tends to simply look at how prices change over time. But an interesting question that might be asked is, How do the relative prices of homes in low-priced zip codes compare to those in high-priced zip codes? What sort of return on investment do low-priced homes earn relative to high-priced homes?

Thinking of a home as an investment, the rent-to-price ratio (rent/price ratio) is the gross yield on the investment—the cash flow claimed by the owner, as a percentage of the price. The inverse of that is the price/rent ratio, which is a measure commonly used to analyze the housing market, similar to the price-to-earnings ratio in the equity markets. One sign that seemed to signal a housing bubble was a rise in the nationally estimated price/rent level far above previous ranges. It seems as if price/rent should be relatively stable across a housing market and across time. But it isn't.

In Los Angeles, for instance, a house that earns about $28,000 in annual rent sells for about $480,000. That is a price/rent ratio of about 17×. So a house that rents for $40,000 might be expected to sell for about $680,000. But it doesn't. A house in Los Angeles with a rental value of $40,000 tends to have a price/rent ratio of about 22×, so that it sells for about $880,000. Notice that, comparing the two houses, the higher-priced house sells for nearly double the price of the lower-priced house, but only about half of that difference is due to its higher rental income. The other half comes from the higher price/rent multiple.

This is systematic across cities and across time. It has nothing to do with the housing boom.

Figure 4-1. Price-to-Rent Ratio by Zip Code, for Dallas and Los Angeles, March 2018

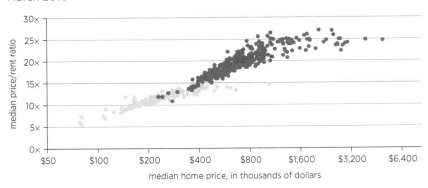

Dallas–Fort Worth zip codes   ● Los Angeles–Long Beach–Anaheim zip codes

Source: Zillow data, http://www.zillow.com/research/data/.

But, at very high prices, price/rent expansion reaches a ceiling. So, in Los Angeles, a house with annual gross rent of about $60,000 would sell for about $1.3 million—a price/rent ratio of about 22×, similar to the $880,000 house. The price difference between the $1.3 million house and the $880,000 house *is* mostly due to the different rental values. Each city has a ceiling price/rent ratio above a certain price level. In many cities, few (if any) zip codes reach a high enough average price level to reach that ceiling. It seems to kick in typically around $500,000, but each city has a different ceiling. In cities such as Dallas and Phoenix, the ceiling appears at less than $300,000, while in Los Angeles it takes effect closer to $800,000. Below the ceiling, in every metropolitan area there is systematic positive feedback from rising prices. In other words, any factor that pushes prices up, including rising rents, causes prices to rise even more than rents.[1] Part of the reason a $400,000 house costs more than a $200,000 house is simply that it gets the benefit of a higher price/rent ratio.

Figure 4-1 shows this systematic positive feedback from rising prices to the price/rent ratio in Dallas and Los Angeles. Each time prices double, price/rent ratios tend to rise by about 3 or 4 points, until they reach the ceiling. As rents increase, the effect of an increasing price/rent ratio pushes prices up even more, until prices reach the point where the price/rent ratio levels off.

Notice that, even though home prices in Dallas are much lower than they are in Los Angeles, both sets of prices line up near a single linear relationship between price and the price/rent ratio, although the peak price/rent ratio is much lower in Dallas. This doesn't mean, however, that higher-priced homes are simply a function of higher ratios. If rents remained level in Dallas but the price/rent ratio on Dallas homes doubled to near the price/rent ratios that are common in Los Angeles, homes in Dallas would still be much less expensive than they are in Los Angeles. (For example, a Dallas home now selling for $200,000 with a price/rent ratio of 11× would sell for $400,000 if the price/rent ratio doubled to 22×. Homes in Los Angeles that sell for $400,000 only sell at price/rent ratios of about 15×. It is the higher rent that makes homes in Los Angeles more expensive, and one reason price/rent ratios in LA are higher is *because* rents are higher.) On the other hand, if *rents* in Dallas doubled, then we should expect price/rent ratios to expand, and home prices in Dallas would begin to reach prices that are common in Los Angeles. (In other words, as rents rise, the price/rent ratio would climb the incline, pushing Dallas price/rent ratios toward the ratios common in Los Angeles, until they reach the level where Dallas price/rent ratios level off.)

This makes intuitive sense because of the tax benefits of homeownership. A home in the highest-income neighborhoods with near-universal ownership rates should have added value worth something close to the marginal top tax rate, since most of the potential tax benefits will be claimed. This fits with research that finds that the tax advantages of ownership are heavily weighted toward high-income households.[2] According to White House estimates for 2017, total tax savings among the three main housing tax benefits are[3]

- nontaxability of imputed rent $121 billion
- mortgage interest deduction $66 billion
- capital gains exclusions $43 billion

Figure 4-2 shows the relative value of the mortgage interest deduction, by income level. In practice, most of the deduction goes to high-income households. Other income tax benefits will also naturally flow more to owners with high incomes and high tax liabilities.

So, if the tax benefits of homeownership were removed, this rising price/rent effect might become much less pronounced. However, the effect may also reflect factors such as the effects of credit constraints, as well as the higher relative cost of being a landlord in lower-priced neighborhoods, less depreciation on properties where value is due to location, and so on, all of which tend to put downward price pressure on less-expensive homes. Whatever the causes are, the positive relationship between price and price/rent ratios is quite strong. As figure 4-3 shows, it remains strong even in a simple, national regression of the two measures (price in a natural log scale and price/rent in a linear scale). Of course, the ceiling

Figure 4-2. US Mortgage Interest Deduction Savings by Income, 2004

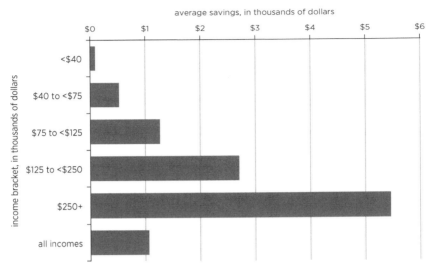

Source: James Poterba and Todd Sinai, "Tax Expenditures for Owner-Occupied Housing: Deductions for Property Taxes and Mortgage Interest and the Exclusion of Imputed Rental Income," *American Economic Review* 98, no. 2 (May 2008).

Figure 4-3. US Price-to-Rent Ratio and Median Home Price, by Zip Code, March 2018

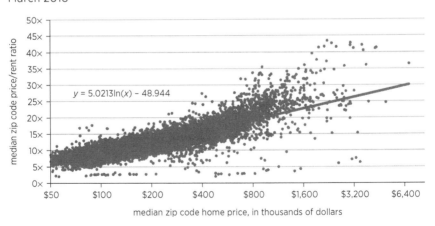

Source: Zillow data, http://www.zillow.com/research/data/.

price/rent ratio will be different for each city, and will reflect local factors such as property tax rates and expectations of future rent inflation.

Broadly speaking, this rising price/rent ratio appears to explain why the value of low-priced houses in Closed Access cities rose relative to high-priced houses, and why that effect was much less common in cities that weren't Closed Access. Low-priced neighborhoods appreciated rapidly in the Closed Access cities because they benefited from both rising rents and an increasing price/rent ratio. In contrast, the *highest-priced* homes in those cities had already reached the ceiling where price/rent levels off. It was the high-end home price/rent ratios rising more *slowly* than homes in the rest of the metro area that explains why lower-priced homes in those areas showed greater price appreciation on average than high-priced homes.

The value of higher-priced homes is a function of the income and tax liabilities of the marginal buyer, the rental value that is untaxed to homeowners, and the tax deductibility of mortgage interest, which would scale with price. Price, rent, and income should all play a role in this effect, and they also correlate strongly with each other between zip codes, so price/rent ratios are higher where incomes are higher, and they are higher where rents are higher. And, however we look at it, they level off at the high end. Figure 4-4 shows price/rent levels in zip codes with different average income levels in Dallas and Los Angeles. Figure 4-5 shows price/rent levels in zip codes in both metro areas with

Figure 4-4. Median Price-to-Rent Ratio and Income, by Zip Code, 2013

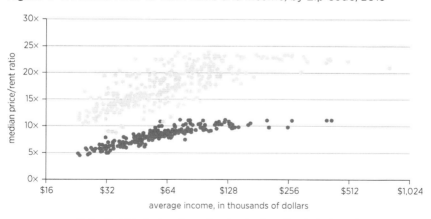

Note: The price/rent ratio is for June 2013; the average adjusted gross income is for 2013.
Sources: Zillow data, http://www.zillow.com/research/data/; IRS, "SOI Tax Stats—Individual Income Tax Statistics—Zip Code Data (SOI)," https://www.irs.gov/statistics/soi-tax-stats-individual-income-tax-statistics-zip-code-data-soi.

Figure 4-5. Median Price-to-Rent Ratio and Rent, by Zip Code, 2018

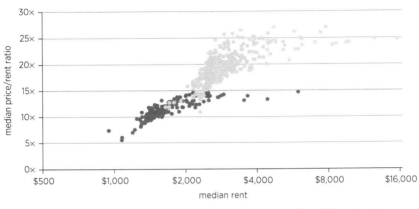

• Dallas–Fort Worth zip codes • Los Angeles–Long Beach–Anaheim zip codes

Note: Data are for all home types.
Source: Zillow data, accessed May 2018, http://www.zillow.com/research/data/.

different median rent levels. In both cases, price/rent is low where rents and incomes are low. It rises systematically as incomes and rents rise. And it levels off in zip codes with the highest income and rent levels. This pattern is universal across metro areas. Metro areas only differ in terms of the price where the price/rent ratio peaks, and what that peak price/rent ratio is.

COMPARING CITIES

Figure 4-6 compares price/rent ratios from Chicago, Seattle, San Francisco, and Los Angeles. In 2013, all cities had a similar pattern, with a surprisingly tight relationship between price/rent and price. Each city had a peak price/rent level that was different. They all flattened out somewhat at the top, but most zip codes fell somewhere on an upward sloping line as prices rose.

At the 2006 peak in housing prices, price/rent ratios were generally higher across almost all zip codes and metropolitan areas. What sets the Closed Access cities apart (San Francisco and Los Angeles in figure 4-6) is not the fact that their price/rent ratios deviated from this pattern. Rather, these cities are distinctive because homes across the entire metropolitan area had reached the point where price/rent levels peak.

As it was, peak price/rent ratios in San Francisco and Los Angeles were not that different from peak price/rent ratios in Seattle. The difference was that in

Figure 4-6. Comparison of Metro Area Price-to-Rent Ratios

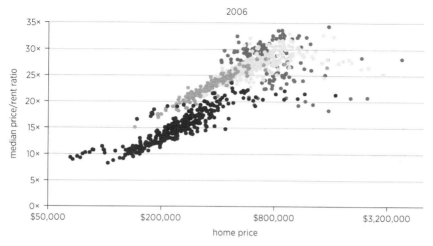

San Francisco zip codes · Los Angeles–Long Beach–Anaheim zip codes
Seattle zip codes · Chicago zip codes

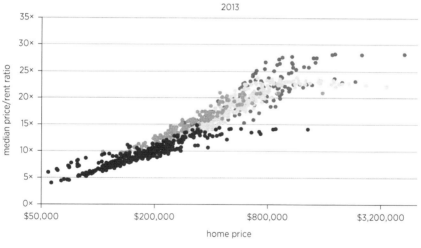

San Francisco zip codes · Los Angeles–Long Beach–Anaheim zip codes
Seattle zip codes · Chicago zip codes

Note: Zillow rent data at the zip code level are only available from 2010 onward, so 2006 rents have been estimated using metropolitan statistical area rent measures.
Sources: Zillow data, http://www.zillow.com/research/data/; author's calculations.

Seattle, there were only a few zip codes where average home prices were above that $500,000 range where price/rent ratios tend to level off. So, while the peak price/rent ratio in Seattle was more than 25×, very few zip codes sold at that level. Most were between 20× and 25×. In Los Angeles and San Francisco, the median home price in most zip codes had reached $500,000 or more, and price/rent ratios were around 25× to 30×.[4] If price/rent levels had continued to rise indefinitely with home prices, then homes at the very high end of the market would have been selling at price/rent ratios of more than 35×.

Now, let's compare the relative price appreciation of homes in these metropolitan areas, by price quintile. Figure 4-7 compares San Francisco, Los Angeles, Seattle, and Chicago. In both Chicago and Seattle, between 1999 and 2006, the relative price change among all zip codes was very similar. Los Angeles and San Francisco displayed the pattern that is peculiar to the Closed Access cities. In those cities, it was the plateauing of price/rent levels in the top quintiles that caused the price appreciation in high-priced zip codes to be less than in low-priced zip codes, where price/rent ratios expanded as prices rose.

Recall that Mian and Sufi pointed to the especially fast price appreciation in low-income zip codes as evidence that the housing boom was triggered by more-generous lending terms. These patterns suggest that lending standards are not the cause of those different price changes. It just happened that price fluctuations in the Closed Access cities were so pronounced that, for the first time, this pattern in price/rent ratios became visible across whole metropolitan areas.

Los Angeles, New York City, and Boston all have a similar pattern. In all three metropolitan areas, all five quintiles of zip codes, by median home price, were below $400,000 in 1999. And, by 2006, prices in all quintiles were pushing toward their ceiling price/rent level. So, in those metropolitan areas, as we move up the price quintiles, each quintile reached that ceiling price/rent level earlier, and so, going from the lowest- to the highest-priced quintile, each quintile had somewhat less price appreciation during the boom. In figure 4-7, in Los Angeles, as prices rise and each quintile in turn hits that price/rent ratio plateau, it peels off from the other quintiles. First the top quintile (in 2003), then the fourth, then the third, and so on, as each quintile reaches that peak price/rent level.

The regularity of this effect is shown by looking at the few other cities where this happened. In San Francisco, both of the top quintiles had already moved above $400,000 by 1999. Both of the top two quintiles had reached their ceiling price/rent ratio by then, so, as figure 4-7 shows, the top two quintiles in San Francisco appreciated at the same rate after 1999. Only the bottom three quintiles appreciated at a faster rate, until each reached the ceiling price/rent level.

Figure 4-7. Relative Price Appreciation, by Metro Area Price Quintile

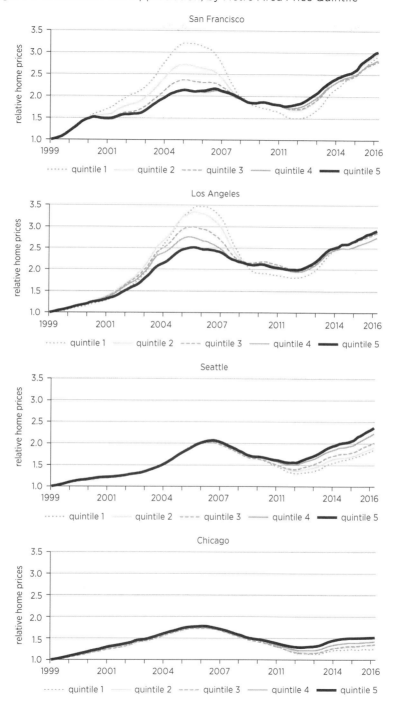

Note: January 1999 prices are set to 1.
Source: Zillow data, http://www.zillow.com/research/data/, sorted by January 1999 price, based on simple average of zip codes, not weighted by population.

At the other end of the spectrum, we have Riverside, California; Washington, DC; and Miami (figure 4-8). These cities began 1999 with all five quintiles well below the ceiling price, and by 2006, only prices in the top couple of quintiles had risen above the ceiling level. So these cities display the opposite pattern from San Francisco. In these cities, the bottom quintiles appreciated at roughly the same rate, and it was only the top quintiles that had begun to appreciate at significantly slower rates.

During the boom, the difference between high-tier and low-tier price appreciation has little to do with credit access. It has to do with this ceiling where price/rent ratios stop rising. In most cities, most home prices never reached this ceiling, so there was little difference in price appreciation within those cities.

Of course, cities with high prices tend to have inelastic supply and homebuyers with strained credit or riskier loan terms, so rising prices in low-priced zip codes will appear to correlate with those factors, too. Models that only look at price changes, without accounting for the relative price/rent ratios across zip codes, will appear to provide convincing evidence that mortgages to credit-constrained borrowers in cities with inelastic housing supply caused their relative home prices to rise. But that correlation between changing prices and credit access is spurious.

It is understandable that this effect has not been properly accounted for. Until services such as Zillow began creating and publishing these data recently, these sorts of patterns would have been difficult to notice. And, even then, it was only when the price shifts in the Closed Access cities became extreme that the effect on relative price changes became clear.

CAUSE OF THE PRICE/RENT RATIO PATTERNS

Income tax benefits of homeownership are weighted toward the top of the market, and they amount to about 25% of net imputed homeowner rental income (after expenses and depreciation).[5] This partly reflects the rising proportion of owner-occupiers as one moves upmarket in a given city. In high-tier markets, most potential buyers are capturing the tax benefits, while in low-tier markets many are not. The mortgage interest tax deduction is famously top-weighted, because it has value only when interest expenses are larger than the standard deduction. Implicit rental income for owner-occupiers is not taxed, which is especially beneficial to taxpayers in the top tax brackets.[6] The capital gains exemption also tends to rise in value along with the price of the home, topping out where the exemption limits are hit, which is at $500,000 for couples.

Figure 4-8. Relative Price Appreciation, by Metro Area Price Quintile: Marginal Cases

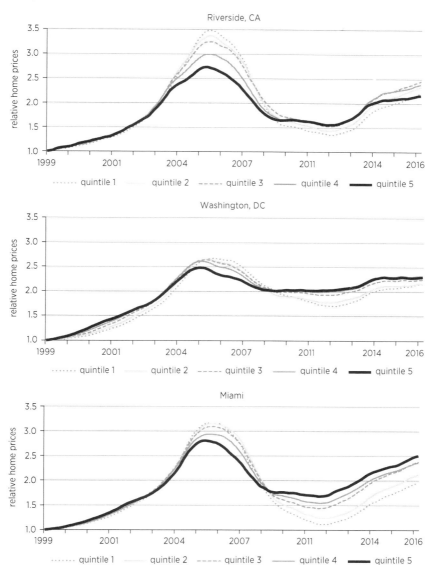

Riverside, CA

.... quintile 1 ——— quintile 2 - - - - quintile 3 ——— quintile 4 ━━━ quintile 5

Washington, DC

.... quintile 1 ——— quintile 2 - - - - quintile 3 ——— quintile 4 ━━━ quintile 5

Miami

.... quintile 1 ——— quintile 2 - - - - quintile 3 ——— quintile 4 ━━━ quintile 5

Note: January 1999 prices are set to 1.
Source: Zillow data, http://www.zillow.com/research/data/, sorted by January 1999 price, based on simple average of zip codes, not weighted by population.

For all these reasons, the value of the tax benefits rises in proportion to home prices up to a level where ownership rates and marginal tax rates are at their maximum, after which the effect levels off. This means that owner-occupier tax benefits can explain much of the price/rent pattern across cities and zip codes.

Recent papers have discussed the effect of tax subsidies on prices.[7] David E. Rappoport estimates that the mortgage interest deduction increases the average home price by about 7%.[8] Christian A. L. Hilber and Tracy M. Turner also find that mortgage interest deduction subsidies are capitalized into home prices.[9] A shift in Danish tax rates provided a chance to estimate the size of this effect; and Jonathan Gruber, Amalie Jensen, and Henrik Kleven find that tax benefits were entirely capitalized into home prices.[10]

But the key point is that the anomalous price behavior in Closed Access cities during the housing boom was in the highest-tier markets, not the low-tier markets. Whatever the specific root causes of that pattern—whether tax subsidies or something else—the pattern itself is systematic and is evidence that low-tier borrowing wasn't the crucial factor. Prices in all markets were changing systematically, and the systematic way in which home prices change includes the effect that prices in high-tier markets in very expensive cities change systematically more slowly than prices in mid- and low-tier markets.

The behavior of collapsing home prices after the boom is also useful evidence regarding the importance of credit expansion versus rising rents as the primary causes of rising prices. Researchers have noted that where prices had risen the most, they also fell the most sharply. Many zip codes lost more ground than they had initially gained. This has been taken as evidence that all prices were unsustainable, and that the low-tier housing markets in the Closed Access cities were propped up by unsupportable lending. According to this view, the eventual collapse led to additional value destruction when households were harmed by the wave of foreclosures and the inability to repay unsustainable debts. While it is understandable that so many observers have reached this conclusion, a careful review of price behavior during the collapse points to a different conclusion.

After the peak of the bubble in 2006, there were two phases of contraction. In the first phase, as home prices sharply declined in 2007 and 2008, prices in the Closed Access cities retreated, quintile by quintile, and a reversal of the price/rent effect occurred. By late 2008, when the broader financial crisis hit, the differences between zip code quintiles had generally been fully erased. Also, in cities like Seattle and Chicago, where low-tier and high-tier prices had risen together, they also retreated together during this period.

So the reversal of prices during this period is explained by the price/rent effect, a reversal of what had occurred over the previous few years. Just as lower-priced homes appreciated more rapidly as they were climbing that price/rent incline, they also declined more rapidly as they descended the incline.

Notice how, in figures 4-7 and 4-8, by late 2008, cumulative price appreciation had reconverged among all price quintiles in all cities. That is because as prices declined, all cities fell back down to a range where most homes were worth less than $400,000 or $500,000, and price/rent ratios declined as prices declined. In cities like Chicago and Seattle, where there was no difference in price appreciation on the way up, and in cities like Los Angeles and San Francisco, where low-tier prices had risen much more than high-tier prices—in all types of cities, relative prices across price quintiles were the same in late 2008 as they had been in 1999.[11]

The second phase of retraction was after late 2008, during the period when regulatory pressures against lending to marginal borrowers were strengthened when the government-sponsored lending organizations were taken over in September 2008 and through new laws such as the Dodd-Frank Wall Street Reform and Consumer Protection Act, passed in July 2010. These actions led to lending standards that were tightened far beyond any other recent standard. During this period, in every city, whether Open Access or Closed Access, there was a separation, and now top-quintile home prices stabilized or increased again, but low-priced homes continued to decline or lagged behind. This *was* a difference caused by changing credit access, and it happened very late in the story.

This period of extreme tightening of credit standards led to the relative decline in low-tier home prices. This was an imposition of national public policy, so this relative decline in low-tier prices was universal across cities during the second phase of the housing bust. It had little to do with what had happened during the boom. In fact, during this phase, low-tier markets in Closed Access cities have performed better than low-tier markets in most other cities, because the relentless march of rising rents in those cities and the continuing sorting of low-income households out of those cities (to be replaced by households with higher incomes) means that prices there continue to rise. And, as prices rise, high-tier zip codes are once again hitting the ceiling price/rent level, while low-tier zip codes keep climbing up the price/rent incline.

Home prices across a metro area have never increased sharply enough at high enough levels for this price/rent pattern to be so noticeable before, so researchers have not accounted for it. John M. Griffin at the University of Texas and Gonzalo Maturana at Emory University have done interesting work quantifying dubious lending practices and found that where dubious lending was more prevalent, prices rose higher than where dubious lending was less prevalent.

Then they found that where dubious lending had been prevalent, prices fell even more sharply than they had risen.[12] It is understandable that Griffin and Maturana would interpret this as strong evidence that credit supply was a causal factor in changing prices. However, recognizing the systematic patterns in price/rent ratios and carefully reviewing the timeline of changing prices leads to a different conclusion.

We should expect that dubious lending would be more prevalent in zip codes where prices have risen to uncomfortable levels, even if high prices weren't *caused* by dubious lending, so the correlation does not prove causation. Maybe high prices led to dubious lending. Griffin and Maturana recognized this problem, so they used various methods to check for causation.[13]

In one test, they controlled for differences in zip codes, and they paired zip codes that had seen similar price run-ups from the third quarter of 2004 to the second quarter of 2006. Then they divided these zip codes into those where dubious lending was more prevalent and zip codes where dubious lending was less prevalent. (Figure 4-9 shows their results.) They treated the period from 2006 to 2012 as a single event, so their conclusion is that normalization of markets after 2006 exposed the excesses of the zip codes where more dubious mortgages had been made, and so prices dropped more in zip codes where dubious lending had driven prices up.[14]

But figure 4-9 actually confirms the description of events that I have laid out above. First, note that Griffin and Maturana find that tightened lending standards came before price declines. They find a pattern where dubious lending declines first, and then prices decline.[15] So the decline in dubious lending is a leading factor. Dubious lending didn't continue for two years after prices peaked. In fact, according to the measure Griffin and Maturana use, dubious lending had generally disappeared by late 2007.

So in Griffin and Maturana's test, by design, prices rise at the same rate until the second quarter of 2006. Now, look only at the two years following that. If the retraction of dubious lending were the cause of falling prices, then we should see prices in areas with dubious lending falling more sharply immediately. On the other hand, if prices were rising and falling for other reasons and were simply following the systematic price/rent patterns described above, then during that time, prices in these zip codes would fall at similar rates, regardless of the prevalence of dubious lending. And that is what the figure shows.

Then there are two distinct points where prices diverge. First, at the end of 2008, prices in areas with more dubious lending decline sharply. After that, in 2009, prices in both sets of zip codes level out. Then another divergence happens when prices fall again after the second quarter of 2010, again falling

Figure 4-9. Price Changes after 2006 in US Zip Codes Where Dubious Loans Were Prevalent

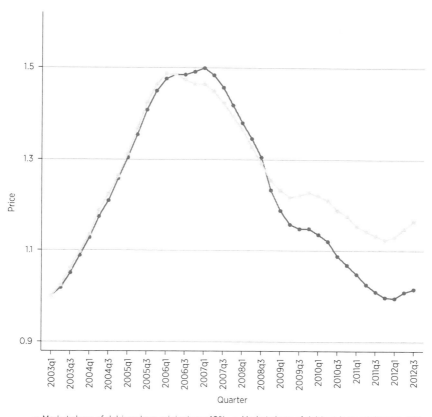

● Market share of dubious loan originators >10%　　● Market share of dubious loan originators <5%

Note: First-quarter 2003 prices are set to 1. Data about average market share of dubious loan originators are for third-quarter 2004 to second-quarter 2006. 858 ZIP codes with a market share of dubious lenders greater than 10% were matched with a control group of ZIP codes that (a) had a market share of dubious lenders less than 5%, (b) were in the same MSA, and (c) which had similar housing returns during the 2003–2006 run-up period. The similarity of the plots from 2003–2006 is by construction. See source for more details.
Source: Figure 2, panel A, in John M. Griffin and Gonzalo Maturana, "Did Dubious Mortgage Origination Practices Distort House Prices?," *Review of Financial Studies* 29, no. 7 (July 2016): 1686. Used by permission.

more steeply in the more dubious zip codes. These points in time happen to coincide with the federal takeover of Fannie Mae and Freddie Mac in 2008 and with the passage of Dodd-Frank in 2010, both of which led to significant tightening of lending standards.[16]

What figure 4-9 describes is a market where dubious or loose lending coincided with rising prices but did not cause unusual price behavior. Then negative credit shocks that happened two and four years after the initial contraction of dubious lending created negative price shocks in credit-constrained zip codes. There were two publicly imposed credit shocks that had little to do with dubious lending. These shocks tightened credit access to levels unprecedented in recent decades, which decimated home-buyer demand in credit-constrained zip codes. These were the same zip codes that would have been more likely to tap dubious loans when prices were high. In short, what we see in this figure is that lending standards had little to do with relative price changes until public policy pushed lending standards far outside any previous norms after the crisis had occurred.[17]

In another test, Griffin and Maturana examined zip codes in cities with elastic housing supply—where homes could be built with few restrictions. Here, they simply compared zip codes with more dubious lending to zip codes with less dubious lending. They found the same pattern.[18] In this case, prices during the boom rose slightly higher in the *less* dubious zip codes. Then prices fell more steeply in the zip codes with more dubious lending. Griffin and Maturana conclude that in cities with elastic supply, dubious lending led to oversupply instead of leading to rising prices, and when the market corrected, the oversupply caused prices in those zip codes to drop farther.

As I have noted, there was never a systematic oversupply of homes.[19] As with Griffin and Maturana's analysis of prices in inelastic markets, the retraction of dubious lending amid a supply overhang in elastic markets should have led immediately to falling prices. Dubious lending had begun to decline in 2006 and disappeared by 2007. Housing starts had begun to collapse in 2006. Surely an oversupply of homes triggered by dubious lending would have led to relative price declines within two years of these developments. Instead, again, prices moved together and only later diverged, in two steps that coincided with two negative credit shocks from the government lending enterprises and from the passage of Dodd-Frank, shocks that occurred long after homeownership rates, housing starts, dubious lending, and home prices had been in steep decline. In Griffin and Maturana's tests, the pattern is the same whether supply is elastic or inelastic.

The decline in home prices that was blamed on dubious lenders in 2004–2006 was actually due to late federal policy choices.

THE SHIFT FROM OWNERS TO INVESTORS

The decline in low-tier prices since 2008 may be thought of as a shift in the price/rent pattern, not a deviation from it. At the low end, there are fewer owner-occupiers, and at the high end, almost all owners are owner-occupiers. So the tax benefits of ownership are gradually priced in as one moves upmarket within a given city. Since 2008, there has been a severe decline in owner-occupier demand because of tighter lending markets. This could certainly be described as a liquidity shock—a lack of funded buyers in the market. But there has been an active all-cash and investor market during this period. The steepening of the price/rent pattern since 2008 could be described as a shift from an owner-occupier market to an investor market. Investors buy the homes that entry-level buyers can no longer get credit for and rent them out to the people who would have bought the homes under the previous and more lenient credit standards.

Landlords have higher costs, and they don't receive as many tax subsidies, so when owner-occupiers were driven out of these markets by tightening credit, prices settled at lower levels.[20] Investors are frequently blamed for driving up prices and pushing owner-occupiers out of the market. Institutional buyers are frequently singled out in this complaint, but landlords for single-family homes are a very localized market. Even after extensive institutional buying after the crisis, institutions own less than 10% of rented single-family homes.[21]

The increase in investor buying since the housing bust has coincided with a decline in low-tier prices, not an increase. Instead of complaining that investors are pushing prices up, we should take investor buying as a sign that some force is pushing prices down. Data reported by the Bureau of Economic Analysis also confirm this. Net rental income has risen since the bust as a percentage of market prices. Yields on housing investments have been strong because investors have been able to buy properties at bargain prices.

These dislocations highlight the symbiotic relationship between a functioning finance sector and working-class households. Access to credit is an important tool for smoothing income and consumption, and for facilitating broad access to ownership and savings. There is also the danger of fraud and abuse, which call for transparent rules and accessible means for resolving disputes and putting a stop to inappropriate lending. Both of these things can be true of credit at the same time. We have thrown out the baby with the bathwater. Working-class households are being damaged. Sometimes, *de*regulation is a matter of social justice. At this time, reducing regulations that make it difficult to build, as well as regulations that make it difficult to take out a mortgage, would improve living standards for Americans with moderate incomes.

CHAPTER 5
Migration and Contagion Cities

Much excellent work has recently been done on the economic costs of Closed Access policies, and there have been endless debates about the role of credit in the housing bubble, yet few have understood how these two issues are related. The key missing piece that connects the two is migration—particularly the way that segregation by income triggered migration from the Closed Access cities to the Contagion cities.

A mass migration *away from economic opportunity* became so intense that it created a Gold Rush–sized housing bubble. If the prices of homes in Phoenix in 2004 and 2005 are viewed only in isolation, it looks like there was a bubble caused by a large spike in demand. But the marginal new homeowners were arriving from the Closed Access cities in California. The buyers driving up home prices in Phoenix were moving away from more prosperous cities in order to reduce their cost of living. Their migration was a direct attempt to *reduce* their individual housing expenditures, even though their arrival meant that demand rose sharply, overall, in Contagion cities.[1]

CLOSED ACCESS CREATED A REFUGEE CRISIS

Rising incomes, rising rents, and inter-city migration explain regional patterns of home price appreciation. A working paper for the National Bureau of Economic Research by a pair of professors at the University of Pennsylvania's Wharton School of Business, Fernando Ferreira and Joseph Gyourko, looked at this from both a metropolitan area–level perspective and a neighborhood-level perspective. Their findings support the passive credit school. Here are the final three out of five points they outline in their abstract:

> Third, local income is the only potential demand shifter found that also had an economically and statistically significant change around the time that local housing booms began. Contemporaneous local income growth is large enough to account for half or more of the initial jump in house price appreciation. While these estimates indicate that the beginning of the boom was fundamentally justified on average, they do not imply that what followed was rational. Fourth, there is important heterogeneity in that result. Income growth is large and jumps at the same time as house price appreciation in areas that boomed early and have inelastic supplies of housing, but not in late booming areas and those with elastic supply sides. Fifth and finally, none of the demand-shifters analyzed show positive pre-trends, but some, such as the share of subprime lending, do lag the beginning of the boom. This suggests that key players in the lending market more responded to the boom, rather than caused it to start.[2]

Ferreira and Gyourko are describing the roots of the Closed Access–Contagion housing problem. Rising incomes in the Closed Access cities led to rising home rents and prices. That triggered households with modest incomes and households that sold homes for windfall gains to migrate to the Contagion cities. In both cases, according to Ferreira and Gyourko, nonconventional mortgages were a reaction to the boom, not the cause. The triggers the authors find for home price appreciation were rising incomes, migration, and low interest rates.

If loose credit actually was luring marginal households into overpriced homes during the housing bubble, wouldn't booming Closed Access cities attract households with lower incomes that now had expanded access to credit? Easy credit would allow in-migrants with limited income to buy into expensive markets, while existing residents with budget constraints would be able to utilize their growing home equity to remain in homes that were otherwise unaffordable. Yet the Closed Access cities actually had declining populations during the height of the boom because both existing renters and homeowners were leaving at higher rates.

The Contagion cities (inland California, Arizona, Nevada, and Florida) experienced the opposite pattern. They did have sharply rising home prices at the peak of the bubble, and they did have rising in-migration, largely coming from Closed Access cities. That in-migration was coming from places where home prices and rents were much higher.

The average population of the US during the 1999–2006 period was about 288 million people. This divides roughly as

Closed Access cities	46,032,093	16%
metropolitan areas in AZ, inland CA, FL, NV	30,260,800	10%
other metropolitan areas	126,834,305	44%
nonmetropolitan areas	85,698,610	30%
	288,825,809	

About half of the metropolitan populations in the Contagion states reached price/rent ratios above 20×. In other words, roughly 5% of the country experienced a housing bubble, as it is generally described. About 16% of the country has high home prices because rents are high and are expected to continue to rise, because these areas have Closed Access housing policies. Most of the country generally exhibited textbook behavior regarding supply, rents, and prices. Prices in some places were moderately higher because real long-term interest rates were low, and a few other places experienced some additional price appreciation that was not as extreme as in the Closed Access or Contagion cities because of some combination of rising incomes, migration pressures, or supply constraints.

Even though the Closed Access cities accounted for about 16% of the US population from 1999 to 2006, they only accounted for about 7% of housing unit permits. Three Open Access cities—Dallas, Houston, and Atlanta—accounted for only about 5% of the US population, but they accounted for 9% of housing unit permits (and Phoenix accounted for another 3%). For that eight-year period, the Open Access cities approved nine housing units per 100 residents. The Closed Access cities approved two. The building boom and the price boom happened in almost entirely different places. About *90%* of the new homes built from 1999 to 2006 were built in metropolitan areas with moderate rents. The *building* boom was an Open Access phenomenon. And, where it happened, moderate home prices generally reflected fundamentals.

What about the bubble cities? They comprised two distinct groups. The Contagion cities have little in common with Closed Access cities, and in fact are their mirror images in many ways.

Figure 5-1. US Closed Access and Contagion Net Domestic Migration

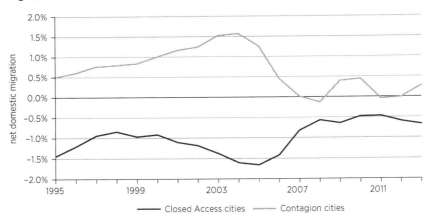

Note: Migration is measured as a percentage of population.
Sources: IRS, "SOI Tax Stats—Migration Data," last modified November 30, 2017, https://www.irs.gov/uac/soi-tax-stats-migration-data, based on number of exemptions reported; author's calculations.

In the Contagion cities, the new homes were meeting the extreme demand from in-migration. The stream of in-migration rose from 0.5% of the resident population in 1995 to 1.5% during the boom (figure 5-1). The Contagion cities never had too many homes. The inventory buildup that started in 2006 was prompted by the end of the inflow of Closed Access refugees. There is no way that any market—planned, regulated, or unfettered—could suddenly shift from net in-migration rates of more than 1% annually to rates of 0% without ending up with some unsold inventory.

In some technical sense, the large amount of unsold inventory in the Contagion cities in 2008 could be called "oversupply." There was certainly a supply of homes that did not have willing buyers. But this is sort of like explaining to a cancer patient that the patient is skinny because he or she isn't eating enough. It is technically true, while entirely missing the point. If the Contagion cities had tried to prevent oversupply by building *fewer* homes in 2003–2005, the price bubble would have been *worse.*

The refugee crisis was connected to an active lending market. But Closed Access lenders weren't funding homeownership by financially marginal households. They were funding homes for high-income, young, aspirational households that had been crammed into rental units. They were accelerating the segregation by income that is created by Closed Access policies.

This migration pattern was also one of the causes of the declining population of the Closed Access cities. Even before the bubble, young people were moving to places like New York City to make their big-city dreams come true, and ending up getting married and starting families. But as such families grow, they tend to look for less crowded, less hectic cities for their children to grow up in, and they move away. So, according to IRS data on the number of exemptions per tax return, households moving into Closed Access cities tend to have about 0.2 fewer members than households moving out. This did not change during the mass migration of the bubble period. In fact, the difference widened as Closed Access families that were homeowners were enticed to take their equity gains and move away. Since the number of new housing units is very limited, this magnified the downward pressure on the Closed Access population.

Figure 5-1 reflects net domestic migration (in-migrants minus out-migrants). Figure 5-2 shows gross migration both into and out of the Contagion cities. Migration into the Contagion cities rose between 2003 and 2005. But once home prices there began to rise, out-migration also increased in 2004 and 2005. These cities were becoming secondary Closed Access cities because the flow of Closed Access migration was overwhelming them, creating a second wave flowing out of them. Then, in 2006, the inflow dropped sharply. Doesn't it seem strange that every location supposedly caught up in a speculative frenzy is characterized by thousands of residents moving away as home prices rose? If the problem in Contagion cities was too many homes, why would these cities see a sudden drop in in-migration and an increase in out-migration?

Figure 5-2. US Contagion Gross Domestic Migration

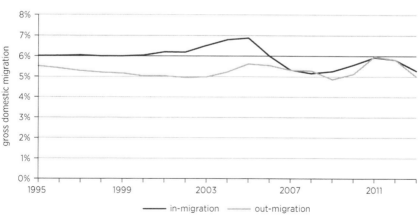

Note: Migration is measured as a percentage of population.
Sources: IRS, "SOI Tax Stats—Migration Data," last modified November 30, 2017, https://www.irs.gov /uac/soi-tax-stats-migration-data, based on number of exemptions reported; author's calculations.

For the collapse in the Contagion markets to have been caused by an oversupply of homes or by a malinvestment into homes that then had to be "worked off," the number of homes built in the Contagion cities would have had to have been doubly extreme. Think of how many extra housing permits would have had to have been issued in the Contagion cities to meet the rapid in-migration and to *overbuild* on top of it—especially for there to still be excessive stock years later.

In the Phoenix metro area, for instance, in 2001, about 42,000 permits for new housing units were issued. By 2005, the number had shot up to 61,000. But net in-migration increased from about 23,000 households to about 44,000 households over the same period.[3] So the Phoenix housing market saw production skyrocket by about 50% in just four years, which seemed to indicate an undeniably frothy market. Yet that growth in units simply met demand from new in-migrants. And, even on the downside, the Phoenix housing market was responsive. In 2006, net in-migration suddenly dropped back to 29,000 households and housing permits followed suit, dropping to 43,000. Meanwhile, rental vacancies remained flat until 2008.[4]

In 2006 and 2007, there was a lot of inventory in Phoenix as sellers held out hope in a buyer's market. But houses in Phoenix generally had occupants. It wasn't excessive building in 2004 and 2005 that caused prices to drop and vacancies to rise in 2008.

Ben Bernanke, referring to housing starts in 2011 that were still at only half the level they have normally been during post–World War II recessions, noted, "To some extent, the drop represented the flip side of the pre-crisis boom. Too many houses had been built, and now the excess supply was being worked off."[5] It isn't hard to find this sentiment, even in 2017, even as housing starts continue to plod along at a depression-level pace after a decade, even as housing units per adult continue to drop ever lower. In fact, there weren't too many homes even in 2006. This is obviously the case in the Closed Access cities— where home prices were far higher than anywhere else while hundreds of thousands of households left town because of a shortage of housing. But it is arguably the case even in the Contagion cities.

INTERNATIONAL MIGRATION

A reasonable question to ask is whether much of this domestic migration was triggered by international migration. Maybe the Closed Access cities are natural entry points for international immigrants, and what the charts indicate is simply a natural outflow of domestic residents from those cities into the rest of the country as immigrant families settle into the US culture and economy.

Foreign migration is a little difficult to track, but the Census Bureau does estimate foreign migration into cities.[6] New York City, San Francisco, and Los Angeles do have strong net foreign migration. But among the Contagion cities, so do Miami and Phoenix; and among the Open Access cities, so do Houston and Dallas. As a group, the Closed Access cities have somewhat more net foreign in-migration than the Open Access and Contagion cities, but the difference is not nearly large enough to explain the systematic differences in migration among these cities (figure 5-3). Thus, foreign migration doesn't appear to have much to do with what makes domestic migration patterns in Closed Access cities different from patterns in the other large cities.

WHO WERE THE MIGRANTS?

The American Community Survey has comprehensive data on US households. Unfortunately, detailed metropolitan area–level data only date back to 2005. But that is far enough to provide a good picture of the migration surge from the Closed Access cities.

The migration away from Closed Access cities is systematically weighted toward younger households with lower incomes (figure 5-4) and less education. At the peak of the outflow, 2% (net of in-migration) of the bottom-income quintiles were moving away annually. Among them, the households between 25 and 35 years old were moving away at a rate of more than 4% per year at the peak. Even after the migration surge ended with the housing bust, households with lower incomes continue to move away (on net) at a rate of more than 1% per year.

These migrants are split between renters and homeowners. Renters were moving in distress, because of rising rents. Homeowners were moving tactically, selling in hot real estate markets and moving away with their windfalls. Figure 5-5 compares these flows in absolute annual numbers of households.

Renters make up most of the persistent outflow of low-income households. Outflows among low-income households did rise somewhat during the boom, but have remained strong even after it.

Closed Access is a regressive policy regime, which is noticeable in figure 5-5. The migrants flooding out of the Closed Access cities consisted mainly of two groups: (1) households with high incomes, which could afford Closed Access homes and thus pocketed gains from the hot market, and (2) households with

Figure 5-3. Net International and Domestic Migration by US Metro Type, 2000–2003

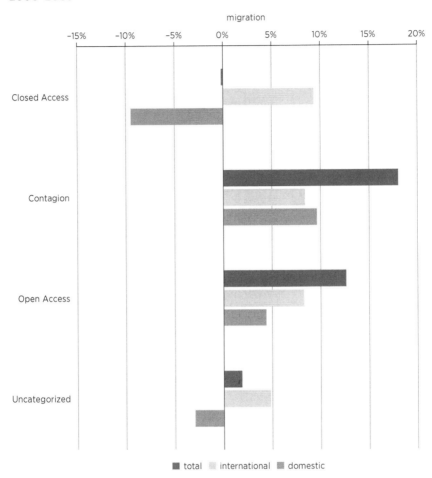

Note: Data are based on estimates from April 2000 to July 2003. Estimates extending to July 2007 appear to reflect a similar pattern. Migration is measured as a percentage of population.
Source: Paul J. Mackun, "Population Change in Metropolitan and Micropolitan Statistical Areas: 1990–2003" (Current Population Report P25-1134, US Census Bureau, Washington, DC, September 2005). Estimates to July 2007 are available in Paul J. Mackun, "Population Change in Central and Outlying Counties of Metropolitan Statistical Areas: 2000 to 2007" (Current Population Report P25-1136, US Census Bureau, Washington, DC, June 2009).

low incomes, which couldn't afford Closed Access homes and were moving away because of high rents.

Make no mistake: homeowners with low incomes did benefit from a tremendous amount of profit-taking. Stated as a percentage of the local population

Figure 5-4. US Closed Access Net Domestic Migration, by Income Quintile

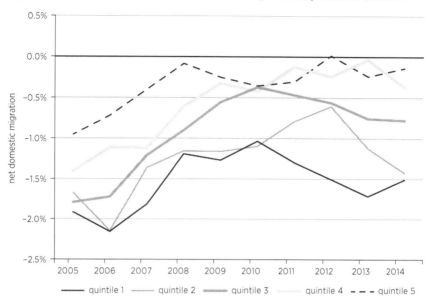

Note: Migration is measured as a percentage of resident households in the same income quintile. Income quintiles are based on national incomes.
Sources: American Community Survey (US Census Bureau); author's calculations.

of mortgaged homeowners with incomes in the middle and lower quintiles, annual in-migration was about 1% and annual out-migration was 4%, meaning that 3% of this population was leaving the Closed Access cities each year. At first glance it seems that the housing bubble could actually be characterized as a bout of wealth redistribution to former Closed Access working-class homeowners who claimed capital gains when they sold their homes. But there just weren't very many of them, in absolute numbers.

What sort of real estate market characterized the Contagion cities—the cities absorbing this wave of migrants? A surge of high-tier homeowners who could afford to buy at the high end combined with low-tier renters fleeing Closed Access cities. The Contagion markets were specifically overcome by a migration event firmly rooted in the problems of Closed Access. This bubble developed primarily in the Contagion cities because of a lack of supply in Closed Access cities. The new homes being built in the Contagion cities were being built for these migrating households, some of which needed rental units and some of which were looking for places to invest their real estate windfalls.

Figure 5-5. US Closed Access Net Domestic Migration, by Income Quintile and Tenure

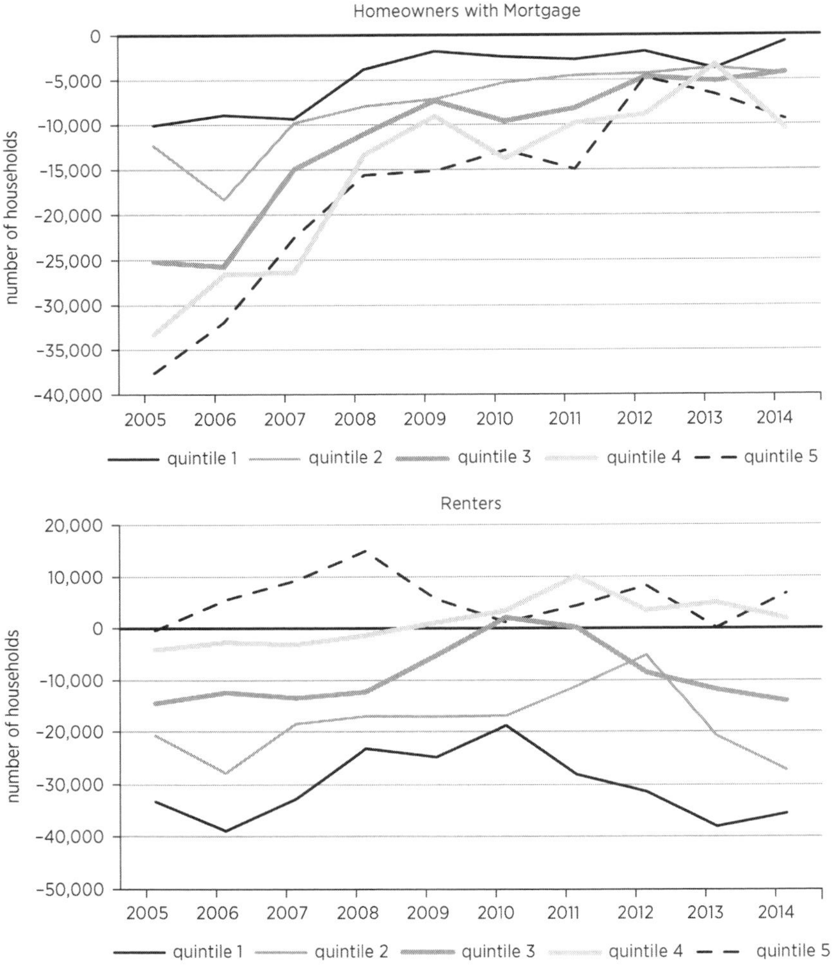

Homeowners with Mortgage

Renters

Note: Tenure is based on tenure at destination. Migration is measured as the total number of resident households. Income quintiles are based on national incomes.
Source: American Community Survey (US Census Bureau).

THE MISSING MIDDLE

Home prices in the Closed Access cities are so high that it is difficult for typical working-age families to own homes there. Ownership rates are generally low in Closed Access cities, especially among working-age, middle-income households. And, increasingly, those types of households don't live in Closed

Figure 5-6. Ownership of US Closed Access Housing Stock by Households with a Mortgage, 2005

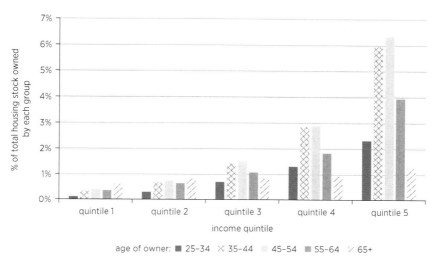

Note: Income quintiles are based on national values.
Source: American Community Survey (US Census Bureau).

Access cities, either as renters or as owners. When households are arranged into national income quintiles, where each quintile should compose about 20% of a city's population, about 30% of Closed Access households are in the top national income quintile. Only about 17% of Closed Access households fall into each of the bottom three quintiles.[7]

Figure 5-6 shows how top-heavy Closed Access real estate ownership is. The figure shows the percentage of the housing stock owned by households with mortgages from each age and income subgroup. For instance, in 2005 about 6% of Closed Access housing stock was owned by 35–45-year-olds with top-quintile incomes and a mortgage. Younger households and households with moderate incomes were much less likely to own homes in the Closed Access cities. Households under 45 years of age with incomes in the median quintile that owned mortgaged homes composed 2.2% of Closed Access households, but composed 4.7% of households in other areas. Households with moderate incomes are less likely to live in Closed Access cities than in other cities, and, if they do, they are much less likely to own homes than they would be in other cities.

All working-age households in the bottom three income quintiles that own their homes and have a mortgage account for only 8% of the entire Closed Access housing stock—half the percentage such households account for in

Figure 5-7. Net Domestic Migration for Selected Metro Areas, 2000–2007

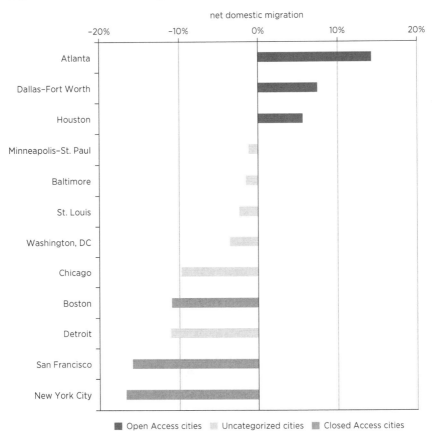

Source: Paul J. Mackun, "Population Change in Central and Outlying Counties of Metropolitan Statistical Areas: 2000 to 2007" (Current Population Report P25-1136, US Census Bureau, Washington, DC, June 2009).

other areas—and typically they purchased their homes long ago. Middle- and low-income borrowers aren't pushing Closed Access prices up. Closed Access prices are pushing middle- and low-income households out.

Figure 5-7 compares domestic net migration for 12 of the largest metropolitan areas from 2000 to 2007. Here we see three of the cities with strong Open Access policies and economic opportunity: Atlanta, Dallas, and Houston. Domestic migrants have been moving into both the core cities and their suburbs.

Despite the strong demand for living space in the Closed Access cities, there is an astounding level of out-migration. New York City, Boston, and San

Francisco have net domestic out-migration levels that look like Detroit's. In San Francisco, even the suburbs experience out-migration.

A Boston Federal Reserve paper calculated that, for 2000–2007, net domestic migration out of New England amounted to about 284,000 residents. Of this out-migration, there was net migration of about 175,000 residents to Florida alone.[8] This pattern explains why the contagion of rising home prices on the East Coast was sharpest in Florida. On the West Coast, the contagion spread inland from coastal California, to the Inland Empire and then to Arizona and Nevada.

In 2005, net migration to Florida from New Jersey, New York, Connecticut, and Massachusetts amounted to about 0.8% of Florida's population. In the same year, net migration from California to Nevada, Arizona, and Oregon amounted to about 1.1% of each state's native population.[9]

To give an indication of the scale of this migration, the average annual population growth of the five largest Closed Access cities since 1995 has been about 0.7%. So, just to handle the out-migration from New York City and Boston in 2005, nearly as many additional homes were being built *in Florida* for New Yorkers and former Boston residents as in New York City and Boston. The rate at which Nevada, Arizona, and Oregon were building homes *just to accommodate refugees* from San Francisco and Los Angeles was higher than the rate at which San Francisco and Los Angeles are even capable of building in total.[10]

The Closed Access cities, where prices were the highest and rose as sharply as they did anywhere, were the places where the base of homeowners with lower incomes was the smallest and where out-migration of such households was the strongest. When high prices spread to the Contagion cities, households with lower incomes there also began to move away. When observers debate the fundamental causes of the housing bubble—aggressive lending, optimistic borrowing, or local crises in housing supply—this pattern is key. The general pattern of migration and ownership was away from the expensive cities and toward cities with *more affordable* housing. It is a lack of local housing that would lead to this pattern.

TRANSFERRING TRADES

One element contributing to the migration pattern that overwhelmed the Contagion cities might be the trend of increasing occupational licensing. Households that are being forced out of the Closed Access cities by the economic stress of high rents frequently face an additional challenge. If household members work in a field characterized by state-sanctioned credentials, they may have incomes bureaucratically tethered to their current locations. A White House report from 2015 found that inter-state migration rates for those in the least licensed occupations were more than 10% higher than inter-state migration rates for those in the most licensed occupations, while intra-state migration rates were similar.[11] Licensed workers have much lower rates of inter-state migration. This presents a problem, especially when local conditions are inducing migration because of economic stress caused by rising costs.[12]

Occupational licensing may have affected the migration patterns at the height of the housing boom. There are frequently regional reciprocity agreements among states with licensing requirements. Contractor licenses are especially prominent in the West. California's Contractors State License Board has reciprocity agreements with Arizona, Nevada, and Utah.[13] This would create an incentive for some California workers in the construction industry to prefer a move to the Inland Empire, or to these neighboring states, even if home prices there were beginning to rise. A move beyond this region would have added risks and costs.

Foreclosures weren't particularly high in places like San Francisco proper. Foreclosures *were* high in suburban California and in cities that became exurbs, such as Sacramento and Riverside and the first line of cities beyond these—Phoenix and Las Vegas. These were the places households were moving to when they moved away from the Closed Access centers in an attempt to lower housing expenses. Often the least disruptive option was the one in which they maintained some access to a high income but took on an unusual amount of housing expense.

WASHINGTON, DC, AND SEATTLE

At first glance, Seattle and Washington, DC, appear to be Closed Access cities, with barriers to building such as down-zoning and height restrictions.[14] Plus, rent inflation in Washington, DC, and Seattle has been similar to rent inflation in the Closed Access cities since the mid-1990s. Rent inflation in all of these cities has averaged about 1% to 2% above US non-shelter inflation for 20 years.

But Washington, DC, and Seattle do not demonstrate the same level of economic distress through domestic out-migration as the Closed Access cities do. Homes can be expensive in these cities, and prices did move up quite a bit during the boom. But they aren't as high as prices in the Closed Access cities, as a proportion of local incomes (figure 5-8).

Rent affordability is manageable in Washington, DC, and Seattle, mostly because incomes are high. Unlike in the Closed Access cities, median household

Figure 5-8. Median Home Price-to-Income Ratio

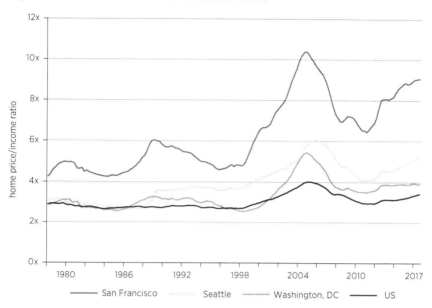

Source: Zillow data, http://www.zillow.com/research/data/.

income in Seattle and Washington, DC, is high both before and after rent, compared to the US average. This is what we should expect to see—housing taking less of the typical household's budget as incomes rise.

There are enough obstacles to housing expansion in Seattle and Washington, DC, to cause households to bid up the rents and prices of prime units. The housing stock in these cities is growing enough for households to keep rental expenses somewhat manageable, even if they have to adjust their real housing consumption downward (through smaller size, fewer amenities, and less desirable location) in order to maintain their housing expenditures within comfortable levels.

This is a different state of affairs than in the Closed Access cities. It may be difficult to afford adequate housing in Seattle and Washington, DC, if you have a low income. But in the Closed Access cities, it is difficult to afford adequate housing even if you have a relatively high income. One could argue that this is a matter of degree, not a matter of kind—that Seattle and Washington, DC, are Closed Access cities, but that Closed Access policies have not yet pushed rents high enough to create the complete signature of Closed Access: rent that claims an unusual portion of incomes even though those incomes are high; high domestic out-migration, especially among households with low incomes; and housing price/rent multiples far above those of other cities. The same could be said of Miami and Chicago. There are some limits to home-building and there are some signs of affordability issues. But all of these cities allow more housing expansion than the Closed Access cities. The ancient pattern of migration flows toward opportunity is generally intact here.

Washington, DC, obviously has a source of income somewhat different from that of the Closed Access cities. Seattle's source of income is tied to frontier information sectors, with firms like Amazon, Microsoft, and Zillow headquartered there. It will be interesting to see how housing policy evolves there and how Seattle deals with the population pressures that will naturally come along with economic success. The choice for Seattle is whether working-class households can move in or whether, eventually, working-class households must move out. In either case, progress means that the city will change. This is the central dilemma for residents who want to preserve the city they knew, and it has no easy solution.

WHO WERE THE BUYERS?

The American Community Survey and the American Housing Survey can provide information about the changing character of homeowners.[15] These data are not based on mortgage applications, so they are not as susceptible to biases about borrower incomes and characteristics due to fraudulent or misstated application information. The sample size is low, especially with the American Housing Survey,[16] but fortunately the story to be told here is so much at odds with conventional wisdom that even these broad indicators are informative.

Figure 5-9 compares buying activity in each city type among high-income and middle- to low-income households, as measured by the American Housing Survey. Buying activity was much higher among households with high incomes during the boom, especially in Closed Access cities where prices were highest.

Middle- and lower-income buying was somewhat strong in the Contagion cities before 2003, but it declined as prices shot up at the peak of the bubble. Everywhere prices were rising, working-class buyers were leaving. Middle- and lower-income buying has remained strongest, relative to the boom, in the Open Access areas. These shifts in buyers reflect three trends created by the housing bust: (1) a decline in homebuying in general, (2) a devastating decline in Contagion city buying across income levels, and (3) a ratcheting up of regional income segregation, meaning only buyers with above-average incomes can buy into Closed Access cities, and middle-class households buy into the other areas.

Figure 5-9. Number of US Homebuyers, by Income Quintile and Metro Type

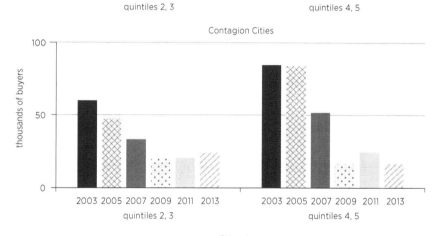

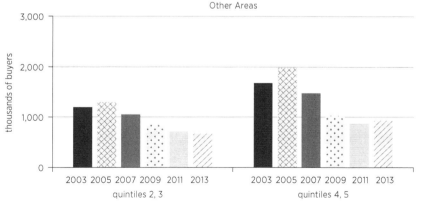

Note: Income quintile 1 is not included because ownership in quintile 1 is too small and idiosyncratic to provide meaningful data. Income quintiles are based on national values.
Sources: American Housing Survey (US Census Bureau); author's calculations. The survey is biennial.

Falling ownership during this period is related to the more than seven million foreclosures that have been completed since the bust. Foreclosures were mostly experienced by the households that had purchased homes late in the boom or that had high leverage.

Figure 5-10 compares changes in mortgaged homeownership from 2005 to 2014 in Closed Access metropolitan areas, Contagion metropolitan areas, and other areas. Groups are arranged both by income quintiles and by age.

Overwhelmingly in the Closed Access cities, the shock to homeownership since the bust has occurred among young households with high incomes. The same is true in all areas, but where prices were more moderate—in the Open Access areas—income was a less important factor. Households with lower incomes weren't buying many homes where nonconventional loans and high prices were the norm. They were buying homes where prices were moderate.

Figure 5-10 shows changes in the homeownership *rate* in each category, but in absolute numbers, households in Open Access metropolitan areas outnumber households in Closed Access metropolitan areas by about 6 to 1 and outnumber households in Contagion metropolitan areas by about 15 to 1. The mass of foreclosures and falling homeownership, in absolute numbers, has taken place across the country in cities where home prices were never particularly high and where foreclosure *rates* were much lower than in the Contagion cities.

Owning a home is mostly a product of age. By the time Americans reach 65 years of age, about 80% are homeowners. That was true in 1995, in 2005, and in 2015. In the first quarter of 2005, 70.1% of 35–44-year-olds owned a home, so we might have expected an additional 10% of those families to become homeowners in the following years. In the first quarter of 2015, a decade later, when those households were now 45–54-year-olds, still 70.1% of them were homeowners. In 2005, their rate of ownership was on the high side, but it wasn't unprecedented. It was about the same as the homeownership rate of 35–44-year-olds in 1982. Now, a decade later, they had a homeownership rate that was 5% below that of any previous generation since at least the 1970s.

In figure 5-10, we can see that the pullback in homeownership has been steepest in the Closed Access cities and the Contagion cities, where the price shock was worst during the crisis, which was to be expected. But we can also see that, around the country, in every market, homeownership has dropped sharply for young households and households entering middle age. These are the households that we would expect to be establishing ownership as part of normal life, and they just happened to be doing that when the crisis hit. These were mostly households with healthy incomes. This wasn't about income. The housing bust was like a depth charge, and it took out small fish and big fish alike.

Figure 5-10. Change in Mortgaged Homeownership, by US Metro Type, 2005–2014

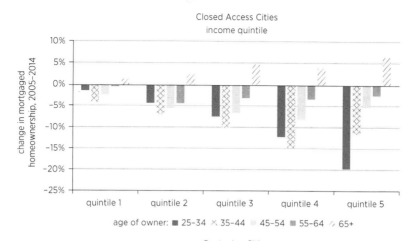

Closed Access Cities
income quintile

age of owner: ■ 25–34 ✕ 35–44 ▨ 45–54 ■ 55–64 ⁄ 65+

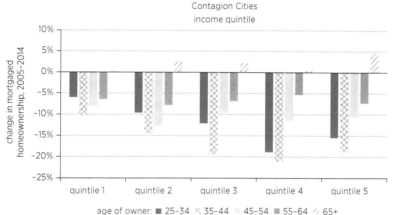

Contagion Cities
income quintile

age of owner: ■ 25–34 ✕ 35–44 ▨ 45–54 ■ 55–64 ⁄ 65+

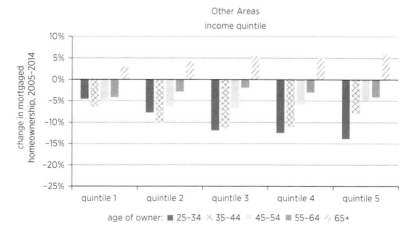

Other Areas
income quintile

age of owner: ■ 25–34 ✕ 35–44 ▨ 45–54 ■ 55–64 ⁄ 65+

Sources: American Community Survey (US Census Bureau); author's calculations. Change is measured in percentage points. (A change from 60% to 65% is shown as a 5% increase.)

THE BORROWING BEHAVIOR OF HOMEOWNERS

Tenure tends to be longer for homeowners with lower incomes and for home-owners in Closed Access cities. Turnover in homeownership is higher among buyers with high incomes and buyers in moderately priced areas. This did not change during the boom.

The American Housing Survey includes measures of households' mortgage payments, the prices they paid for their homes, and the current values of their homes. The data referenced in this section are from that survey. These data allow some broad inferences about the behavior of American homeowners.

Average mortgage payments can be compared to the average original price paid for homes. With a fixed-rate mortgage, the mortgage payment remains the same over time. If the ratio of the average mortgage payment to the average purchase price rises over time, this would suggest that households, on average, are taking on extra mortgage debt from growing home equity or are buying homes at higher interest rates. If it decreases over time, this suggests that households are refinancing, are purchasing at lower rates, or are paying down mortgages (figure 5-11).

In areas outside Contagion and Closed Access cities, existing homeowners were, on net, reducing their mortgage payments over time during the housing boom—as shown in figure 5-11. Their payments in 2006 were a little more than 10% lower than their payments in 2000 had been. For instance, in the median income quintile, in 2000, the average price they had paid for their homes was about $73,000, and by 2006, that had risen to $101,000. But, over the same period, their average mortgage payment increased from $737 to only $940.[17] Lower interest rates, net prepayments, or both held their payments down. In Closed Access and Contagion cities, homeowners with high incomes were also reducing their mortgage payments over time. Middle- and lower-income households in Contagion and Closed Access cities were fairly evenly balanced between households lowering their payments and households increasing their payments. Tactical refinancing at lower rates was roughly being balanced out by some cash-out refinancing.[18] Low-tier Closed Access zip codes are where Atif Mian and Amir Sufi found that cash-out refinancing was most prevalent, and American Housing Survey data appear to confirm that pattern.[19]

Also, remember that most homeowners who are older or who have low incomes do not have any mortgages at all. That's why the measures shown here have been limited to households with mortgages. For households that owned their homes free and clear, obviously all price changes would have been taken

Figure 5-11. Change in US Ratio of Mortgage Payments to Home Purchase Prices, 2000–2006

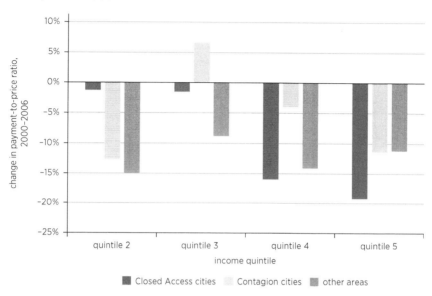

Note: Income quintile 1 is not included because ownership in quintile 1 is too small and idiosyncratic to provide meaningful data. Income quintiles are based on national values. Data are for homeowners with a mortgage.
Source: American Housing Survey (US Census Bureau), 2001 and 2007 surveys.

as capital gains, and those gains would have accrued most heavily to the lower-income quintiles—much of them to retired households.

Another comparison that is informative is average home value compared with the average original price paid (figure 5-12). This is simply a measure of unrealized capital gains for the typical homeowner. For instance, looking again at the median income quintile in the areas outside Closed Access and Contagion cities, in 2000, mortgaged homeowners had paid an average price of $85,000 for the houses they lived in, and those houses' market values now averaged $128,000. In 2006, those numbers had risen, so that owners had paid an average price of $118,000 for homes now worth, on average, $196,000. In stable markets, both figures will rise over time, but the ratio will remain about the same. On average, outside the Closed Access and Contagion cities, in all income quintiles, the typical mortgaged homeowner lived in a home worth about 50% more than he or she had paid for it, in both 2000 and 2006.

Figure 5-12. Comparison of Home Market Value and Price Paid, by Income Quintile and US Metro Type

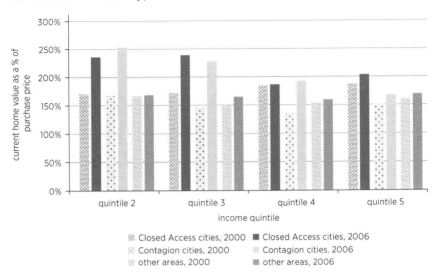

Note: Income quintile 1 is not included because ownership in quintile 1 is too small and idiosyncratic to provide meaningful data. Income quintiles are based on national values. Data are for homeowners with a mortgage.
Source: American Housing Survey (US Census Bureau), 2001 and 2007 surveys.

In the year 2000, when prices had only just begun to rise, all areas had similar ratios. At that point, the higher-income households in Closed Access cities tended to be sitting on more capital gains.

By 2006, the housing bubble had shown up in the Closed Access and Contagion cities, and homeowners, on average, were sitting on more capital gains than usual. Households with lower incomes were seeing the most gains. In the Closed Access cities, though, the primary reason lower-income households were pocketing more capital gains wasn't that their home prices had risen more.

In 2000, Closed Access mortgaged owners in the top income quintile had paid an average price of $230,000 for a home that was now worth an average of $431,000. By 2006, they had paid $398,000 for a home that was worth $810,000. Since high-income owners were active buyers, the typical owner lived in a home that was worth 88% more than it had been worth in 2000, but he or she also had paid 73% more for that home than the typical owner had in 2000.

Also in 2000, Closed Access mortgaged owners in the median income quintile had paid an average price of $155,000 for a home that was now worth an average of $267,000. In 2006, these owners had paid an average price of $217,000 for a home now worth an average of $518,000. For mortgaged owners in the median income quintile, their homes' average value had risen by 94%, but their average price paid had risen by only 40%. That is because households with incomes at or below the median had little to do with the hot housing markets in Closed Access cities during the bubble.

The reason middle- and lower-income homeowners in the Closed Access cities had more capital gains wasn't that their homes had increased in value by more than the homes of high-income homeowners. Prices on their homes had risen just a little bit more than prices on homes owned by households with higher incomes. The primary reason low- and middle-income homeowners in Closed Access cities had more capital gains was that they were less likely to have bought their homes during the bubble.

Finally, another useful set of measures for comparison are the average mortgage payment and the average current value of a home (figure 5-13). This comparison gives a broad indication of how much of the average homeowner's capital gains are being eaten up by cash-out refinancing or by purchasing new

Figure 5-13. Change in US Ratio of Mortgage Payments to Market Value, 2000–2006

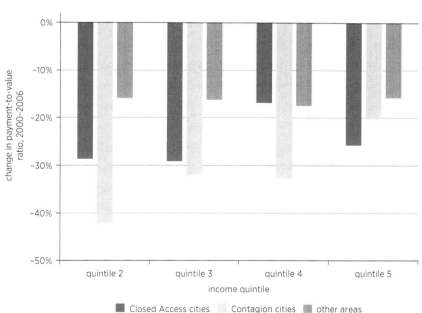

Note: Income quintile 1 is not included because ownership in quintile 1 is too small and idiosyncratic to provide meaningful data. Income quintiles are based on national values. Data are for homeowners with a mortgage.
Source: American Housing Survey (US Census Bureau), 2001 and 2007 surveys.

homes at new, higher prices. Outside the Closed Access and Contagion cities, homeowners were generally lowering their mortgage expenses by refinancing at lower interest rates. so, just as we saw that the typical mortgage payment declined by a little more than 10% for all income groups (compared to their purchase prices), payments also declined by a little more than 10% compared to market values.

Since home prices were rising at unusually high rates in the Contagion and Closed Access cities, homeowners there were capturing capital gains. In the Contagion and Closed Access cities, households with lower incomes appear to have been retaining more of those rising market values than households with higher incomes were.

Most of the new buying activity occurred among households with higher incomes, and Closed Access and Contagion homeowners with lower incomes had been in their homes longer, on average. So households with lower incomes were more likely (1) to have taken some of their capital gains in the form of cash-out refinancing and (2) to still have retained more capital gains from their rising property values than typical homeowners with higher incomes had. And, even with some cash-out refinancing, their total mortgage payments remained more moderate than the mortgage payments of home-owners with higher incomes, compared to their homes' market values. This was because, even though lower-income owners used capital gains to access some home equity credit, households with higher incomes were the main source of new buying during the housing boom, so their mortgage payments, on average, were increasing because more of them were buying homes at higher prices.

Of course, households with lower incomes were tapping home equity during the boom. This is bound to happen, regardless of the cause of the rising prices. But the source of demand for new homes was households with higher incomes. They might have required nonconventional loans to fund homes at Closed Access prices, but they had the wherewithal to pay off these mortgages. These high-income homebuyers were simply accelerating the process of economic segregation set in motion by Closed Access housing policies. On net, the homeowners with lower incomes were selling and leaving the city.

HOME EQUITY, SPENDING, CREDIT, AND MIGRATION

In hindsight, it has become clear that rents and prices in Closed Access cities continue rising persistently regardless of the leniency of lenders or of trends in homeownership. Prices are rising persistently because they are claims on politically exclusive properties. In that light, it makes sense to think of a Closed Access homeowner as the holder of a valuable permission slip—like a taxi medallion. There are different ways to use or claim this value.

Some homeowners who don't need credit will simply let that value sit in the form of growing home equity. Other homeowners may claim the value by selling the home and moving to a different city. Such households will not be vulnerable to credit shocks.

Other households, trying to move into the exclusive cities, may take out risky loans to buy in. Still other households, ones that own homes and need cash, may tap their homes for credit. These households will be vulnerable to credit shocks.

Mian and Sufi found that an increase in home prices of 20% was associated with an increase in cash-out refinancing of 3 percentage points. They also found that the tendency to refinance was 60% weaker among households with higher incomes (households with adjusted gross incomes of $100,000 or more).[20] But we should note that households were also claiming their newfound home equity by selling and moving. In 2005, when prices increased by more than 10%, among mortgaged homeowners, about 2.1% of owners in the top income quintile moved away from the Closed Access cities. The rate of migration was higher where incomes were lower, such that about 4.6% of homeowners in the bottom income quintile moved away.[21]

Households were naturally claiming their gains in the various ways they could, in predictable patterns. They each chose different amounts of risk when balancing their choices between spending and savings, and between remaining in place and moving. There has been a lot of focus on credit, because there was a presumption that high prices in Closed Access cities were credit-induced and unsustainable. But there has not been so much focus on the out-migration. Credit expansion might have allowed households to remain in overpriced homes and to spend more than their incomes would allow. But, on the other hand, moving away and selling to a new, leveraged buyer would have added to the supply of homes for sale, helping moderate home prices. And for the new owners, the mortgage would be a drag on their nonhousing spending.

Mian and Sufi note, "The house price recovery from 2011 onwards did not contribute as much to economic activity as the 2002 to 2006 housing gains. Our results suggest that this might be because the borrowing channel was effectively shut down for those most responsive to house price gains."[22]

Inflated borrowing against home equity was a phenomenon limited to areas where (1) owners were credit-constrained and (2) limited housing supply pushed home prices much higher. Borrowing was more subdued among more credit-worthy households in the expensive cities, and it was also more subdued among all households in the more moderately priced cities.[23] Mian and Sufi conclude that this inflated borrowing was a primary cause of rising prices in the low-tier markets of the Closed Access cities where it occurred.[24] In chapters 3 and 4, I argue that they were mistaken. Yet the idea that credit was the cause of rising prices led to the general belief that blocking the extension of mortgages to many families was prudent. The primary effect of this has been to limit credit where neither borrowing nor home prices had ever been unusually high. The most financially vulnerable households have been left out of the recovery in a mistaken attempt at prudence. Shutting down lending to these families slowed down the broader recovery by impairing their home equity and by preventing them from using what equity they had to support spending when they needed to.

WHO LOST THEIR HOMES, AND WHEN?

The American Community Survey can give a direct view into what happened as the bust began. Was the private securitization boom the last gasp of predatory lending? Did households that had mortgages they couldn't afford finally break down and default, leading to a broader contagion that spread into the rest of the housing market, eventually leading to the Great Recession?

There wasn't much of a shift in homeownership in the bottom two income quintiles during the boom. New homeownership tends to happen in the top three income quintiles. So, to compare changes in mortgaged homeownership at the margin to changes in the top tier of the market, figure 5-14 compares changes in middle-income mortgaged homeownership rates to top-quintile mortgaged homeownership rates in Closed Access areas, Contagion areas, and all other areas outside the Closed Access and Contagion cities, indexed to 2005.

According to the Survey of Consumer Finances, mortgaged homeownership rates had been generally rising by about 1% per year for these groups since the mid-1990s. The first drops in mortgaged ownership were among high-income owners in Contagion and Closed Access cities in 2006 and 2007. In 2006, homeownership rates in the middle-income quintile continued rising across the country, as they had for a decade; they leveled off in 2007. In 2008, the decline in mortgaged homeownership hit middle-income owners in Contagion cities, as home prices there collapsed especially hard, while homeownership for households with the highest incomes declined more sharply in all regions.

Some of this decline was likely related to a decline in first-time homebuyers. Looking at credit scores, Christopher L. Foote, Lara Loewenstein, and

Figure 5-14. Change in US Mortgaged Homeownership Rate, by Income Quintile and Metro Type

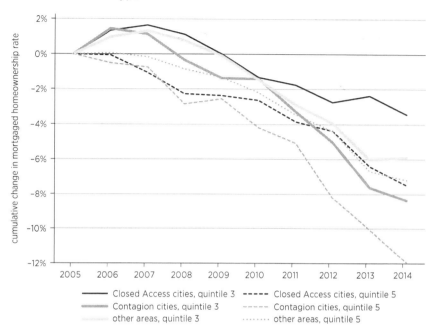

Sources: American Community Survey (US Census Bureau); author's calculations. Change is measured in percentage points. (A change from 65% to 60% is shown as a 5% decrease.)

Paul S. Willen find that first-time homebuyers tend to be mostly borrowers with stronger credit.[25] Some of this decline was likely related to tactical defaults in areas where prices had already begun to decline.

Middle-income declines in mortgaged ownership were a remarkably lagging factor. Middle-income mortgaged homeownership rates didn't really fall below 2005 levels in Closed Access cities and in most of the moderate parts of the country until 2010—three or four years after top-quintile ownership had begun to fall! It is true that middle-income homeownership rates were declining in all areas by 2008, but even in 2008, top-quintile ownership was falling more sharply.

Research has found that defaults tended to be overwhelmingly triggered by collapsing prices, not by borrower characteristics.[26] This pattern also shows up in measures of sales turnover and home prices. The top-tier markets in Closed Access and Contagion cities started to collapse first in 2006.

By a long shot, the groups that experienced the mildest collapse in mortgaged ownership were the lowest-income quintiles in the priciest housing markets. The popular story has this completely backward. Reckless mortgages to households with low incomes didn't create a housing bubble, then a bust in 2007, followed by the Great Recession. The collapse of the housing market was associated mainly with defaults by households with higher incomes and negative equity, because they were the most active group of recent buyers. Subsequently, US policy choices and the Great Recession caused a broad cross section of households to lose their homes in 2009 and after.

PART III

SYMPTOMS OF THE URBAN HOUSING SHORTAGE

CHAPTER 6
Closed Access to Labor

losed Access housing has become such a high barrier to the free movement of capital to its most-valued use[1]—normally a cornerstone fringe benefit of living in a free society—that the US population appears to be fleeing prosperity. The effect this is having on our national standard of living—especially for households with lower incomes—must be significant. Figure 6-1 compares the median income in 2005 for the 20 largest metropolitan areas with the net domestic migration from 2000 to 2003 for each metropolitan area, according to the Census Bureau.[2] The graph shows that rising income is associated with migration *away* from a city. We should surely expect migration patterns in a liberal society to operate in the opposite direction, with households moving into cities with opportunities. But through local housing constraints, we have created an economy that is shaped by exclusion. In this kind of economy, income is determined by access, and households are pushed away from affluence. Figure 6-1 is an emblem of a broken economy. Exclusionary housing policies are the root cause of wage stagnation, asset inflation, income inequality, and the "bubble" economy.

REVERSING THE BALANCING FLOWS OF AN OPEN ECONOMY

Incomes converge naturally when labor and capital are allowed to be mobile. When the Bureau of Economic Analysis began tracking incomes by region in 1929, there were large differences in per capita income levels between different regions of the country. Incomes in the South, the Plains, and the Rockies were

Figure 6-1. Income and Migration Patterns, 20 Largest US Metro Areas

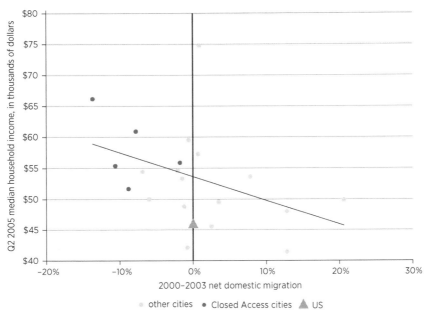

Sources: US Census Bureau, *Population Change in Metropolitan and Micropolitan Statistical Areas: 1990–2003*, September 2005; Zillow data, http://www.zillow.com/research/data/. The outlier with nearly $75,000 median income is Washington, DC.

roughly half the level of incomes in the coastal West and the Northeast. Over time, the progression of technology and investments in infrastructure pulled incomes toward a national mean by allowing capital and labor to move and to be more connected. As figure 6-2 demonstrates, this convergence was largely complete by 1980. Since then, regional incomes have generally moved in parallel, within 10% to 20% of the national average.

This is the sort of convergence that liberal economies tend to create. The old saying that "a rising tide lifts all boats" is actually an understatement for an economy where capital and labor are newly mobile. In more recent years this convergence has taken place globally, since incomes in newly liberalized economies are rising toward the level of the developed world.

These regional shifts play an important role in the variance of incomes within the United States over time. Until 1980 these regional convergences naturally reduced the variance of individual incomes, but since then the potential for these regional convergences to pull incomes toward the mean has been mostly tapped. And meanwhile a new trend has developed, but this trend is intra-regional. Now certain cities have created obstacles to housing

Figure 6-2. Regional Incomes Relative to the US National Average

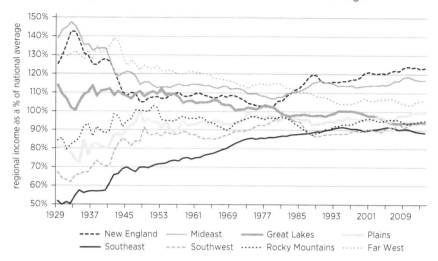

Source: Table SA1 (Personal Income, Population, Per Capita Personal Income, Disposable Personal Income, and Per Capita Disposable Personal Income) from Bureau of Economic Analysis, available at https://apps.bea.gov/iTable/index_regional.cfm.

expansion, which thus act as obstacles to both labor mobility and capital mobility.

The sharp rise in home prices in the high-priced cities cannot be explained by a rise in construction costs.[3] But neither political restrictions on building nor simple consumer preferences would be likely to lead to such high rents and prices on their own. That is because some households on the margin would migrate to lower-cost areas as costs rose. However, if there is a sustainable local source of high wages in cities with high costs, then households will push up the prices of homes, in terms of both rent and price, before the higher costs induce out-migration.[4]

In a paper published through the Institute of Labor Economics, Lena Edlund, Cecila Machado, and Maria Sviatschi have documented a shift in urban population patterns since the 1980s.[5] High-income households have been moving to metropolitan core cities. There have been simultaneous shifts toward more variance in incomes, toward more work and less leisure for high-income households, and toward urban residential locations for households with high incomes and less leisure. Highly skilled, highly educated high-income households are working longer relative to households with less education and income.

Edlund, Machado, and Sviatschi document how jobs requiring more education have shifted to city cores while jobs requiring less education have shifted away. This means that lucrative employment opportunities have moved to city cores, and highly skilled workers will demand residential locations that minimize commuting time. The relative shift in home prices between core cities and suburbs, and between high-income metropolitan areas and metropolitan areas with moderate incomes, reflects a substitution between these households based on the value of time and the opportunity cost of commuting.[6]

The rise in urban home prices has been concentrated in the city cores. At the aggregate metropolitan area level, rents remained moderate until the mid-1990s. From 1980 to 1990 the new value of core city real estate was counterbalanced by a relative decline in suburban real estate values. But in the early 1990s, this mitigating factor dissipated, and prices stabilized in the suburbs while they continued to rise in the core cities.

During the 1980s and early 1990s, highly skilled and highly educated households were working longer hours, earning high incomes, and moving to locations that both leveraged their skills and reduced their commutes. But by the mid-1990s, the housing constraints in the most economically dynamic cities were beginning to prevent these migrations. This pushed home prices higher throughout the economically dynamic cities, until migration *between* metropolitan areas was induced.

So the importance of location has been increasing since at least 1980. Over that time, the pressure on prices has moved away from the core cities as the relative scope of the problem of constricted housing supply has grown. From 1980 to 1990, prices were appreciating in areas less than five miles from the core, and over time, that pressure has increased prices farther from the core, and eventually beyond the boundary of the city. On the West Coast, as the housing supply remained constricted and economic growth and opportunity continued to add value to location, the pressure on housing supply moved to the Inland Empire and finally even to places like Phoenix and Las Vegas.

If the Closed Access cities had not had artificial constraints to new housing, a shift of workers with high incomes into the Closed Access cities would have happened, but high-income workers would have moved into *new* housing in the city cores. Low-income households would not have been forced by rising costs to migrate to suburbs or to other cities. There would have been much less dislocation and economic stress.

A flood of working class out-migrants is not a natural outcome of a growing city. It is the outcome of successful cities that refuse to grow. Compared to other metro areas, Closed Access cities are outliers in terms of the low number of homes that are permitted, the high rate of domestic out-migration they induce, and the low incomes of the households that do migrate away from them.

CITIES AREN'T NATURALLY THIS EXPENSIVE

It is tempting to dismiss the recent problem of urban housing constraints as simply the normal effect of urban population density. Figure 6-3 compares metropolitan areas by size and by the ratio of the 90th percentile wage to the 10th percentile wage (a measure of income inequality). The graph contrasts Closed Access cities (coastal California, New York City, and Boston) and other cities. As the figure shows, income inequality does tend to rise with city size. All the Closed Access cities have more inequality than normal, even adjusting for size.

In an article published in 2017, Peter Ganong and Daniel Shoag connect land use regulation, income-segregating migration patterns, and housing prices. They find many of the patterns being described here. Restrictive land use policies have caused migration patterns to shift so that high-income workers move to areas with high *income potential* and low-income workers move to areas with low *cost*. Ganong and Shoag find that for high-income households, migration patterns today are similar to migration patterns of previous decades—workers

Figure 6-3. City Size and Income Inequality, 2013

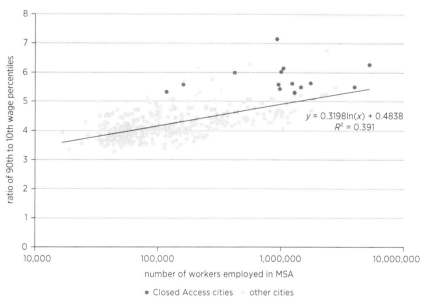

$$y = 0.3198\ln(x) + 0.4838$$
$$R^2 = 0.391$$

● Closed Access cities · other cities

Note: MSA = metropolitan statistical area.
Source: J. Chris Cunningham, "Measuring Wage Inequality within and across US Metropolitan Areas, 2003–13," *Monthly Labor Review* (Bureau of Labor Statistics), September 2015. Cunningham's study uses a different specification for metropolitan areas than the one I use. Some of the areas marked "Closed Access" are cities like Newark, New Jersey, which elsewhere in this book is included in the New York City MSA.

move to where there are income opportunities. For low-income households, migration patterns are similar to past patterns in net terms—households move to where incomes are higher, after housing expenses. But since housing expenses have become dominant, this means that in terms of gross income, the migration pattern of low-income households has reversed. They now move to areas with lower gross income potential.[7]

This is really important. Declining prospects for households with lower incomes might be the single most debated issue in the country today. Whatever defenses there are for such tight political restrictions on housing expansion in our dynamic cities—and there are some—those restrictions have unintentionally removed an age-old source of improvement for free people—the right to move to opportunity. And, in practice, the removal of this right has disproportionately impacted economically disadvantaged households.

In a 2010 article, Alicia Sasser explored the issue of migration patterns and home prices, treating population changes as depending on unemployment, incomes, and housing affordability as the independent variables. If unemployment goes up, if local incomes go down, or if houses get more expensive, we would expect to see slower population growth. The article summarizes the relative importance of the three variables over three periods of time: 1977–1986, 1987–1996, and 1997–2006.[8]

During the 1977–1986 period, housing affordability appears to have played no role in migration patterns into and out of New England. When relative unemployment in the area was low or when incomes were rising, workers moved into the area to take advantage of economic opportunities, as we would expect. By 1997–2006, declining unemployment and rising incomes only slightly encouraged in-migration, whereas housing expenses were a factor keeping population away. It may be useful to think of Boston as having a fairly hard upper limit on housing expansion. So the dependent variable, net migration, is now more or less fixed.

A strong economy in Boston is still a draw to new residents. What has changed is that Boston is no longer willing to accommodate much population growth. Thus, when migrants are drawn in, home prices must rise to a level that forces a similar number back out.[9] This is a subtle but important point. Price is simply the means of rationing the approximately five million spots available in the Boston area. It doesn't matter whether the average Boston home costs $100,000 or $430,000. Five million people, give or take, will live there next year. If we institute some sort of price control that forces the home price down to $100,000 without fixing the underlying supply problem, we are simply giving some household a $330,000, nontransferable subsidy to claim a home that millions of other Americans are excluded from.

There has been an endless stream of articles about the rise and fall of cities. Do young people still want to live there? Why aren't as many people migrating to places where there are jobs as in the past? Are implicit subsidies of automobiles and roads favoring sprawling suburbs over dense urban cores? These factors are beside the point. Regardless of any marginal changes in preferences, five million people will live in Boston. The only question is who. This fact is purely a function of artificially constrained supply. The limit on the supply of residences available in Boston is a form of economic waste, regardless of whether the housing units for those five million people are rationed through price, public dispensation, or queuing. Public policies meant to bring down prices and rents or to subsidize units are policies that address the *method* of rationing an arbitrarily scarce resource. To reduce the waste, policies must address the arbitrary scarcity itself.

STRESS FROM HOUSING EXPENSES FALLS MOSTLY ON THE WORKING CLASS

For the median household in Closed Access cities now, it appears that even though it has a much higher gross income than the median household in other cities, after housing expenses, its income is the same or lower. But the stress is not symmetrical.

In figure 6-4, average adjusted gross income for each zip code is shown on the *x*-axis. The farther to the right a dot is, the higher that zip code's gross income is. Estimated income after rent is shown on the *y*-axis. The higher the dot, the more income is left after rent. The graph distinguishes between Closed Access zip codes and all other zip codes.

At the top right corner of the graph, high-income households move into the Closed Access cities. In the zip codes with the highest incomes, where gross incomes are similar, incomes after rent are also similar in Closed Access cities and other cities. But as we look at zip codes with lower gross incomes (moving to the left), incomes after rent in Closed Access zip codes become lower and lower compared to incomes after rent in other places. At the low end, there is a distinct difference between Closed Access zip codes and zip codes everywhere else.

Households with high incomes can take advantage of the exclusively high incomes of the Closed Access cities by substituting their consumption away

Figure 6-4. Scatterplot of US Incomes before and after Rent, 2013

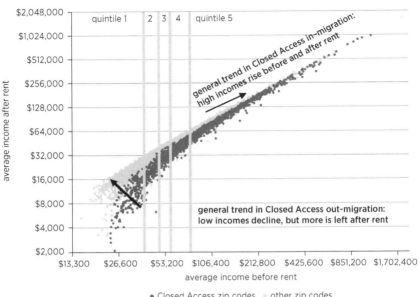

Note: Zip codes comprise 1,670 Closed Access zip codes and 14,154 other zip codes.
Sources: IRS, "SOI Tax Stats—Individual Income Tax Statistics—Zip Code Data (SOI)," https://www.irs
.gov/statistics/soi-tax-stats-individual-income-tax-statistics-zip-code-data-soi; Zillow data, http://
www.zillow.com/research/data/.

from housing by living in less comfortable units than they could afford in other cities. So, when they move to Closed Access cities, they shift both to the right and up on the graph. They get access to career opportunities, and they cut back on housing expenses.

For the lowest quintile, however, rent expense is the critical issue of household finances. Notice how, below the median income, there is a sharp downward curvature in the cloud of Closed Access zip codes. Plus, there is very little overlap between Closed Access zip codes and other zip codes. The cloud of Closed Access dots curves downward and the other dots form a relatively straight line. In the Closed Access lower-income quintiles, gross incomes are higher than elsewhere, but incomes after rent are much lower. That is why these households tend to move away from Closed Access cities. For households with lower incomes, moving away from Closed Access cities may lower their gross incomes but raise the income they have left after rent—moving them to the *left* and *up* on the graph.

Many of the households in the lowest-income Closed Access zip codes are hanging on, thanks to rent control, which is a common Closed Access policy. Often the difference between the controlled rent and the market value of a unit becomes great enough that a landlord sells the property and the rent-controlled household is forced to move, and no similar units are available for the household to move into. Ellis Act evictions in San Francisco, one step in a process landlords use to evict tenants in order to sell the property, are correlated with home prices.[10] The stresses and dislocations created by Closed Access policies are numerous.

Exclusion is the act of enforcing a division between haves and have-nots, whether by means of money and wealth or of political power and public subsidy, whether motivated by explicit bigotry or by individuals with local political power who worry that a new 30-unit condo building will cause traffic to be a little worse or that a new high-rise apartment will cast a fleeting shadow on a beloved park. Regardless of the excluders' intentions, the costs inevitably fall on the most marginalized and powerless families. And these costs have become large enough to shape the financial character of a generation.

CHAPTER 7
Broader Economic Implications
of Closed Access Cities

There has been a growing perception that wages are stagnant, incomes are becoming less equal, and national income has been accruing more to asset owners than to workers. This situation is frequently blamed on corporate power or market deregulation. But a significant cause of this economic malaise is the exclusion created by Closed Access housing.

In fact, the Closed Access housing problem sheds light on how important free and open capital markets are for the well-being of the typical worker. Houses are essentially pure forms of capital—deferred consumption, the textbook definition of capital. The act of building a house is purely the act of forgoing the immediate consumption of goods and services to create shelter that will be consumed for many years into the future. The rental value of a home—the value that is consumed today—is almost purely a transaction between a consumer and capital, free of organizational intermediaries. Especially for homeowners, there is no network of firms and workers that must produce, administer, and deliver that shelter each month.

Furthermore, what the experience of Closed Access cities has made clear regarding this pure relationship between consumer and capital is that, first and foremost, where capital is obstructed from entering competitive markets, consumers are harmed. Especially consumers of limited means.

The migration flows that have developed because of the Closed Access housing problem remove any doubt about this. Households with the lowest incomes systematically move away from cities where capital is obstructed from being used for housing and move to cities where capital flows relatively freely.[1]

This pattern is true of capital markets more generally, though it can be harder to see in most sectors, where the relationship between capital, laborer, and consumer is more complicated. Open Access economies tend to provide a larger share of income to laborers. Where rule of law is universal and freedom of contract is protected, capital has fewer systemic risks, and new entrants bid profits down. For instance, investors in developing markets tend to require higher expected returns on investment than investors in developed markets. Labor's share of income in developed economies tends to be about 65%–70%. In developing economies, it tends to be about 55%–60%.[2]

The same pattern occurs within markets. Investors tend to demand lower returns for taking risks during long periods of expansion, such as the 1960s and 1990s. Unemployment also declines. Expected stability lowers the share of income earned by firms.[3]

When poor countries improve their local institutions to make the market for new capital more stable and safe, capital tends to flow to these economies, and wages rise. Because these economies begin with low wages, low wages are erroneously viewed as a competitive advantage that attracts capital. But capital doesn't flow to where wages are low and will remain so. Capital flows to where wages are *rising* because local institutions are improving, productivity is rising, and ultimately the returns required by investors are declining. Where capital flows, wages rise and working people benefit.

In this respect, Closed Access cities resemble less-developed economies.[4] Capital income is bloated by limited entry. But because limited entry happens through the housing market in Closed Access cities, workers act as conduits for the bloated capital income—earning it first as gross wages before transferring it to landlords as rent. So migrants crossing America's southern border from Latin America are attempting to increase their incomes, and migrants crossing the borders of America's Closed Access cities as they leave are attempting to decrease their cost of living. But, fundamentally, the cause of the migration is the same. The lack of open and stable capital markets in the places these migrants are moving away from creates inequitable economic conditions.

THE VALUE OF EXCLUSIVITY

Comparing the total value of residential real estate to aggregate personal income provides a measure of the value (and cost) of exclusion. Figure 7-1 shows this ratio for the Closed Access cities, and compares it to the ratio for all areas outside the top 20 metropolitan areas. The value of residential real estate outside the top 20 metropolitan areas might be considered a measure of the value of real

Figure 7-1. US Residential Property Value Relative to Personal Income

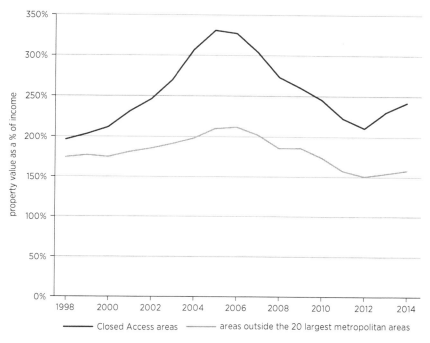

Closed Access areas ——— areas outside the 20 largest metropolitan areas

Sources: Total residential property value estimate provided by Zillow upon request; table CA1 (Personal Income, Population, Per Capita Personal Income) from Bureau of Economic Analysis, available at https://www.bea.gov/iTable/index_regional.cfm.

estate as shelter. The difference between these two ratios gives an estimate of the additional value of Closed Access real estate as a source of exclusivity.

In 1998, real estate outside the major metropolitan areas was worth about 174% of annual personal incomes. In the Closed Access cities, real estate was worth about 196% of incomes. These ratios at the time were at the low end of the 20-year range, and in both sets of cities they basically reflected the value of shelter.

During the housing boom, the ratio increased only slightly outside the major metropolitan areas, reflecting falling real long-term interest rates. The ratio topped out in 2006 at about 212%. The value of real estate in the Closed Access cities, on the other hand, shot up to about 330% of income.

By 2014, outside the largest metropolitan areas, the ratio was down to 158%. That was low because obstructions to mortgage credit were holding housing prices down, but prices relative to incomes were still within long-term norms.[5] The Closed Access problem, which was not fixed by tightening credit markets, remained. Real estate values in Closed Access cities diverged from those of the rest of the country during the boom, and that divergence has never ended. So, in 2014, Closed Access real estate was worth about 242% of local personal incomes—still about one and a half times larger than the value of property outside the major metropolitan areas (242% vs. 158%).

Closed Access incomes are a third higher than incomes in other areas. So, in 2014, Closed Access real estate, per capita, was worth about 323% of the per capita income outside the largest metropolitan areas. If we think of Closed Access home values as toll booths barring the path to exclusive economic opportunity, then roughly half the value of Closed Access homes is the value of exclusivity. It takes about 160% of the typical Open Access American income to purchase shelter. It takes an additional 160% of an Open Access income to gain access to the Closed Access cities, where typical incomes are 34% higher.

WHERE DOES THE INCOME COME FROM?

The higher incomes in the Closed Access cities have three basic sources:

1. *Composition*. The economic segregation set into motion by Closed Access policies could mean that more-productive workers are more numerous in Closed Access cities. In other words, the median household in San Francisco may have more valuable job skills than the median household in Atlanta because Americans are self-segregating, according to income, into and out of Closed Access cities.

2. *Productivity*. There could be qualities about these cities that allow workers to be more productive. Networking potential for, say, tech designers in San Francisco or investment bankers in New York City is an example of how urban labor markets can increase productive opportunities for their workers. Economists sometimes call these "agglomeration economies."

3. *Monopoly*. Limited entry can create monopoly profits. Here, the source of limited entry for workers is Closed Access housing.

Changing composition could lead to higher incomes, but in that case, we would expect workers to continue to spend a normal proportion of their incomes on housing. Even in a city with some limits to housing expansion, households tend to adjust the location and amenities of their homes to keep housing expenses in a comfortable zone.[6]

A city that enables workers to be more productive could experience an outcome similar to that of a city with changing composition. Incomes might rise, but there would be no reason to expect housing expenses to rise, as a portion of income. Because of the recent prevalence of the Closed Access problem, high housing costs for rich households have become the norm, but it is worth revisiting what a strange outcome this is. When countries like South Korea and Taiwan attained the status of developed economies, rents didn't eat up all the wage increases workers gained there. Even in the United States, there are cities that have been attracting productive workers while also allowing a reasonable number of new homes to be built.

Austin, Texas; Denver; Seattle; and Washington, DC, attract many productive workers. All of these metropolitan areas approved more housing units than the US average during the housing boom. They all have housing markets that look like housing markets should look in productive cities. Incomes are strong, and workers spend a comfortable portion of their incomes on rent. Figure 7-2 compares rent affordability in these metro areas with rent affordability in the Closed Access metropolitan areas.

But we shouldn't expect local incomes to rise too far because of high productivity. As the highly productive workers arrive, all the workers that fill in

Figure 7-2. Incomes and Rent Affordability in Productive Cities, 2017

Note: Data are for the third quarter of 2017.
Source: Zillow data, http://www.zillow.com/research/data/.

the economic ecosystem around them, to provide various local services, would also arrive. Furthermore, the rise in productivity that is due to local economic advantages should mostly accrue to consumers rather than to workers. When Rockefeller was consolidating the oil industry and Carnegie was consolidating steel, workers' wages were rising a bit, but the primary effect of rising productivity was falling prices. In an open market, productivity flows largely to the consumer, even in cases where producers are powerful. So, while the composition of workers could lead to some rising incomes, rising local sources of productivity should mostly lead to consumer benefits. In a city without Closed Access limits to entry, new firms and workers would enter the market. Even if firms have monopolistic profits from patents or network effects, firms should retain those profits in a city where workers are free to move in and bid wages down.

The taxi industry is a good recent example of the power of limited entry versus productivity when it comes to wages. Uber and Lyft allow drivers to be much more productive. This has greatly increased the market for ride-hailing services. But what the taxi companies had that Uber and Lyft didn't were taxi medallions—government permission to operate in a field protected from competition. Those medallions used to be very valuable. Uber and Lyft bring two features to a local ride-hailing market—tools that make the service more productive and open access for potential new drivers. The combination of higher productivity and open competition lowers prices and increases quantity, but it does not increase wages.

Among cities with thriving tech sectors, workers in Austin are more like Uber drivers, and workers in San Francisco are more like taxi drivers. The rents on San Francisco homes are like the fee for using a taxi medallion.

This brings us to the third source of higher incomes: monopoly, or limited entry. Limited entry is the most powerful source of persistent excess income. It can ensure that the producers retain the new wealth that is created by higher productivity. Economists call this excess income "economic rents," not to be confused with the rental value of a home. In the Closed Access cities, the productivity is created by the workers and the firms they work for, but it is real estate owners who earn excess income from limited access. In order for the real estate owners to collect their *economic* rents (which, here, do happen to come in the form of rental value on properties), the workers must first collect them as higher wages before transferring them to landlords as rent payments. As transfer agents, the workers are a cost to the firms and a benefit to the real estate owners. For limited access to be profitable, the real estate owners must have a source of geographically captured productivity that produces the income. So, fundamentally, it is a limit on the supply of residential space that creates the monopoly power, but that power is only profitable because it creates a limit on the supply of labor where that labor is productive enough and geographically captured enough to be able to pass on the higher costs to the firm and the consumer.

We can surmise that demand for skilled Closed Access labor is quite inelastic, because if there were easy substitutes for it, the extremely high costs wouldn't be sustained. On the other hand, supply of workers should be fairly elastic because, on the margin, workers will move to other cities if their after-rent income is pushed too low in the Closed Access cities. In fact, basic observation, confirmed by migration data, tells us that on the margin many workers are leaving or staying out of the Closed Access cities because of the high costs. Many workers are moving away from Closed Access cities while certain kinds of firms move into Closed Access cities. The demand for Closed Access labor is inelastic, but the supply is elastic.

So the end result of the Closed Access problem is that some amount of income is claimed that would mostly have otherwise accrued to consumer surplus (figure 7-3). This income is routed through Closed Access worker wages, raising gross wages but ultimately ending in the pockets of landlords.

This is not a story against the importance of urban productivity. This added housing cost is only possible *because* Closed Access cities have some geographic monopoly on certain kinds of productive work. And this is also not a story against the market mechanisms that give postindustrial firms that operate in these cities high profit margins and market power. Again, it is only because of that market power that they can pay such high wages and pass them on to consumers. These factors all interact with one another to create this outcome. It is access to Closed Access labor markets that is a primary source of market power; otherwise tech startups would be distributed across the country instead of being focused in Silicon Valley, and investment banks would move inland.

Also, there are many other industries and sectors in a city that don't have the market power of the postindustrial frontier firms. For these sectors, there is more of an effect on quantity. The high costs do lead to substitutions away from workers in *these* sectors. These are the workers who are moving away from the Closed Access cities by the millions, or who don't move in. These are the service-sector workers, construction workers, and so on. These services are harder to come by in Closed Access cities, and they are more expensive. So, much of the added cost for the highly skilled, geographically captured workers isn't routed directly to their landlords. It is routed to many of the high-cost service-sector workers, who then rout much of *their* wages to landlords. Because of all of those substitutions, Closed Access workers substitute goods and services that can be sourced outside

Figure 7-3. Supply and Demand for Skilled Closed Access Labor

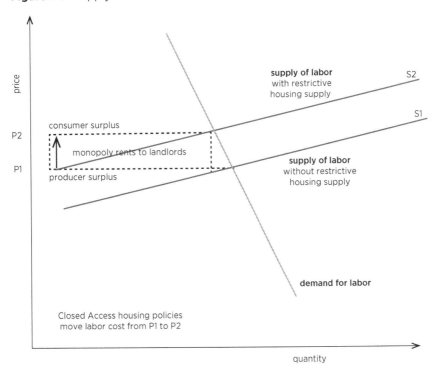

their cities for the sorts of services that must be provided locally.[7] In real terms, this substitution away from expensive local services is most obvious in their real consumption of housing—first, by switching to smaller, less convenient units, and finally by leaving the city altogether.

These effects on the price and quantity of various types of labor are a significant factor in the forms of economic stagnation that have been worrying economists for the last couple of decades.

THE MOST IMPORTANT ECONOMIC CHART

Since the later decades of the 20th century, the US and other developed economies appear to be characterized by slower growth and an increase in variance of incomes compared to previous decades. Some claim that this trend stems from an increase in the power of corporations to capture more income relative to labor. This apparent problem has become a popular topic.[8] Thomas Picketty published the most famous recent book on this topic, *Capital in the Twenty-First Century.*[9]

Figure 7-4. The Gap between Productivity and Wages

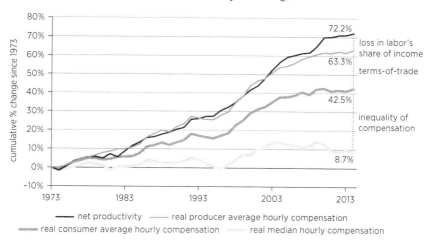

Note: Data are for all workers. *Net productivity* indicates the growth of output of goods and services minus depreciation, per hour worked.
Sources: Josh Bivens and Lawrence Mishel, "Understanding the Historic Divergence between Productivity and a Typical Worker's Pay: Why It Matters and Why It's Real" (Briefing Paper #406, Economic Policy Institute, Washington, DC, September 2, 2015), used with permission. Data are originally from the Bureau of Economic Analysis, the Bureau of Labor Statistics, and Current Population Survey Outgoing Rotation Group microdata.

The Economic Policy Institute published an extensive report on the divergence between median pay and productivity growth since the 1970s.[10] In this report, authors Josh Bivens and Lawrence Mishel analyzed a version of what Atif Mian and Amir Sufi have called "The Most Important Economic Chart" (figure 7-4).[11] This chart shows the gap between productivity growth (the top line) and growth in median real hourly compensation (the bottom line) from 1973 to 2014. Working down from the top, Bivens and Mishel found that the loss in labor's share of income accounted for only a small portion of the gap—only about 12% of the total (and this coming almost entirely in the period of dislocation after the 2008 recession). About 30% of the gap is explained by consumer inflation, which has been higher than producer inflation, which created a drag on workers' real wages. And about 60% of the gap is due to a widening variance between the incomes of wage earners.

Much of the divergence Bivens and Mishel found can be attributed to Closed Access housing policies. The plight of workers may be real, but it has almost nothing to do with a rising share of income going to employers. It has more to do with a rising share of income going to landlords in certain cities.

Loss in Labor's Share of Income

Bivens and Mishel found that very little of the gap between rising productivity and compensation of the median worker has been due to claims on that income by firms. This confirms the work of Matthew Rognlie of MIT and the Brookings Institution, who looked at capital's share in many countries. He found that the rise in the share of income going to capital reflects gains in rental income earned by housing.[12] As I have explained, this is true in the United States.

One reason that some have pointed to rising corporate incomes as a culprit for stagnant median incomes is that, recently, corporate profits have been high. But corporate profits are a poor indicator of total income to firms. As a share of national income, corporate profits can be high because corporate interest expenses are low. Interest expenses can be low either because interest *rates* are low or because firms are funding operations more with equity than with debt. Both of those factors are currently operative.

Over the long term, more firms have taken on the corporate form instead of being run as proprietorships. That also has increased the share of national income that is labeled "corporate profit."[13] Corporate profit is a poor indicator of the domestic earning power of firms.

A better way to measure the total operating income of firms over time is to simply consider the combination of proprietor income, after-tax corporate profit, and interest income. Figure 7-5 is a stacked line graph of these forms of income, going back to 1929, when Bureau of Economic Analysis data begin. Over the entire period, *total capital income has been quite level*—remarkably flat after adjusting for cyclical variations.[14] In fact, it would take an economic upheaval larger than anything experienced in nearly a century for the split in capital-labor income to account for more than a few percentage points of difference in total labor compensation. It would be nearly impossible for a persistent shift in capital income to firms to be a significant cause of The Most Important Economic Chart.

Figure 7-6 compares shares of housing income, labor income, and other capital income to show the proportion of total domestic income going to each category. The most significant change since the 1970s has been a shift from labor income to housing income—most of which is taken by owner-occupiers and some of which is claimed by mortgage lenders and landlords.[15]

Total net capital income to homeowners and lenders has increased from about 4.0% to 7.4% of net domestic income over the 40 years since the 1970s.[16] Much of that increase in income to housing has been a transfer to existing owners in Closed Access cities, through rent inflation on existing properties. This is *not* income that is increasing because more homes are being built. This

Figure 7-5. US Capital Income Relative to Net Domestic Income

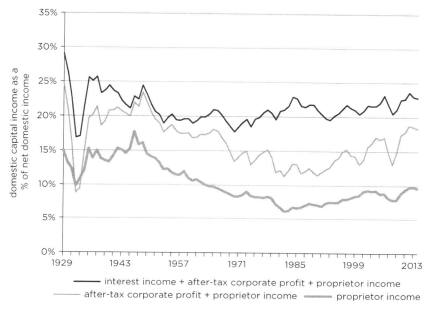

Note: Proportions are based on net domestic income after the consumption of fixed capital.
Source: Table 1.10 (Gross Domestic Income by Type of Income) from Bureau of Economic Analysis, available at https://apps.bea.gov/iTable/index_nipa.cfm.

is income that existing owners receive in cities where new homebuilders are locked out. This is income for *not* building.

The *only significant decline* in the share of income to housing since the 1970s came when housing starts were strong. In the mid-1990s, as housing starts recovered from the contraction of the early 1990s, housing income leveled off at about 6.8% of net domestic income. From 2002 to 2006, at the height of the housing boom, when supply was pushing down rent inflation, housing income declined from 6.9% to 6.1%. After 2006, housing starts dropped sharply, and by 2009, housing's share of domestic income was back to new highs.

Figure 7-6 shows that the decline in labor compensation has paralleled the rise in income to housing. Measuring from peak to peak, compared to the 1970s, the share of income going to labor has declined, but when labor and housing income are added together, the total is at about the same level as it was then. The decline in labor compensation share has been caused by a transfer to housing.

Ironically, in order to reduce the income going to capital and increase the income going to labor, cities need to allow *more* capital investment in residential housing. More investment in Closed Access housing would reduce

Figure 7-6. US Labor Compensation, Housing Income, and Nonhousing Capital Income, Shares of Total Domestic Income

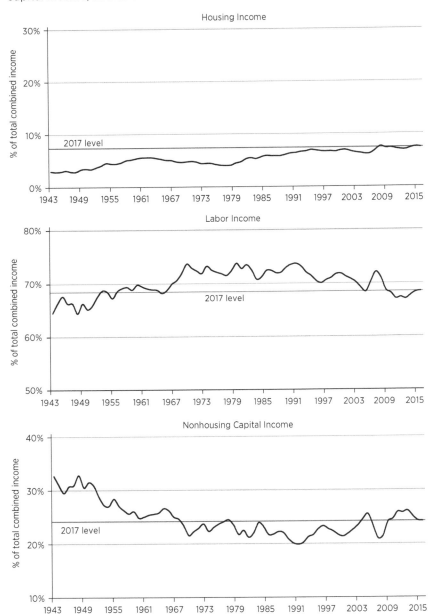

Housing Income

Labor Income

Nonhousing Capital Income

Note: Housing income = housing net operating surplus (meant to capture both the owner and the lender portions of housing net income). *Other capital income* = other capital net operating surplus. *Labor income* = compensation of employees. Total domestic income in this figure is the sum of these individual shares, so that the three measures add to 100%. Some other minor components of domestic income are not included.
Source: Table 1.10 (Gross Domestic Income by Type of Income) and table 7.4.5 (Housing Sector Output, Gross Value Added, and Net Value Added) from Bureau of Economic Analysis, available at https://apps .bea.gov/iTable/index_nipa.cfm.

income to Closed Access housing. Every homeowner group fighting against a new apartment building and every monetary official warning that "hot" real estate markets could cause a destabilizing collapse in real estate prices understands this. Their only error is in trying to *stop* it.

Homebuilding is frequently cited as a way to raise compensation by creating construction jobs for the new units. But, more importantly, homebuilding increases real net compensation by reducing rents on all units and lowering the cost of living.

"Terms of Trade" Gap from Consumer Inflation

Looking back at The Most Important Economic Chart (figure 7-4), this growth in housing income generally comes through the "Terms of Trade" gap. That was the gap created by consumer inflation, which has been higher than producer inflation. In other words, to some extent workers have been earning higher wages, but the prices of things workers consume have risen more than the prices of things firms buy. Figure 7-7 compares consumer inflation, with and without shelter, to the GDP deflator since 1973.[17] About half the gap between the GDP inflation measure and consumer price index inflation between 1973 and 2017 is accounted for by shelter inflation. In other words, half the gap between rising productivity and rising wages, what Bivens and Mishel call "Terms of Trade," is due to rising rent, much of the increase coming from the bidding war workers have to engage in to get into the Closed Access cities.

Inequality of Compensation

The largest gap between the growth of productivity and the growth of median compensation, in the Most Important Economic Chart, is from "Inequality of Compensation"—in other words, median wages have not risen as strongly as top wages. Clearly high incomes have become very geographically concentrated. The economist James K. Galbraith and his coauthor, Travis J. Hale, in research with the University of Texas Inequality Project, have shown that incomes between states have converged over the past 40 years, but incomes between counties within states have diverged. Since the mid-1990s, just a handful of counties have been responsible for much of the rise in geographic income inequality.[18]

In some ways, this phenomenon also causes the gap between median incomes and higher incomes to be overstated, because much of the shift has come from migration—low-income households moving to low-cost cities and

Figure 7-7. Consumer Inflation vs. the GDP Deflator

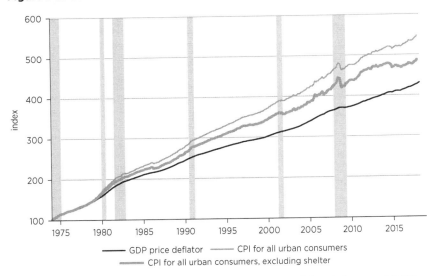

Note: CPI = consumer price index. Shaded areas indicate US recessions. All three indices are set to 100 for November (or fourth-quarter) 1973.
Sources: Bureau of Economic Analysis, "Gross Domestic Product: Implicit Price Deflator" (GDPDEF), and Bureau of Labor Statistics, "Consumer Price Index for All Urban Consumers: All Items" (CPIAUCSL), and Bureau of Labor Statistics, "Consumer Price Index for All Urban Consumers: All Items Less Shelter" (CUSR0000SA0L2), retrieved from FRED, Federal Reserve Bank of St. Louis.

high-income households moving to high-cost cities. The net gains and losses in income are generally mitigated by changing housing expenses. Thinking in terms of the "Most Important Economic Chart," the gap is overstated, because both the higher rents and the higher incomes are concentrated in Closed Access cities. Rents for the median worker are lower than average, because the median worker is likely to live outside the Closed Access cities. The national consumer price index understates price inflation in Closed Access cities and overstates the price inflation of workers outside those cities. Much of this is a result of the migration itself—of workers sorting according to cost of living—aligned with their own earning potential.

This part of the gap between median wages and productivity growth has many complex causes, which are beyond the scope of this book. But the deep effects of exclusion that have led to self-segregation and migration away from opportunity centers is an important factor. One sign that this gap has more to do with geographical exclusion than with corporate power and corporate income is that this income pattern has not been limited to workers. Firms have experienced a similar pattern.

Jason Furman, who was the chairman of President Barack Obama's Council of Economic Advisers; and Peter Orszag, who had been the director of the Congressional Budget Office and then director of President Obama's Office of Management and Budget, came to the same conclusion in 2015 about how changing income shares are not attributable to an aggregate rise in corporate incomes. The increases have largely been related to rising rental incomes from a constrained housing supply: "Zoning and land use restrictions can potentially discourage low-income families from moving to high-mobility areas—effectively relegating them to lower-mobility areas, reinforcing inequality. Accordingly, housing rents have important implications for both aggregate growth and its distribution."[19] Furman and Orszag show how rates of return on investments have increasingly diverged among firms, with high returns generally being *shared* with labor. Workers who appear to have similar levels of skill and productivity earn higher incomes if they work at high-return firms. Plus, these high returns and wages within certain firms are persistent over time.[20]

Furman and Orszag note a decline in mobility among both workers and firms. In an age when human capital is becoming the dominant source of corporate economic value added, geographic frictions in the labor market *are* geographic frictions in the capital market. The same housing issues that are increasing variance among labor incomes should also be increasing variance in rates of return to firms.

Furman has also written separately on this topic, where he has addressed more directly the connection between housing constrictions and economic dynamism:

> Understanding the connections among zoning, affordability, mobility, and income inequality is important because of the substantial rise in overall inequality observed over the last several decades. . . . Reduced labor mobility may be a contributing factor to both increased inequality and lower productivity growth in the United States. . . . Businesses are creating and destroying jobs at a lower rate and fewer new businesses are being formed, both of which could be causes or consequences of a decline in labor mobility.[21]

Among workers with fewer skills, incomes have been converging geographically for decades, and continue to converge—incomes in poor cities are growing faster than incomes in rich cities. But recently, incomes of high-skilled workers have stopped converging. In cities such as San Francisco, Boston, and New York City, incomes for high-skilled workers have been especially strong.[22] Closed Access cities limit the spots available for workers to access more economic opportunity, so highly skilled workers outbid workers with fewer skills for those limited spots. One reason that the lack of labor mobility Furman and Orszag identify leads to income inequality is that mobility into the Closed Access cities is only available for those who can afford it. So Closed Access opportunity is only available for the most productive producers—and this applies to both firms and workers.

Jae Song, David J. Price, Fatih Guvenen, and Nicholas Bloom quantify how the unequal growth in wages has been largely the result of unequal outcomes among firms. In the abstract of their paper, "Firming Up Inequality," they write,

> Covering all U.S. firms between 1978 to 2012, we show that virtually all of the rise in earnings dispersion between workers is accounted for by increasing dispersion in average wages paid by the employers of these individuals. In contrast, pay differences within employers have remained virtually unchanged, a finding that is robust across industries, geographical regions, and firm size groups.[23]

In other words, the rise in income inequality has been a rise in inter-firm income inequality, not intra-firm income inequality.

Potential reasons given by the authors, and others, for this situation include the possibility that there is now more sorting of workers between firms by productivity, or that the rise of superstar firms in sectors like tech or finance has produced specialized firms that have attracted the most productive, highly skilled workers.

The authors find that the pattern generally holds, even within counties or within geographic regions. So much of what is going on here is due to nongeographic factors. But, in the authors' geographic regions (South, West, Midwest, and Northeast), inter-firm income inequality has risen more in the West and Northeast regions, where the Closed Access cities are located, suggesting that Closed Access costs could be one factor at work.

High local costs from Closed Access policies can explain all the trends I have described above: relatively level capital income for firms, more wage disparity, more disparity of profits between firms, highly profitable firms paying high wages, rising consumer cost of living, rising income to housing. The coexistence of these trends has been a mystery to those who have tried to understand them by placing corporate power at the center of the story. Closed Access housing solves that mystery. I don't propose that it is the entire story, but it is an important part of the story.

For example, Stephen Lake, a cofounder of Thalmic Labs (a tech firm located in Toronto that creates innovative wearable digital interface devices), published an essay in December 2016 titled "Debunking the Myth of Higher Pay in Silicon Valley," with the tagline "Don't leave Toronto-Waterloo expecting a higher quality of life in the Bay Area."[24] Lake notes that an entry-level STEM graduate making Can$65,000 in Toronto could make Can$140,000 in San Francisco. That is a 115% wage gap for the same worker, simply based on geographic location.[25] He estimates, though, that after subtracting taxes and living expenses, the worker would have about Can$18,000 left in Toronto and only Can$1,900 left in San Francisco.[26]

Lake is interested in convincing tech workers to consider moving to Toronto. But the fact is that Thalmic has operations in both Toronto and San Francisco. The company has less of a footprint in San Francisco than many tech firms do, so it might benefit from workers' willingness to work in Toronto instead of San Francisco, but even with these extreme differences in cost, Thalmic needs a San Francisco presence. San Francisco has what amounts to a geographic monopoly control of some portion of the tech sector.

This example shows how geography can explain much of the rise in income inequality. Lake's essay also reveals another effect of Closed Access policies. Since taxes are paid on gross income, which must be high in order to pay the real estate entry fee into Closed Access labor markets, many workers making high incomes have to pay very high taxes even though they have very little discretionary income left after housing expenses. In Lake's examples, the Bay Area workers had higher taxes—more than triple the taxes of the Toronto workers.[27] This is one reason why it was advantageous for Closed Access workers to become homeowners, even at a high cost: to capture the income tax benefits of homeownership.

THE COSTS TO THE US ECONOMY

The Closed Access housing problem imposes three significant costs on the domestic economy:

1. An indeterminable number of innovations simply haven't happened because innovators are locked out of the creative mileu of the innovative skill centers. In 2017, 81% of all venture capital was invested in five cities—San Francisco; New York City; Boston; San Jose, California; and LA—the Closed Access cities.[28] These are cities that, according to the Bureau of Economic Analysis, have general price levels about 19% higher than average, mostly attributable to housing costs.[29]

2. American consumers pay higher prices for goods and services that come out of these labor markets (finance, technology, biotech, etc.).[30] The consumer surplus that should have been created by recent US innovation booms has been cut short because the wages of workers who have developed these innovations have been inflated in order to pass on excess returns to owners of urban real estate.

3. Economic opportunities are denied to struggling workers who would move to the Closed Access cities to work in service sectors. Thriving service sectors in these cities would attract spending from the high-income workers there who have significant disposable income.

In a widely cited recent work, Chang-Tai Hsieh from the University of Chicago and Enrico Moretti from the University of California, Berkeley, estimate that housing constraints have reduced aggregate US GDP by 13.5%.[31] Removal of these constraints in high-income cities, according to their model, would lead to an annual wage increase for the average worker of $8,775. More than two-thirds of this drag on domestic income is due to just two metro areas: New York City and the San Francisco–San Jose area.

On the margin of new growth, the United States has largely transitioned to the postindustrial economy. This is a transition of economic growth from extraction and physical production to education and human cooperation. This should be a cause for celebration. But this transition requires a new wave of urbanization, and because our dynamic cities will not allow that, there is now a surcharge on these innovations with human capital, with the proceeds paid to rentiers.[32]

Keep in mind that American metropolitan areas currently tend to have low population densities. Even European cities, which tend to have tight height restrictions, have densities that run twice the level in US cities, including New York and San Francisco.[33] Also, the densest core cities in the US are only dense during the day. Manhattan nearly doubles its population from night to day.[34] So increasing density, in many ways, would actually be less taxing on city infrastructure because of reduced commuting. American cities have plenty of room to grow. In fact, the cities of Washington, DC; Boston; and Manhattan all had larger populations decades ago. If their infrastructure is being stressed, it is not by too much residential density.

Places like Manhattan have no trouble allowing *commercial* density. Figure 7-8 is a striking graphic comparing nighttime and daytime density in Manhattan. We assume that this is just the natural way that cities develop, but it's not. It's the result of a long buildup of peculiar policies and trends in governance. Trillions of dollars' worth of untapped resources, in the form of empty

Figure 7-8. Density of Manhattan, Night and Day

Wednesday at 2 a.m.

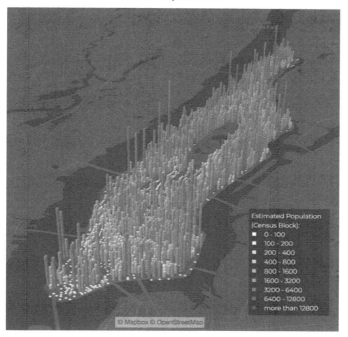

Wednesday at 2 p.m.

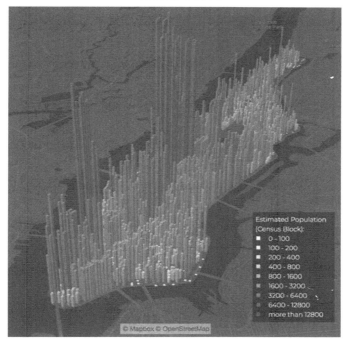

Source: Manhattan Population Explorer, designed by Justin Fung, Oak Ridge National Laboratory, Urbica Design, using Mapbox GL JS, accessed August 29, 2018, http://manpopex.us/.

cubes of air dozens of feet above the ground in our major core cities, could be released if we just enclosed those cubes of air with some steel and gypsum board. If you think that our cities are geographically constrained, keep in mind that they are already relatively dense. They just force their daytime residents to go to New Jersey or the Inland Empire to sleep each night.[35] Nobody marches at the planning department to protest that the new skyscraper in the financial district will have rents that are unaffordable for investment bankers or will ruin the character of the neighborhood. So commercial building meets less resistance.

One reason productivity and real growth have been low is that instead of building housing that consists of $100,000 of building materials and unlocks $400,000 of intrinsic location value in core cities,[36] households substitute housing outside the cities that consists of $100,000 of building materials and unlocks $50,000 of intrinsic location value.

CLOSED ACCESS POLICIES LEAD TO LOWER PRODUCTIVITY

Many of the workers whose productivity is boosted in Closed Access cities are in innovative industries and service industries, where hedonic comparisons are difficult. When Thalmic Labs creates a new prosthetic arm that gives its wearer control over the motion of mechanical fingers, how in the world can the real value of that new equipment be estimated? If it sells for $50,000 instead of $10,000, the Bureau of Economic Analysis has no way to decide whether $40,000 of consumer surplus has been lost. Such products are revolutionary.

Since consumer surplus can't be measured directly, the tradeoff between consumer surplus and producer surplus goes mostly unnoticed. The added value of revolutionary innovations is transformative. But some portion of this abundance gets captured. Where high wages are transferred to landlords, they increase measured inflation, appropriately decreasing measured real production. But, to the extent that limited entry into Closed Access markets protects firms and workers from some competition, high wages are measured as increased productivity, when they are really just a transfer from consumer surplus to producer surplus.

The real estate market also provides a window into the effects of Closed Access policies on productivity. Figure 7-9 is a graph of the components of private fixed residential investment. Each measure is stacked on top of the lower measures to show cumulative totals, as a proportion of GDP. The long-term decline in multifamily investment is a measure of the long-term refusal to develop the tremendous value of high-density urban areas, especially in the past 20 years.

Figure 7-9. Private Residential Fixed Investment Relative to US GDP

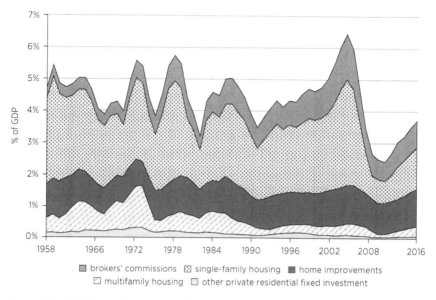

Source: Table 5.4.5 (Private Fixed Investment in Structures by Type) from Bureau of Economic Analysis, available at https://apps.bea.gov/iTable/index_nipa.cfm. Measures are stacked.

When single-family investment is stacked on top of multifamily investment and improvements, the chart shows that total private fixed residential investment (before adding brokers' commissions) had been in slight decline as a portion of GDP for decades. In 2004–2006, total residential investment in structures did briefly reach levels typical in the 1970s. The substitution of material-heavy single units in the heartland for high-value multi-unit housing in the Closed Access cities probably required additional fixed residential investment of 0.25% to 0.50% of GDP at the peak of building, compared to where residential investment would have been if units of similar value had been built in Closed Access cities.

Brokers' commissions are a component of private fixed residential investment, and they were inflated during the decade after 2000. The reason is that home values in the Closed Access cities were very high compared to incomes. Commissions are usually based on a proportion of the sales price, and because of the structure of the real estate broker industry, they do not adjust easily. This led to a boom in real estate brokers. The number of real estate agents in California doubled during the housing boom because of these extra profits from commissions.[37]

The effort required to sell a home had not changed, but the fee taken for it had. In other words, there was de facto price inflation for brokers' services. These fees are counted statistically as investment, but the higher fees brokers received added little to the economy's productive capacity. Measures of return on national investment would naturally be lower because of this.

If brokers' commissions are removed from the measure of residential investment, the actual level of investment in structures had been relatively low, and only briefly reached the highs of earlier peaks at the point that was considered to be a "bubble."

INVESTING IN A FIXED PIE ECONOMY

In a Closed Access context, wealth comes from *not* producing. One of the symbols of long-term stagnation has been the decline in domestic productive capital and the rise in real estate values compared to domestic production. These trends come from the same source: real estate has *replaced* productive capital as a source of income. We have replaced new and efficient or innovative assets with overpriced housing units that stand as gatekeepers to new capacity and innovation. This trend of rising real estate values and stagnant productivity has been widely blamed on "financialization" of the economy. That conclusion mistakes the symptom (increased mortgage levels and asset valuations) for the cause (high prices for exclusive locations).

In previous eras, firms in competitive industries took on extra expenses to fund new production facilities that increased their ability to produce. But postindustrial firms aren't generally funding physical capital in new factories. They are funding human capital that creates new software, constructs financial securities, develops networks for streaming entertainment, and so forth. That human capital comes with a high price tag, in large part because of the high cost of living in Closed Access cities. So, some of the extra expense of developing new, disruptive capital in Closed Access cities is fundamentally an expense that is funding immobility, exclusion, and stagnation. The extra expense that ends up being funneled to landlords is a payment for the value of excluding others instead of a payment for producing more. Imagine if, in the 1960s, Ford had sought to increase its market share not by spending a billion dollars on a new automobile factory, but by spending a billion dollars to *prevent* General Motors from building a new factory. Today, when firms in Closed Access cities hire new workers, they have no choice but to invest in exclusion. Part of the excessive cost of Closed Access hires is a payment for preventing other workers from being hired in Closed Access cities, because each new worker will take one of a limited number of spaces, and those spaces are rationed through cost.

CLOSED ACCESS, LABOR MOBILITY, AND TRADE

Closed Access prevents American laborers from making adjustments in the face of economic changes. There is nothing new about these changes. In 1840, agriculture claimed about 70% of the American labor force. That declined by about 5% per decade until 1970, when it only claimed about 5% of the American labor force. In 1950, manufacturing claimed about 35% of the American labor force. That declined by about 5% per decade until 2010, when it only claimed about 10% of the American labor force. These regime shifts in employment have been happening for a couple of centuries now. But recently, laborers have had a harder time adjusting to these shifts.

Some of the most recent and interesting work on this topic has come from economists David H. Autor, David Dorn, and Gordon H. Hanson. They have found that in areas with sectors that have been affected by declining manufacturing employment because of import competition, workers have faced persistent dislocations. This situation has developed during the period when Chinese manufacturing has been ascendant, and the US has experienced a growing trade deficit. The authors conclude that these developments are all related.[38]

Autor, Dorn, and Hanson's most interesting finding isn't the fact that this dislocation happens. All progress creates dislocations. The challenging part of their findings is the apparent difficulty the communities that suffer those dislocations have in recovering.

During the shift out of agriculture, millions of Americans were freed to labor in other sectors. The level of technology and burgeoning transportation options at the time meant that, over time, many of those laborers shifted to large-scale, centralized manufacturing. Large-scale, centralized manufacturing meant growing cities. From 1860 to 1930, the population of the United States grew from 31 million to 123 million—an increase of 320%. During the same period, some of America's oldest cities—such as Boston, Philadelphia, and New York City—grew at roughly the same rate as the rest of the country, while many other cities grew by thousands of percent. Tens of millions of Americans piled into these growing cities.

Then, in the latter half of the 20th century, this process slowed down. Automobiles, communications and transportation technology, and the relative decline of manufacturing employment made it easier for households to escape the stresses of urban living. But pressure toward urbanization resumed at the turn of the 21st century. Cities today aren't characterized by large manufacturers attracting large numbers of unskilled or semiskilled workers. Today, the fundamental draw to cities is a core of highly skilled information workers. That, by itself, wouldn't create pressure for multimillion-resident mega-cities. But, just as the shift out of agriculture was paired with a shift into manufacturing, the shift out of manufacturing has been paired with a shift into services. Many services are in nontradable sectors.[39] While an increase in large, centralized manufacturers meant that labor had to flock to the cities to be near production, an increase in nontradable services means that labor has to flock to the cities to be near customers. These financial, trade, and technology workers bring with them doctors and nurses, teachers and tutors, counselors, fitness instructors, and baristas.

At the core of this new urbanization is a strong component of complementarity among those skilled workers. They need to live in urban centers because they need to be close to one another to innovate. It may seem like this can't be the source of the population surge, because those workers represent less than a quarter of any given city's population. It is the combination of network effects among those highly skilled workers and the new shift of the labor force into nontradable sectors that move along with them that creates a surge of demand for urban living.

The primary obstacle to labor mobility is the lack of housing where the new jobs are in the nontradable sectors. Ironically, the growth of construction spending in the Open Access parts of the country during the decade after 2000 is frequently cited as a problem—malinvestment. But, to the contrary, the primary problem was in the cities where real housing investment is severely limited. The malinvestment wasn't due to building unneeded homes. It was due to not building homes where they were demanded.

Autor, Dorn, and Hanson find that from 1999 to 2011, upward of two million workers across the country were displaced, which the authors attribute principally to Chinese import competition.[40] This was worsened by the lack of a migration response, so that job loss from a specific sector spread around the other sectors in that geographic area.

During the same period, net domestic migration away from Closed Access cities amounted to more than 1 million households—mostly residents with associate degrees or less. This pattern should be reversed. Instead of creating a million migrant households for the rest of the country to absorb, the Closed Access cities should be absorbing migrants—hardly an extreme expectation for a country's most economically successful cities.[41]

Autor, Dorn, and Hanson recognize the fundamental place of labor mobility at the center of the problem of geographic labor stagnation.[42] But the problem of immobile labor isn't a fixed problem. It appears to have gotten worse with the rise of China, but the rise of China just happens to have coincided with the rise of the Closed Access housing supply problem. Labor can be more mobile. There is little use debating the plausibility or fairness of expecting some small portion of the labor force to relocate in the face of economic shifts if the most clear destinations for that relocation have been cut off by political fiat.[43]

The 2010 article cited in chapter 6 found that improving economic prospects do not lead to much of an inflow of population to Boston anymore.[44] Autor, Dorn, and Hanson have found the corollary to that: employment loss related to import competition has recently led to little population outflow.[45] This means that where there are shocks to local manufacturing employment, now the population tends to remain stable, leaving nonemployment persistently elevated.

Free trade is supposed to raise incomes. But standard models of the economy suggest that changing patterns of production triggered by new trade can only lead to widespread prosperity if, on the margin, labor can be mobile and can shift to regions where trade has boosted local production.[46] Autor, Dorn, and Hanson outline how the American economy doesn't seem to be measuring up to the expectations of the standard model:

> When faced with greater import competition, an open economy normally reallocates resources out of some tradable industries into others, at least under balanced trade. If, however, the trade shock is accompanied by a rise in the trade deficit, then the reallocation from exposed tradables into tradables not exposed to China may be delayed, shifting employment into non-tradables instead. While this reasoning still predicts a long-run employment reallocation towards non-exposed tradables, the large and growing U.S. trade deficit during the period under study may have significantly slowed such a reallocation.[47]

Furthermore,

> That this neoclassical[48] prediction does not appear to hold even approximately over the span of a decade suggests that the labor market impacts of trade shocks are likely to be amplified by slow and incomplete adjustment: rather than modestly reducing wage levels among low-skill workers

nationally, these shocks catalyze significant falls in employment rates within trade-impacted local labor markets.[49]

In another paper, the authors explain,

> Theory suggests that trade with China yields aggregate
> gains for the US economy. Our study also highlights the
> distributional consequences of trade and the medium
> run efficiency losses associated with adjustment to trade
> shocks. The consequences of China trade for US employ-
> ment, household income, and government benefit
> programs may contribute to public ambivalence toward
> globalization and specific anxiety about increasing trade
> with China.[50]

In these passages, we can see that Autor, Dorn, and Hanson view the trade
deficit as a factor delaying the transition of workers to new sectors, that neoclassical economic models fail to account for these delays in labor transition, and
that the costs of these delays fall disproportionately on displaced workers. For
the economy as a whole, the gains from trade are significant, but "the ultimate
and sizable net gains are realized only once workers are able to reallocate across
regions in order to move from declining to expanding industries."[51]

This suggests that an overreliance on neoclassical economic models has
harmed vulnerable workers and led to a backlash. But the key problem with
the neoclassical economic models is that they assume that capital can be freely
allocated to its best and most-valued use. The Closed Access cities have thrown
a monkey wrench into a key adjustment mechanism of the economy. The solution to this isn't to rid ourselves of neoclassical economic models. The solution
is to rid ourselves of Closed Access housing obstruction.

Trade with China isn't the fundamental problem here. It may have been one
of the symptoms that exposed the problem. But the fundamental reason that
economic growth and trade have not been broadly shared is the rise of Closed
Access.

The empirical findings of Autor, Dorn, and Hanson are a clear window
into the costs of what has happened. The widespread and strongly held premise that there were too many houses in the United States when these labor
mobility issues developed diverts our eyes from the obvious implications of
their work. That premise needs to be shifted radically. There were never too
many homes in the United States. There has been an endemic shortage of

homes. Once we accept this radical shift in the premise, its position as a fundamental cause of the economic paralysis Autor, Dorn, and Hanson identify becomes obvious.

SUPPLY AND DEMAND FOR UNSKILLED AND DISPLACED LABOR

Now, let's revisit supply and demand for Closed Access labor. Figure 7-3 described supply and demand for skilled labor in Closed Access cities. Figure 7-10 describes supply and demand for less-skilled labor in Closed Access cities. Demand for this labor is more elastic than demand for skilled labor. This means that higher costs lead to a greater decline in quantity. We can also surmise this from the hundreds of thousands of households with low incomes flooding out of Closed Access cities, and the millions of workers identified by Autor, Dorn, and Hanson who would work in the new nontradable sectors, but who lack opportunities and who can't afford to move to Closed

Figure 7-10. Supply and Demand for Unskilled Closed Access Labor

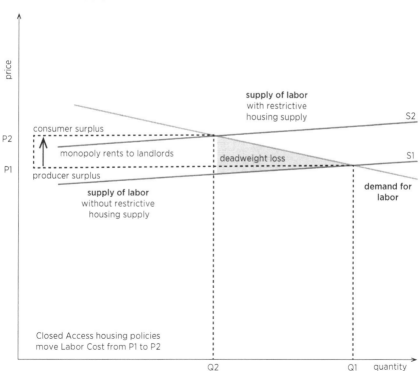

Access cities in search of them. Incomes in Closed Access cities for less-skilled workers don't seem to rise high enough to pay for higher rents, so that market rents in zip codes where incomes are lower claim a large portion of resident incomes. The turnstile migration pattern in the Closed Access cities is a direct effect of the different demand elasticities for less-skilled and more-skilled laborers.

In comparison to the market for workers with high skills, this means that there is more deadweight loss in low-skilled labor markets. Deadweight loss is the loss in economic benefits resulting from the economic activity that simply doesn't happen when costs rise. In the skilled labor markets there may not be much deadweight loss, because the firms that tap into those markets are still drawn to the Closed Access cities. The effect of Closed Access may be mostly to raise the price of their labor, with less effect on quantity. But, with less-skilled labor, there is less pricing power, and so the quantity of low-skilled Closed Access employment declines so much that it has triggered significant out-migration.

These supply-and-demand graphs represent human stories. In the skilled labor supply saddled with higher costs, we can see the tech worker in San Francisco who can't seem to retain any savings even though she is earning $100,000 a year. In the monopoly rents to landlords, we can see the middle-class couple who bought their Closed Access home 30 years ago and who sell it today, retiring to the mountains with a windfall. In the deadweight loss, we can see the millions of workers who could provide many personal services to the skilled workers that populate the Closed Access cities, but for whom no job materializes.

A NOTE ON MONOPOLY RENTS

The high income earned by firms in the postindustrial sectors derives from many factors. Some of the largest firms in the world now are American technology firms that have very high gross margins, because of the winner-takes-all character of parts of the technology sector. It is interesting that those high profits don't appear to have increased the domestic capital income share, as I outlined above. But the supply-and-demand curves shown above apply just as well to monopoly power of firms as they could to monopoly power of real estate owners. For a tech firm with significant market power, even without the Closed Access cost shift, supply would have already been shifted to the left.[52]

So, to the extent that firms faced with Closed Access housing costs have monopoly power from factors other than housing limits, they were already capturing consumer surplus by reducing output. In that case, when the high costs of Closed Access housing captured monopoly incomes for real estate owners, some of this income was being taken from the firms, not from the firms' customers.

As I noted above, it appears that varying rates of income growth among workers are the result of varying rates of income growth among firms. Just as the demand for labor can be more or less elastic for different types of workers, the demand for the output of firms can be too. So these effects operate on a scale. Some firms may have had complete monopoly control over some product or service, so that monopoly rents claimed by landlords came entirely from monopoly rents those firms were already claiming. Other firms may have had little market power, but the demand for the output of their industry niche as a whole was inelastic. In those cases, firms would not have been claiming monopoly rents, but when they were faced with Closed Access costs, their prices would have risen to account for those costs, and the monopoly rents claimed by landlords would have come entirely from consumer surplus.

It is beyond the scope of this book to quantify how much of the cost of Closed Access came from firm profits and how much came from consumer surplus. These processes can be quite complicated. If a firm has high profits because it is the current "winner" among its immediate competitors, the fact that those profits can be siphoned away would still lead to changes in patterns of investment. If being the "winner" is less lucrative, then less capital will be invested in disruptive competition to topple the current "winners."

One of the clichés of the past two decades has been that we created a stock market bubble and then we replaced it with a housing bubble. But that description is based on the premise that those bubbles grew out of irrational exuberance, loose money, and loose lending. If, instead, our premise is that strong incomes in the Closed Access cities were the source of the high asset valuations, then those bubbles are still related. But, according to this premise, much of the stock market bubble was based on the expected monopoly profits of the tech "winners." Those monopoly profits didn't go away. Today, the tech giants really do dominate the equity market. Some of their profits were just siphoned away by Closed Access real estate owners. We still had a stock market bubble and replaced it with a housing bubble, but these bubbles were based on monopoly rents.

In the first quarter of 2000, the market value of US nonfinancial corporations was $21 trillion (in 2017 dollars), and real estate owned by US households was worth $17 trillion, for a combined value of $38 trillion. By the second quarter of 2006, the combined value had grown to $46 trillion, but now it was divided between $16 trillion of corporate value and $30 trillion of real estate value.[53] The total value had risen by a moderate 3% annually, in real terms, but it had been shifted from corporations to real estate owners.

The financial crisis that followed collapsed all asset values, and it was 2014 before the total value recovered back to 2006 levels. One reason the recession of 2008 was so much more damaging than the recession of 2001 was that the first stock market collapse was partly the result of a transfer of income from one asset class to another, while in the second stock market collapse, the lost value of real estate simply disappeared. Rents are still high, so the earnings to housing still justify high prices, and Closed Access real estate still claims monopoly rents from productive activity, but the valuations fell and didn't recover. That has created a permanent wealth shock. Homes that are owned by the resident household have ever-rising rental values but have market prices that were pushed well below their previous prices. For these families, the reduced market prices and the lack of access to home equity credit hurts. The added rental value means nothing to them. They don't write a rent check to themselves each month. They aren't saying to themselves, "Aren't we lucky that our home earns inflated rents because of a nationwide credit shock!"

Regarding the shift in monopoly rents from firms to real estate, not all monopoly rents are created equal. The firms are earning those profits in very competitive and innovative markets, so the quest to get at those high profits draws new investment into those industries, and consumers benefit in the long run. Nobody benefits from the legislated monopoly power of real estate owners. It is simply a tax on productive tenants.

As the housing supply problem continues to push up housing costs, even as the housing bubble slowly fades into the past, the proper role of the housing shortage in all these economic challenges is becoming clearer. The White House issued a report in September 2016 directly addressing the number of ways that urban housing constraints are creating economic stress and inequality and limiting real income growth.[54] A radical change in the premise about the housing bubble is necessary in order to fully come to grips with the solutions to this problem. Fundamentally, our problem is that there are not and have never been too many houses. There haven't been enough. The backlash against the financial markets that fund new housing supply has been quite damaging in this regard.

As for the Closed Access cities, the fact of the matter is that marginal new households are moving *somewhere*. They are changing the fabric of the city, the character of the neighborhood, *somewhere*. Why should LA, San Francisco, Boston, and New York City be the places that especially don't allow this to happen? *San Francisco and New York City*. Cities with neighborhoods that have names like Little Italy and Chinatown. Places, for the love of Pete, that for centuries have been teeming with hopeful immigrants. Cities that were designed *centuries ago* for just this purpose—for density and change and dynamism.

Think of the miracle of human forethought that these cities represent. They boast broad thoroughfares and the ability to hold and move massive numbers of people, *yet they were largely designed before the automobile and before the skyscraper.* These places are miracles handed to us by our forebears, and we are demeaning their legacy.

CHAPTER 8
Closed Access and International Trade

T he underemployed workers that David H. Autor, David Dorn, and Gordon H. Hanson found were displaced by import competition, but if the fundamental cause of labor immobility is Closed Access housing rather than import competition, then why does the American trade deficit coincide with the labor immobility problem? It could be that they *are* related, but that the causation goes in the other direction.

There are at least four sources of pressure on the US trade balance that could originate in Closed Access housing markets, discussed here in the likely order of importance.

The first source of pressure is *consumer surplus*. As shown in figures 7-3 and 7-12, the added cost of limited housing acts as a tax on labor, paid to real estate owners. That tax largely comes out of consumer surplus. So for transactions within the United States, there is a transfer from the consumers of the goods and services produced by skilled Closed Access workers that ultimately flows to Closed Access real estate owners as rent payments. This is a drag on the US economy because it shifts income from productive activities to passive rentiers. But, in terms of total income, it is neutral. One American pays it and another American receives it.

The same tax applies on goods and services that Closed Access workers sell abroad. But, in that case, the loss of consumer value falls on the foreign buyer, and American real estate owners collect the transfer. Since much of the value-added of highly skilled postindustrial workers in Closed Access cities is embedded in goods and services sold through foreign subsidiaries in complex supply chains and financial networks, the bloated income from this transfer is frequently recorded as foreign income rather than as exports. This foreign income can then be used to purchase imports.

The second source of pressure is *consumption smoothing*. Especially during the housing boom, Closed Access housing valuations rose to very high levels. Closed Access homeowners were borrowing from their home equity or selling their homes and pocketing those gains, and they were using some of the cash from those activities to consume more. This increased demand for goods and services above the level of concurrent American production, and triggered a rise in imports.

Empirically, this claim is not new. The normal explanation for some of the spike in the trade deficit during the boom was that Americans were using mortgage debt to overconsume. But that explanation places credit expansion at the base of the series of events, and paints that consumption as unsustainable. In hindsight, the Closed Access housing markets that funded the bulk of that consumption are not dependent on risky credit markets, and the high home values in Closed Access locations are sustainable because of the limits to new supply.

It is more accurate to say that the consumption fueled by home equity was mostly consumption smoothing. Closed Access homeowners had control of a persistent flow of economic rents. Those rents were capitalized into the prices of their homes, and they could draw on those values to consume some of their future rents immediately. With any newly discovered wealth, consumption smoothing will inevitably be employed.

The third source of pressure is *substitution* away from local services. For the skilled Closed Access workers with high incomes, the potential benefit of working in Closed Access cities came from a series of substitutions. Workers earned high incomes, but costs for housing and local services were high. Raising the price of local services led to consumption substitutions away from local services and to goods and services that could be sourced from low-cost locations. A portion of those substitutions would have been to international goods and services. This is related to the deadweight loss of the American workers locked out of Closed Access cities, which I discussed in chapter 7. Transactions that didn't happen were replaced with international transactions in which Americans received foreign goods, and those dollars were invested back into American assets, such as mortgage securities that were helping Closed Access workers to purchase expensive homes.

The fourth source of pressure is the *high profits* of existing Closed Access firms. Many postindustrial firms exist in markets where startup costs are high and the profits of sector winners are high as a result. A market where the costs of new entry are inflated would slow down disruptive innovators, and could allow existing firms to monetize their older technologies more. Recent returns of US firms in global markets have been strong, coinciding with the rise of the Closed Access economy.[1] This would have similar effects as the first source of pressure on exports, since it would increase the profits of foreign subsidiaries of those firms.

All of these factors suggest that the causal direction of the rising trade deficit during the housing bubble was rising Closed Access incomes, not a glut of foreign saving. And one significant piece of evidence in favor of this interpretation is the fact that, throughout the housing boom, incomes from foreign investments owned by Americans were growing faster than incomes from American investments owned by foreigners. As a percentage of GDP, net American incomes on foreign investments have never been higher. This is because the flow of imports and financial assets into the US was funded by Closed Access wealth and income, not by American profligacy or foreign saving.

THE SUSTAINABLE TRADE DEFICIT

Figure 8-1 compares US net foreign income (US foreign income minus US income to foreign savers) to the trade deficit and net foreign investment (foreign capital inflows minus US capital outflows). Notice that the US has earned more income abroad than foreign savers have earned on American assets for many decades. After the 1970s, foreign savers began to bridge that gap. The US ran a trade deficit. On net, foreigners used the proceeds of exports to the US to invest in US assets for income, rather than to buy US exports. This caused foreign income from the US to catch up with US income earned abroad, and by the late 1990s, international capital income flows were roughly in balance. Foreign investors were earning as much on their American assets as Americans were earning on their foreign assets.

But notice what began to happen after the late 1990s. Foreign capital inflows to the US greatly accelerated. These capital inflows had to be funded with dollars, and those dollars generally had to come from selling imports to US consumers. So the trade deficit moved in tandem with the capital inflows. But a strange thing happened. These new massive inflows of capital did nothing to boost foreign income. In fact, net US income on foreign assets has grown to a higher proportion of GDP than ever.

Part of the explanation is a matter of semantics. The super firms of the new economy generally sell software and services, which can be sold directly from foreign subsidiaries. So, to an extent, this is simply a problem of mismeasurement. The services some US firms sell abroad do not register as exports. They

Figure 8-1. Trade and Capital Flows Relative to US GDP

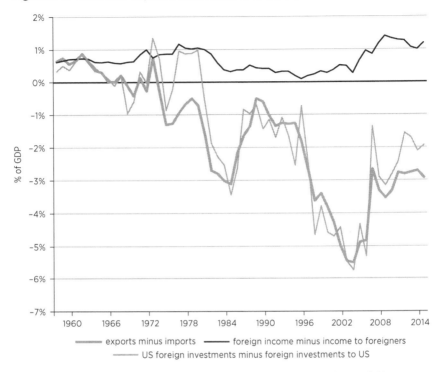

Source: Table 1.1 (U.S. International Transactions) from Bureau of Economic Analysis, available at https://apps.bea.gov/iTable/index_ita.cfm.

register as the sales of foreign subsidiaries. Plus, profits reinvested in those foreign subsidiaries don't register as international capital flows, because the capital never crosses the US border.

Figure 8-2 clarifies this issue a bit. It compares the market value of foreign assets owned by Americans and US assets owned by foreigners. But notice even here that the US has a net negative position. This should coincide with net negative income. Or, at the least, if US foreign income tends to be more profitable but riskier, it should coincide with positive US foreign income that is occasionally rocked by cyclical disruptions. But, instead, the US enjoys steadily growing net foreign capital income.

One way to think of this is that US corporations earn foreign income, and as a result, US owners use that income to purchase imports, in a perfectly sustainable set of transactions. Here is some simple arithmetic to help think about this. Imagine that a US firm has a $1 billion foreign investment earning 10%

Figure 8-2. US Foreign Assets and Liabilities Relative to US GDP

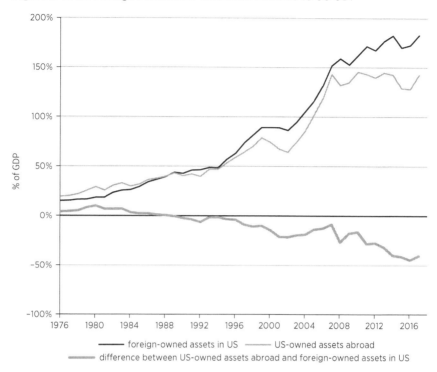

foreign-owned assets in US ——— US-owned assets abroad

difference between US-owned assets abroad and foreign-owned assets in US

Source: Table 1.1 (U.S. Net International Investment Position at the End of the Period) from Bureau of Economic Analysis, available at https://apps.bea.gov/iTable/index_ita.cfm.

returns, and foreign savers have $1 billion invested in US bonds that earn 5% returns. The US firm would earn $100 million this year, and the foreign savers would earn $50 million. If the US firm reinvests that $100 million, next year its income will be $10 million higher ($100 million × 10%). If the foreign savers reinvest their US income, they will only increase their income by $2.5 million ($50 million × 5%). In order to simply maintain neutral net foreign income, foreign savers would need to invest an additional $150 million into the US with 5% returns. To a certain extent, this is what is happening. Foreigners must maintain a trade surplus with the US each year to earn dollars that they can invest into US assets, just to maintain a neutral foreign income level.[2]

Using the market value of foreign assets, the net change in international asset ownership since the mid-1990s has been an increase in US foreign liabilities of about 40% of GDP. (Foreign savers have increased the value of their US holdings more than US savers have increased their foreign savings by an amount equal to 40% of GDP.) This amounts to roughly 1.6% per year. Since the mid-1990s, US net income on foreign assets has averaged about 0.7% of GDP. The amount of new foreign capital invested into the US each year is much larger than the net amount of profit Americans earn on their foreign investments. Despite all of this extra saving, foreign investors still can't keep pace with US-owned foreign profits. US-owned assets abroad continue to earn more than US assets owned by foreigners. Talk about a financial treadmill!

This suggests that the US has a tremendous advantage in foreign investment returns. And those excess returns have increased in tandem with excess wages and rents in the Closed Access cities.

Harvard economist Ricardo Hausmann and former president of the Central Bank of Argentina Federico Sturzenegger explain this mismatch between measured foreign assets and foreign income with the term "dark matter"—American assets abroad that have a true value that is higher than their measured value.[3] They count at least three sources of such investments.

First, American foreign direct investments earn higher returns than foreign investments in the US partly as a result of American organizational capital, expertise, and so on. Foreign investments into the US tend to be more weighted in low-risk debt securities. Second, the dollar provides stable liquidity in world markets, so US savers invest in productive foreign assets while some foreigners get liquidity value just from holding dollars. Third, because developing markets lack a stable source of safe investments, foreign savers are willing to invest in low-yielding, safe US assets while risk-seeking US savers buy riskier, high-yield foreign assets. In short, the US is selling knowledge, liquidity, and insurance in complex ways that don't always show up on official balance sheets put out by the Bureau of Economic Analysis.

These explanations are somewhat satisfying, and they go a long way toward explaining the mystery. Yet notice the coincidence that the scale of the gap surged at the same time that Closed Access took hold of the American economy. Beginning in the late '90s, US foreign income shot up as our net foreign asset position dropped.

American savers have long earned excess returns on foreign assets, compared to foreign investors in US assets.[4] In other words, some of the sources Hausmann and Sturzenegger give for our net foreign income have been around for a long time. It could be that the explosion in international asset holdings—from about 50% of US GDP in the 1990s to about 150% of US GDP in the decade after 2000, for both liabilities and assets—simply expanded this advantage arithmetically. But I would suggest a fourth recent source for Hausmann and Sturzenegger's dark matter: Closed Access rents and profits.[5]

Figure 8-3. Home Prices and Capital Flows, 2001-2006

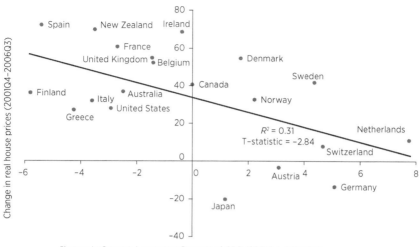

Change in Current Account as Percent of GDP (2001Q4–2006Q3)

Sources: Ben S. Bernanke, "Monetary Policy and the Housing Bubble" (speech at the Annual Meeting of the American Economic Association, Atlanta, Georgia, January 3, 2010). Data are from the International Monetary Fund, Haver Analytics, and Federal Reserve staff calculations.

Figure 8-3 is a slide from a presentation by Ben Bernanke. Bernanke (and Alan Greenspan) argued that a savings glut in the developing world was the causal factor bringing capital into the developed world, pushing down real interest rates, and thus pushing up property values. He is correct that this had little to do with monetary policy. But his explanation leaves many mysteries, including the first obvious question: Why did that capital flow to Australia but not to Germany? This is similar to the question that should be asked about the US housing bubble: Why did low interest rates or predatory lending lead to home prices doubling in coastal California but not in Texas?

The answer to both of these questions is that the unstoppable force of postindustrial urbanization met the immovable object of constrained urban housing supplies in Australia and California, but not in Germany and Texas, and that was the development that set these global capital flows in motion.

THE GLOBAL SAVINGS GLUT

If the savings glut explanation were true, then that savings would fund excess housing, pushing *down* rents in countries with current account deficits. But the reverse is the case. Higher home prices are associated with *rising* rents—

certainly in the US, and, it seems, internationally. Closed Access policies suck in rents, goods and services, profits, wages, and capital from the rest of the world, and much of that income must be used in the bidding war to get into Closed Access cities.

Upon reflection, the conventional explanation for the various factors involved in the bubble include two odd bedfellows. In the conventional version of events, there were foreign savers seeking safety with unleveraged, low-yield savings, and there were other investors who were bidding down risk spreads and leveraging risky securities in a reckless attempt to increase profits. Somehow there was a surge of investors seeking risk and seeking safety, both serving as explanations for the same phenomenon. But, if the cause of these capital flows was Closed Access incomes, those various savers are not such important inputs in the story.

If low-risk savers were bidding down the yields of securities, the natural reaction of risk takers shouldn't have been to double down on leveraged holdings of those securities. It should have been to shift to securities that had a higher risk premium built into the expected return. The internet boom is a good example of this. Stock prices shot up and investments into equity were strong. Since savers *were* risk takers then, risk-free interest rates were higher. Real Treasury rates in the late 1990s were above 3.5%. They were generally below 2.5% in the decade after 2000.[6] That is because investors in the late 1990s sought profit in equity markets, where higher risks may lead to higher returns, rather than in safe bonds. During the height of the private securitization boom (2004–2007), the S&P 500 rose by 9%, 3%, 14%, and 4%. This is not what risk-taking behavior looks like. The stock market nearly matched this four-year rise in 1997 alone. Then did it again in 1998. That's what risk-taking behavior looks like.

The global savings glut theory raises at least two questions:

1. Why would the capital flows be so selective? And why would they be associated with housing bubbles?

2. If housing bubbles are caused by developing market capital flows, why would they cause rents to go up in the destination countries?

Economist Paul Krugman told the Financial Crisis Inquiry Commission,

> It's hard to envisage us having had this crisis without considering international monetary capital movements. The U.S. housing bubble was financed by large capital inflows. So were Spanish and Irish and Baltic bubbles. It's

a combination of, in the narrow sense, of a less regulated
financial system and a world that was increasingly wide
open for big international capital movements.[7]

At first glance, this explanation seems obvious. But how well does it hold up if
all the facets of the housing boom are considered? The inflow of capital lowered interest rates in Dallas just as much as it did in Los Angeles. In the Open
Access cities, that capital funded lumber, labor, gypsum, and more products.
In the Closed Access cities, most of that financial capital funded transfers to
landowners, taxes, fees, and various other claims that bridge the gap between
building costs and market values, but little physical investment.[8]

Does this make sense as an explanation of how a global glut of capital fueled
a housing bubble? Is there an economic model that says capital will be drawn to
places where asset values are inflated because new, competing capital is taxed
and burdened? If this were true, then shouldn't global capital just remain in the
developing economies? If the glut of global capital were searching for safe markets, wouldn't that capital be attracted to places that *don't* have housing bubbles,
where the home values are stable because they are near the cost of replacement?

All things considered, the idea that global savings would naturally correlate
with housing bubbles has a number of conceptual hurdles to clear. Locations
incapable of bearing real investment would not be the obvious destination
for capital in search of safety, and even if they were, they would have limited
ability, on net, to actually serve as the destination for that capital—for the
simple reason that it is not easy to actually transform financial capital into
physical capital there.[9]

As for the question about why housing bubbles would cause rents to go up
in the destination countries, it is useful to turn to Dallas and Los Angeles again.
It appears that Open Access areas took in and transformed their fair share of
financial capital. Even the capital that entered the Closed Access cities was transferred via existing homeowners. Millions of those homeowners moved away,
took that capital with them, and reinvested it in new homes in Open Access
America. The American migration pattern is part of this capital flow.

If the global glut of capital had been the cause of the housing boom, then
capital flowing in should have increased the supply of homes and reduced
rents. Bernanke's regression line in figure 8-3 would have a positive slope. The
countries with low home prices would have had large capital inflows that would
have funded new homes, and countries where there were limits to housing supply expansion would have had less capital inflow. Rents would have declined
in the low-priced countries that would have allocated so much capital to new

Figure 8-4. Rent Inflation in the Two Americas

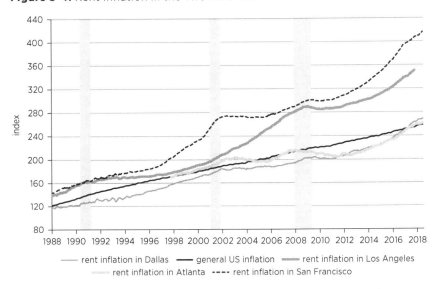

Note: CPI = consumer price index, OE = owners' equivalent. Shaded areas indicate US recessions. Inflation measures are set to 100 in 1982–1984.

Sources: Bureau of Labor Statistics (BLS), "Consumer Price Index for All Urban Consumers: Owners' Equivalent Rent of Primary Residence in Dallas–Fort Worth–Arlington, TX (CBSA)" (CUURA316SEHC01), and BLS, "Consumer Price Index for All Urban Consumers: All Items Less Food and Energy" (CPILFENS), and BLS, "Consumer Price Index for All Urban Consumers: Owners' Equivalent Rent of Residences in Los Angeles–Riverside–Orange County, CA (CMSA) (DISCONTINUED)" (CUURA421SEHC), and BLS, "Consumer Price Index for All Urban Consumers: Owners' Equivalent Rent of Primary Residence in Atlanta–Sandy Springs–Roswell, GA (CBSA)" (CUURA319SEHC01), and BLS, "Consumer Price Index for All Urban Consumers: Owners' Equivalent Rent of Primary Residence in San Francisco–Oakland–Hayward, CA (CBSA)" (CUURA422SEHC01), retrieved from FRED, Federal Reserve Bank of St. Louis.

housing stock. Rents would have declined, but by less, in the countries that built fewer homes and had higher price appreciation.

To the contrary, in America, no major housing markets have experienced persistently falling rents. Rent inflation, on average, has been high. While rent inflation in Dallas and Atlanta did tend to decline when homebuilding was more active, generally—over the course of 20 years—these cities have had rent inflation roughly in line with core inflation. Los Angeles and San Francisco, on the other hand, have had rent inflation far above core inflation (figure 8-4).

Figure 8-5 suggests an international relationship between incomes and price/rent ratios. The net importer countries had higher income growth and an increase in price/rent ratios. The pattern that has developed in the United States appears to be fairly uniform across developed economies. This suggests that the Closed Access phenomenon is operating internationally much as it is within the United States. Places that have transitioned more into

Figure 8-5. Income, Home Price-to-Rent Ratio, and Trade

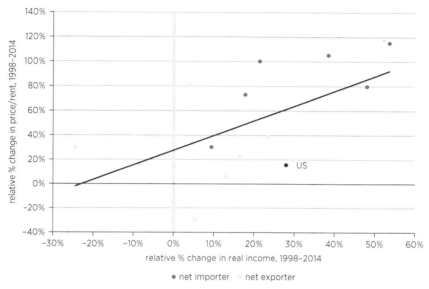

Note: Net importer countries are the US, Australia, Canada, Denmark, France, New Zealand, and the United Kingdom. Net exporter countries are Belgium, Finland, Germany, Italy, Japan, South Korea, and Switzerland. Sweden was removed because of income data that were incongruous. It should be noted, though, that Sweden is an exception in that it has urban housing constraints but also a trade surplus. See Giang Ho, "Housing Supply Constraints in Sweden," in *Sweden: Selected Issues*, IMF Country Report No. 15/330 (Washington, DC: International Monetary Fund, 2015).
Sources: Organisation for Economic Co-operation and Development, "Focus on House Prices," http://www.oecd.org/eco/outlook/focusonhouseprices.htm; World Bank, "Current Account Balance," http://data.worldbank.org/indicator/BN.CAB.XOKA.CD.

the postindustrial economy have higher incomes, but they have run into urban housing constraints that cause home prices to rise. And this combination of factors fuels a trade deficit and capital inflows.

In general, the Organisation for Economic Co-operation and Development data used in figure 8-5 don't show strong relationships between rent and income, or between rent and home prices. On a national level, this is the same in the US. That is what has thrown off so much of the analysis of the US market. During the housing boom, on the national level, it looked like home prices were skyrocketing but rents were fairly level. Yet an examination of individual metropolitan areas shows that rent and price were related.

On an international level, the same sort of inter-metropolitan analysis is necessary. For instance, the United Kingdom appears to have a similar pattern to the US, with a very expensive economic center in London and cities with much less expensive housing, such as Birmingham, Leeds, and Glasgow. France has very expensive Paris and less expensive Marseille, Lyon, and Toulouse. According to work from researchers at the Reserve Bank of Australia, recent shifts in local zoning restrictions have triggered much of the increase in Australian home prices, especially in urban cores.[10]

On the other hand, Germany, which did not have a housing bubble and is a net exporter, has relatively inexpensive housing across cities such as Berlin, Hamburg, Munich, and Cologne. Because local factors can dominate in real estate and because international cost and income comparisons are difficult, this is a complex topic. Plus, many factors influence trade patterns.[11]

Qiao Yu, Hanwen Fan, and Xun Wu summarize this issue with references to many of the papers on the topic.[12] They conclude that the global savings glut hypothesis fails several empirical tests. As with most criticisms of the glut hypothesis, they stress a relationship between loose monetary policy and housing prices during the boom.

As I have demonstrated in earlier chapters, loose monetary policy isn't necessary to explain housing bubbles. Prices in Open Access cities were somewhat sensitive to long-term real interest rates, as we would expect, but they weren't outside historical norms. Prices in Closed Access cities are reasonably explained by high and rising rents. And, in both the US and Europe, cities or countries that shared monetary regimes had vastly different housing markets.

This issue was an important factor in key monetary decisions leading up to the financial crisis. A global savings glut was seen to be the cause of low interest rates and high home prices. Long-term interest rates remained low even though the Federal Reserve had lifted short-term rates by 4% from mid-2004 to mid-2006. Federal Reserve leaders thought that those rates remained low because of the global savings glut. They thought that those low interest rates were stimulative to the American economy. They thought that, even though they were tightening monetary and credit conditions, foreign savers were continuing to flood the American economy with capital.

I pointed out above that the growth of American net incomes on foreign assets should raise considerable doubt about the idea that the trade deficit was due to American profligacy being funded by foreign savers. Interest rates also don't really point to foreign savers as a strong causal force. In the early- and mid-1990s, the trade deficit and the flow of financial capital into the US were both about 1% of GDP. They had grown to about 4% of GDP by the year 2000. But interest rates were still very high in the year 2000. The real interest rate on 30-year inflation-protected treasuries was still nearly 4%. Most of the increase in the trade deficit and foreign capital flows happened without any significant shift in interest rates.

From 2002 to 2005, the trade deficit and the capital flows surplus would increase to nearly 6% of GDP while the interest rate on inflation-protected 30-year treasuries declined to about 2%. For that specific period, declining interest rates and rising foreign capital inflows coincided. This also coincides with the period when Closed Access real estate owners were capturing more monopolistic rents and were consuming from their newly found wealth.

If capital flows were largely the result of incomes flowing into Closed Access cities because of these monopolistic forces, then low interest rates were more likely already a sign of declining economic prospects. From 2005 to 2007, homeownership was declining, first-time homebuyers were decreasing, former owners were selling out, and many former Closed Access homeowners were selling and moving to less-expensive cities. Increasingly, the source of the glut of savings in search of safe assets was American housing markets, where sentiment was turning, potential new homeowners were waiting, and former homeowners were liquidating home equity and reinvesting into other, safer assets. By 2006, when housing starts and private investment began to collapse, falling long-term real interest rates should especially have been a reasonable concern. But the idea that easy global capital was the trigger for low interest rates diverted attention from that concern. These two potential causes for declining interest rates call for opposite monetary reactions, beginning as early as 2005 and 2006. In hindsight, it is worth considering whether we chose the wrong reaction.

A GLOBAL BARRIER TO THE POSTINDUSTRIAL ECONOMY

The countries that have had trade deficits, high home prices, and rising incomes also share another commonality. Figure 8-6 compares countries according to the proportion of their workforce employed in the manufacturing sector. Of the twelve countries, other than the US, for which the Bureau of Labor Statistics has long-term employment data, eight have had home price appreciation at least as strong as in the US. All eight of those countries have low and falling manufacturing employment—falling from between 22% and 32% of the labor force in 1970 to between 8% and 13% of the labor force in 2012.

Of the four countries with less price appreciation than the US, Italy did have a price run-up by some measures, though it was smaller and temporary. Germany, Japan, and South Korea all maintained moderate home prices throughout the period. In all four cases, manufacturing remains a stronger part of the economy—between 16% and 20% of the labor force in 2012.

Figure 8-6. International Trends in Manufacturing Employment

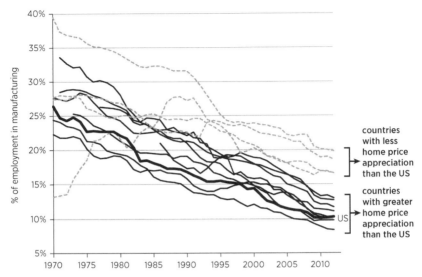

Note: Countries with greater home price appreciation than the US are Australia, Canada, France, the Netherlands, New Zealand, Spain, Sweden, and the United Kingdom. Countries with less home price appreciation than the US are Germany, Italy, Japan, and South Korea.
Source: Table 2.8 (Percent of Employment in Manufacturing) in Bureau of Labor Statistics, "International Comparisons of Annual Labor Force Statistics, 1970–2012," June 7, 2013, https://www.bls.gov/fls/flscomparelf/lfcompendium.xls; Organisation for Economic Co-operation and Development, "Focus on Home Prices," accessed 11 September 2018, http://www.oecd.org/eco/outlook/focusonhouseprices.htm. Home price appreciation categories are based on real price changes during the Closed Access era after the mid-1990s.

It seems as though there is a fairly universal trend of developed economies (and cities) becoming postindustrial economies and developing a problem of urban housing constraints.

Figure 8-7 shows the per capita GDP growth over time in Australia, Canada, the US, and the UK (housing bubble countries) and in Germany, Switzerland, Italy, and Japan (non–housing bubble countries). During this period, incomes have been growing faster in the countries with expensive housing. If we were hocking our futures to foreign savers in order to overconsume, isn't it strange that the countries that look like us—countries with housing bubbles, trade deficits, and foreign capital inflows—are systematically countries with high and growing incomes? This is because the economic arguments have had the story reversed. These capital flows are being set in motion by high incomes in countries that are pushing into the postindustrial economy and are running up against urban housing constraints.

In a way, both supply and demand inputs are required for a price spike. But

Figure 8-7. International Growth in Per Capita GDP since 1991

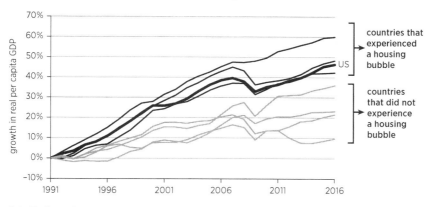

Note: Real growth rates are estimated using purchasing power parity. Countries that experienced a housing bubble were the US, Australia, Canada, and the United Kingdom. Countries that did not experience a housing bubble were Germany, Italy, Japan, and Switzerland.
Source: Organisation for Economic Co-operation and Development, "Level of GDP per Capita and Productivity," http://stats.oecd.org/Index.aspx?DataSetCode=PDB_LV#.

removing credit and money from the US economy, the policy that has been pursued for a decade now, will not erase the difference in housing markets between San Francisco and Omaha. If credit and money are allowed to flow more liberally, prices will rise. But they will only rise to "bubble" levels in San Francisco, not in Omaha. Those two cities have distinctly different housing markets, regardless of how much credit is flowing.

In Omaha or San Francisco, Manchester or London, home prices will move up or down with changing monetary, credit, and capital flow limitations, but these influences will do nothing to bring rents in London down to the level of rents in Manchester. Rent is the flow of income that is, in the end, the determining factor in this trend. Rent is what connects the postindustrial economic transition to housing bubbles.

The limits of housing access in cities with highly skilled labor networks are creating economic rents from exclusion and barriers to entry that suck income from both the surrounding regions of those countries and from other countries. In the end, the consumers of software and financial services in Omaha, Marseille, and Manchester are paying for those overpriced homes in San Francisco, Paris, and London.

Countries characterized by high incomes, high home prices, trade deficits, and declining manufacturing employment also tend to have rising income inequality. Thomas Piketty, Emmanuel Saez, and Stefanie Stantcheva find that the income share of the top 1% has increased significantly in the US, the

UK, Canada, and Australia; and it has not in Germany, Switzerland, and Japan. They also find that this difference is correlated with changes in top marginal tax rates.[13] Countries that have reduced rates farther than others have seen a rise in the share of income claimed by the top 1%. Much of the rise in the incomes of the top 1% has also happened since the mid-1990s.

It appears that a set of countries has attracted firms of the postindustrial economy. Possibly the lower tax rates helped. But it is plausible that the innovative economic growth in those countries may have more influence on rising income inequality than tax rates do, per se. And that inequality is worsened by the effects of urban housing constraints.

LET'S BE EXCEPTIONAL FOR THE RIGHT REASONS

A class of dynamic cities have set themselves up to be the productive centers of the new economy. The networks of creative human capital seem to create productivity through levels of residential density that are above the level postindustrial cities are politically willing or able to allow. It seems a mystery why these cutting-edge sectors are attracted to these housing-constrained cities, even as costs skyrocket above normal costs in other cities. Why don't cities with lower costs attract some of these economic activities with pro-growth, pro-density local governance?

The cultural and technological character of our age calls for a new urbanization. Certain countries have succeeded at cultivating innovation and abundance in cities that have become crucial to facilitating this flourishing and sharing it equitably. But at the same time, political tools that block new entrants from moving to these cities are preventing all the countries' citizens from reaping the rewards of innovation and cooperation.

Equitable abundance just might require a housing bust. But this would be a bust that resulted from breaking the urban housing cartels. They block access to our era's source of opportunity for millions of Americans and for millions of people throughout the developed world.

As economist Edward L. Glaeser recently quipped, "Educated people, apart from making productivity work, they are also really good at erecting barriers to building. Right? It's one of the things that educated people are fantastic at doing, is coming up with reasons why you can't build where they live."[14] Although the local politics are more complicated than that, it is odd that the cities with inflows of information-sector workers seem to universally have this problem.

Yet even the Open Access cities would have difficulty developing a core city as dense as Manhattan. The cities that manage to grow at rates much faster than the national average have done it, so far, by growing out, not up. I think this is essentially the problem. Cities like New York City have become creative centers because the cores of those cities developed before modern aesthetic sensibilities and local political control limited density. So density has become a sort of natural resource, like gold. We have a fairly fixed amount of "reserves" of high-density urban centers, which can only be expanded with great effort. Cities like Austin can take on some secondary roles, but the center of gravity of the major information sectors can't shift from those legacy cities because we aren't capable of building cities like that today. A new city in the West likely wouldn't even come close to the density of Manhattan before sclerosis set in.

Economist Paul Romer has promoted the idea of charter cities in developing economies, those that can import developed-world governance into developing economies.[15] Maybe this idea needs to be applied to developed economies. Maybe we need a charter city that imports urban density into a developed economy.

In the civil rights era, federal limits on local governments were used to enforce more-universal civil rights. In a similar way, state or federal limits on the ability of local governments to limit the mobility of households and firms through building codes might also be an important tool for addressing Closed Access problems.[16] This seems to be one factor that has helped Japan avoid rising home prices.[17] Recently, State Senator Scott Wiener has been active in pressing for these sorts of changes in California. Whatever the method, Closed Access is the problem that must be solved to escape the "bubble" economy.

CHAPTER 9
A Moral Panic and a Financial Crisis

The presumption that unsustainable flows of credit and money were the fundamental causes of the housing boom and bust during the decade after 2000 has led to a damaging misconception about the shape of the US economy. Housing, instead of being seen as a part of the solution, is seen as a bandage on stagnant employment—one that only leads to later busts. Actually, construction employment was not unsustainably propping up employment. It was part of the natural shift of employment to new sectors, a shift that should have been even stronger than it was, but for Closed Access obstructions.

Kerwin Kofi Charles, Erik Hurst, and Matthew J. Notowidigdo from the University of Chicago have researched recent employment trends. The abstract of their April 2017 paper is a good summary of what seems to be the growing consensus regarding labor markets during the boom-and-bust period.

> Using a local labor markets design, we estimate that manufacturing decline significantly reduced employment between 2000 and 2006, while local housing booms increased employment by roughly the same magnitude. The effects of manufacturing decline persist through 2012, but we find no persistent employment effects of local housing booms, likely because housing booms were associated with subsequent busts of similar magnitude. These results suggest that housing booms "masked" negative employment growth that would have otherwise occurred

> earlier in the absence of the booms. . . . Applying our local labor market estimates to the national labor market, we find that roughly 40 percent of the reduction in employment during the 2000s can be attributed to manufacturing decline and that these negative effects would have appeared in aggregate employment statistics earlier had it not been for the large, temporary increases in housing demand.[1]

As with so much research that has been completed since the housing boom, the presumption that the housing boom was an unsustainable bubble sneaks into the conclusion. As a consequence, the authors treat this potential source of economic support for less-educated men as only a temporary mask that couldn't have provided ongoing opportunity. This calamitous point of view appears to be the consensus today among academics, the press, and policymakers.

During the housing boom, new mortgages allowed borrowers to claim better units, such as by buying nicer units; moving out of crowded, shared, rental units; and so on. Since the Closed Access cities have a relatively fixed number of units, this led to an outflow of population from the Closed Access cities, so that housing had to expand more in the rest of the country. What looked like a national story—lost manufacturing jobs masked by construction that inevitably collapsed—didn't actually happen anywhere.

The first pull of aspirational workers into the Closed Access cities in the late 1990s had stuffed millions of new residents into a fairly stagnant housing stock (figure 9-1). At the national level, the number of new residents per new housing unit permit during the boom was no less than it had been at times in the 1970s and 1980s. The number of new residents per housing unit permit during the 1990s had been quite high by historical standards. But the number of new residents piling into new units in the Closed Access cities was even higher throughout the 1990s than it had been at the national level.

In the decade after 2000, the number of new residents per new housing unit permit plummeted in the Closed Access cities. But that wasn't the result of a surge of housing units. It was because Closed Access residents were moving away.

This made it look like there was a national housing bubble in the decade after 2000 that was unsustainable. The appearance of a housing bubble came from two factors. First, there was a tremendous amount of pent-up demand for housing units, stemming from low unit growth in the 1990s. Second, because this lack of unit growth was focused in the Closed Access cities, the rest of the country had to make up for it.

Figure 9-1. US Population Growth per Housing Permit

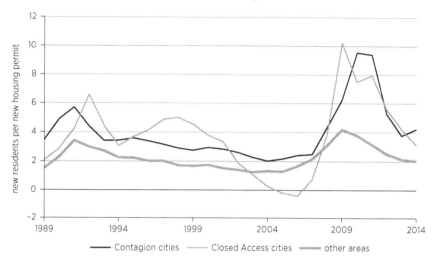

Sources: US Census Bureau, "Building Permits Survey," last modified May 1, 2018, http://www.census .gov/construction/bps/; Bureau of Economic Analysis, table CA1 (Personal Income, Population, Per Capita Personal Income) from Bureau of Economic Analysis, available at https://www.bea.gov/iTable /index_regional.cfm.

The expansion of mortgage credit was funding an expansion of housing consumption by young, highly skilled Closed Access workers. They had been packed into the Closed Access cities like sardines, and new credit options allowed them to spread their elbows a bit.[2] The problem is that the housing stock in those cities can only expand slowly. So, when mortgage access allowed these workers to expand their utilization of housing, it actually caused the populations of those cities to shrink.

This was not an unsustainable expansion. This was a correction toward more normal housing consumption after a decade of overcrowding into the existing housing stock. But since housing in Closed Access cities can't expand much, the new housing that was built to accommodate the more comfortable utilization of existing housing stock had to be built outside the Closed Access cities— much of it in the Inland Empire, Nevada, Arizona, Florida, and so on. Some households had to migrate in order to fill those new homes.

So it appeared as if there was an unsustainable national expansion of the housing stock, because—compared to recent experience—there was an increase in the number of units built relative to population growth. But unsustainable building was not happening anywhere.

Clearly, the housing boom wasn't "masking" employment losses in the Closed Access cities. First, a sustainable level of housing construction in those cities would have required much higher levels of construction employment than existed in the decade after 2000. Second, employment was not weak in those cities. They have the country's strongest local economies. They were depopulating in spite of their strengths.

In the rest of the country, houses were being built in large numbers because of the massive inflow of Closed Access refugees. Only in the cities where new housing couldn't keep up with the in-migration did prices spike.

So there were two types of cities that had high home prices and rising employment rates. Closed Access cities had high prices because they weren't building many homes, and employment rates were rising because workers were leaving. The employment rates in those cities were strong, in part, because the denominators were shrinking.

The cities whose economies were built around in-migration had rising construction employment because the migration created construction demand. Those cities were growing, so stagnation in manufacturing employment was not a problem. Those cities weren't having the transitional problems described by David H. Autor, David Dorn, and Gordon H. Hanson. They had plenty of jobs.

Some other cities, such as St. Louis and Detroit, had stagnant economies because of manufacturing declines. But those cities didn't have housing bubbles, either in price or in quantity. Those cities didn't experience sharply rising construction employment, because they had plenty of houses. The unemployed workers in those cities could have used *more* houses in the Closed Access cities, so that they could move to the cities that were rich with economic opportunities.

Figure 9-2 compares Los Angeles, Phoenix, St. Louis, and Detroit. St. Louis and Detroit did not have a construction bump during the 2003–2006 boom. In Phoenix, there was a bump in construction, but it is a fast-growing city. Figure 9-3 compares the growth rates of nonconstruction employment in each city. Phoenix didn't need a construction boom to maintain employment growth. It had a construction boom *because* it had strong employment growth. In Los Angeles, construction employment did rise somewhat, along with home prices—all the way up to the construction employment level of Detroit.

These relationships, observed at the national level, really do look like they describe a country that masked a manufacturing decline with an unsustainable housing bubble. But the cities in manufacturing slumps didn't have home price booms or construction employment booms. The Closed Access cities had home price booms, but they didn't have construction employment booms or problems of stagnating local economies. The Contagion cities had home price

Figure 9-2. Construction Employment in Selected Metro Areas

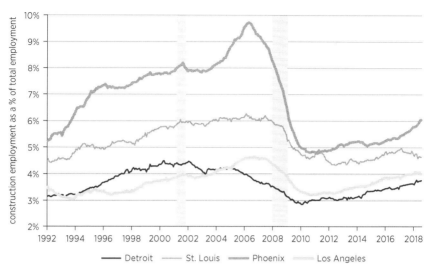

Note: This measure of total employment excludes farm employment. Shaded areas indicate US recessions.
Source: Bureau of Labor Statistics (BLS), "All Employees: Mining, Logging, and Construction in Detroit-Warren-Dearborn, MI (MSA)" (DETR826NRMN), and BLS, "All Employees: Total Nonfarm in Detroit-Warren-Dearborn, MI (MSA)" (DETR826NA), and BLS, "All Employees: Mining, Logging, and Construction in St. Louis, MO-IL (MSA)" (STLNRMN), and BLS, "All Employees: Total Nonfarm in St. Louis, MO-IL (MSA)" (STLNA), and Federal Reserve Bank of St. Louis, "All Employees: Construction in Phoenix-Mesa-Scottsdale, AZ (MSA)" (SMU04380602000000001SA), and BLS, "All Employees: Total Nonfarm in Phoenix-Mesa-Scottsdale, AZ (MSA)" (PHOE004NA), and Federal Reserve Bank of St. Louis, "All Employees: Construction in Los Angeles-Long Beach-Anaheim, CA (MSA)" (SMU06310802000000001SA), and Federal Reserve Bank of St. Louis, "All Employees: Total Nonfarm in Los Angeles-Long Beach-Anaheim, CA (MSA)" (SMS06310800000000001), retrieved from FRED, Federal Reserve Bank of St. Louis.

booms and construction employment booms, but those cities had already been growing. Their labor markets were strong enough to support population growth. The abstract evidence of a credit-fueled housing frenzy seems so clear on the national level. The description of the period as one boosted by unsustainable construction employment has been canonized. Yet this unsustainable housing frenzy didn't actually happen anywhere, locally.

THE SELF-FULFILLING PROPHECY

The University of Chicago IGM Forum regularly surveys leading American and European economists on important topics. In October 2017, the forum asked economists to rate "Factors Contributing to the 2008 Global Financial Crisis."[3] Here are the 12 options, in order of the importance they were given by the voters:

Figure 9-3. Growth Rate of Nonconstruction Employment in Selected Metro Areas

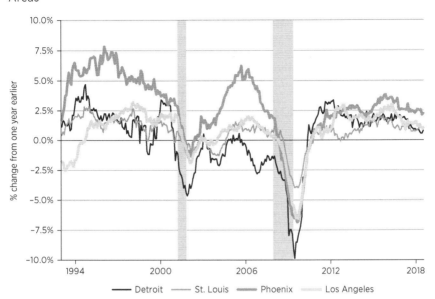

Note: This measure of nonconstruction employment excludes farm employment as well as construction employment. Shaded areas indicate US recessions.
Sources: Bureau of Labor Statistics (BLS), "All Employees: Mining, Logging, and Construction in Detroit–Warren–Dearborn, MI (MSA)" (DETR826NRMN), and BLS, "All Employees: Total Nonfarm in Detroit–Warren–Dearborn, MI (MSA)" (DETR826NA), and BLS, "All Employees: Mining, Logging, and Construction in St. Louis, MO–IL (MSA)" (STLNRMN), BLS, "All Employees: Total Nonfarm in St. Louis, MO–IL (MSA)" (STLNA), and Federal Reserve Bank of St. Louis, "All Employees: Construction in Phoenix–Mesa–Scottsdale, AZ (MSA)" (SMU04380602000000001SA), and BLS, "All Employees: Total Nonfarm in Phoenix–Mesa–Scottsdale, AZ (MSA)" (PHOE004NA), and Federal Reserve Bank of St. Louis, "All Employees: Construction in Los Angeles–Long Beach–Anaheim, CA (MSA)" (SMU06310802000000001SA), and Federal Reserve Bank of St. Louis, "All Employees: Construction in Los Angeles–Long Beach–Anaheim, CA (MSA)" (SMU06310802000000001SA), retrieved from FRED, Federal Reserve Bank of St. Louis.

1. Flawed financial sector regulation and supervision

2. Underestimated risks

3. Mortgages: Fraud and bad incentives

4. Funding runs

5. Rating agency failures

6. Housing price beliefs

7. Household debt levels

8. Too-big-to-fail beliefs

9. Government subsidies: Mortgages, homeowning

10. Savings and investment imbalances

11. Loose monetary policy

12. Fair-value accounting

This list is most interesting for what is *not* on it. Uncontroversially, the overwhelming reason for the global financial crisis was that residential real estate in the United States lost a quarter of its value suddenly over a two-year period. If that had been on the list, it should have ranked first. Hypothetically, if all you knew about an economy was that residential real estate had lost a quarter of its value over a two-year period, you really wouldn't need to know anything else to expect it to have had a financial crisis.

Tightening credit markets with a sharp decline in incomes and economic production also were uncontroversially part of the developments that led to the crisis. And, again, these factors were not listed as options for the survey recipients.

As for the factors that are on the list, the fourth most important factor on the survey—funding runs—is more of a description of the development of a financial crisis, and the twelfth most important factor could have worsened the crisis irrespective of the direct causes. The other ten factors all would be more accurately described as factors contributing to a bubble, with the assumption that a bust was inevitable. They are all descriptions of too much—too much money, too much credit, too much risk, too much optimism, and so on.

In the literal sense, no bank has ever failed because of too much money or too many potential borrowers. Banks fail because of the opposite situation—a lack of money, a contagion of pessimism, and a seizing-up of credit.[4] Clearly those conditions were in place by September 2008, when the collapse metastasized. They were already explicitly in place by the summer of 2007, when rating agencies downgraded mortgage bonds, in part because home prices were expected to sharply decline. Beginning in March 2007, the statements the Federal Reserve released after each meeting specifically mentioned an "ongoing" housing adjustment or correction.

So why didn't any of the respondents express dissatisfaction with the fact that the clear primary and secondary causes of the crisis were not on the list?[5] The list of factors itself *depends on the presumption of an inevitable bust*. No major economist seems to have a problem with that.

The debates about the bust have all centered on the supposed causes of the unsustainable bubble. No one has debated whether the bust was inevitable. This has been accepted as self-evident.

If there is a certain amount of public control over monetary and credit conditions, and the overwhelming consensus about a contracting housing market is that prices were too high, owners were too optimistic, lenders were unscrupulous, money was too loose, banks were too big, and debt was too high, then a crisis *was* inevitable. Its inevitability had been stipulated by those very economists and the public at large.

At the end of 2008, in the midst of the tightest credit markets, the most pessimistic sentiment, and the most enervated labor markets in decades (the factors that actually cause financial crises), the overwhelming public complaint against the Federal Reserve and the Treasury was that, even at that late date, they were daring to prevent the inevitable. Stability was derided as a "bailout."

Many have complained that the bailouts were given to Wall Street and not to families. But Wall Street bailouts typically came in the form of emergency lending. Who was demanding more lending to households at the time? The demands were centered on transfers and subsidies like forced principal reductions on outstanding mortgages. Households needed the same thing that Wall Street needed—some credit. And, because of the false premise that an oversupply of housing had been funded by unsustainable credit, denying households the very thing they needed was the most popular policy position of the entire episode. If there was anything the public was not going to accept, it was any policy that would have extended mortgage credit to marginal buyers or that would have led to a recovery in home prices.

NOT A BOOM BUT A BUST

The premise that the extreme rise in home prices and mortgage debt was related to excessive homebuilding and thus oversupply seemed so obvious that the entire public conversation has proceeded without ever confirming the premise. There is an awkwardness in the credit-bubble story, though, which was solved by invoking behavioral finance. Buyers and lenders were irrational, and a collapse was unavoidable. This story features a number of unrelated irrational actors—federal housing advocates, an overly loose Federal Reserve, predatory lenders, overly optimistic homebuyers, greedy speculators, devious investment bankers—who parade in turn as deus ex machina to explain why the numbers don't appear to add up. This is *theory by attribution error*. A model whose very specifications are that buyers and sellers are unmoored from objective reality is difficult to falsify. So, as home prices rose higher and higher in 2004 and 2005, even as the Fed raised the fed funds rate, the model was adjusted to account for buyers and lenders who must have been even more irrational than previously thought.

The problem is that, if a behavioral model influences policy, then collapse is imminent whether the model is right or wrong—if not because of agent irrationality, then because of model error. Those who "called" the bubble have regarded the collapse as confirmation that there was a string of irrational players. Today, many are warning of new bubbles.[6]

What if model error in public policy was the primary cause of the collapse? What if the collapse was inevitable because its inevitability had been stipulated? What sort of economic asceticism are we imposing on ourselves if rising valuations are *incorrectly* treated as irrationality and falling valuations are treated as a return to normalcy? What level of certainty should we require in our models of the economy before we impose policies predicated on the need for a contraction?

Closed Access home prices continue to climb relentlessly, compared to home prices in other cities. Rents—the proper measure of housing affordability—are now rising nearly everywhere. Other major countries with urban housing supply challenges avoided the depths of the recession, and their home prices continue to rise more sharply than US home prices have. Collapse wasn't inevitable or helpful. On August 7, 2007, when home prices nationally were still within a few percentage points of their mid-2006 high, the press release from the Federal Reserve's Federal Open Market Committee (FOMC) announced that the fed funds rate would remain at 5.25% and said, "The housing correction is ongoing."[7] Who could disagree? For the next 19 months, home prices nationally would fall at an average of *1% per month*. And, in the previous 19 months leading up to that, housing *starts* had already fallen by 40%.

That model of the housing market seemed to be confirmed. Those falling prices seemed like a correction. Note the root of that word—"correct."

The following text is from the transcription of an October 2015 interview of Ben Bernanke on the *Diane Rehm Show*:

> REHM. It's remarkable that you said that the recent financial crisis was the worst in human history, even worse than the Great Depression. But that's where I think an awful lot of people wonder, if it was so big, why didn't you see it coming and why couldn't you have done something to stop it before it happened?
>
> BERNANKE. Well, again, we were aware of the fact that house prices were very high. And we thought it quite possible that they would correct at some point. By 2006, 2007, we also were aware of the problems in the subprime

> lending market. What we did not anticipate and no one
> anticipated was the vulnerability of the financial system
> overall to a run, a panic.[8]

There is that word again: "correct." Bernanke's use of that word here is simply a reflection of the consensus that was clear in the IGM Forum survey cited earlier. A drop in home prices, whether it would turn out to be 5%, 20%, or 40%, had been accepted, a priori, as correct. Disastrously tight monetary policy and epochal shifts in lending standards surely were major factors in the scale of the final collapse. But, in this frame of mind, they were simply adjustments made to help with the "correction."

This presumption runs throughout the literature on the crisis. Prices at the peak are treated as anomalous, and prices at the subsequent bottom are treated as the "correction." Deep drops in prices are taken as proof of the irrationality of the peak. In truth, the "correct" price is somewhere between the peak and the nadir. The contents of this book suggest that, in fact, the "correct" price for houses probably is closer to the peak than to the nadir.

The existing literature rarely, if ever, even acknowledges that gray area. The world is treated as binary: a place where high prices were wrong and the collapse, wherever it happened to settle, was the "correction."

It is true that there were mortgage products that were especially prone to systematic destabilization, including questionable mortgages by investors with little equity as a buffer. But the mortgage cohorts from 2006 and 2007, which had, by far, the worst default performance, were originated in a market that already had sharply collapsing buyer activity and building rates.[9]

A reasonable response to this is, as Warren Buffett would say, "Only when the tide goes out do you discover who's been swimming naked." That is certainly plausible. Extreme prices together with the existence of a large number of non-conventional mortgages at the time seems damning. But this is still a case of begging the question.

The idea that companies that engaged in acts of desperation in 2006 and 2007 were responsible for the crisis is a product of this presumption that the crisis was inevitable. The premise, not the facts, is guiding public policy. If home prices fall sharply, for any reason, lenders will face difficulties in proportion to the risks they were taking. And many principals, in the face of collapse, will be tempted to push ethical limits to escape bad deals. That fact tells us little about what was causing the collapsing prices. The idea that those lenders were responsible for the crisis is entirely a result of the presumption that the collapse was "correct." And the effect that that presumption had, in real time, on the willingness to allow or applaud the collapse and crisis was significant.

MORAL PANIC

A lack of adequate housing supply caused home prices to rise, and this was mistaken as a surplus of demand—too much credit and too much money. This led national policy down a tragic path. A scarcity of credit and money was demanded to remedy a phantom demand problem. Since the real problem was a lack of supply, each time this process of deprivation ratcheted up, the dislocation and economic stress increased. This in turn increased the anger and resolve about implementing the disastrous prescriptions while failures and financial losses mounted. Sure, many innocent homeowners and workers were drawn into the crisis. But what were policymakers supposed to do? Support stable prices and financial markets? That's just what the speculators and predatory lenders would want. Bail *them* out? The ones that *did this to us*?

The answer to the question of whether public policy could have provided more stability is not particularly in dispute. The answer to the question of whether public policy *should* have provided more stability depends on the premise—on the determination of what is "correct." A brief summary of the timeline of the crisis follows.

March 2006

Ben Bernanke and the FOMC had been raising the target interest rate since mid-2004, and it had nearly reached the 5.25% level, where it would remain until September 2007. Home prices had peaked. Housing starts had begun to fall precipitously. Bernanke remembers the March meeting—his first as chairman:

> My colleagues and I were upbeat. We saw the cooldown in housing as mostly good news. A decline in construction and the flattening of house prices would let some air out of any potential bubble and help slow overall economic growth to a more sustainable level, reducing the risk that inflation might become a problem.[10]

In the year previous, almost a quarter of a million households, on net, had moved away from the most expensive and most economically rewarding cities, for lack of housing.

Late 2005 to Early 2007

The private securitization boom, consisting of subprime and Alt-A mortgages, lasted from about the beginning of 2004 to early 2007. From 1995 to 2004, an average of 2% of households each year were first-time homebuyers. By 2005, the rate had fallen to about 1.7%, and it continued to fall after 2005.[11]

Investment banks collected capital from investors and used it to make subprime and Alt-A mortgages. As borrowers paid back those mortgages, the investors' claims on those payments were divided up into "tranches" by various risk characteristics. Some investors took on more risk as holders of the equity tranches, or the low-rated tranches that paid higher yields, which were mortgage-backed securities (MBSs) with lower ratings, such as a "B" rating. Other investors took on less risk by, for example, being the first priority in the payback schedule, and earned lower yields. Theirs were the AAA-rated MBSs.

Another type of financial security called collateralized debt obligations (CDOs) had been around in several asset classes for many years. Beginning in late 2005 and continuing until the collapse in 2007, a large number of MBSs were used to fund these CDOs, and CDOs became much more numerous. A CDO was much like an MBS, but instead of investing in mortgages, CDOs invested in the lower-rated securities of the MBS pools. By doing this, they could repackage those securities and divide up the payouts again into several tranches of new securities. As with the basic MBSs, different CDO tranches allowed investors to take on different amounts of risk. Some investors accepted more of the risk in exchange for higher yields on their investments, and other investors were promised a priority position in exchange for accepting a lower yield. In this way, a group of B-rated MBSs could be pooled and resold to CDO investors, and many of the CDO investors could buy AAA-rated tranches because other investors in the CDO pool agreed to accept the risk of nonpayment. There was tremendous demand at the time for safe securities. It was the AAA-rated securities that investors really wanted, and the demand for those drove the CDO market.

It turned out that the one factor those CDOs were highly susceptible to was a nationwide housing collapse that would lead to high defaults across time and geography. Eventually, even the highly rated tranches of those CDOs lost most of their value.

It is important to distinguish between the basic MBSs, where all privately securitized mortgages were placed, and the later, smaller CDO market. The AAA securities from the basic MBSs were susceptible to excessively weak underwriting, and the lower-rated MBSs were meant to protect them from some range of defaults. Most of the AAA-rated securities from the basic

MBSs were downgraded during the panic, but in the end, only about 10% of them had impairments. Even considering the depth of the crisis, the lower-rated tranches basically did their job.[12] All of these securities were subject to a panic in 2007, but it was the CDOs that took large, permanent losses even for the "AAA" tranches. In 2018, there are many basic AAA-rated MBSs that were issued before 2008 and are still providing income to investors.

The question is, what led to the rise of CDOs? They were created because there was a tremendous amount of capital in search of *low-risk* investments, and there weren't enough willing or able mortgage borrowers to feed the frenzy of investors, so the existing low-rated MBSs were packaged up to create new pools that could issue new AAA-rated securities. The CDOs were used to create low-risk securities for investors because, without new mortgages, the MBSs couldn't meet the demand.

As the story goes, mortgages were being handed out to anyone with a pulse, and by 2007, in spite of lowering standards, the mortgage originators had run out of suckers. This would make perfect sense if the private securitization boom was actually built on the backs of borrowers who had little means to make their mortgage payments.

But what if that story is wrong? What if the income of the typical homeowner had never declined, even when homeownership was rising? What if CDOs and most of the basic MBSs rose up amid a massive *outflow* of equity from the housing market?

In 2004, Karl Case and Robert Shiller, who are widely credited with calling the bubble and bust, had written,

> Judging from the historical record, a nationwide drop in real housing prices is unlikely, and the drops in different cities are not likely to be synchronous: some will probably not occur for a number of years. Such a lack of synchrony would blunt the impact on the aggregate economy of the bursting of housing bubbles.[13]

If the bust they described had happened, the CDOs, which were vulnerable to nationwide generalized collapse, would have performed relatively well. When the collapse did spread across the nation, the reaction to these developments, *because the underlying premise was wrong*, was to insist on tightening access to mortgage credit, tightening monetary policy to reduce borrowing and investing, and accepting unprecedented declines in housing prices in order to impose discipline on the market. Yet the markets had shifted to a bias of fear and protection long before. That wasn't widely appreciated because the CDO market was treated as if it was a product of *risk-taking*—as if rabid demand for AAA-rated securities while short-term interest rates were hiked up and investment was collapsing was a sign of recklessness.

Descriptions of the CDO market are usually couched in language about leverage. But the global capital flows that were fueling this demand weren't leveraged. Nor were the expanding domestic money market funds that were seeking safe assets. Investors were seeking secure cash flows.

By the second half of 2006, mortgage growth was slowing. This is the period normally associated with declining lending standards. How can that be? If standards had become so lax, why were they attracting a declining number of borrowers? It is because this was the beginning of the crisis. Fear had already taken hold, and qualified borrowers were exiting home equity. It was the sharp decline in qualified borrowers that made the new pool of borrowers look worse, not an increase in less-qualified borrowers. And, because homeowners were cashing out and exiting the market well before the collapse of the CDO market, many of the homebuyers in 2006 and 2007 were investors rather than homeowners. Many of the early defaults were from investors, who are more likely to default tactically when prices fall than homeowners are. The reason so many of the recent buyers were investors is that homeowners had been selling their homes and either moving to less expensive cities or cashing out of homeownership altogether and sticking that cash into things like AAA-rated securities.[14]

August 2007

Housing starts continued to collapse, along with residential investment and homeownership. Some local prices had begun to fall, but nationally, home prices had been generally flat since early 2006. A panic was brewing in mortgage CDOs. The Federal Reserve held the target fed funds rate at 5.25%, citing inflation fears and noting again that "the housing correction is ongoing."[15] During this period, US home prices diverged from the trends of a dozen other countries and began to move sharply lower.

Before the August Fed meeting, the *Wall Street Journal* had this to say:

> Naturally the wounded are clamoring for the Federal Reserve to ride to the rescue with easier money when it meets tomorrow, even though the Fed helped create this mess.
>
> Credit panics are never pretty, but their virtue is that they restore some fear and humility to the marketplace.[16]

After the meeting, the panic in CDO markets heated up. This panic was based mainly on expectations. AAA-rated securities, even in the CDOs that would eventually be impaired, were still receiving their cash payments.[17] But expectations of *future* declines in home prices unprecedented in post-Depression markets, and defaults that were expected to be triggered by those declining prices, caused markets for those securities to freeze up. President George W. Bush responded, "It's not the government's job to bail out speculators or those who made the decision to buy a home they knew they could never afford."[18]

Rates of default on securitized mortgages made in 2006 and 2007 were high because prices on many of those homes were already in decline, but it was the persistence of those high default rates over several years that eventually caused impairments that reached into the AAA tranches. When the crisis is reviewed without the premise that collapse was inevitable or warranted, it is staggering how often, as with the president and the *Wall Street Journal* above, the explicit choice of collapse over stability was made—quite universally. There is little question that mortgage defaults that happened in 2008 and after—which are the vast bulk of defaults—could have been minimized with a concerted effort at stabilization and monetary stimulus. This is not to say that it is the job of the Federal Reserve to prevent every asset class from experiencing the occasional "correction."[19] But those defaults happened very late. They were the *result* of the recession and the clampdown on lending, not the cause of it.[20]

September 2007

The Fed had been trying to patch up the panic that had ensued, but even at the September meeting, the support for further instability was strong:

> As in August, we again discussed the issue of moral
> hazard—the notion, in this context, that we should refrain
> from helping the economy with lower interest rates
> because that would simultaneously let investors who had
> misjudged risk off the hook. Richard Fisher warned that
> too large a rate cut would be giving in to a "siren call" to
> "indulge rather than discipline risky financial behavior."[21]

Bernanke and other FOMC leaders managed to convince the committee to lower interest rates, though in the FOMC press statement they continued to refer to the housing bust (which by now meant average home prices dropping sharply in most cities) as a "correction."[22]

What if the market didn't need discipline? What if the market needed a couple of million homes in productive urban centers?

October 2007 to August 2008

From September 2007 to May 2008, the fed funds target rate was lowered quickly to 2%, where it remained until October 2008. To be fair to the FOMC, measured inflation was not declining during this time, and one of the committee's primary functions is to maintain consumer price levels. However, even though these rate drops are generally attributed to Fed easing, this was arguably not the case. The way that monetary policy is normally thought of, the Federal Reserve injects cash into the economy by purchasing Treasury bills with newly created cash. But during this time, interest rates were falling because of the panic, not because of Fed cash injections.

During this period, the Fed frequently made emergency loans to panic-suffering banks, but when it made those loans, it would purposefully *sell* an equal number of Treasuries into the market in order to suck cash back *out of the economy*. The Fed was selling Treasuries during this period, not buying them.[23]

Figure 9-4. Monetary Base and Federal Reserve Treasury Holdings

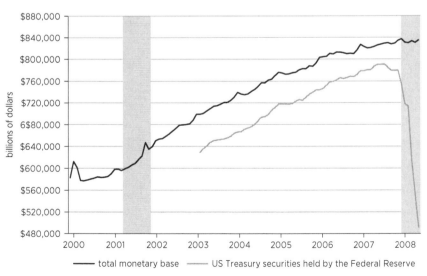

Note: Shaded areas indicate US recessions.
Sources: Board of Governors of the Federal Reserve System, "Monetary Base; Total" (BOGMBASE), and Board of Governors of the Federal Reserve System, "U.S. Treasury Securities Held by the Federal Reserve: All Maturities" (TREAST), retrieved from FRED, Federal Reserve Bank of St. Louis.

Beginning in 2007, the Fed was making emergency loans in some panicked markets, but, as figure 9-4 shows, at the same time it was selling hundreds of billions of dollars' worth of Treasuries in order to suck up cash and arrest the growth of the monetary base. During this period, several credit markets with little connection to subprime mortgages also were seizing up.

September to December 2008

By September 2008, home price declines nationally were approaching 20% from their previous highs. The federal government took control of Fannie Mae and Freddie Mac, the private-public mortgage giants, in September. In both cases, the takeovers came when regulators determined that future credit losses and foreclosures that hadn't even been experienced or accounted for yet would be so severe that the government-sponsored enterprises would not have taxable income for the foreseeable future.

Vexingly, less than two weeks later, the day after Lehman Brothers failed, the FOMC had a regularly scheduled meeting in which it agreed to hold the fed funds target rate at 2%, based on inflation fears. Chaos broke out. Over the next week, the Fed and the Treasury pushed the Troubled Asset Relief Program (TARP), a number of emergency measures, and many actions commonly referred to as bailouts. Amid all the extraordinary actions taken that week, the fed funds rate—the *ordinary* monetary tool—sat at 2%. It would take three months for the Fed to pull it down to nearly zero, and during those three months, while the fed funds rate certainly was set above the neutral rate that would have prevented a deflationary collapse, the Fed implemented interest on reserves. In other words, it offered to pay banks to send cash back to the Fed's vaults instead of lending cash out into the economy.

In effect, the Fed didn't have the means to pull liquidity out of the economy in the form of cash anymore,[24] because it was running out of Treasuries that could be exchanged in liquid markets for cash, so it pulled liquidity out of the economy by paying banks not to provide liquidity.[25] The Fed's balance sheet did begin to bloat at this time, but it is important to remember that this was before quantitative easing (QE).[26] This wasn't because the Fed was trying to inject cash into the economy. This was because the Fed was trying to make emergency loans to banks *without* injecting cash into the economy. It was loaning them cash, but then at the same time it was offering to pay interest to them if they would simply return that cash back to the Fed.

While all of this was happening, the Fed was mostly being castigated for "bailing out" Wall Street. Yet the *Wall Street Journal* did have praise for its decision to keep interest rates at 2% the day after Lehman failed. The *Wall Street Journal* editors still saw value in panics.

> These columns have been tough on the Federal Reserve in recent years, so it's only fair to praise the central bank when it does the right thing. And that's what it did yesterday by holding the federal funds rate stable at 2%, despite the turmoil in financial markets and enormous Wall Street pressure to reduce rates further.[27]

The private securitization market was gone. Banks were lame ducks. The powers that be had just engineered the worst financial crisis in generations. And, amid all of this, the new federal conservators decided that lending standards at Fannie and Freddie needed to be tightened extraordinarily. During this time, the average FICO score of an approved mortgage moved up 40 to 50 points.[28] That is a huge shift. There isn't much evidence of a shift in the other direction during the boom. At most, the average score shifted by a few points. This was a colossal change in the standard used to determine who can get a mortgage.

Only after all these steps had been taken did the worst period of home price declines, the sharpest climb in delinquencies, and the losses that eventually led to the impairment of AAA-rated mortgage securities occur. Hundreds of articles were written about subprime borrowers in 2007 who were unable to make their payments because of poor loan terms. In the scheme of things, those defaults are barely a bump on the road to the crisis. It took years of public policy specifically geared toward cutting down residential investment, standing aside as panics developed and credit markets seized up, and sucking cash and credit out of the economy to create the defaults that impaired those securities.

2009 and After

With the implementation of QE1,[29] the Fed did something that it hadn't done since the summer of 2007. It created some currency and bought some treasuries. Still, though, most of that currency was "loaned" back to the Fed as reserves. But it did finally provide some needed liquidity.

Treasury secretaries Henry Paulson and Timothy Geithner both claim that the conservatorship of Fannie and Freddie was crucial in creating stability during this period. They are right, in a way. In neighborhoods where household financial qualifications met the new standards, the housing market did sta-

Figure 9-5. Delinquencies over Time

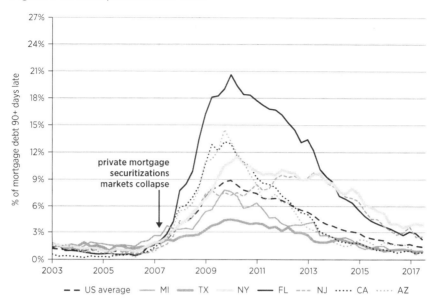

Source: Federal Reserve Bank of New York, Center for Microeconomic Data, "Household Debt and Credit Report," https://www.newyorkfed.org/microeconomics/hhdc.

bilize. But for the bottom tier of the housing market, which was cut out of the new credit regime, this was actually the most *destabilizing* period. Demand for homes for owner-occupiers in those neighborhoods was wiped out. It was nearly impossible for them to get mortgages. Whether 2006–2008 had ever happened or not, for these neighborhoods, 2009–2010 by itself was a generation-defining collapse in home values and household net worth.

Recall that in most cities, there had been no unusual rise in home prices in lower-tier markets. In every major metro area, price collapses in lower-tier markets in 2009 and 2010 moved the prices in these markets much lower, relative to the prices in higher-tier markets.

Figures 9-5, 9-6, and 9-7 tell the tale in pictures. Figure 9-6 shows the rate of mortgage delinquencies over time, with the mountain of delinquencies coming in 2009–2012.

The bulk of delinquencies and foreclosures happened years after homeownership rates had peaked, the rate of first-time homeowners had begun to decline, and housing starts had collapsed. They happened after prices had collapsed. And, as figure 9-6 shows, they happened after credit standards had been tightened sharply.

Figure 9-6. US Mortgage Originations by Credit Score

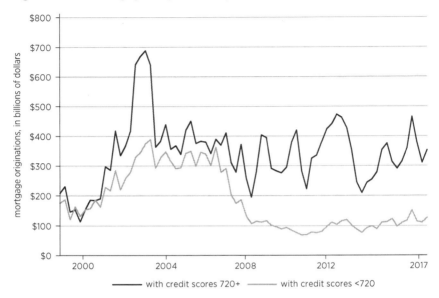

Source: Federal Reserve Bank of New York, Center for Microeconomic Data, "Household Debt and Credit Report," https://www.newyorkfed.org/microeconomics/hhdc.

The average American consumer credit score tends to be a bit under 700.[30] For decades, two-thirds of American households had been homeowners. The proportion of lending to borrowers with low credit scores was not unusual during the boom, as shown in figure 9-6. About half of mortgage originations were to borrowers with FICO scores below 720. But, between the second quarter of 2007 and the end of 2008, mortgage credit to all but the financially strongest households was drastically cut. This created a vicious cycle, where homebuying demand dried up in areas that depend on functioning credit markets, which drove prices down, which destroyed home equity for existing owners, wiping out their financial safety net, and so forth. The bulk of foreclosures happened well after this extreme shift in lending standards was imposed.

Figure 9-7 shows the rise and fall of home prices, in the least expensive and the most expensive quintiles of zip codes, in Atlanta and Seattle. Seattle is among the more expensive cities outside the Closed Access cities, and Atlanta is relatively inexpensive. But Atlanta and Seattle were similar to most cities in that prices increased relatively evenly across each metro area during the boom. Low-tier and high-tier prices within each metro area increased by similar amounts.

Figure 9-7. Price Changes over Time, Seattle vs. Atlanta

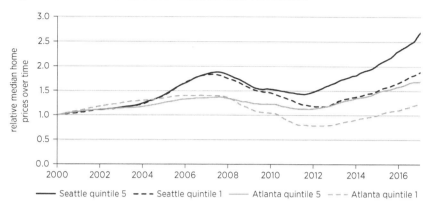

Note: All prices are indexed to 1 at January 2000. Zip code quintiles are arranged by median home price.
Source: Zillow data, http://www.zillow.com/research/data/.

In the year leading up to the collapse of the private securitization market, prices were relatively level in Atlanta and were rising moderately throughout Seattle. Then, in the year after the collapse of the private securitization market, prices fell in both cities by about 5% to 10%, at both the high and low ends of the housing market. That, in and of itself, was a sharp price shock, something a city would not generally face very often. If there had been a reason for a price shock in either of these cities, the drop-off they had already experienced should have gone a long way toward taking care of it. But, unfortunately, for both of these cities, and for most other cities around the country, the worst was yet to come.

In September 2008, the federal government took over Fannie Mae and Freddie Mac, and even though the demise of the private securitization market had removed significant lending potential from the housing market, federal regulators pushed Fannie and Freddie to curtail lending even more. In the following year, ending August 2009, home prices in each city fell by 10% to 15%. In Seattle, low-tier homes were still holding on, but in Atlanta, by 2009, the low end of the market was starting to decline more than the high end.

Prices leveled off somewhat between the summer of 2009 and the summer of 2010, and they were probably boosted by a first-time homebuyer tax credit that expired in the summer of 2010.[31]

Then, in July 2010, Dodd-Frank was passed. In the year from August 2010 to August 2011, prices notched down again, in both cities. For the least-expensive zip codes, after having made it through three heart-wrenching years of losses, the year after the passage of Dodd-Frank was the single worst year for both Seattle and Atlanta. The next year after that, prices finally began to stabilize, but still, low-tier homes were lagging high-tier homes. The effect of this has been so strong that homes in the lowest-price quintile in Seattle have roughly matched the price changes of homes in the highest-price quintile in Atlanta.

The housing bust was not caused by too much money, too many mortgages, or too many homes. It was caused by not enough. *We had the premise wrong,* and unfortunately, we had the ability to impose the consequences of that premise on ourselves.

Epilogue

The financial crisis was simply a tragic, extreme side effect of the more general problem of Closed Access. Because of this problem, there is a growing sense that the spoils of growth are only shared by a select few. The politically imposed limit on how many people can share in prosperity undermines the communal support for growth.

The extreme valuation of Closed Access housing is a measure of how crippling this exclusion is. Since these high prices have been blamed on credit and money, the true source of our discontent has been misunderstood.

INSISTING ON STAGNATION

Home values are high because of fundamentals (high and rising rents), yet they have been universally treated as if they are a product of irrational exuberance, predatory lending, and a too-generous Federal Reserve. A context of deprivation that imposes high costs means that Americans need support and growth. But instead, we have collectively acted as if we needed to be punished and disciplined, and the arguments about the correct policy approach have mostly centered on *who* should be disciplined. What perversity!

The moral panic that led to the financial crisis was the most acute form of this perversity, but this sense of communal flagellation has been guiding us since the turn of the century.

Here is an example of this common approach:

> San Francisco Fed President John Williams said in a speech
> on Sept. 28 [2015] that he sees "signs of imbalances" emerg-
> ing in asset prices—especially real estate. After saying that
> conditions haven't yet reached a tipping point, he recalled
> that in the mid-2000s it was too late to "avoid bad out-
> comes" by raising interest rates once the housing boom was
> in full swing.
>
> Williams told reporters on Oct. 1 [2015] that his hous-
> ing market warning is "not about fighting bubbles, or try-
> ing to deal with financial stability"—it's more a response
> to why interest rates need to rise even though inflation
> remains low. "The reason you don't just let an economy
> rip—let it grow, and grow, and grow, and just see what hap-
> pens, is because that usually ends badly," he said. . . .
>
> From his seat at the San Francisco Fed, Williams has a
> bird's-eye view of one of the hottest housing markets in the
> country, which may inform his assessment. . . .
>
> . . . The Fed has learned a "sobering message" that it's
> hard to contain an existing crisis after the housing crash,
> said Stephen Oliner, a scholar at the American Enterprise
> Institute and former Fed Board research director. That's
> given them a new focus on preemptive policy, even if it
> only helps at the margin, he said. "They can nudge things,
> and I think that's really about all," Oliner said, adding that
> policy makers are "acutely worried" about fueling asset
> bubbles with easy policy. "It's going to be something you
> hear about from more Fed officials."[1]

If supply is the core problem, this widely shared idea that our mistake was to
not reduce demand early enough is downright frightening.[2] What Americans
need is to *let it rip*. Toward the end of 2005, we were beginning to solve the
rent problem. Rent inflation briefly dropped to about 2%, along with general
inflation. The reason that development was disruptive was that there is such a
bottleneck for supply in the Closed Access cities that it led to a migration event
in the Contagion cities. If the Fed had aimed for stronger growth instead of for
declining residential investment, rents would have continued to fall. We are
now afraid of growth.

Here is another example of the common thinking. In a newsletter published by Bloomberg in November 2015, under the tagline "Bubble Watch," the introduction opened with the following observations:

> Earlier this month, the Boston Fed's Eric Rosengren wondered aloud in a speech to the Portsmouth, Rhode Island, chamber of commerce whether the swelling number of cranes dotting Boston's skyline should be a source of worry. In September, San Francisco's Fed President John Williams voiced similar concerns about U.S. "imbalances" in the form of high asset prices, "especially in real estate."
>
> Some Fed members might be hesitant to drop the "B word"—bubble—but other market observers are being a bit more blunt.[3]

Rosengren's speech was made just before the Federal Reserve raised interest rates after a lengthy period of historically low rates. This was in late 2015, but it might well have been in early 2004. In either case, Boston would have been similarly dotted with cranes. At either time, both Boston and San Francisco would have been permitting new housing units at an annual rate of about 1 per 300 residents (figure E-1). Compare this to the US as a whole, which from 1960 to 2007 issued permits within a range of 1 unit per 100–300 residents, only briefly falling to 1 per 300 at the nadir of a few recessions.[4]

What had Rosengren worried was construction. What state of events could have led to such widespread concern about "bubbles" amid such highly depressed construction activity? At these permitting rates, 15,000 to 20,000 residents have had to move away from Boston and San Francisco in a typical year, for lack of housing.

In 2004, at least parts of the country were building enough homes to accommodate the households that needed them. But in 2015, housing permits at the national level were at nearly the same level that produces out-migration from Boston and San Francisco.

Nobody would explicitly call for this policy. Nobody argues that we need to deprive working-class families of housing in order to maintain price stability. The argument should run in the other direction. "Too much" housing would cause prices to fall back toward the *actual market price that would reflect unencumbered costs of building.* This return to functionality would be destabilizing in an asset market that has developed based on exclusion. By framing exclusion as normal and the building that would defeat that

Figure E-1. Permits Relative to Population

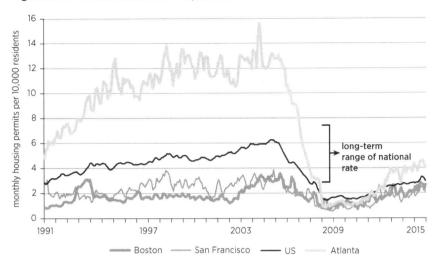

Note: Data for number of housing permits are monthly.
Sources: US Census Bureau, "Building Permits Survey," three-month moving average, http://www
.census.gov/construction/bps/; Bureau of Economic Analysis, table CA1 Population, https://www.bea
.gov/iTable/index_regional.cfm.

exclusion as abnormal, exclusion can be enforced without ever coming to terms with it.

So new building can proceed without caution in Open Access cities because prices are near replacement cost, and new supply will not be disruptive. Ironically, it is only where housing has been severely *under*supplied that locals fear disruption from perceived *over*supply. That is because undersupply has lifted rents and prices so far above replacement cost that new supply *will* be disruptive. In Open Access cities, rent inflation tends to follow general inflation levels; sometimes it is slightly higher, and sometimes it is slightly lower. But the perverse effect of extreme undersupply on local economic stability in Closed Access cities means that rent inflation in those cities runs high, but rarely runs low—because as soon as it does, locals look for ways to cool down the market to prevent disruption, and the undersupply problem only worsens. True oversupply would mean that prices have declined to somewhere below replacement cost, and in Closed Access cities this would require decades of active construction far above levels residents currently will allow.

The key here is simple. The bubble that needs to be popped is the one in Closed Access *market rents*. That is fundamentally what is out of order. The only sustainable solution to that problem is politically difficult, but conceptually simple—more supply. Tightening the money supply and credit conditions does nothing to solve this problem, and it creates many other problems.

If new supply can ever come online in amounts high enough to actually lower rent levels to a true reflection of the cost of shelter, that will indeed be disruptive to the Closed Access economies. Trillions of dollars of real estate equity will be lost. Yet clearly the idea that a crisis is necessary in order to correct markets can be quite popular. We just need to support the crisis that actually solves the problem.

THE CHARACTER OF AN OPEN SOCIETY

Douglass C. North, John Joseph Wallis, and Barry R. Weingast's "limited access orders" and "open access orders" categorization offers a conceptual framework for thinking about the current challenges regarding urban housing.[5] (I have borrowed their terminology in my categorization of cities, using "Closed Access" to describe cities where housing supply is so constrained that it creates economic rents for owners and high wage earners within the city.) They describe the evolution of civil societies from limited access orders, where elites negotiate access to ownership and legal protections in an ongoing balance of power between individuals and shifting alliances. Modern, affluent, liberal societies have made the difficult transition from these limited access orders to an open access order, which, in addition to a perpetually lived state (and other institutions that aren't defined by their current leaders) and consolidated political control over violence, has the following characteristics:[6]

- a widely held set of beliefs about the inclusion of and equality for all citizens;

- entry into economic, political, religious, and educational activities without restraint;

- support for organizational forms in each activity that are open to all (for example, contract enforcement);

- rule of law enforced impartially for all citizens; and

- impersonal exchange.

We have reached an odd disequilibrium in the development of the modern city—especially, it appears, in countries that are heirs of British cultural and political heritage. Dense urban economic centers have become valuable for highly skilled information-age workers. This should be cause for celebration.

These cities have existed for centuries, and they were built for the kind of density that now provides value.

The evolution of capitalism has led to almost universal acceptance of middle-class values. Whereas the elite of most societies have sought control and leisure, these few modern open access societies have a citizenry that seeks to be productive, to cooperate, and to innovate. It is common to hear complaints that wealthy children today have an unfair advantage because they can access the best schools, get the best education, and therefore perpetuate inequality by working in the most lucrative careers. But everyone should appreciate how revolutionary this is. Elites of the past would scoff at the notion that this even describes elites. Elites don't need to be productive. Elites have access and control.

Those associated with wealth and income today are people in places like Manhattan and San Francisco, working through these dense, productive core networks of human capital. People developing apps, social networks, and smartphones, and making the financial arrangements for a global economic uprising that is pulling billions out of poverty and providing technological wonders our grandparents only dreamed of. This flourishing of human interaction is facilitated by urban density.

Yet, at the same time, the development of political influences and processes within these cities has set up roadblocks in the way of building the residential density that is the core source of transformative value in our time. Instead of a world that continued to benefit from the equalizing influence of wealth and technology in a productive open access order, the economy is returning to the context of the 19th century—a context North, Wallis, and Weingast might identify as a limited access order.

Hernando de Soto has famously documented the sorts of obstructions that stand in the way of economic opportunity in undeveloped economies, where ownership for the average citizen is difficult to establish and governance is not transparent or impartially applied. In Peru, it took de Soto's team 289 days to register a business. A private bus service required 26 months to complete the registration process. The story is similar in many undeveloped economies. De Soto's team found that it could take years to establish legality for housing or business ventures, and typically required dozens or hundreds of steps. As a result, much of the economic activity in such countries is informal.[7]

In a way, advanced countries have created a more virulent form of limited access. Because of the rule of law and the capabilities of enforcement, their limited access orders can be enforced. In Closed Access cities, the mitigating relief of informal markets is severely limited by the well-organized state.[8]

As Edward L. Glaeser, Joseph Gyourko, and Raven E. Saks state in the abstract for a study of this problem, governance in some cities has evolved:

> [Changes include] changing judicial tastes, decreasing ability to bribe regulators, rising incomes and greater tastes for amenities, and improvements in the ability of home-owners to organize and influence local decisions. Our preliminary evidence suggests that there was a significant increase in the ability of local residents to block new projects and a change of cities from urban growth machines to homeowners' cooperatives.[9]

Granted, there are stresses from dense urban living that naturally mitigate its ample benefits. But there are always tradeoffs. It is possible for a polity to be too effective at managing its discomforts. A common example is the use of walls to keep people in or out. The Closed Access cities have built some of the most effective walls in the world, even if they are only figurative walls. But these problems aren't eternal. These cities have evolved to this state, and they can evolve to a new equilibrium.

For Closed Access housing developers in the most constrained areas, the 289 days it takes to register a business in Peru would seem like a miracle pace. Planning Commission review and objections from interest groups routinely hold up projects for years.

NO SHADOWS IN MY PARK

Here are excerpts from a single article published in the *San Francisco Chronicle* in April 2016 about a proposed pair of skyscrapers with two million square feet of commercial and residential space, to be called Oceanwide Center.[10] Note how thoroughly this project is characterized by its limited access order context. Every paragraph is an exercise in the forms of rent extraction and posturing that citizens of limited access orders are forced to engage in. (Emphasis mine—I have underlined examples of limited access postures and boldfaced examples of the imposition of **fees and taxes**.)

> The project, which heads to the Planning Commission on Thursday for approval, would generate **$117 million in one-time impact fees**, which would probably be paid in November, when Oceanwide is expecting to obtain

construction permits. In addition, it would pay about **$647 million in Mello-Roos special taxes over 30 years**, which would fund infrastructure in the Transbay district, including a possible Caltrain rail extension into the Transit Center.

But critics argue that economic benefits don't justify a violation of 1984's Proposition K—the "Sunlight Ordinance"—which blocks construction of any building over 40 feet that casts an adverse shadow on Recreation and Park Department property unless the Planning Commission decides the shadow is insignificant.

The project would throw a shadow on Portsmouth Square between 8:05 and 9:10 a.m. from late October to early February. It would shadow St. Mary's Square, also in Chinatown, in March and September. It would also shadow Justin Herman Plaza, at the foot of Market Street, from mid-October to late February, and Union Square from early May to early August.

"It really clobbers Portsmouth Square," said Allan Low, an attorney and a member of the Recreation and Park Commission.

After six months of negotiating with the city, Oceanwide Holdings—a Chinese developer that also has projects in New York and Los Angeles—has agreed to mitigate the shadows with a **$12 million endowment for recreation and parks programming** in Chinatown, a fund that will help pay for amenities like sports, after-school programs and senior fitness programs, said Low, who helped hammer out the deal.[11]

"I am loath to negotiate a cash-for-shadow deal, but to their credit, Oceanwide did recognize the significant impact their project will have on Portsmouth Square and the Chinatown parks," he said.

He said funding for programming is desperately needed.

"We can build the parks, but we have to have money for programs and services for the people in the parks," Low said. "For the majority of people in Chinatown, the parks and recreation centers are the only open spaces to go outside of their SRO [single room occupancy] rooms."

The commitment to Chinatown recreation is not enough to appease those who have fought to keep shadows out of city parks. Bill Maher, a former supervisor and director of the Department of Parking and Traffic who wrote Prop. K, said trading shadows for dollars is "flatly illegal." Prop. K's shadow-limiting powers are clear, he said.

"Planners have completely disregarded the voters' decision on Prop. K," Maher said. "They have simply administratively overruled the voters. They have changed the rules, without legal authority, to say the economic value of the project is the driving force. If that is the case, no park will survive."

He added: "Once you build a building, you can never get the park back. Downtown will become a perennial wind tunnel of darkness."

Attorney Sue Hestor, who also worked on Prop. K legislation, agreed.

"Everyone throws money at things, but shadows are shadows," said Hestor, who has long been involved in battles over development. "Portsmouth Square is the living room for people who live in 10-by-10 rooms," she said.

In addition to the shadow issue, Oceanwide has faced blowback from affordable housing proponents, who contend the project will exacerbate already inflated housing prices. The Oceanwide project will probably stand out even in a neighborhood becoming defined by high-end buildings like Lumina and Millennium Tower. Plans call for a 17,000-square-foot, ultra-luxury penthouse at the top of the taller tower, the city's largest. No price has been set, but it is likely to surpass the $49 million being asked for the 15,000-square-foot penthouse at nearby Lumina.

To meet that headwind, Oceanwide has agreed to pay **$40 million for off-site affordable housing**, $33 million of which would go toward making permanent existing affordable housing stock within a mile of the project, according to Jeff Buckley, senior housing policy director for Mayor Ed Lee.[12]

"Over the past several months, Oceanwide has worked closely with affordable housing and park advocates on a comprehensive community benefits package that will improve Chinatown parks and allow the city to secure affordable housing sites and SRO hotels within a 1-mile radius of the project," said Boe Hayward, who led the negotiations on behalf of Oceanwide.

The $33 million would target apartment buildings and residential hotels in Chinatown, an area that is increasingly attractive to investors looking to take advantage of the city's astronomical rents.[13]

In sum, the fees and taxes specific to this project amount to about $470 million.[14] That is $235 *per gross square foot* in fees and taxes. The political process in San Francisco for determining building density requires an assumption that the housing supply problem will not be solved. These fees would not be affordable to a developer who expected there ever to be a functional housing supply policy in the region, because these fees are more than the total cost of new housing in a functional housing market.

This is the description of a limited access negotiation, and all the players are engaged in limited access posturing. How might this project help mitigate the housing supply problem? That topic is only explicitly mentioned where "affordable housing proponents" claim it will lead to *higher* rents.[15] Later, kickbacks for affordable housing units are identified as a way to protect affordable units from investors "looking to take advantage" of high costs. Investors and developers are not explicitly identified as part of any solution, even though their activity is key to every city that has affordable housing. And note the number of times that the housing problem itself is used as a reason to block development. Dallas does not have neighborhoods full of people in living in 10-foot cubes, so Dallas can develop housing without working out half a billion dollars in payoffs.[16]

The groups in the constant state of negotiation and compromise in limited access orders aren't acting out of bald-faced self-interest. As North, Wallis, and Weingast point out, the negotiations are part of a process of social management. They are attempts at stability, at the avoidance of violence and conflict. But limited access orders make conflict inevitable.

Open access orders are an anomaly in human society—an incredibly successful anomaly. The citizens of the Anglosphere's major metropolitan areas have lost this marvelous anomaly. Limited access orders are characterized by instability and conflict, and as this problem enmeshes more major economic centers, so does it enmesh the wider economy. The stress this causes has led to public anger, but the anger is misplaced, because the problem is not properly understood. Nationalist movements on the right and redistributionist movements on the left both reflect stress, but the source of that stress isn't primarily corporate power or competition from foreigners.

WHAT COULD GO WRONG?

It may be that open access orders are not easily maintained. The reason is that economic rents will tend to gather naturally in open access orders. The way that economic rents can still accumulate, even in an open system, is through sunk costs, survivorship bias, and geographic advantages that come from path-dependent development.[17]

Detroit is a prime example of the previous generation of this sort of development. The early years in the automotive business were highly competitive and tumultuous. As the industry matured, the number of producers decreased. The producers that remained earned high returns on their invested capital. This happened for several reasons.

- The amount of total invested capital in the industry was large, but much of that investment failed. So a comparison of gains to capital taken at a point in time tended to overstate the total returns to the industry, because failed capital investments would fall off the aggregate balance sheet when firms failed.

- The returns of the remaining firms also tended to naturally be high because the competitive advantages that led to their success would also be likely to lead to higher returns. Firms with losses fail, so subpar returns fell off the aggregate income statement.

- The development of a particular industry, possibly from some initial local advantages, can have positive feedback mechanisms that increase those local advantages. Specialization of the local labor force, dense supply chain connections, and other economies of scale can lead to excess profits for the firms that survive there.

These developments would normally lead to an inflow of population in competition for the high local incomes. These natural sources of rents eventually pull local governance back into the mode of limited access orders. This is because access to the high profits of the surviving firms is related to geography. Even if the industry as a whole exists in an open access order where total returns (including failed firms) have been bid down to the competitive level, the returns of the geographically captured surviving firms contain economic rents which can be taken.

In other words, because of the factors and history described above, the remaining firms at any given time have excess profits that are somewhat tied to place. Previous, failed competitors naturally had poor returns on investment, counterbalanced by the above-average returns of the surviving firms. As a result, on average over time, a sector can have average profits while the remaining firms have above-average profits. These above-average profits are maintained by a combination of sunk costs, network effects, operational knowledge, and cultivated relationships with local managerial and labor talent. And, because they are somewhat geographically bound by some of those advantages, firms can't move away and keep those profits. So those profits can be taken politically, reducing the profits of the remaining firms through taxes, legislated advantages to local labor, and so on.

Detroit came to prominence in the age of physical capital and mass production. Firms maintained economic profits by investing in new production facilities that used the local labor and supply networks. Unionization was a way for local labor to capture some of those economic rents, by negotiating higher wages from the firms and by restricting the entry of non-union labor to the local source of higher incomes. But generally, when Detroit was ascendant, its population was rising. Americans were moving to opportunity. Firms increased their competitive advantage through more productive physical capital. And, to the extent that rents were captured by labor, they were captured by middle-class workers.

Eventually, though, competition from foreign firms pushed the profits of the Detroit firms down. Then the collection of organizational inefficiencies, high union wages, and other local forms of rent extraction was not easily dislodged. Detroit once held a competitive advantage, but now even foreign firms choose to open new US plants in other regions. And the results in Detroit are devastating.

THE ROLE OF RENT CONTROLS

When economic subsistence depends on access to various forms of limited access subsidies and control, movements to open access feel like a loss to locals. Local housing advocates usually complain that one reason markets can't be trusted to fix their housing supply problem is that when officials *do* allow new market-based housing expansion, it inevitably is built to serve only the "luxury" market. The reason usually assumed for this is that luxury homes are more profitable than low-cost homes, and so developers will only build for the luxury market unless they are forced to do otherwise.

Ironically, this sort of thinking attributes problems that are created in the broken markets of Closed Access areas to Open Access markets. There are two problems with this observation. First, of course new housing tends to supply the top end of the market. That's how functional housing markets work. When high-end tenants move into their new luxury units, households in the rest of the income distribution move up to fill in the existing stock. We don't insist that auto manufacturers only produce new cars that are worse than the existing used cars in order to be equitable.

Second, the claim that developers only build luxury units is untrue for any market outside the Closed Access cities. Other cities have plenty of supply of low-end and mid-low-end rental housing—some of it even new stock. Markets, when they operate openly, have no problem serving all sorts of owners and tenants.

Yet Closed Access policies do create a ratcheting effect on household budgets, which causes rent expenses to rise as a portion of income. This is especially hard on households at the low end of the income distribution, because they have less room to adjust their discretionary expenses. So, at the top end of the income distribution, households in Closed Access cities reduce their real housing expenses (say, by living in a very small unit) in order to keep their housing expenditures at a comfortable level similar to that of households in Open Access cities. Their reaction to Closed Access housing policies is to curtail real housing consumption.

But at the bottom end of the income distribution, there is a physical limit to how much adjustment can be made. The size of the unit cannot go any smaller, or the commute cannot functionally be any longer, and so on. So these households adjust to Closed Access housing policies by holding their real housing consumption constant while increasing their nominal housing expenditures and decreasing other expenditures. (They keep paying more for the same unit.) For some, this adjustment becomes unsustainable, and they migrate.

How does this situation affect the reaction of a city's populace as new units are added? Where is the pent-up demand? Which group has been reducing its real housing consumption because of Closed Access policies? High-income households that would be in the "luxury" market. That is the natural market for new *real* housing stock. When that new stock is added to the local market, it will also tend to bring down rents. In fact, high-income households will only be moving into those new units because of declining rents caused by the new supply. This is what helps low-income households. They aren't looking for an expansion of the housing stock, per se; they need lower costs. And when lower rents come, they will not respond by increasing their housing consumption. They will instead gratefully enjoy the reprieve from rising rents. The main sign of healing for them will be a decline in out-migration, not an increase in housing consumption.

This phenomenon makes it difficult to gather support for policies that could functionally expand Closed Access housing. The first step in the process would make the Closed Access cities look more like Seattle. Thousands of new "luxury" units would be filled by affluent households, while households with lower incomes would still be living in their old units. This would appear to be an elitist, "trickle down" policy. But it would be a tremendous improvement over the status quo, under which hundreds of thousands of households with lower incomes must move away from prosperous cities. When new units don't "trickle down" to households with lower incomes, households with lower incomes have to "trickle down" to Phoenix or Las Vegas.

Local housing policy that includes demands about increasing the real stock of "affordable" units has never coincided and will never coincide with falling prices. Because that is the essence of Closed Access governance. For a developer to be induced to build units below the market price, the city has to confirm that the Closed Access policies that maintain the inflated price of the "market rate" units will remain in place. A housing policy that requires "below market" units is a housing policy that is committed to maintaining Closed Access exclusion.

This is the irony of the complaint that market-rate builders only build luxury units, and therefore don't help to solve the housing problem. Those multi-million-dollar units in San Francisco and Los Angeles aren't valuable because of their material amenities. Larger, more beautiful homes are available in cities across the country. What makes them a luxury is their location. A luxury good is one that conveys status because its supply is limited. All new market-rate units in Closed Access cities are luxury units, by definition. The complaint that we should obstruct the development of market-rate units in Closed Access cities because market-rate units are all luxury units is an exercise in eating one's own tail.[18]

Closed Access cities tend to develop rent-control policies, which are themselves an attempt to capture economic rents, to compensate for rents that rise when supply is obstructed. New York City has had various rent control rules since World War II. California famously passed Proposition 13 in the 1970s, which was a limited access negotiation to allow existing owners to live in their artificially overpriced homes at a lower cost by limiting property tax increases. Soon after, rent controls in California were passed that were a limited access negotiation to allow existing renters to live in their artificially overpriced homes at a lower cost. Eventually, the city of Santa Monica went so far as to deny landlords the right to remove their rental units from the market, and this was upheld by the California Supreme Court. California then passed the Ellis Act to confirm the right of owners to evict tenants in order to sell or change the use of their properties.[19]

This is parallel to problems typical in less-developed economies, where existing factions receive political favors and new entrants are disfavored. In a less-developed economy, someone might have special permission to distribute a good—say, fuel—in an area because the person's cousin has a prime political position or because the person has bribed the right officials. In California, these favors have been developed democratically, so they are captured as voting blocks of certain special interests or preferred interests. At their broadest, they are favors bestowed on existing residents at the expense of potential new residents.

If the Ellis Act protects the ability of owners to freely contract, it does so at the peril of renters who have grown accustomed to an opaque transfer of benefits they have been taking from their landlords. They feel justified in taking these benefits because the high rental value of the property is truly unnatural. Their controlled rent seems more just than the market price. These intuitions are valid. This is why so few countries have made the transition out of limited access orders. Limited access quarrels *feel* like moral battles. It *is* a moral battle to help a poor elderly person remain in her below-market rental unit at the expense of the landlord. Why should the landlord be pocketing $4,000 per month on a unit that, by all rights, should cost $1,000? Then one thing leads to another, and eventually advocates for affordable housing are making seemingly moral demands that add up to fees and kickbacks of $235 per square foot for new units.

The problem isn't that anybody is morally depraved. Limited access negotiations always appear, individually, to be solutions when, in the aggregate, they are the problem.

INCIVILITY AND INEQUITY

Eventually, the whole notion of a market is undermined. What is the market price? There is one market price for the owner who pays taxes adjusted from the original purchase date in 1994, another for the renter who moved into the unit in 2006, yet another for the new tech worker who just moved into town and has no grandfathered tax treatment or rent level, and another for the prospective developer who would have to pay reparations to the tenant, pay off the local affordable-housing advocates, negotiate a range of development fees, and raze the property to build a condo for the aforementioned tech worker. This is the literal context of limited access, where impersonal exchange is unavailable. The value of the property depends on who's asking.

Duke economist Michael Munger has further developed the idea of an open access order to an even more pure conception of universal liberty, which he calls "euvoluntary exchange."[20] The idea is that voluntary exchange is the economic behavior enabled in open access orders that leads to the abundance and growth that has characterized our age, but even economic activity that seems voluntary can be imperfect. Perfectly voluntary exchange—euvoluntary exchange—requires conventional ownership; it requires the ability to transfer and transact without coercion, uncompensated externalities, or regrets; and, most importantly, it requires reasonable alternatives.

This is what is so important about freedom of entry into a market and the ubiquity of impersonal exchange. In Closed Access housing markets, the obstruction of new supply removes alternatives for all residents and potential residents. But worse is the destruction of impersonal exchange.

Let's say you are renting a unit at $2,000 per month because of rent control, and there are other similar units renting for $4,000. This preferential treatment transforms the market from one that favors landlords who maintain their properties and treat their tenants well into one that favors landlords who drive tenants out and abuse the arbitrary sets of rules that determine individual rental rates. Any life-cycle changes that might trigger a marginal change in an individual's housing needs also trigger an added fee when rents or taxes reset with each transaction.

Even without rent control, rents of existing units tend to lag the market. Among the reasons for this is the fact that, in an Open Access market, landlords incur expenses to find new tenants, and they run the risk of taking on bad tenants.[21] Both the tenant and the landlord have a significant motive to act in each other's best interest. As tenants' tenures lengthen, their rents tend to fall below the market rate. Attracting and keeping good tenants is an important part of a landlord's business. This naturally incentivizes the landlord to be civil and accommodating to existing tenants, and the macro data confirm that stable tenants are so valuable that landlords charge them lower rents. Lower rent, in turn, incentivizes the tenant to respect the property and the landlord.

But consider a rent-controlled apartment, where a landlord has been prevented from raising the rent at market rates. An apartment worth $2,000 in monthly rent, which the landlord might have rented to the existing tenants for

$1,900 in an open market, might have a legal cap well below that price. Now the incentives are reversed. The landlord would prefer to replace the tenant or sell the property at its market price. A relationship that could be naturally symbiotic becomes hostile. Limited access order policies change both the behavior of existing renters and landlords toward each other and the types of people who are attracted to businesses that operate under such rules.

This is the source of conflict. Limited access orders make everyone beholden to a certain negotiated capture of economic rents. Limits to entry create deprivation, so, whereas battles to claim economic rents in a previous generation (in a place like Detroit) were fought over the gains from economies of scale or improved productivity, fights today are for respite from deprivation.

Ironically, we have come to a point in history where the questions "Why is Latin America economically stagnant?" and "What is the problem with the world's richest cities?" share an answer—limited access orders are intractable. And, as North, Wallis, and Weingast point out, there really isn't a solution to this problem.

The twist we have put on the limited access problem is that limited access cities are embedded in open access societies. Policymakers can impose limited access negotiations on capital, but with the exception of some issues like increasing barriers to entry from occupational licensing, open access attitudes still generally prevail in other realms. No one would stand for laws limiting the ability of workers to move to a city, for instance. Free entry of labor pushes prices up, and a lack of free entry for capital prevents them from coming back down.

The cost of building a new development is pulled up from the cost of building to the market price by the imposition of public obstacles and fees. New developers will be drawn to the city unless those fees and impositions rise high enough to reduce their expected profits to a normal rate of return. But the developer can only justify building under these conditions if housing policy is sufficiently dysfunctional that the developer can count on being able to charge high rents for many decades. So, instead of having an equilibrium price that settles where supply and demand meet, as it would in an open access context, the equilibrium price settles where the fees and kickbacks extracted by local power brokers meet the expected level of future dysfunction, so that the developer can earn a market return.

Free entry is key to the equity produced by open access orders. Workers and developers are free to enter Closed Access cities, so they don't generally retain excess incomes. Even if their incomes are high, their incomes are claimed by high rents, fees, and taxes. Existing real estate owners and city officials do control limited resources, so they are able to impose high rents, taxes, and fees, and they retain those gains as excess profits and public revenues.

BOOTLEGGERS AND BAPTISTS

The economist Bruce Yandle has a useful framework for thinking about certain political and economic issues, which he calls "bootleggers and Baptists."[22] In short, the most potent and immovable regulatory interventions are frequently those that pair a moralizing front with an economic special interest. For example, bootleggers profited from the prohibition of alcohol, but they would not have had much power to implement prohibition on their own. Only the rise of morally confident teetotalers could engender enough political support to implement prohibition. Frequently, without collusion, both groups working toward the same goal can create a powerful political movement. Closed Access housing seems to be a good example of this phenomenon.

The political features of this issue can easily push observers into partisan teams. Forces lined up against housing expansion in the Closed Access cities can include existing homeowners, residents of exclusive enclaves protecting the socioeconomic profile of an area, local businesses trying to avoid competition, environmental and historical conservationists, renters' advocates, affordable-housing advocates, advocates for marginalized resident groups that would be displaced by in-fill development, existing residents in gentrifying neighborhoods, and so forth. Plenty of blame can be selectively spread without upsetting anyone's personal, preexisting lineup of good guys and bad guys.

The problem seems to fall along partisan lines. The Closed Access cities (New York City, Boston, San Francisco, Los Angeles) are reliably Democratic and the Open Access cities with high population growth (Dallas, Houston, Atlanta, Phoenix) are in reliably Republican areas. All of these metro areas have existing homeowners, elite suburban enclaves, and rent-seeking business interests. These generally fit the "bootleggers" category—those whose self-interest is served by regulatory limits.

What sets the Closed Access cities apart are the "Baptists"—activists, conservationists, advocates, renters, and displaced residents. These groups are either socially sympathetic or putatively advocating for some sympathetic idea or group. It is the bootlegger and Baptist combination that creates the political problem.

This is especially the case on this particular issue, since much of the current set of "bootleggers" in Closed Access cities are themselves victims of the problem. They are homeowners who had to buy into the expensive housing market to access lucrative labor markets. The middle-class families who origi-nally owned most of those homes and who sold out and moved with their bankroll to less-expensive Open Access areas realized the gains of limited access rents at the new owners' expense. A return to functionality will mean a significant capital loss for many "bootleggers" who didn't particularly gain from the original economic rents.

It would be easy to conclude that causality runs from the appearance of "blue" activists in a city to the development of dysfunctional housing policies. But that causality may be a little too simplistic.[23]

There is also another dichotomy between the Open Access and Closed Access cities, and that is density. The Open Access cities have grown outward, not upward. In fact, the Closed Access cities tend to build more new homes in high-density neighborhoods than the Open Access cities do.[24] Most cities, even on an international scale, have become less dense in the last several decades, but Open Access cities do not have cores that create as much value from high density, so they have not run up against this density problem.

Manhattan was most dense in the late 1800s and early 1900s, when parts of the island were filled with tenements. The rise of zoning, building codes, and community regulators on development were, in part, reasonable reactions to the worst aspects of the conditions at that time. But it is surprising to consider that the peak in urban density happened before the propagation of the mod-ern high-rise building. This may be hard to believe for young workers living in such cities, but much of the decline in urban density has come from a rise in the residential floor area claimed by each resident. Population and residents per square foot of living space both peaked in Manhattan in the 1910s. Population has fallen by about a third on the island while the number of residents per square foot has fallen by about half. Living space has been added to the island, just not enough to make up for changing standards regarding residential spaces.[25]

There are certainly obstacles to residential mobility far out into the suburbs, especially in the Closed Access cities. But the dense urban cores should be a natural focus for change. This is because (1) these areas were built and inhab-ited with a bias for—even pride in—their dynamism; (2) they have developed the most value, because of that dynamism and their ability to accommodate enough density to create value from highly skilled, innovative networks; and (3) high-rise buildings naturally can be built to tap into that value in a fruitful way and greatly expand the housing stock.

This is quantifiable. The price of residential real estate in Manhattan and in the city of San Francisco can run $1,000 or more per square foot. The differ-ence between the prices of residential housing in those core locations and the unencumbered cost to build new housing there is extreme. Where the distortion is greatest, the need for change is greatest.

As for causation, the stresses of urban living naturally lead to the development of public forms of communal support and control. These include the imposition of standards for living conditions, municipal support of economically marginalized residents, and advocacy for historical and environmental preservation. These forces can be for the good.

The problem in the 21st century is that some aspects of these forces on local governance have attained enough supremacy to create problems, frequently focused on the marginalized residents that advocates had intended to aid. These problems are now bleeding into the hinterlands surrounding these cities, across the entire country—even creating costs globally.

There are many interests in balance here. There is a balance between the interests of different residents of a city. Between the interests of the current residents of a given city and those of its potential residents. Between the interests of the city and those of its surrounding host country. Public betterment invariably revolves around the evolution of those balances. That evolution is invariably slow and frequently painful, as is clear in the history of racial and gender inequities. Yet Open Access societies are especially adept at facilitating that evolution. In a way, our frustration at the delays and pains associated with those evolutions exists because we take for granted that our world, in particular, is capable of change. It is helpful to think about these dislocations in terms of open access versus limited access rather than in terms of "red" versus "blue."

A better way to think about these challenges may be that the challenges of urban density are what turn a city "blue." Urban stresses create a need for progressive, communal actions. The Closed Access cities are "blue" because they are dense. So factional politics is probably not the framework that best addresses the challenge of finding the most equitable form of governance for these cities. The challenge is to create a structural framework for governance that allows a progressive local regime to address the challenges unique to the urban context without leading to a collective action paradox that ends up harming the very constituents that the progressive regime was intended to help. One way to address this problem is to implement civil rights policies from higher levels of government, such as the state or federal level, that limit the ability of local residents to block the entry of new homes and families.

Some level of historical, neighborhood, or environmental preservation is beneficial. But in the Rube Goldberg machine of intended and unintended consequences, limited access orders invariably harm the least powerful, most vulnerable residents, even when the original intent of their policies was benign.

The development and subsequent regulatory blockage of microhousing in Seattle is a good example of the snowballing effect of regulatory demands that seem reasonable individually, but that add up to obstruction and to a cultural shift in which it becomes more acceptable to amplify the concerns of locals who oppose new building. This situation is enabled by the difficulty of quantifying those concerns easily. Those concerns were addressed in Seattle— concerns about aesthetics, parking, building standards—all reasonable, in their way. And when they were addressed, they effectively blocked a form of afford able housing.[26]

Think of the attorney in the Oceanwide case who, in response to a shadow cast from 8 a.m. to 9 a.m. for three and a half months on a small park, said, "It really clobbers Portsmouth Square." New development encounters a dozen different sources of obstruction, each with their own separate complaint, levied with a similarly elastic sense of scale and importance. The existence of the limited access order—the ability to force others to negotiate regarding each concern— induces an inflation of stated concerns, because in a context where scale is imprecise, the inflation of concerns is a natural, unavoidable product of the negotiation. Modern societies strive for universal fairness so that all concerns will be heard—on the principle that everyone has a right to have a say in the development of a community. Yet, ironically, this undermines the very foundation of a fair and open society.

There are two separate issues here: (1) support for vulnerable residents, social safety nets, and management of change, and (2) an unwillingness to let progress and growth emerge in a liberal and open society.[27] Progress is change. Change causes dislocation. Especially because progress in a liberal society is frequently associated with some innovation or application of capital, there is usually someone who is profiting as others are disrupted. This is aesthetically and morally off-putting. But in the process of stopping profit that comes from progress, growth, and innovation, more profit has been created that creates more losers, more refugees, and more inequity. Moralistic attempts at local optimization that focus on individual developments have pushed the Closed Access cities far from their global, citywide optimums. Good intentions do not change that fact.

The same framework can be applied to broader national policies. In effect, the reactions to the housing bubble have led to limited access policies in housing markets across the country. This is especially true in mortgage markets, where federal control has been used to enforce strict access to credit. As is typical of limited access policies, this trend has imposed harm on American households in inverse proportion to their economic well-being.

The broad solution is simple—build. The local political battles are so complex that they may be intractable. Economic growth and the stress of Closed Access policies are unavoidably intertwined. The constrained mortgage market is what is holding back growth today. But, just as surely as expanded mortgages will help to recover growth, they will also push prices in the Closed Access cities back up, probably prompting renewed migration into and out of the Contagion cities. One process can't happen apart from the other. We have been engineering slower economic growth to slow down the inevitable stress of Closed Access. Anyone watching cities like San Francisco knows that the stress of Closed Access is building anyway.

Closed Access may be an intractable problem. What about the rest of America? Let's let it rip.

APPENDIX: HOME PRICES

The different mental frameworks we use when we think about different classes of assets have a significant effect on our response to changing values. We think of bonds in terms of yield. This is because bonds tend to be issued at a standard face value (say, $100), and so bond buyers think in terms of how much income they will receive for each $100 investment. Newly issued bonds have a fixed price, so when market yields change, it is cash flows that adjust. If yields were 3% last year and are 2% this year, then bondholders in both years think of their investment as a $100 investment that last year earned $3 and this year earns $2. But, for long-term bonds that were issued last year, the bonds' market value will rise substantially in the second year as a result of those falling yields. When new bonds only fetch $2, existing bonds that pay $3 are worth much more than $100.

Since bonds tend to differ in maturity dates, so that a yield change affects each bond's price differently, it is easier to think of bond markets in general in terms of yield, and then to apply that yield to each individual bond to estimate the price.

But, since homes have no maturity date, if they are properly updated and maintained, they are essentially perpetuities. This means that changing yields have a similar effect on all home prices. Furthermore, rents are very stable in the short term. When yields change on bonds, cash flows change along with them. But when yields change on homes, rents remain stable. This means that price is the variable that must change in response to short-term changes in yield. So, in homes, we think in terms of price.

These different mental framings lead us to discuss bonds and homes in opposite ways. Any change in yield on any financial security reflects a transfer between future owners and past owners. When yields decline, past owners receive a capital gain on the basis of the changing market value, and future owners receive lower incomes on the basis of falling yields. But these are mathematically two sides of the same coin. Price is the inverse of yield:

$$Yield = \frac{Income}{Price}.$$

So, when yields fall, we think of homes as having rising prices, and we note that owners have gained wealth, even though their rental incomes have not changed. (In fact, in Open Access cities, their rental incomes should fall as new capital is attracted into the homebuilding market, increasing the competition for rents.) At the same time, we think of bondholders as losing, and public discussions revolve around the problem of savers and pensioners receiving lower incomes. But, at least if we compare homeowners to owners of very long-term bonds, we are basically describing the same circumstances.

If we presume that homebuyers are simply agents of demand, with no rational pricing discipline, then it is easy for this mental framing to lead us to conclude that increases in home prices are temporary outcomes of having too much credit or too much money. In that case, it would look like high home prices created a "wealth effect" where households were enticed into spending more than they really could afford, because their inflated home values caused them to overestimate their wealth.

However, if we presume that home prices do tend toward no arbitrage prices (in the loose sense) relative to other assets,[1] then this is a case where the cause of the price change is important. If the price change is due to changing yields, then the wealth effect is probably not significant, especially in Open Access cities where building will be triggered. But if the price change is due to rising rents, then the wealth effect is not temporary. Then the wealth effect reflects higher income expectations from future rents. Since rising local rents for entire metropolitan areas are only sustainable over the long term when they are paired with rising local incomes, the rising rents themselves reflect higher incomes.

The Reserve Bank of Australia has done research on this topic, finding that when home prices increased, instead of seeing a pure wealth effect among only homeowners, both owners *and* renters increased their spending. "The conclusion . . . is that it is a common third factor such as higher expected future income, or less income uncertainty, that is, at least partly, responsible for the observed association between housing wealth and spending."[2]

MORTGAGES AS OBSTACLES TO OWNERSHIP

While incomes and expected incomes are an important factor in home prices, there are natural factors that moderate prices. Since homes cannot be easily purchased piecemeal, as one might purchase shares of a firm, access to credit serves as an obstacle to demand. People with only a small amount of savings can buy a few shares of Berkshire Hathaway or a mutual fund more easily than they can buy real estate.

High transaction costs also limit demand for homeownership. High transaction costs mean that if prospective buyers expect to live in a home for less than several years, the expected return to buying a home is probably not worth the purchase cost.

This factor limits demand, pulling owner-occupied home values down, making values dependent on tenancy. The longer an owner lives in a home, the higher the yield will be on his or her investment, after transaction costs.

There is a similar effect in the market for firms. Privately held firms usually sell at a discount. In other words, they earn a higher return for their investors. And the reason they do is that it is more difficult to find a buyer for such firms. Google, on the other hand, can be bought and sold in bits and pieces, by investors who can even buy shares with borrowed money. So a firm like Google trades at nearly its full value, with little discount required to account for liquidity. The market for Google shares is very liquid, so the return on investment for speculators that hold shares for weeks or months isn't much less than the return on investment for long-term holders.

The effect of transaction costs and market liquidity is asymmetrical. Adding costs can lower the price and raise the yield of a security, but once a market is sufficiently liquid, adding more liquidity will not continue to boost the price. If brokers decided that Google could be traded with a margin account leveraged up to 90%, this wouldn't move the price of shares much, because there are many potential sellers who will sell shares when they think the price is too high.

This same asymmetry applies to housing markets. Homeowners may be less likely to sell, for personal reasons or because of the high cost, so there is some additional danger of added liquidity pushing home prices above a sustainable level, where yields on investment are temporarily lower than they are for assets with similar risks. But the flight of homeowners out of Closed Access cities and the decline in the national homeownership rate that began a couple of years before prices peaked suggests that there are sellers willing to react to rising prices.

In general, with a decade of hindsight, it seems reasonably accurate to suggest that Closed Access home prices reflected rising rents along with some boost in liquidity from lenient credit markets, akin to the price boost a firm would receive by changing from a privately held firm to a publicly traded firm. Conditions in the Contagion Cities became peculiar enough to trigger a true bubble, where prices, for a short time, seem to have objectively moved higher than was justifiable.

That being said, housing values generally seem to have a similar asymmetry to equity markets. As I described in chapter 4, lenient credit during the boom didn't push prices in credit-constrained zip codes to relatively higher levels in most cities. But tight credit applied after the housing boom has been so extreme that it has pushed prices down in credit-constrained zip codes compared to less-credit-constrained zip codes.

It is possible for improvements in credit access and declines in transaction costs to create a broad rise in home values. That is a benign outcome. It is possible for that to be the case in most contexts, even if there are isolated contexts, as in the Contagion cities, where prices temporarily become "bubbly." On average, homeowners who remain in homes for more than a few years, so that they minimize transaction costs, earn yields that are higher than yields on comparable assets. According to the American Housing Survey, homeowners with lower incomes tend to have been in their homes for longer than homeowners with higher incomes. Mortgage access that facilitates this activity is generally benign.

MORTGAGES ARE SAVINGS

Conceptually, there is another reason why growth in mortgages, in and of itself, should be considered benign. Effectively, mortgages are a sign of saving as much as of borrowing. The "housing ATM" is a colloquialism typically applied to the run-up in debt. Certainly, households utilize home equity for spending at times, and this would especially apply to markets where prices are rising.

There are measures of equity withdrawal that attempt to quantify the "housing ATM," but in the end, money is fungible, and it is not really possible to know the net effect of new purchases, refinancing, and so forth on household cash flow. To the extent that mortgages are utilized as purchases, they are the product of a decision to buy instead of to rent. The decision to buy is a decision to save. What is a primary means of saving for middle-class households? Buying a house. And what do they need to do to initiate that saving? Take out a sizable mortgage. Mortgages are a sign of saving.

And, since the conventional approach to homebuying pairs a nominal mortgage with a real asset (the house), the purchase creates an asset-liability mismatch. Even if we ignore amortization, the house-mortgage pairing creates a natural stream of equity accumulation by the owner, in real terms. In normal markets, if mortgage rates are 6%, representing a 4% real yield and a 2% inflation premium, then we would expect the average homeowner to make payments worth 6% of the mortgage (plus amounts due for amortization), collecting roughly 4% of the home value in (imputed) rent while the home gains about 2% in value, on average, over the year due to general inflation.

The initiation of a mortgage is the initiation of an unbooked savings plan. Leveraged homeowners must commit to making payments that are higher than the expected net rent yield. The inflation portion of those payments is actually a form of equity purchase. But we don't account for them that way. We account for them as interest income for the mortgage lender, even though in real terms it isn't income at all.[3] And, while net worths of households rise as these imputed transfers accrue, the Bureau of Economic Analysis (BEA) does not account for capital gains as income. So new homeowners with mortgages create a mirage where the real incomes of financial intermediaries and the financial expenses of homeowners are overstated while real household savings are understated.

Under the presumption that the housing boom was caused by excess credit, high home prices seem to be unsustainable, so we have tended to think of the "housing ATM" as a boost to spending that was coming from capital gains that would eventually be reversed. But what if limited supply was the cause of rising prices, and high home prices in the Closed Access cities are related to high incomes and will persist until the Closed Access policies are overturned? If this is true, then households were effectively saving at higher rates than our system of measurement accounts for. And low real interest rates meant that the real portion of interest income for financial intermediaries in the decade after 2000 was a smaller proportion of measured incomes than it had been in the 1990s.

THE DOUBLE BONUS OF THE MORTGAGE INTEREST TAX DEDUCTION

On the other hand, the substantial income tax benefits of homeownership make owning a home more valuable, and this pushes the *pretax* yield on homes down—meaning that prices are pushed higher. As I have noted elsewhere, these tax benefits are highly weighted toward more expensive homes with high-income owners, especially leveraged owners.

In the decade before the tax code change that made the mortgage interest deduction more important in 1986, household mortgage debt had averaged about 32% of real estate value. By 1996, that had increased to 42%. It was still at 41% in 2005, at the peak of the housing boom.[4]

The boom itself was not associated with rising leverage. But the tax value of leverage on high-priced homes for high-income owners certainly accommodated the rising valuations of homes in Closed Access cities where young, high-income households were buying homes with leverage that were highly likely to accrue capital gains because of rent inflation.

The mortgage interest deduction is only a part of this factor. The fact that owner-occupiers don't pay income tax on the rental values of their homes is a larger benefit. Property taxes are an indirect way of taxing the rental income of owner-occupiers. But if property taxes are applied to both owned and rented properties, then there is still a tax disadvantage that raises costs for renters compared to owners. One way to erase that difference would be to reduce income taxes on landlords, or to reduce income taxes on capital income in general. Reducing taxation on capital income may, on net, lead to a more progressive tax code, by eliminating the tax on rental income that currently applies to renters but not owners.

We can think of these tax benefits as a government requirement to buy an annuity when you buy a house, and since most owners have some mortgage debt, that annuity is fully leveraged. In other words, you might want to buy a house that is worth $200,000. Because of income tax benefits, that house may sell for $250,000 instead. So the government is basically saying that if you want to buy a house for $200,000, you have to also get a loan for $50,000 and invest it in an annuity that pays you back over time in the form of tax subsidies. If you can't claim those tax benefits, that annuity will be a total loss for you. If you have a high marginal tax rate and a large mortgage, then your returns on that annuity will be very high.

It would be socially beneficial if we stopped making homebuyers purchase fully leveraged annuities that only pay out to highly leveraged, wealthy families.

Given the current policy regime, we have two countervailing factors in housing markets: illiquid markets and transactions costs tend to keep home prices lower, but tax policy tends to push prices higher. The net effect of these factors seems to be to make aggregate pretax yields on the national housing stock similar to pretax yields on inflation-protected Treasuries.

LANDLORDS VS. OWNERS

In markets with a sufficient number of rental units, we should expect investor-owners to be concerned with yields and to bid prices up or down in concert with other types of income-earning assets.

Owner-occupiers differ from investors because they have a control premium. They have the valuable ability to change or upgrade their home to satisfy their own tastes and needs, without asking for permission, and to decide when they will or will not dispose of it. In addition, under our current tax regime, owner-occupiers enjoy substantial tax preferences. But, to gain these benefits, owner-occupiers are limited to a single property, or at least a small number of properties, so that they cannot attain the benefits of diversification.

The control and tax premiums are benefits; thus they reduce the cash returns homeowners require. The lack of diversification is a cost to owner-occupiers. This means they need to earn more income on a home to justify owning over renting.

Unfortunately, the control premium and the diversification premium would be difficult to measure. There is no market-based measure of these premiums.

Figure A-1. US Landlord vs. Owner Returns on Investment

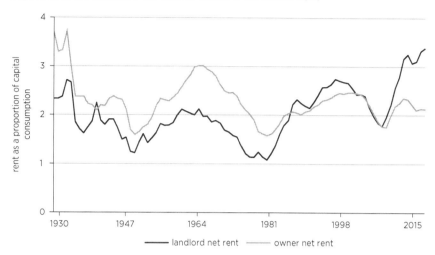

Note: Rental income is the income that would be earned if all properties were unleveraged—similar to the "operating profits" of a firm. Capital consumption is the natural rate of depreciation.
Source: Table 7.4.5 (Housing Sector Output, Gross Value Added, and Net Value Added) and table 7.12 (Imputations in the National Income and Product Accounts) from Bureau of Economic Analysis, available at https://apps.bea.gov/iTable/index_nipa.cfm. In both tables, operating surplus = rental income after expenses and capital consumption + net interest, to reflect the total net income of the properties.

Since the BEA tracks incomes and expenses for both owned and rented properties, we can compare the returns on these different sets of properties. The BEA has data back to 1929. In order to compare the two types of properties, figure A-1 shows the operating surplus (net rent after expenses and consumption of capital) as a ratio of consumption of capital.

We can see parallel movement over time, suggesting that prices for owner-occupied properties reflect fundamentals, similarly to prices for investor-owned properties. There is some drift downward in relative returns to owners over time. The value homes had in the 1970s for hedging against inflation (and the tax implications of inflation) may have helped pull down the required return on owned houses, and the relative tax advantage of the mortgage interest tax deduction also pulled down the required return on owned homes relative to rented homes.

For my purposes here, the important points to consider are (1) there appears to be long-term parallel behavior between yields on owned versus rented homes, (2) looking only at the period from about 1985 to 2005, yields on both rented and owned homes tracked very closely together and were within long-term ranges, and (3) since 2006 and 2007 when housing starts and the mortgage

Figure A-2. Rent Relative to US GDP and Homeownership

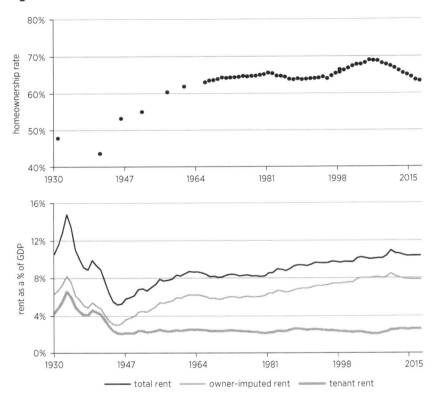

Sources: Table 1.5.5 (Gross Domestic Product, Expanded Detail), table 7.4.5 (Housing Sector Output, Gross Value Added, and Net Value Added), and table 7.12 (Imputations in the National Income and Product Accounts) from Bureau of Economic Analysis, available at https://apps.bea.gov/iTable/index _nipa.cfm; US Census Bureau, "Housing Vacancies and Homeownership (CPS/HVS): Historical Tables," last modified April 26, 2016, http://www.census.gov/housing/hvs/data/histtabs.html.

market collapsed, housing yields have risen, and they have risen especially in rented units because tight lending since the crisis has increased the demand for rental units and decreased competition from buyers. This is a reflection of the collapse of prices in low-tier markets. The sharp decline in homeownership has created a set of renters without other options.

We can see in figure A-2 that the democratization of homeownership after the New Deal raised both homeownership and housing expenditures until the mid-1960s. In other words, before that time, frictions in the marketplace prevented households from accessing credit and created obstacles to owning. The development of credit markets helped to facilitate ownership, which allowed households to capture those control and tax benefit premiums, inducing new households into ownership and inducing more spending on housing in general, because households were effectively consuming the control premium of ownership that had previously been unavailable to them.

There are two separate considerations here regarding past differences between owner and landlord returns. One is access to credit and to ownership, and the other is the value of tax benefits. Concerning access, it appears that the reforms coming out of the New Deal created real benefits. Liquidity in markets is a public good. As a public good, it is especially difficult to measure, because liquidity manifests itself through lower incomes. Liquid markets mean that investors have lower risks and more control, and so investors systematically require lower returns from liquid markets. The value capital searches for is *not* income; it is *risk-adjusted* income. This is one of the difficulties in recognizing the tremendous value that a functional financial sector brings to an economy. A functional financial sector should reduce the relative income required by capital. This is not a transfer from capital investors, as we normally think of it, because investors happily earn less in liquid markets because the liquidity lowers risk.

However, in Closed Access housing markets, more-liquid credit markets only induce demand for a relatively fixed stock of housing, pushing up both rents and prices. In Open Access housing markets, more-liquid credit markets mean that better or more homes are built. Since real estate investors demand lower returns, new supply lowers rents. Demand for housing increases as a result, but this is met with real gains in the available housing stock.

But tax benefits do not necessarily provide public benefits. There is a balance between the control and tax benefits and the cost of lack of diversification. If tax benefits induce households to purchase homes or to consume more housing, in effect, government is inducing them to take on more of that nondiversification risk. Again, because these costs are conveyed through risk premiums, the effect on incomes is not easily measured. If the added tax benefits induce a household to take on nondiversification risk by owning a more valuable home, then the household appears to get higher rental consumption that looks free in absolute terms. But it isn't free. It's just that the cost is in the form of higher risk.

This can be conceptually difficult to understand, but it is easy to understand in practical terms. Many households lost homes to foreclosure during the crisis and suffered tremendous financial burdens as a result. This is a cost of nondiversification. Those same families might not have fared so poorly if they had been renters and, instead of making down payments on homes, they had invested in a broad basket of financial securities. As things were, the tax benefits of homeownership may have increased their (imputed) incomes, generally, but the cost of nondiversification is volatility and unevenly distributed financial catastrophe.

To put this another way, if credit access allows households to make the jump from renter to owner, they capture the onetime gain of control over their homestead. This also comes with a cost of nondiversification, since they must expose themselves to the changing value of a single large asset. Most households clearly perceive a net benefit from that trade. If tax benefits cause the typical value of the home they own to increase—in either real or nominal terms—that does not change the basic value of control that they gained by becoming an owner, but it does increase the cost of nondiversification by increasing the value of their single large asset.

The takeaway from all of this is a contrarian point of view regarding the housing boom and bust. First, there wasn't a particular increase in housing consumption during the boom; and there was no obvious, significant change in tax benefits related to housing. To the extent that access to mortgages and homeownership improved during the period, this is the sort of change we should support. Reducing the tax benefits of homeownership while increasing access to ownership through more accessible avenues to partial ownership or mortgages would bring net benefits. Improvements in mortgage access during the boom, all things considered, were focused on younger households with high incomes more than they were focused on households with lower incomes that may have been taking on more risk than was advisable. Yet we *should* be finding ways for lower-income households to capture the value of control, where control would have value for them. The best way to do this may be outside a highly leveraged mortgage arrangement with terms that trigger cyclical defaults. But the goal is something we should be aiming for, not something to fear. Unfortunately, the misinterpretations of the housing boom and the misplaced fears these interpretations have created have probably taken us a large step backward in this regard. For the decade since the boom, the tax benefits that push prices up have remained in place, and prices have been tamped down by aggressively denying households access to credit.

HOUSING YIELDS VS. REAL TREASURY YIELDS

Housing yields (net rental value as a percentage of market value) have ranged between 2% and 4% since at least 1946.[5] Housing yields generally ebbed and flowed along with general levels of real long-term interest rates, rising after World War II, falling during the 1970s, rising again in the 1990s, and falling in the decade after 2000. As we see in figure A-3, housing yields were low in the decade after 2000, but they weren't outside the historical range.

It is difficult to assemble accurate data on long-term real interest rates before the 1990s, because inflation risks in the 1970s and 1980s complicate the division

Figure A-3. Housing Yield and 30-Year Real Treasury Yield

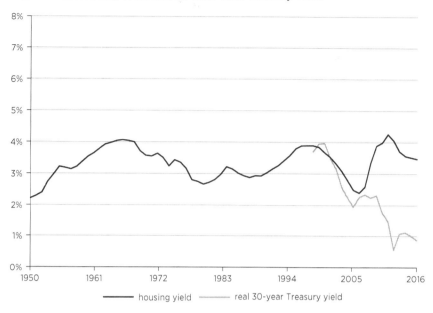

Note: Housing yield estimated by dividing aggregate rental and interest income of owner-occupied houses by the aggregate market value.
Sources: Table 7.12 (Imputations in the National Income and Product Accounts), Line 159 (Net Interest) + Line 163 (Rental Income of Persons with Capital Consumption Adjustment) from Bureau of Economic Analysis (BEA), available at https://apps.bea.gov/iTable/index_nipa.cfm; Board of Governors of the Federal Reserve System, "Households; Owner-Occupied Real Estate Including Vacant Land and Mobile Homes at Market Value" (HOOREVLMHMV), retrieved from FRED, Federal Reserve Bank of St. Louis; "30-Year 3-5/8% Treasury Inflation-Indexed Bond, Due 4/15/2028" (TP30A28), retrieved from FRED, Federal Reserve Bank of St. Louis; Board of Governors of the Federal Reserve System, "30-Year Treasury Inflation-Indexed Security, Constant Maturity" (FII30), retrieved from FRED, Federal Reserve Bank of St. Louis.

of nominal interest rates between the real portion and the inflationary portion, and before the 1970s, data on rates are less available. But the market for Treasury Inflation-Protected Securities (TIPS) does provide a market yield for real long-term Treasuries over the past 20 years. From the mid-1990s to 2007, real long-term Treasury yields moved within the long-term range of real housing yields, and housing yields and long-term real Treasury yields moved together.

After housing starts and mortgage credit markets collapsed in 2006 and 2007, housing yields and real long-term Treasury yields diverged in a way that they have not before. *This* is the period when housing markets have been far outside the norm, because yields have been too high (which is the same as saying prices have been too low). (And this is using a measure for only owner-occupied housing. As noted above, rental housing yields have moved even higher.)

Another way to loosely measure the efficiency of home prices is to compare mortgage rates and housing yield.[6] These represent the two forms of ownership of owner-occupied real estate—the debt position and the equity position. Since mortgages are generally paid in nominal terms (a rate that includes an inflation premium on a fixed face value) and homes are real assets (they have a face value that rises with inflation so that inflationary gains are captured as capital gains instead of through rental income), and since both tend to have relatively low-risk premiums, the difference between mortgage rates and housing yields should track inflation expectations.

This is what we see in the data in figure A-4. The "implied inflation" line is the difference between the effective mortgage rate on mortgages (which includes an inflation premium) and the effective rental yield on homes (which does not include an inflation premium). So, if home prices are relatively reasonable, that

Figure A-4. Housing Yield, Effective Mortgage Rate, and Implied Inflation

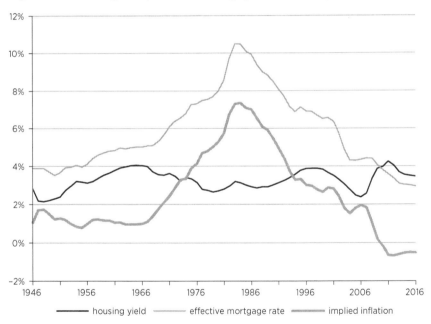

Note: *Housing yield* equals the sum of total net interest and rental income (after costs and capital consumption of owner-occupiers) divided by market value of owner-occupied housing. *Effective mortgage rate* equals net interest of owner-occupied housing divided by home mortgage liability of households and nonprofit organizations. *Implied inflation* equals effective mortgage rate minus housing yield. Sources: Table 7.12 (Imputations in the National Income and Product Accounts) from Bureau of Economic Analysis, available at https://apps.bea.gov/iTable/index_nipa.cfm; Board of Governors of the Federal Reserve System, "Households; Owner-Occupied Real Estate Including Vacant Land and Mobile Homes at Market Value" (HOOREVLMHMV), retrieved from FRED, Federal Reserve Bank of St. Louis; Board of Governors of the Federal Reserve System, "Households and Nonprofit Organizations; Home Mortgages; Liability, Level" (HHMSDODNS), retrieved from FRED, Federal Reserve Bank of St. Louis.

difference should approximately equal expected inflation. We do not have market estimates of expected inflation before TIPS bonds, but the relationship follows values that appear reasonable. Before the inflationary period that began in the late 1960s, and coming out of the 1980s, implied inflation expectations were reasonable: below 2% in the 1950s and falling back to about 2% in the decade after 2000, in line with movements in inflation and expected inflation at the time.

Here, again, we see that it is the period since 2006 that demonstrates a clear deviation from reasonable valuations. In fact, since 2010, the real housing yield has been higher than the nominal effective aggregate mortgage rate, implying deflation. In other words, the average leveraged homebuyer today would have a solid return on investment even if homes never appreciate another dollar. This is not reflective of general inflation, which continues to be low but positive, and it is certainly not true of rent inflation, which has been running above 3% during the recovery from the recession.

The stark difference between the data and the general consensus about the housing boom and bust should not be understated here. In the period that has been commonly described as a bubble, there is no signature of excess at all. Mortgage rates, housing yields, and implied inflation in 2005 were all similar to levels from the late 1940s and early 1950s, which were also years where both real rates and inflation were low. The average leveraged homeowner required 2% annual rent inflation to break even on his or her home at given aggregate-level interest rates and home prices. The rent inflation required to justify prices had actually been declining for some years when the boom peaked.

And, on the flip side, in the period since 2006 these measures have taken a sharp turn from levels that would imply efficiency. Since then, housing yields have been far too high (meaning prices have been too low).

A SIMPLE GORDON GROWTH MODEL OF HOME PRICES ACROSS METROPOLITAN STATISTICAL AREAS

The basic relationships in yields explained in the previous section can be applied at the metropolitan level. Because some cities have developed obstructions to housing supply, rent inflation specific to each metropolitan area has become an important determinant of price. Using a simple valuation formula, we can estimate the amount of rent inflation required to justify rising prices in each city.[7]

I believe that this is similar to other models of home prices, such as the model put forth by Charles Himmelberg, Christopher Mayer, and Todd Sinai, who come to some of the same conclusions that I will with my version of the model.[8] However, I will account for the finding of Edward L. Glaeser, Joshua D. Gottlieb, and Joseph Gyourko that home values have not been as sensitive to long-term real interest rates as we might expect a very long-term asset to be.[9] I will do this by making sensitivity to real risk-free rates only 40% of the full rate movement, which I have denoted with the constant C:[10]

$$Home\ Price = \frac{Rent}{C \times Discount\ Rate + Property\ Tax\ Rate - Growth\ Rate}.$$

Thus, we can construct a basic expectation about home prices in a metropolitan area with just four inputs:

1. *Rent*. This, after expenses, is the cash flow for a home.[11]

2. *Discount rate*. The discount rate is set in the model to equal the estimated 30-year real risk-free rate in 1995.[12] Then changes in the discount rate after 1995 are equal to 40% of the change in the 30-year real risk-free rate.

3. *Property tax rate*. The median property tax rate for each city.[13]

4. *Expected excess rent inflation*. In a city with persistent rent inflation attributable to Closed Access housing policies, expected future changes in rents will be expressed as a growth rate in the values of homes. Remember, homes are real assets, which we are discounting with real bonds, so the growth in expected rent inflation is only the rate of rent inflation above general non-shelter CPI inflation.

Since we have good estimates of price, rents, property tax rates, and real risk-free rates, we can treat expected rent inflation (the "growth rate" in our model) as a dependent variable in the valuation model and consider whether the expected future rent inflation is reasonable, given what we know about housing in each city.

This, then, becomes a test of irrational exuberance. In effect, if home prices were too high, it would, mathematically, be because growth expectations were too high. This is a better measurement of demand-side excess than surveys of expectations about home prices, for two reasons. First, this is based on market prices—the marginal buyer and seller—which are more informative than survey information. Second, framing the market in terms of expected price appreciation mixes up general inflation, local rent inflation, changing interest rates, local neighborhood trends, and so on. The results of this model provide clear information about the expectations required to justify given prices.

CASE-SHILLER AND CPI DATA

One way to compare relative metropolitan home prices is to use the Case-Shiller price index in each city as a proxy for price,[14] the consumer price index for owners' equivalent rent in each city as a proxy for rent, and the discount rate described above. These data are available for all the Closed Access cities, for Atlanta (an Open Access city), and for several other cities, plus for the US as a whole.

Since the price and rent proxies here are indices, not absolute measures, we need to normalize them to reflect absolute prices. Fortunately, the period that seems to be characterized by these Closed Access problems began in about 1995. This year appears to work well as a target date for normalizing measures. Figure A-5 shows how rents changed in each metropolitan statistical area (MSA) compared to non-shelter consumer prices. In other words, if national non-shelter consumer prices increased by 2% and rent in a city increased by 3%, then the measure for that city would rise from 1.00 to about 1.01 for that year, because rents there increased by 1% more than non-shelter prices.

There had been a period in the late 1970s and early 1980s when Closed Access cities experienced rent inflation. But this had subsided by the late 1980s. So, by

Figure A-5. Rent Change Compared to Change in Non-shelter Prices

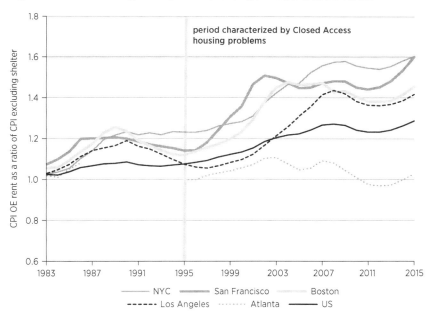

Note: CPI excluding shelter also excludes food and energy.
Source: Bureau of Labor Statistics. For example, Boston ratios are from "Consumer Price Index for All Urban Consumers: Owners' Equivalent Rent of Residences in Boston–Cambridge–Newton, MA–NH (CBSA)" (CUURA103SEHC) and "Consumer Price Index for All Urban Consumers: All Items Less Food, Shelter and Energy" (CUSR0000SA0L12E), retrieved from FRED, Federal Reserve Bank of St. Louis.

1995, all cities had either low rent levels or flat or falling trends in relative rent inflation that had been persistent for at least five years. As a first approximation, we can set the model for all cities so that *Growth Rate* (the expected excess rent inflation) in 1995 is assumed to be zero. Using these proxies, the model for each city *i* over time *t* will be[15]

$$Case\text{-}Shiller\ Index(i,t) =$$
$$\frac{CPI\ Owners'\ Equivalent\ Rent(i,t) \times Constant(i)}{0.4 \times 30\text{-}Year\ TIPS\ Yield(t) + 2.5\% + Property\ Tax\ Rate - Growth\ Rate(i,t)}$$

Solving for *Growth Rate*,

$$Growth\ Rate(i,t) = 0.4 \times 30\text{-}Year\ TIPS\ Yield(t) + 2.5\% + Property\ Tax\ Rate$$
$$- \frac{CPI\ Owners'\ Equivalent\ Rent(i,t) \times Constant(i)}{Case\text{-}Shiller\ Index(i,t)}$$

For each MSA, *Constant(i)* will be set so that the expected *Growth Rate* in 1995 is zero.

EXPECTED RENT INFLATION VS. ACTUAL RENT INFLATION

Figure A-6 shows the excess annual rent inflation in several cities. As outrageous as home prices had become in some cities, they required a relatively low expectation of excess rent. That is because much of the rise in prices comes from past rent increases that make homes in Closed Access cities expensive both to rent and to own.[16] Also, when real long-term interest rates reached the low levels of 2003 and after, small shifts in rent inflation expectations had a more powerful effect on prices.

On a year-to-year basis, rent inflation expectations tend to reflect trends in actual rent inflation. When rent inflation was very high in San Francisco and Boston in the late 1990s until about 2002, prices there implied the highest future rent expectations. Then rents in Los Angeles began to outpace rents in the other cities, and home prices in Los Angeles also began to reflect higher rent expectations.

We see the same pattern in the Open Access city included here—Atlanta—and in the broader national US measure. There are two humps in rent inflation, generally across cities, followed by dislocation after 2007. But, in Atlanta and most of the rest of the US, excess rent inflation and expected future rent inflation never strayed far from zero for long.

In the following analysis, I will use 2005 as the reference year to estimate the peak in expected rent inflation (the model's growth rate).

Figure A-6. Excess Rent Inflation, by Metro Area

Note: Excess rent inflation is annual change in the ratio of the MSA owner-equivalent rent price index over the US consumer price index for all items less food, shelter, and energy.
Source: Bureau of Labor Statistics. For example, Boston ratios are from "Consumer Price Index for All Urban Consumers: Owners' Equivalent Rent of Residences in Boston–Cambridge–Newton, MA–NH (CBSA)" (CUURA103SEHC) and "Consumer Price Index for All Urban Consumers: All Items Less Food, Shelter and Energy" (CUSR0000SA0L12E), retrieved from FRED, Federal Reserve Bank of St. Louis.

THE GROWTH RATE: EXPECTED RENT INFLATION PLUS PRICE/RENT POSITIVE FEEDBACK

As I discussed in chapter 4, there is a systematic relationship, both nationally and within metropolitan areas, between price and the price/rent ratio. For each doubling of home prices, price/rent ratios increase by about three (say, from 10× to 13×).[17] This could reflect income tax benefits less depreciation expense on lot value versus home value, or it could reflect some other factors. In any event, the relationship is universal across cities. So, if real prices double in a city, then we should expect the price/rent ratio to increase by about three even if there is no expectation of future rent inflation.

In the model, I apply this effect to all real growth in home prices, whether from excess rent inflation, from declining interest rates, or from rent expectations. The unexplained portion of the price that remains after accounting for this effect is the portion I attribute to expected rent inflation.

As discussed in chapter 4, this effect only applies up to a certain price level, above which level price/rent levels do not continue to rise. In the Closed Access cities, where a substantial portion of the market had reached the peak price/

rent level, and in Miami, where portions of the high-tier markets had reached the peak, this effect is reduced in the model to account for that situation. For instance, in San Francisco, I estimate that this effect only increased the aggregate price/rent level by about 1× for each doubling in prices. In the most expensive cities, rising prices did mostly reflect rent expectations.

THE SCALE OF EACH FACTOR IN CHANGING HOME PRICES

We can use this model to compare home prices and rents between MSAs, and to note the portion of the home price that may be attributable to each factor. This can give us a sense of the scale of each factor in explaining changing home prices.

To help visualize the scale of the factors, the following graphs show the stacked effect of each factor on a city's relative home price, over time. The first measure will be the US CPI for all items less food, energy, and shelter—basically, core CPI without rent. The next measure will be the estimated additional rise in home prices that I attribute to changing interest rates. Moving up, the next measure will be the city's measure of owners' equivalent rent CPI. This will give a sense of by how much rising rents in a city have outpaced other prices. The next measure (which I have rendered only as a point at 2005) will be an estimate of the price/rent effect described in chapter 4. Finally, the last measure will be the actual home price indexed to 100 in 1995. If the actual price is higher than the price predicted by the other factors, then excess rent inflation will be necessary to justify the price. This is the portion of the home price that might also be attributed to irrational behavior, excess demand, and so on. The question, as I frame it here, is as follows: What expected growth in rent is needed to justify the price, and is that level of growth reasonable for the city in question?

I will use the national measure as an example of how to read these tables. For the US, home values rose an average of 112%. Of that number, 18% is attributable to general non-shelter inflation, 21% is attributable to changing real interest rates, 14% is attributable to excess rent inflation above general inflation, and 20% is attributable to the systematic rise in price/rent levels described in chapter 4. This explains all but 8% of the rise in home prices. The remaining 8% rise in home prices implies that expected future excess rent inflation would average 0.3% per year.

Since excess rent inflation for the previous decade had averaged more than 1% per year, this expectation would not be unreasonable. Some selected cities follow (figures A-7, A-8, and A-9), using this same method of estimating the expected future rent inflation and comparing it to past experience.

There are 16 cities with both CPI data and Case-Shiller price indices covering this period, plus the US average. The other Closed Access and Open Access cities have patterns similar to those shown in the figures.

Figure A-7. Home Price Factors in the US (Aggregate)

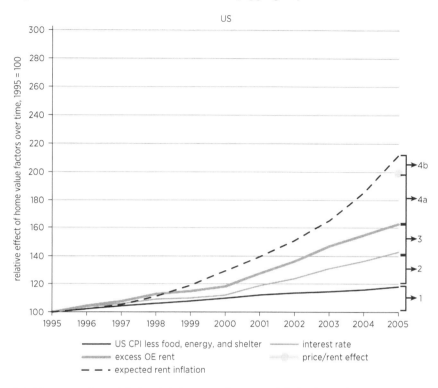

Note: The perpetual future inflation rate is the expected excess rent inflation that would be required, in perpetuity, to justify the home price in the model. Alternatively, one could assume a 20-year period of excess rent inflation, followed perpetually by zero inflation. For cities with the highest rent expectations, the 20 years of rent inflation required to justify 2005 home prices would be roughly double the given perpetual rate of rent inflation.

Total appreciation, 1995–2005	$1.18 \times 1.21 \times 1.14 \times 1.20 \times 1.08 - 1 = 112\%$
Median property tax rate	1.0%

Price appreciation from 1995 to 2005 attributable to each factor:

1: Core inflation minus shelter	18.0%
2: Changing real interest rates	21.0%
3: Past excess rent inflation	14.0%
4a: Price/rent effect	20.0%
4b: Expected future rent inflation	8.0%

Annualized inflation rates:

1995–2005 excess rent inflation	1.3%
2000–2005 excess rent inflation	1.5%
Implied perpetual future inflation	0.3%

Unfortunately, all of these data aren't available for this time frame for Las Vegas or Phoenix. But we do have data for Tampa, Florida, and for Miami, both of which I include with Phoenix and Las Vegas in the category of Contagion cities. If there were any cities where we would expect home prices to exceed rea-

Figure A-8. Home Price Factors in Atlanta (Example of an Open Access City)

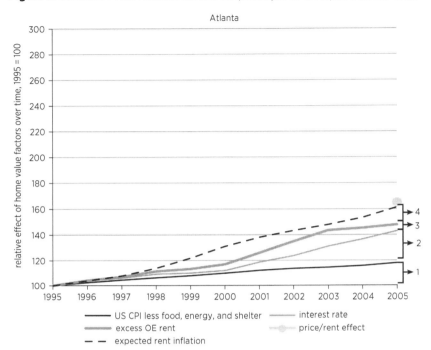

Note: The perpetual future inflation rate is the expected excess rent inflation that would be required, in perpetuity, to justify the home price in the model. Alternatively, one could assume a 20-year period of excess rent inflation, followed perpetually by zero inflation. For cities with the highest rent expectations, the 20 years of rent inflation required to justify 2005 home prices would be roughly double the given perpetual rate of rent inflation.

Total appreciation, 1995–2005	61.0%
Median property tax rate	1.0%

Price appreciation from 1995 to 2005 attributable to each factor:

1: Core inflation minus shelter	18.0%
2: Changing real interest rates	21.0%
3: Past excess rent inflation	3.0%
4a: Price/rent effect	11.0%
4b: Expected future rent inflation	−2.0%

Annualized inflation rates:

1995–2005 excess rent inflation	0.3%
2000–2005 excess rent inflation	−0.2%
Implied perpetual future inflation	−0.1%

sonable expectations, it would be these. Yet even in Miami and Tampa, where we definitely see sharply rising prices late in the boom, those price increases are related to rising rents, related rent expectations, low interest rates, and the systematic rise in price/rent ratios that those changes triggered. Miami home

Figure A-9. Home Price Factors in San Francisco (Example of a Closed Access City)

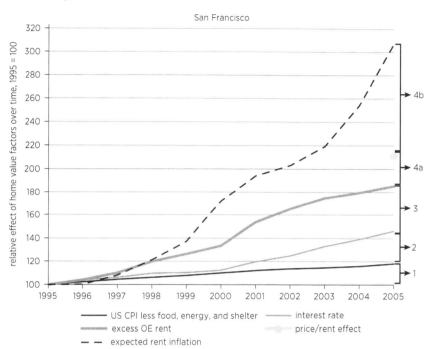

Note: The perpetual future inflation rate is the expected excess rent inflation that would be required, in perpetuity, to justify the home price in the model. Alternatively, one could assume a 20-year period of excess rent inflation, followed perpetually by zero inflation. For cities with the highest rent expectations, the 20 years of rent inflation required to justify 2005 home prices would be roughly double the given perpetual rate of rent inflation.

Total appreciation, 1995–2005	207.0%
Median property tax rate	0.5%

Price appreciation from 1995 to 2005 attributable to each factor:

1: Core inflation minus shelter	18.0%
2: Changing real interest rates	24.0%
3: Excess rent inflation	27.0%
4a: Price/rent effect	13.0%
4b: Expected future rent inflation	47.0%

Annualized inflation rates:

1995–2005 excess rent inflation	2.4%
2000–2005 excess rent inflation	1.3%
Implied perpetual future inflation	1.2%

prices imply perpetual excess rent inflation of 0.8%, and five-year and ten-year average excess rent inflation had been 2.7% and 1.6%. In Tampa, implied expected rent inflation was 0.4% and past five-year and ten-year average excess rent inflation had been 2.0% and 1.4%. It might be the case that Florida should more accurately be thought of as a mixture of Contagion and Closed Access factors. In-migration was less pronounced there during the bubble, and parts of Florida seem to have more limits to building than the Western cities do. Using this same method, Phoenix and Las Vegas are more likely to have approached values in 2005 that were not justified by past rent inflation.

Expectations of future rent increases within each city were strongly related to persistent rent behavior in that city. Figure A-10 compares five- and ten-year trailing annual excess rent inflation (2000–2005 and 1995–2005) in each city to the perpetual future excess rent inflation that would be required to justify home prices in 2005.

These relationships have the signature of reasonable values. Future inflation expectations didn't rise to match recent-past rent inflation.[18] They rose to less than one-fifth of the excess rent inflation of the past five years. In other words, for each 1% of annual excess inflation in a city from 2000 to 2005, home prices in that city rose enough that future excess inflation of about 0.19% was necessary to justify those prices.

As excess rent inflation persists, expectations of future rent inflation firm up, so future rent inflation expectations climbed to about one-third of the excess

Figure A-10. Past Rent Inflation vs. 2005 Rent Expectations

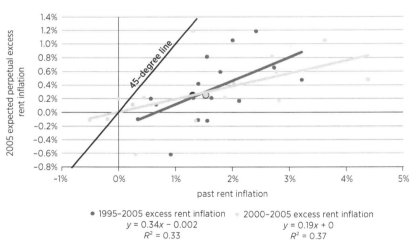

Note: The large, darker dots are the data points for the US aggregate.
Sources: Author's calculations. Past excess rent inflation is based on metropolitan statistical area owners' equivalent rent CPI relative to US CPI for all items less food, energy, and shelter, for the periods given. Expected perpetual rent inflation is the excess rent inflation that would be required in the future to justify the average metropolitan statistical area home price at a given point in time, on the basis of the model described above.

Figure A-11. Past Rent Inflation vs. 2005 and 2014 Rent Expectations

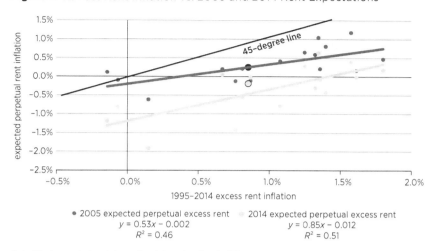

Note: The large, darker dots are the data points for the US aggregate.
Sources: Author's calculations. Past excess rent inflation is based on metropolitan statistical area owners' equivalent rent CPI relative to US CPI for all items less food, energy, and shelter, for the periods given. Expected perpetual rent inflation is the excess rent inflation that would be required in the future to justify the average metropolitan statistical area home price at a given point in time, on the basis of the model described above.

rent inflation that had persisted for a decade. For each 1% of annual excess inflation from 1995 to 2005, home prices in the typical city required future excess rent inflation of 0.34%.

Figure A-11 shows the relationship between rents of the previous 19 years and rent expectations in both 2005 and 2014. A rate of 1% average annual excess rent inflation in a city from 1995 to 2014 is associated with an expected perpetual excess rent inflation in 2005 of 0.53%. The relationship is even stronger in 2014. By 2014, for each 1% of past excess inflation, 0.85% of future excess inflation is expected. But prices in all cities have been brought down so much because of tight credit markets that most cities don't require excess rent inflation at all in order to justify prices, and homes in cities that have not had excess rent inflation could earn reasonable returns even with significant future rent deflation.[19]

Now, it is possible, of course, to tweak the model—to raise or lower the risk premium, or to change the sensitivity to real interest rates. This tends to raise or lower the implied future rent inflation rate across all cities, but doesn't change the strength or slope of the relationship very much. In all cases, whether the risk premium is high or low, or whether sensitivity to real interest rates is high or low, there tends to be a correlation of expected future rent that is about one-third of the rent inflation of the past five years, one-half of the past ten years, and three-quarters of the past nineteen years.[20]

Furthermore, remember that the model is calibrated to 1995, when prices were low. So it is difficult to argue, using this model, that prices in individual metropolitan areas were overpriced in 2005. They appear to have reacted to rent inflation systematically. It is possible to argue that home prices throughout the country were overpriced in 2005, but to do that, one would need to claim either that homes had been just as overpriced in 1995, that home prices have zero sensitivity to interest rates, or that the positive feedback effect I have found in price/rent ratios is not applicable. But none of those factors creates a substantial change in the relationship between past rent inflation and expected future rent inflation.

I think it is interesting to compare the rent inflation from 1995 to 2005 to the rent inflation from 2000 to 2005. Notice how national excess rent inflation was slightly higher in the later period, but also notice that mostly what we see is a stretching-out of the variance between Closed Access cities and Open Access cities. This is the inevitable outcome of economic expansion when the most economically dynamic cities have Closed Access policies. This increased variance in rent inflation was caused by economic growth. Increasing rents in the Closed Access cities were a product of demand from households in their capacity as tenants. At the high point of credit and homebuilding expansion, in the 2000–20005 period, credit and homebuilding markets were having the effect we would expect them to have where they can actually create activity—they were pulling rents down in the Open Access cities. So, during that time, rent inflation increased in Closed Access cities and decreased in Open Access cities. Expanding credit markets were *pulling down* housing costs where supply was elastic.

Economic growth, itself, will inevitably cause rents to rise (and thus home prices to rise) in the Closed Access cities. Economic rents from Closed Access policies are the source of those housing rents. Since growth in mortgage credit tends to rise and fall coincidentally with economic growth, it will inevitably take the blame for this.

The housing bubble was a supply deprivation bubble, and it was conveyed more through rising rents than through loose credit. Overactive credit markets were the effect, not the cause. It was Closed Access housing policies that were forcing homeowners to be speculators on future rent increases in their home cities. And homeowners were bidding those homes up to prices tentatively reflecting those rising rents.[21]

THE INFLUENCE OF CREDIT AND INTEREST RATES ON HOME PRICES

Many studies of the various influences on home prices find various levels of support for changing credit standards, real interest rates, and inflation.[22] But, clearly, a lack of supply is a necessary precondition for any of these forces to raise prices. Prices are proportionately sensitive to rising rents. Rising rents require both a lack of supply and a sustainable local source of elevated incomes.

It is possible that the lack-of-supply response makes Closed Access real estate more sensitive to declining real interest rates, so that real interest rates are a key reason for rising prices, which might explain why prices tend to be high in some cities, both in the US and internationally, even when cities provide a moderate amount of new supply, but not enough to lower rents.

It is possible that loosening credit markets could increase demand for housing by allowing some households to increase their housing consumption. This would lead to rising rents in supply-constrained markets. It is true that during the housing boom, rents seem to have diverged between Closed Access and Open Access cities. But, as the housing boom proceeded, it appears that rent inflation, in general, was moderating across cities (figure A-6). Rent inflation, aggregated nationally, was moderating during the boom. So it appears that in the US, the effect of new credit to expand housing supply in the Open Access areas was more powerful than the effect of new credit on Closed Access housing demand and rent inflation. The high-cost refugees flooding out of the Closed Access cities in 2004 and 2005 would be influenced by both (1) the problem of high costs in their cities and (2) the opportunity of lower costs in other cities. Mortgage lending standards have tightened in the decade since, and migration flows have slowed. And rent inflation has returned.

In the end, though, however we model these various effects, they all correlate strongly with supply. Supply weakens all of these effects. Would we be better served by figuring out whether foreign investors, low interest rates, or loose credit standards cause supply-constrained home prices to rise? Or would we be better served by solving the supply problem that is the root cause of rising prices, regardless of which of these factors might facilitate them?

What if we determined that, without a doubt, credit access or foreign savings or low interest rates can be statistically fingered as the cause of rising prices? That is only true for Closed Access cities or cities that were overwhelmed by Closed Access refugees. It's not true for Dallas or Atlanta or a hundred other regional centers where credit was flowing. Their prices were within long-term ranges.

Is the answer to constrain borrowing access or nominal economic activity in the two-thirds of the country that has a functional housing market so that the dysfunctional cities are relieved of volatility? That seems wrong. But that is, unfortunately, the path we seem to have chosen.

HOW MIGRATION PATTERNS FEED SEEMINGLY EXCESSIVE PRICES

One measure of home affordability that has generally seemed dependable in the past has been the ratio of the median home price to median income. This has always moved within a relatively narrow range, until home prices shot up in the decade after 2000. It seems only reasonable that this would be a measure of sustainability. If prices move far outside the typical price/income range, it seems as if houses must be priced above the level that households can continue to support.

Price/income levels tend to run around two to three times income in Open Access cities, but since households in Closed Access cities spend more of their incomes on rent, and since they expect those rents to continue to rise, they tend to spend more than four times their income on homes, an amount that has risen to more like eight to nine times their income during and after the boom.

But there is an apparent incongruity here. If the median Closed Access household is already spending 35%, 40%, or more of its income on rent, how can rent inflation be expected to continue to rise at a rate 2%–3% above that of general inflation? Maybe this is the source of irrational exuberance. If rent inflation continues, then eventually the median Closed Access household will be spending 60%, 70%, 100% of its income on rent. It's unsustainable.

This is where the migration patterns come into play. There is a significant circular flow of households into and out of the Closed Access cities. When rents rise, they eventually do become unsustainable, typically for a household at the bottom of the income distribution. Since these cities have sustainable sources of employment opportunities, when rents hit unsustainable levels, they don't stop. They simply trigger this migration, and a housing unit trades up to a new household with higher income after the previous tenants leave the city.

This migration pattern is palpable in the newspapers in places like San Francisco. Local activists blame the in-migrating households, which sort of misses the point—even while the activists' experiences and frustrations cannot be denied. Closed Access policies inevitably lead to anger, public clashes, and factionalism.

So rents continue to march higher, not because the existing households continue to pay unsustainable rents, but because new households move in, push the median income of the city up, and thus raise the ceiling on potential rents.

And, because prices can be incredible conveyors of information, the prices of houses bear the inevitable bad news. Those rising rents mean that your city eventually isn't going to have room for you any more. You may not know it, but the price of your house knows it. So the prices of houses in Dallas and San Francisco both continue to reflect long-standing patterns in the price/income ratios of the median homes and the median households that will live there. The thing that makes San Francisco different is that the city is committed to making sure that the household that lives there now will not be the household that lives there in the future. The house in question will someday fetch the rents that a new household can afford, but the current tenant can't. Owning a house means paying the present value today of all those future imputed rents that the high-income tenants of the future will be willing to pay.

The reason more demand doesn't cause prices to rise in Dallas is because, in an Open Access city, high-income households tend to be the households that create new housing stock. So, in most cities, today's upper-middle-class housing stock becomes tomorrow's middle-class housing stock, and eventually maybe lower-middle-class housing stock. Practically every city has neighborhoods where there are mostly working-class households and a few remaining retirees who still live in the houses they bought when the neighborhood was full of accountants and salesmen. But the Closed Access cities have reversed this pattern. Since new housing is so limited, now high-income households move into old neighborhoods.

THE DESTABILIZING COMBINATION OF LOW RATES AND GROWTH EXPECTATIONS

Another factor that pushes Closed Access prices up is the inverse relationship between yield and price.

Low rates and growth are a dangerous combination. As the denominator in the valuation model used above approaches zero, price approaches infinity. Since price and yield are inversely proportional, the price/rent ratio can become wildly volatile while the yield (rent/price) appears to follow along within long-term ranges. In addition, California has relatively low property taxes, a situation that also leads to pretax yields that are lower. In fact, applying valuation models like the model I used above to the various cities, low property taxes can explain much of the difference in prices between California and Texas. A 1% difference in property taxes should have the same effect on price/rent ratios as an expectation of 1% rent inflation. Property tax rates didn't necessarily change much during the boom, but they had more of an effect on price as rent inflation and falling discount rates reduced net yields. Because of the inverse relationship between price and yield, an expectation of 1% excess rent inflation or 1% lower property taxes has less of an effect on prices when housing yields are at 4.50% than it does when housing yields are at 3.25%.

FALSIFIABILITY

In the end, while many of the models and methods I use here are, individually, simple, they form a dense web of interconnected explanations. They must form some body of results that appears reasonable, given my hypothesis. If I attribute high prices in the Closed Access cities to high rents and high rent expectations, there is a range of mathematical relationships that I must confirm in order for my hypothesis to remain viable. If prices were actually double or triple what I might estimate with standard models of valuation, then my hypothesis has little credibility.

The demand-side explanation is typically a behavioral finance explanation. Prices were in a bubble. They were unsustainable, because they were higher than reasonable buyers would be able to justify. Irrational exuberance.

There is a problem with these behavioral explanations. Once you plug irrationality into your model, scale goes out the window. Scale imposes discipline on our explanations.

Ask yourself a question. Is there any level of home prices that would have given you pause regarding a demand-side explanation, where you would have said, "Hmm. At this point, irrationality or bubble behavior probably can't explain this anymore"? If the average home price had risen to $500,000, or $1 million, or $2 million, would you have decided that the scale had outgrown the ability of behavioral explanations to explain it? It appears to me that what happened was that the higher prices went, the more convinced everyone was of the bubble story. Now there's a model, huh? Can irrationality have confidence bands?

BLAMING CREDIT IS COSTLY FOR LOW- AND MIDDLE-INCOME HOUSEHOLDS

Following the intuition that blames rising prices on irrational buyers is especially corrosive because homes in low-priced neighborhoods can provide very high returns for owner-occupiers. As shown in figure A-12, the returns as a percentage of market price, before taxes and costs, for low-priced homes are much higher than the returns for high-priced homes. Some of that difference isn't captured by low-income owners because they are not able to take advantage of many of the tax benefits, but clearly the return on investment for low-tier homeowners is quite high.

Another problem is that much attention concerning the housing bubble and homeownership in general has been focused on price appreciation. This has been averred as the primary motivation for homebuyers when prices were rising. But price appreciation is probably the third-most-important source of financial gain for homeowners. The most important source is rental income.

Figure A-12. Gross Returns to Housing

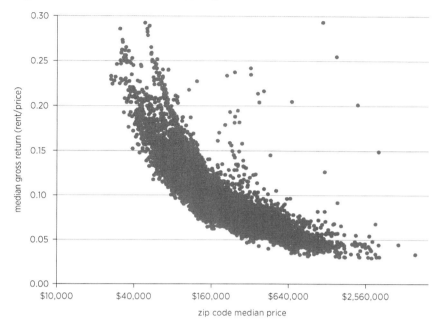

Note: These data are from March 2016. Data include 13,271 zip codes, from median price and price/rent measures.
Source: Zillow data, http://www.zillow.com/research/data/.

For owner-occupiers, the combined net rental income (after costs) plus price appreciation should generally be similar to the cost of renting the same unit to a tenant. A renter doesn't avoid the capital cost of homeownership. The renter simply has a landlord as an intermediary for those costs. There is no reason to equate ownership with higher costs. In fact, in today's market, many tenants would dramatically cut their monthly expenses if they could purchase their homes using new mortgages. For homeowners, income comes from the rent one pays to oneself. In a recent working paper that quantified returns on a range of assets, Òscar Jordà and coauthors find that over a broad historical and international sample, returns to homeownership are similar to returns on corporate stocks, but with less risk.[23]

One common complaint about low–down payment mortgages is that they create homeowners in name only. These "owners" have no capital on the line, so they are really just tenants with a call option on speculative gains in home prices. But there is an additional gain that would be especially valuable to owners of low-priced homes. That is the value of control. Some of that value is nonmonetary. It is the ability to maintain the unit to one's own liking, and also to maintain it more optimally for long-term value. These benefits do not necessarily show up in an annual profit-and-loss estimate for a given home, but they are important.

But, more relevant to the point, there is a monetary gain to owner-occupiers, especially at the low end of the market. One of the costs to landlords is the risk of having bad tenants. Rents must be high enough to account for the costs of dealing with bad tenants and the risks of not being able to predict the character of tenants. Owner-occupiers can pocket the portion of the rent that accounts for those costs and risks. Additionally, the natural alignment of incentives for an owner-occupier will typically lead to more optimal usage and management of the unit. These costs tend to be higher in neighborhoods with lower rents, so there are more potential gains available to low-end owner-occupiers.

The concern about the owners-in-name-only is that they were paying, say, 7% in mortgage payments plus planning to capture some optimistic annual gain in price appreciation, instead of spending, say, 5% of the home's value in rent. But annual rent in many homes is more than 10% of the home's value. Factoring in the relatively low price/rent ratio of homes in low-priced neighborhoods and the control-to-risk premium that owner-occupiers can pocket, those who are able to secure financing are likely to pocket gains over renting even without counting on price appreciation. That is certainly true in a lot of places in 2016. It might have been true in fewer places in 2005, but it would still have been in effect in the lower-priced zip codes of most cities.

In general, the gains of ownership for responsible households in low-income categories are higher than for responsible households in high-income categories. The misidentification of the housing boom with reckless low-end mortgages has removed this source of de facto income equalization. In housing markets with generous supply and generous credit, the market is rigged *in favor* of low-tier homeowners. They naturally earn much higher returns on their investments in neighborhoods where annual rent is 15% of a home's market price than wealthy homeowners earn in neighborhoods where rent is only 5% of the market price.

It is unfortunately common to see economists discuss homeownership as if homes that don't gain value over time are bad investments. This is horribly naïve. If you buy a 10-year bond for $100, and then in 10 years you receive the $100 back, that doesn't mean the bond was a bad investment. It tells you nothing about the return on the investment. Homes are no different. There are homes across the Rust Belt that will provide excellent returns for their owners even if they never appreciate by a penny.

NOTES

INTRODUCTION

1. A thoughtful response to this argument might be that excessive credit and money were allowing buyers to buy homes that were larger, increasing demand along with supply, so that rent inflation might still rise even as new homes were being built. But rent inflation on rented units has been rising even more sharply than rent on owned units, where we would expect credit to fuel demand.

2. Manufactured homes traditionally have been more popular in rural areas, especially in the South. Less complicated regulatory restrictions in rural areas are clearly one reason for this, but there appear to be many reasons for differences in popularity over geographic areas and over time. The rise of manufactured home shipments in the 1990s was related to financing options that became unstable. Since then, in all areas, including the South, deliveries have collapsed. In all areas, placements have declined by 75% or more since the early 1980s.

3. Additionally, since home values above cost naturally accrue to the value of the land, as local supply constraints drove home prices to well above replacement cost, the number of tear-downs increased. Richard Peach of the New York Federal Reserve told the Federal Open Market Committee in June 2005, "Now, I haven't done this in the most scientific way, but if you just take periodic estimates of the stock of housing, whether from the Census or from the American Housing Survey, and try to line up changes in the stock with new production, it appears that we're in a period when a lot of destruction of old housing is taking place. As you mentioned, the average estimate on tear-downs is 300,000, but I've seen estimates as high as 700,000 units." Transcript of Federal Open Market Committee meeting, Board of Governors of the Federal Reserve System, June 29–30, 2005, Washington, DC, https://www.federalreserve.gov/monetarypolicy/files/FOMC20050630meeting.pdf. This would also cause the measure of housing starts to overstate the net growth rate of the housing stock.

CHAPTER 1

1. As of 2017, it would take about four million additional homes to match the number of homes per adult that the US had in 2006, and about six million additional homes to match the number of homes per adult in 1991. One might make an argument that changing cultural or demographic factors would have led to a natural reduction in housing units. The rise in the number of units during the 1980s is related to changing norms about family composition, rising divorce rates, single-parent families, etc.

   There isn't an obvious reason for there to have been a reversal since 1990. In fact, currently there is a demographic bulge of baby boomers in their 50s and 60s, millennials in their 20s, and more healthy retirees living in single-family units. If anything, these age groups might lead to a rise in the number of units per capita. But certainly since 2006, the overwhelming factor has been economic upheaval and the collapse in mortgage availability.

   There is a well-known demographic predicament on the horizon: the time is coming when there will be many older, retired households and fewer workers. When that time comes, there will be many more consumers than producers. This problem cannot be easily solved by saving, because much consumption is produced in the same period that it is consumed. No matter how much is saved in preparation for that time, there will still be pressure to consume the output of the dwindling number of active workers.

   Housing provides one avenue for smoothing production on a large scale. Housing is almost pure capital. Very little of it is consumed in the same period that it is produced. If more housing is produced in earlier periods, where there are still abundant workers, this frees up labor to produce other, less durable goods and services when workers are more scarce. In fact, the inducement of capital into housing when workers are nearing retirement and there is downward pressure on interest rates may be a natural, emergent form of this production smoothing.

One might even go so far as to suggest that a household that today builds a vacation home or a second home is indirectly fending off this coming predicament by building a home today that may become a primary residence in the future, freeing up capital and labor in that future time for more immediate consumption needs.

The imposition of a housing bust for this past decade has prevented this sort of production smoothing from happening. But even without the bust, the existence of the Closed Access housing problem also prevents this production smoothing. Closed Access residents frequently complain about out-of-town homebuyers who buy precious Closed Access units and leave them standing empty. In other cities, this is not a problem. But in Closed Access cities, this becomes a claim on a limited resource. It becomes one more force excluding the households that would live in that city today, given the opportunity.

2. I generally limit my quantitative analysis to the 20 largest cities because they capture the bulk of the aggregate story. So there are some smaller cities that were noticeable parts of the housing bubble story that are not listed here because they were relatively small. Las Vegas would be a Contagion city, as well as some additional inland California and Florida cities. And many growing regional centers in the nation's interior are examples of Open Access cities.

3. Most of the cities fit easily into their group. Miami does not. On the basis of the statistics for each group, I include Miami in the Contagion group, but there do seem to be some obstacles to housing expansion there, and the importance of retirees and international migrants in the Miami market make the city a little more difficult to analyze quantitatively.

4. When I discuss "Dallas" throughout this book, I typically mean the Dallas–Fort Worth MSA.

5. Labor markets are analogous to housing markets. Employment tends to rise slowly, generally in line with population, but is prone to negative shocks. Imagine that the conversations about the labor market over the past decade had been similar to the conversation about the housing market. There would have been a consensus that the problem was that there were too many jobs in 2005 and that real wages were growing too fast. We would have watched unemployment shoot up to 10% without attempting to stabilize it because we would have considered that spike to be a correction following the period of excess. We would have begrudgingly started trying to stabilize the labor market only after the employment shock became so bad that wages began to fall sharply. And all the debates about what went wrong would focus on how we ended up with too many jobs in 2005. Were employers irrationally optimistic? Were investors naïve? Was the government too friendly to employers or workers? We would be arguing about how to fix those problems before they happen again, so we don't again end up with too many jobs.

6. Figure 1-1 in Gregory D. Morrow, "The Homeowner Revolution: Democracy, Land Use, and the Los Angeles Slow-Growth Movement, 1965–1992" (PhD diss., University of California at Los Angeles, 2013), 3.

7. Zillow data, http://www.zillow.com/research/data/, using price/income measure for metropolitan areas.

8. This is a conventional treatment of the subject of rent. Some of the data I use come from Zillow, where you can see Zillow's estimated rental value of your own home, even if you own it. Federal statistical agencies, such as the Bureau of Labor Statistics and the Bureau of Economic Analysis, also refer to the rental value of homes, whether they are rented or owned.

9. Edward L. Glaeser, Joshua D. Gottlieb, and Joseph Gyourko, "Can Cheap Credit Explain the Housing Boom?" (NBER Working Paper No. 16230, National Bureau of Economic Research, Cambridge, MA, July 2010).

10. Washington, DC, has high incomes and high rents. But rent is not high *relative to those high incomes*. In Washington, DC, *rent* is high because *incomes* are high. In Closed Access cities, housing constraints have become so severe that they feed high incomes. The ancient right of free people to move toward opportunity, moderating incomes and costs, is violated. In Closed Access cities, to some degree, *incomes* are high because *rents* are high.

11. This estimate is lower than some measures, probably because it is based on median measures. Price/rent estimates based on aggregate values or value-weighted averages tended

to increase more because price appreciation was strongest in homes with prices above the median price. This caused the mean value to rise more than the median value.

12. Notice how most of the outlier cities with very high rents and prices fall above the linear regression line, while the bulk of normal cities doesn't stray far from the proportional line.

13. This is not a pattern we would necessarily always see. As late as 2001, median price/income levels didn't differ that much across metro areas, even though there were large differences in median rent/income levels. This suggests that, where rents were high relative to local incomes, they were expected to decline back toward the norm. But by the peak of the boom in 2005, price/income levels for each metro area were positively correlated with rent/income levels, suggesting that during the decade after 2000, there was a regime shift, and now where rents were high they were expected to continue to rise.

    Between 2005 and 2017, mortgage markets, housing starts, sales, and homeownership all collapsed, yet the positive correlation remains. The collapse of the homebuyer market and the financial sector that facilitates it did tend to pull home prices down from their boom-level highs, but it did nothing to bring back expected mean reversion of rents.

14. Paolo Gelain, Kevin J. Lansing, and Gisle J. Natvik, "Explaining the Boom-Bust Cycle in the US Housing Market: A Reverse-Engineering Approach" (Working Paper 2015-02, Federal Reserve Bank of San Francisco, February 2018).

15. By real housing consumption, I mean the actual attributes of the home: size, location, amenities. This is different from the amount of money spent on housing. As an analogy, let's say the average person spends $3 each morning for a large coffee. Let's say that a drought causes a shortage of coffee beans, doubling the price of coffee. The person might now buy a medium coffee for $4. Because the medium coffee is smaller than the large, the person is reducing real consumption (drinking less coffee) even while increasing total spending.

16. This can be seen by comparing the expensive central city of most metropolitan areas to the suburban sections. Homes may have similar values in both areas, but housing units in the central area will tend to be smaller. To move to central areas with more amenities and location value, we intuitively understand the tradeoff we make between location and the material value of the space. This is why cities with only some of the characteristics of Closed Access cities—such as Seattle and Washington, DC—have tended to have persistently high rent inflation while rents and home values relative to incomes have remained closer to the national norm. In these cities, the problem is still manageable enough that households can react to rising rents by reducing their real housing consumption—moving to smaller units or to units in less-desirable locations. This does create some economic stress for households that live in these cities, and as households downsize to the edge of their range of comfort, nominal housing demand becomes somewhat less elastic. This phenomenon probably helped push home prices up more than usual in these semi–Closed Access cities during the bubble period, but not nearly to the same extent as in the true Closed Access cities.

    Median rents and home prices are rising in the Closed Access cities even after the location-amenities tradeoff has been made by local residents. This is one reason why these stresses are especially hard on low-income households. Such households have less room to adjust—for instance, by compromising on size, quality, or relative location within the metro area. Partly, what appears to have happened in Contagion cities such as Riverside, California, at the height of the bubble is that the housing price stresses in Closed Access cities became strong enough to push households so far out that the Contagion cities were increasingly acting as exurbs of the Closed Access cities and starting to take on the valuation characteristics of the Closed Access coastal housing market. Wes Woods II, "Inland Empire Residents Commute Outside the Region," *Redlands Daily Facts*, March 13, 2011.

17. This is just another way of stating what figure 1-8 shows: that in cities where rents have risen, prices have risen even higher. When viewing the pattern in terms of the price/rent ratio, it may be easier to see the systematic effect of rent on accelerating prices.

18. Todd Sinai and Nicholas S. Souleles, "Owner-Occupied Housing as a Hedge against Rent Risk," *Quarterly Journal of Economics* 120, no. 2 (May 2005): 763–89.

19.   Economic rents are profits gained above economic cost, usually because of ownership of a limited resource.

20.   Figure 2.1 in Robert J. Shiller, *The Subprime Solution: How Today's Global Financial Crisis Happened and What to Do about It* (Princeton, NJ: Princeton University Press, 2008), 33.

21.   I want to give great credit to Shiller et al. here, both for doing the difficult and essential work of developing these data, and for very generously making the data public for other researchers to utilize, improve upon, and critique.

22.   The data used in figures 1-10 and 1-11 are from Robert Shiller's web page, which he generously makes available for use by other researchers.
      The various home price indices referred to as "Case-Shiller" indices are now maintained and published by CoreLogic®, https://us.spindices.com/index-family/real-estate/sp-corelogic-case-shiller.

23.   One reason that high interest rates due to inflation may not have a strong effect on home prices is that high inflation has two contrasting effects. It limits access to credit because it increases monthly payments. But it also increases the value of homes as tax shelters. Also, in an environment of rising inflation, homes retain their real value compared to long-term fixed-rate bonds, which lose value as rates increase. For a discussion of these effects, and for an alternate measure of price/rent ratios that ran high during the late 1970s, see Monika Piazzesi and Martin Schneider, "Inflation and the Price of Real Assets" (Research Department Staff Report 423, Federal Reserve Bank of Minneapolis, April 2009).

24.   Intrinsic value is a term of art in finance. It refers to the value of an asset based on its expected income. The market price is our best guess at the intrinsic value of tradable assets. Much of financial analysis involves second-guessing the market price in order to earn trading gains. Referring to a market as a "bubble" is equivalent to saying that market prices have moved significantly above intrinsic values. An increase in prices because households are using cheap credit *might* lead to a bubble. By definition, an increase in prices because of rising intrinsic values would not be a bubble.
      Here it is important to think carefully about the difference between the rental value of a home and ownership of a home. Setting aside the physical form of the home itself, homeownership is like owning a bond, and the future rental value is like the coupon payments that would be made on the bond.

25.   I am using the concept of efficiency as it is used in finance. An efficient market is one where prices generally reflect known value and risks, and investors don't push prices to values that would provide predictably higher or lower returns than those known values and risks would call for. To refer to a market as a "bubble" is to imply an inefficient market, since a bubble market should provide predictable gains to those who expect the bubble to collapse.

26.   The nominal interest rate is the stated interest rate paid by the borrower. That rate is a combination of the expected rate of inflation and a real interest rate that would exist in the absence of inflation. If inflation is expected to be 2%, then the interest rate must be 2% higher than the real rate to account for the dwindling value of the future dollars that will repay the loan.

27.   This should be obvious, in any case, since many neighborhoods are full of households that have not remotely maxed out their credit access: prices in those neighborhoods do not perpetually rise until households have used up their credit.

28.   For about 15 years after World War II, homeownership rates increased with the help of New Deal financing programs. Spending on housing recovered from Depression-related declines. By the early 1960s, homeownership rates leveled out. Consumption of housing also leveled out, in terms of rental value. During the half century since then, total nominal spending on housing has been flat, at about 15% of personal consumption expenditures, with little deviation. This would, more or less, be the case whether the real housing stock were 20% larger than it is or 20% smaller. Housing is mostly sunk costs. The problem of Closed Access cities has generally meant that the real housing stock has been shrinking relative to other expenses. (Households in Closed Access cities have been moving into smaller homes with fewer amenities, relative to their rising incomes.)

Since aggregate spending on housing is mostly a product of income, real housing growth and housing inflation are like a seesaw. Over reasonable periods of time, all else being equal, if one goes up, then the other goes down. Because of the Closed Access problem, over the past couple of decades there have been barriers to increasing the real stock of housing, and so housing (rent) inflation has been high.

The idea that too many houses were built is deceptively incoherent. It seems coherent, because at very local levels, local shifts in incomes and population might cause overbuilding—leaving speculative neighborhoods with temporary vacancies, for instance. But at the aggregate level, if the housing boom had somehow increased the real housing stock to 20% above trend, people would have simply filled in that 20% larger stock while continuing to spend 15% of personal consumption expenditures on it. This isn't like spending on leisure activities, where people suddenly realize they don't have the income for trifles, and entertainers or chefs must shift to another line of work. The work has been done on the house. It is a nearly pure form of delayed consumption—capital. The house is ours, and the amount we will pay for it is largely a product of our nominal income. Our nominal income, in the end, is entirely a product of monetary policy. Regardless of the real production we create, our income is in the form of dollars, and the nominal total is entirely a function of the number of dollars we have decided to use to represent that real production. At the aggregate level, there is no reason to expect a rise in the real value of the stock of housing to revert down to some mean level. The housing that has been built is here, and it's ours to keep. And it appears that we are willing, in the aggregate, to spend 15% of our total personal expenditures on it.

One might respond that the market for new units is more volatile than the entire housing market, so small shifts in supply can lead to local economic volatility. This is true, and in some ways, one could describe what happened in the Contagion cities this way. But if this is what happened, a collapse in rents should have occurred in those cities as rates of new building started to decline. The opposite happened.

This effect is not symmetrical, however. Where supply is greatly constrained, nominal spending on housing is not stable. So, while it is difficult to build too much housing, it is possible to have too little. In cities where households are spending an uncomfortably large amount of their incomes on rent, they will respond to an expanded real stock of housing by reducing their nominal spending on housing. In other words, new supply will cause rent deflation, but households will not fully increase their real housing consumption (in size, location, and amenities) to compensate. They will allow their nominal spending on housing to decline to more comfortable levels. In other words, when supply has been constrained, demand for housing is inelastic.

Ironically, then, markets that were supposedly overbuilt would not tend to be susceptible to sharp declines in housing expenditures. Only in markets that were severely constrained, which need an increase in the housing stock to allow households to reduce their housing expenditures to comfortable levels, could there be sharp declines in nominal housing consumption (i.e., rent expense). But such sharp declines would be a result of solving a supply constraint. They would not be the result of some capital that was misallocated into unneeded housing. Only housing that was desperately needed would trigger the market collapse in nominal housing expenditures that most observers mistakenly think occurred.

To state this more concisely, a city where the median household spends 40% of its income on rent is more susceptible to a housing price shock than a city where the median household spends 25% of its income on rent, because, given the opportunity, households will adjust their housing consumption downward until it is in that comfortable 25% range. That is what they spend in every city that allows enough housing to be produced. The only way that additional supply could realistically cause a sharp market collapse is if the additional supply became available in a market that desperately needed it.

29. For an explanation of the nominal interest rate, see note 26.

30. Staff, "Political Intelligence: No Wall Will Stop the Wave," *Texas Observer*, November 16, 2007.

31. Alyssa Katz, "How Texas Escaped the Real Estate Crisis," *Washington Post*, April 4, 2010.

32. American Housing Survey (US Census Bureau).

33. In the simplest terms, think of real housing expenditures as what house you live in and nominal housing expenditures as the money you pay for it. Increasing real housing expenditures (or consumption) means, for example, moving to a larger house. Increasing nominal housing expenditures means spending more on rent, regardless of which house you live in. In the aggregate, we have been paying more for less.

34. The brief period where housing consumption grew at a similar rate to total consumption after 2008 is the result of stagnating total consumption, not growing housing consumption.

35. Susan Wharton Gates, *Days of Slaughter* (Baltimore: Johns Hopkins University Press, 2017), 32–33.

CHAPTER 2

1. For an excellent and thorough review of housing in London, see Mayor of London, "Housing in London, 2018: The Evidence Base for the Mayor's Housing Strategy" (London: Greater London Authority, 2018).
   London has many similarities with the American Closed Access cities, including substantial levels of domestic outmigration. Recent trends in London may be toward more expansion of the housing stock.

2. Depending on how wide a net one casts and the measure one uses, the Netherlands and Italy might be included in the list of countries where high prices collapsed far enough to be called a bust. Some minor countries have been omitted because of limited historical data.

3. William A. Fischel, *Zoning Rules!* (Cambridge, MA: Lincoln Institute of Land Policy, 2015), 353.

4. Randal O'Toole, *American Nightmare: How Government Undermines the Dream of Home Ownership* (Washington, DC: Cato Institute, 2012), 241. See also Colin Wiles, "German Lessons," *Inside Housing*, January 26, 2012; Colin Wiles, "German Lessons—Part 2," *Inside Housing*, March 26, 2012.

5. Robin Harding, "Why Tokyo Is the Land of Rising Home Construction but Not Prices," *Financial Times*, August 3, 2016. Harding points out that a Japanese tendency toward teardowns is part of what leads to these higher starts numbers, but that even so, the replacement units will tend to create greater density where it is demanded.

6. Man Cho and Kyung-Hwan Kim, "Housing Policy, Mortgage Markets, and Housing Outcomes in Korea," *Korea's Economy* 26 (May 2011). Here is a description of housing policy developments in South Korea leading up to the housing boom, according to the Korea Economic Institute (Cho and Kim):

   > The 1989–92 drive to build two million new dwelling units was a major milestone as it led to a 30 percent increase in housing stock between 1988 and 1992. Thanks to the massive increases in *new supply*, housing prices did start declining in 1991 and remained stable throughout the mid-1990s. Although this ambitious government campaign helped resolve the housing shortage within a short time period, it also showed that housing supply was a political parameter under government control rather than a response of housing producers and the factor markets to changes in demand conditions.
   >
   > As the housing shortage was perceived to be under control, government instituted a number of policy changes in the mid-1990s: *lifting price controls* on new apartments in phases starting in 1995; *deregulating* the housing finance market by *inviting* new mortgage *lenders* while *privatizing* the Korea Housing Bank, the government-owned monopolistic housing finance institution, in 1997; and *relaxing regulations* on the conversion of agricultural land near the outer edge of built-up urban areas in 1994. . . .

There no longer exists an overall housing shortage in Korea, as the number of houses exceeds that of households in the country as a whole. Instead, the problem is the mismatch between demand and supply in local markets. . . . Despite the localized nature of the house price run-up, the government went back to its arsenal of traditional weapons to suppress speculators. . . . For example, the comprehensive *real estate tax* on expensive condominiums was introduced in 2005, and the *capital gains tax* was raised, in particular, for owners of two or more houses. The government also introduced various regulations covering housing development, including a series of new *restrictions on redevelopment* as well as reinstitution of the *price controls* on new apartments that had been lifted in 1999. In addition, the government set a *limit on the loan-to-value* (LTV) ratio and *debt-to-income* (DTI) ratio to discourage home purchases via leverage in those hot markets. . . .

Household debt, including home mortgages, has increased substantially in Korea during the past 10 years. . . . Micro analyses show, however, that the explosive increase in consumer lending in Korea during the past decade was concentrated in high-income households and that those high-income consumers used the borrowed funds predominantly for acquiring real estate. . . . A more fundamental issue is that more than 90 percent of mortgage loans outstanding in Korea are still adjustable-rate mortgages (ARMs). . . .

A major conclusion is that significant progress has been made on mortgage financing since the 1997 Asian crisis but that no fundamental changes have been brought to the housing supply system. This poses a serious issue, as the combination of inelastic supply and demand increases will lead to a highly volatile housing price path. (emphasis mine)

Maximum LTV ratios were set as low as 40% in some cases. These restrictions actually led to price declines in 2003 and 2004. But, as South Korea experiences the same pressures of demand for urban housing, will a shift in focus from massive new supply to controls on borrowers eventually lead to the secular increases in housing costs that other growing economies are experiencing?

7. Japan, South Korea, Germany, and Switzerland also all have disincentives for taking on high loan-to-value ratios. Christopher Crowe et al., "Policies for Macrofinancial Stability: Options to Deal with Real Estate Booms" (IMF Staff Discussion Notes No. 11/02, International Monetary Fund, Washington, DC, February 25, 2011). This might help to keep urban price/rent levels low by limiting demand for ownership of constrained urban real estate to households that already have substantial wealth.

8. The difference between these countries is the extent of their supply problems. To the extent that fiscal or demand-side policies have an effect, the removal of owner-occupier tax benefits and implementation of higher property tax rates can remove some volatility in home prices—and the Open Access cities tend to use some of those policies. But these policies work by changing the underlying, intrinsic value of properties. They allow the price mechanism to work. They don't bring prices down by blocking access to ownership. They bring prices down by *creating* access. The association of housing dislocations with deregulation is pernicious. Closed Access cities in the boom had deregulated credit and regulated supply. Open Access cities in the boom had both deregulated supply *and* deregulated credit. Now, because of limitations on mortgage lending, Closed Access cities have both regulated supply and regulated credit, and Open Access cities have deregulated supply and regulated credit. Which of those four contexts is the most just, fair, and functional? Is there any question? It seems clear that the answer is Open Access cities, with both lightly regulated supply and lightly regulated credit policies.

The United States has imposed the worst set of policies at every shift of the housing market. First, we imposed severe supply constraints in our most economically dynamic cities and combined that policy with an innovative financial sector that created financial access to those highly sought-after markets—sometimes with securities that contained risky terms like low down payments and resetting of amortization schedules. Then we imposed financial suppression, but not by eliminating favorable tax treatments or other reductions to the financial advantage of owning property. The set of responses we imposed have resulted in a dysfunctional mortgage market where value is not the constraining factor in housing demand—access is. *Qualifying* for a mortgage has become more constraining than being able to afford a mortgage. We have imposed both supply and demand dysfunctions. Instead of creating a housing market where buyers can make decisions on the margin, we have created a binary market. Can I get a rent-controlled apartment or not? Can I satisfy all the local interest groups in order to build a new condo building or not? Can I qualify for a mortgage or not? Do I initiate a short sale and put the negative equity on the bank or not? Do we make a go of it one more year in the Closed Access city, or do we migrate?

Binary decisions lead to stress, anger, and social dissonance. Policy should always aim to allow decisions to be made on the margin. This is the foundation of a liberal, civilized society. Even worse than the high costs created by limited supply is the lack of marginal choices.

9. If there is no lender recourse, then in a foreclosure a lender is limited only to the home itself in its effort to recover its losses.

10. Nobody should dispute the fact that if we make it difficult to purchase a type of asset, the price of that asset will decline and the yield earned by investors in that asset will rise. There are already significant obstacles to homeownership, such as high transaction costs, that push yields on homeownership above where they would otherwise be.

11. The estimated rental value of owner-occupied properties is also useful information that is affected by many local supply and demand factors other than credit access.

12. These "demand" factors appear to be compelling on the surface, but they are not as compelling as they seem when viewed in a new light. I will address these factors in the following pages.

13. Wikipedia, s.v. "Subprime mortgage crisis," accessed April 5, 2017.

14. Giovanni Favara and Jean Imbs, "Credit Supply and the Price of Housing," *American Economic Review* 105, no. 3 (March 2015).

15. Timothy Howard, *The Mortgage Wars* (New York: McGraw-Hill Education, 2014), 66–67.

16. Fannie Mae 10-K filings and Information Statements for periods before 2002: "SEC Filings," Fannie Mae, last revised November 20, 2018, http://www.fanniemae.com/portal/about-fm/investor-relations/sec-filings.html.

17. Age groups below 65 had returned to roughly their pre-1982 peak levels, and the age group 65 and over increased its ownership rate over time, as average active lifespans increased.

18. Table 17 (Quarterly Homeownership Rates by Family Income: 1994 to Present) in US Census Bureau, "Housing Vacancies and Homeownership (CPS/HVS): Historical Tables," last modified April 26, 2016, http://www.census.gov/housing/hvs/data/histtabs.html.

19. This is an example of Simpson's paradox. Much of the increase in ownership has been from the natural rise in ownership as baby boomers have aged into the homeowning phase of their lives. The increase in homeownership overall was greater than the increase for every individual age group (except the small 75+ group).

20. Foote, Loewenstein, and Willen, "Cross-Sectional Patterns," 2.

21. Table 9 in Board of Governors of the Federal Reserve System, "Survey of Consumer Finances," last modified November 15, 2017, http://www.federalreserve.gov/econresdata/scf/scfindex.htm.

22. To derive this estimate from the Survey of Consumer Finances data, one has to assume that the average value of unencumbered homes within each quintile is the same as the average value of mortgaged homes. American Community Survey data suggest that this is roughly true.

23. Atif Mian and Amir Sufi, *House of Debt: How They (and You) Caused the Great Recession and How We Can Prevent It from Happening Again* (Chicago: University of Chicago Press, 2014), 19–25.

24. For details, see the detailed tables on "Distribution of Wealth and Debt" from the US Census Bureau, accessed February 2016, https://www.census.gov/data/tables/2005/demo/wealth/wealth-asset-ownership.html and https://www.census.gov/data/tables/2011/demo/wealth/wealth-asset-ownership.html.

25. Stefania Albanesi, Giacomo De Giorgi, and Jaromir Nosal, "Credit Growth and the Financial Crisis: A New Narrative" (NBER Working Paper No. 23740, National Bureau of Economic Research, Cambridge, MA, August 2017).

26. Atif Mian and Amir Sufi, "Household Debt and Defaults from 2000 to 2010: The Credit Supply View" (Kreisman Working Papers Series in Housing and Law Policy No. 28, University of Chicago Law School, Chicago, June 2016), 1.

27. In addition to Albanesi, De Giorgi, and Nosal, "Credit Growth and the Financial Crisis," and Foote, Loewenstein, and Willen, "Cross-Sectional Patterns," see Manuel Adelino, Antoinette Schoar, and Felipe Severino, "Loan Originations and Defaults in the Mortgage Crisis: The Role of the Middle Class" (Working Paper No. 2546427, Tuck School of Business, Dartmouth Center for Corporate Governance, Hanover, NH, March 2016); Christopher L. Foote et al., "Subprime Facts: What (We Think) We Know about the Subprime Crisis and What We Don't" (Public Policy Discussion Papers No. 08-2, Federal Reserve Bank of Boston, May 30, 2008).

28. Albanesi, De Giorgi, and Nosal, "Credit Growth and the Financial Crisis."

29. Closed Access governance of all types—whether in the context of banana-republic land-owners, zoning-protected owners of urban residential property, or state-approved alcohol distributors—benefits existing owners and producers at the expense of potential new entrants and of consumers. Figure 2-11 is the signature of the Closed Access phenomenon's central role in the housing bubble. The value of existing properties (which are what is measured by the Case-Shiller index) have been inflated. Open Access is defined by the ability of new entrants to compete with existing owners or producers. Where there is Open Access, there can be many new entrants or properties, and values of neither existing nor new properties are inflated.

30. Private securitizations are sometimes referred to loosely as "subprime" loans, but they can also be categorized more specifically as either subprime, which usually are issued to borrowers with lower credit scores, or Alt-A, which are usually near-prime loans that don't meet conventional standards. In this quotation the authors are using the more specific description.

31. Gene Amromin et al., "Complex Mortgages" (FRB of Chicago Working Paper No. 2010-17, Federal Reserve Bank of Chicago, Chicago, November 2010).

    If I may make one pedantic point, these borrowers did expect house price growth, but they also expected growth in local rents, which is certainly a reasonable expectation. These borrowing decisions always seem to be framed with price expectations, which makes buyers look like speculators, when it would be more accurate to frame them with rent expectations, which would make buyers look more like hedgers seeking safety. I don't mean to single out Amromin and his coauthors. This is a rhetorical tendency found throughout the literature.

CHAPTER 3

1. This is not equivalent to saying that there is *no* desperation borrowing or lender or borrower excess. It is also not equivalent to saying that credit excesses weren't more common when prices and credit were at high levels. But it does suggest that lending to households that had incomes too low to be homeowners was not systemically important.

2. J. W. Mason, "Income Distribution, Household Debt, and Aggregate Demand: A Critical Assessment" (Working Paper No. 901, Levy Economics Institute of Bard College, Annandale-on-Hudson, NY, March 2018).

3. This is the term for debt taken out by borrowers who previously did not have access to credit. "Intensive margin" is the term for increasing debt levels among existing borrowers.

4. Data are from Zillow, provided to the author upon request. This is the aggregate value of all real estate (labeled by Zillow as Metro TotalMarketValue), so the relative rise in Closed Access real estate values has happened even while Closed Access cities add to their physical stock of housing at a much slower pace than the rest of the country. These numbers are based on the 20 largest metropolitan areas, which are the areas I have focused on throughout my analysis. There are some smaller cities in inland California, Nevada, Arizona, and Florida that followed a Contagion pattern and are not included here. So, a comprehensive summation of Contagion cities—one that pulled in every small metropolitan area—would be somewhat larger than 6%–8% of the US real estate market, but the pattern would be the same.

5. I will provide more detail on the migration portion of the story in chapter 5.

6. Atif Mian and Amir Sufi, "The Consequences of Mortgage Credit Expansion: Evidence from the U.S. Mortgage Default Crisis," *Quarterly Journal of Economics* 124, no. 4 (2009).

7. For a good summary of the credit supply argument, see Atif Mian and Amir Sufi, "Household Debt and Defaults from 2000 to 2010: The Credit Supply View" (Kreisman Working Papers Series in Housing and Law Policy No. 28, University of Chicago Law School, Chicago, June 2016).

8. Atif Mian and Amir Sufi, "Fraudulent Income Overstatement on Mortgage Applications during the Credit Expansion of 2002 to 2005," *Review of Financial Studies* 30, no. 6 (2017): 24–25.

9. Figure 3-2 uses a natural log scale, which accounts for compounding. The log scale is useful for computations, but it actually visually understates the difference between the cities because it compresses the stated change when changes are extreme.

10. "County-level changes in income, home prices, or other variables that uniformly affect ZIP codes in a given county are removed." Mian and Sufi, "Consequences of Mortgage Credit Expansion," 1465.

11. Or they had little need for credit if they were moving away with a capital windfall after selling a house in a Closed Access city.

12. Chris Mayer and Karen Pence, "Subprime Mortgages: What, Where, and to Whom?" (FEDS Working Paper No. 2008-29, Divisions of Research and Statistics and Monetary Affairs, Federal Reserve Board, Washington, DC, December 2007).

13. Mian and Sufi, "Consequences of Mortgage Credit Expansion," 1490.

14. Mian and Sufi, "Household Debt and Defaults," 11.

15. Atif Mian and Amir Sufi, "House Prices, Home Equity-Based Borrowing, and the US Household Leverage Crisis," *American Economic Review* 101, no. 5 (August 2011): 14.

16. Collateralized debt obligations used mortgages and financial engineering to create new financial securities with various terms, risks, and payout schedules for investors.

17. Yuliya S. Demyanyk, "Quick Exits of Subprime Mortgages," Federal Reserve Bank of St. Louis *Review* 91, no. 2 (March/April 2009).

18. Here, I report the percentage change in an arithmetic scale. In figures 3-7, 3-8, and 3-9, the changes are shown in log scale so that upward and downward changes are proportional. This is why the change referenced is larger than the changes shown in the figures. When growth is high, the log scale is more compressed.

19. This is true for the 20 largest MSAs (the ones that I include in my analysis). A few of the MSAs have some anomalous zip code price changes, but none have a systematic difference across quintiles, as the Closed Access MSAs do.

20. Of the 20 largest MSAs, Baltimore is the only city that lacks a significant income-related pattern in bust period price trends.

21. In figure 3-10, the big cloud indicating low-priced homes with little change in value are zip codes in areas that were less metropolitan, which generally did not have a boom or a bust, so

that the pattern of the bust has been V-shaped. The most-expensive and the least-expensive zip codes have increased their values moderately since the peak of the boom, and the mid-priced zip codes, which are generally in non–Closed Access metro areas and the low tiers of the Closed Access cities, have declined in value sharply. While national indices of home prices are near the 2006 peak levels, many of these midrange zip codes remain well below the peak.

CHAPTER 4

1. Market bubbles are an example of positive feedback. Rising home prices draw in speculators or allow existing buyers to releverage their growing equity. That source of positive feedback has been so thoroughly identified and discussed that it tends to be broadly accepted as the source when positive feedback has been measured in housing markets. In this chapter, I describe a persistent source of positive feedback in housing markets that is largely unrelated to credit markets and buyer sentiment. This source of positive feedback is a better explanation for some rising home prices than credit or sentiment.

2. This situation also worsens the Closed Access migration pattern. For instance, homes in Los Angeles that might have the potential to provide significant tax benefits to a leveraged owner are worth much more to a high-income in-migrant than they are to a low-income current resident. So the tax benefits of homeownership that are weighted toward higher-income owners are yet another factor passively pushing lower-income families out of their home cities. Income tax policy increases the gentrification process by making housing units in rising neighborhoods much more valuable for high-income owner-occupiers than they are for either low-income owner-occupiers or renters.

3. Table 13-1 in Office of Management and Budget, *Fiscal Year 2019 Budget of the US Government*, 2018, p. 157, https://www.whitehouse.gov/wp-content/uploads/2018/02/ap_13_expenditures-fy2019.pdf.

4. In 2006, there were some zip codes in San Francisco with anomalously low price/rent ratios. Perhaps this reflects certain policies, such as rent control, which might have caused price distortions in certain parts of the city when prices were changing rapidly. Anomalous zip codes tend to be in parts of the city of San Francisco and in Marin County.

5. Here, I mean depreciation in the general sense, not in the sense of tax accounting—in other words, the general rate of decline of a property. The Bureau of Economic Analysis refers to this as "consumption of capital."

6. Just as every shareholder values a stock differently, every homeowner has a different personal context, and on a given street each owner captures a different amount of the available tax benefits. It is the marginal buyer—that potential new buyer who is the next buyer to enter the market if the price falls by a small amount—who determines the price. We can think of that buyer as an archetype: the "typical" family that would buy a certain house. This is a more coherent way of thinking about price than comparing the current tax benefits taken by the existing owners, especially in the Closed Access markets, where new buyers who represent current demand are likely to have much higher incomes than the existing owners who bought the homes years ago and now live in real estate whose value far exceeds any price they would have ever been able to pay.

7. Kamila Sommer and Paul Sullivan, "Implications of US Tax Policy for House Prices, Rents, and Homeownership," *American Economic Review* 108, no. 2 (February 2018); David E. Rappoport, "Do Mortgage Subsidies Help or Hurt Borrowers?" (FEDS Working Paper No. 2016-081, Board of Governors of the Federal Reserve System, Washington, DC, October 2016).

8. Rappoport, "Do Mortgage Subsidies Help or Hurt Borrowers?"

9. Christian A. L. Hilber and Tracy M. Turner, "The Mortgage Interest Deduction and Its Impact on Homeownership Decisions," *Review of Economics and Statistics* 96, no. 4 (October 2014).

In other words, "There ain't no such thing as a free lunch." If a home is worth $100,000 and a new law creates $10,000 worth of tax subsidies for the homeowner, then new buyers won't continue to pay $100,000 for the house, receiving a free $10,000 bonus. The market price will tend to move up to $110,000. Consider: if that newly subsidized house were selling for $101,000 and you were a buyer, wouldn't you be willing to outbid the other buyer for it?

Prices don't have to be precise and exact in all cases for this to be true. In a way, prices are like tides on a beach. The tide ebbs and flows. There is nothing exact about the "level" of the ocean at the beach. But if Greenland's ice caps melt, the sea level will predictably rise. Likewise, the "$100,000" house might sell for $95,000 or $105,000, depending on the economy, the negotiating skill of the buyer and seller, etc. But, even though the market price isn't exact, we can still recognize that the subsidy will have a predictable effect. In aggregate data, such as the data I am discussing here, the fluctuations of individual properties wash out, and the predictable macro-effects are more clear. That is even true of differences between neighborhoods, so that, for instance, when zip codes in Seattle are divided into five quintiles by price, all five quintiles have nearly identical behavior during the housing boom, even though clearly some parts of town are in relative decline while others boom.

10. Jonathan Gruber, Amalie Jensen, and Henrik Kleven, "Do People Respond to the Mortgage Interest Deduction? Quasi-experimental Evidence from Denmark" (NBER Working Paper No. 23600, National Bureau of Economic Research, Cambridge, MA, July 2017).

11. Even though the pattern of price/rent ratios that rise with home prices until they reach a ceiling level seems to be universal among the major metro areas, the price level at which that price/rent ceiling is reached is different in every city. If tax effects are the primary cause of this effect, then variables such as local tax rates, local rental levels, incomes, etc., would create local differences.

Home prices in Seattle are not that much lower than they are in Boston. Yet Boston price/rent ratios had leveled off in much of the city by 2005, whereas price/rent ratios in Seattle were still rising in all but the priciest zip codes. So low-tier prices rose higher than high-tier prices in Boston, but they didn't in Seattle. One reason might be that the median rent in Seattle was still quite a bit lower in 2005 than in Boston, and untaxed rental income is an important component of the tax benefits of homeownership.

12. John M. Griffin and Gonzalo Maturana, "Did Dubious Mortgage Origination Practices Distort House Prices?," *Review of Financial Studies* 29, no. 7 (July 2016).

13. Griffin and Maturana, 1673–1674, 1687–1689.

Two of their checks involved distinct credit policy shifts in certain locations where they could measure how prices reacted to distinct changes in credit access. In both cases, they found that restricted credit access did create price shifts. But in one case, where they looked at a local credit program in Chicago, the price shift was of a relatively small scale.

In the other case, they compared changing prices in states that introduced new anti-predatory laws (APLs) in 2004 and 2005 to states that did not have anti-predatory laws. Here they built on Raphael W. Bostic et al., "State and Local Anti-predatory Lending Laws: The Effect of Legal Enforcement Mechanisms," *Journal of Economics and Business* 60 (2008). Griffin and Maturana find strong statistical evidence that anti-predatory laws reduced home price appreciation by almost 10% annually during the bubble.

This seems to corroborate evidence at the metropolitan area level. The private securitization market, which surged at the end of 2003, was especially strong in California, although much of the activity was in Alt-A loans, which tend to go to more qualified borrowers. According to median home price data from Zillow, home prices across Los Angeles and San Francisco accelerated at that time compared to the rest of the country. Massachusetts passed an APL in the third quarter of 2004, and after that, prices in Boston didn't rise as sharply as they did in California. Prices in New York City didn't rise as sharply as in California either, but prices in Boston moderated after 2004, even compared to New York City. The difference between Boston and the California cities roughly parallels the findings of Griffin and Maturana. Prices in the California cities outpaced prices in Boston during the private securitization boom by about 10% annually.

Price declines in Boston were also more moderate after the crisis than they were in the other Closed Access cities, which also seems to confirm the effect of the APLs. On the other hand, prices began to recover in 2012, and prices in the California cities have recovered that lost ground. Even though there is no active private securitization market today, home prices in Boston, LA, and San Francisco are all at similar levels today compared to 2005. This combination of evidence suggests that APLs may have moderated the effects of the boom and bust in Boston by lowering the number of marginal recent borrowers who were hit by collapsing markets after 2007, but that prices in California are rising more sharply than in Boston for other reasons.

Also, in this test, Griffin and Maturana compared prices from twelve states—five that passed APLs and seven that didn't. These were states that fit the two categories that Griffin and Maturana were trying to compare, but it is a bit of a hodgepodge. The states with no APLs include Arizona, Washington, and Montana. The states with APLs include Wisconsin, South Carolina, and Indiana. During the 2004–2007 period, there were many different extreme forces at play in these different states. It would be hard to isolate the effects of APLs.

Among the list of states, Massachusetts is a state that passed an APL in 2004, and New Hampshire is a state that did not have an APL. Also, South Carolina passed an APL in 2004, and Tennessee did not. Of the states that were tested, these are the best examples of states that might have had similar pressures on their housing markets, where having an APL might have made a difference. Using the median home price for each state from Zillow, prices in New Hampshire and Massachusetts behaved very differently than in any other of the 12 states in the test, and they moved nearly in lockstep with each other. There was also little difference in price behavior between Tennessee and South Carolina. In the two cases where we can come close to comparing apples to apples, the APLs that were passed don't appear to have made much difference. To be fair, Griffin and Maturana used more sophisticated methods than I have in an attempt to control for differences, but it seems unlikely that an APL in Massachusetts would have been precisely countered in New Hampshire by factors I have not controlled for.

Bostic et al. note that, in the case of these laws, the devil is in the details. (New Mexico and Arizona are among the twelve states in the test, but New Mexico was subjected to much less of the migration wave than Arizona was, so those two states don't offer as much of an apples-to-apples comparison as geography might suggest. One could argue that there is a channel of causality from loose lending to in-migration, but in the case of Arizona, there is a history of exposure to Californian migration.)

It could be that well-implemented APLs can prevent predatory or systemically destabilizing lending, but that they aren't that much of a factor behind rising prices.

14. Griffin and Maturana, 1685–1687.

15. Figure 7 in Griffin and Maturana, 1705.

16. A temporary tax credit for first-time home buyers, which expired in April 2010, also probably contributed to the brief period of stabilization between 2008 and 2010.

17. A reasonable reader might wonder how I can give little weight to the effect of credit access on boom prices before 2007 but then assert that credit access is very important for prices after 2008. That seems like a contradiction.

    In most analysis of prices in the financial literature, restricted access can push yields on certain assets well above yields on other assets (thus pushing prices down), because restricted access creates less competitive markets. But, once access to a market has approximated a competitive model, adding more access does not push prices above the competitive price level that provides a yield on investment similar to that of other types of assets. The effect is asymmetrical. The idea that looser credit in 2005 only had small effects on prices while very tight credit after 2008 had large downward effects on prices is in line with standard financial models regarding liquidity and competitiveness.

    We can think of this in terms of monopsony power. If limited access to the buyer's market creates a monopsonistic market, then prices will fall. But prices in a relatively competitive market will tend to approximate prices in a perfectly competitive market. As markets become more competitive, market prices converge on the competitive price, so the effect on price of marginal new entrants becomes less important. It may seem like the housing market is too broad to have monopsonistic price effects, but consider typical low-tier market renters today. In many cases, they could significantly lower their monthly costs by purchasing their homes with a mortgage rather than renting, but they are unable to qualify for a mortgage. In those cases, the monopsonistic advantage of the landlord is clear. Where housing costs (in rental terms) were highest, in the Closed Access cities, that effect was more likely to be in place in 2005 than it was in other cities. Tenants with high incomes were renting units that would require nonconventional mortgages. This would dampen home prices. Supply constraints may have created monopoly power for homeowners, but also monopsony power for buyers who didn't require nonconventional credit. In that context, we should expect the development of more flexible mortgage markets to push prices up more than they would have been pushed up in less-expensive markets. Thus, localized expansion of nonconventional lending that coincided with rising prices in expensive cities might reflect a movement toward prices that were closer to a competitive equilibrium rather than prices that were pushed above a competitive equilibrium. In Contagion cities, the bubble was more short-lived and temporary, so in those cities, the combination of disruptive levels of migration, cash buyers who sold Closed Access homes, subprime owner-occupiers, and speculators is more likely to have driven prices temporarily above justifiable levels.

Even if prices in the California Closed Access cities in 2005 can be justified, in hindsight, by high rents and supply bottlenecks, the situation still points to deregulated lending as a source of disruption. Looser lending accelerated workers' ability to sort into and out of those cities according to their income potential. The quick shift to broader lending increased demand for housing in Los Angeles and San Francisco, triggering the migration event. The outflow of housing refugees was disruptive regardless of whether Closed Access prices were sustainable. The new lending increased demand, but prices were moderated by out-migration.

Or, thinking in terms of market segmentation, market prices in 1995 and 2005 generally reflected owner-occupier price levels in most cities, and credit access didn't have much effect on what those price levels were. But tightening credit after 2008 effectively eliminated the owner-occupier market in many low-tier markets, so the declining price levels after 2008 reflect a regime shift from owner-occupier price levels to investor-landlord price levels.

18. Figure 5 in Griffin and Maturana, 1693.

19. Among the 20 largest metro areas, the Contagion cities were the only cities where rental vacancy rates systematically increased as a result of the whipsaw in migration, but even there, rental vacancy rates didn't rise until 2008—nearly two years after housing starts had begun to collapse. There was an oversupply of *sellers* with homes on the market, but in terms of *tenants* the vacancies in the Contagion cities came rather late, after the migration event suddenly stopped, and there was never a rise in tenant vacancies associated with the housing collapse in most other cities. See table 4a (Rental Vacancy Rates for the 75 Largest Metropolitan Statistical Areas: 2005 to 2014) in US Census Bureau, "Housing Vacancies and Homeownership (CPS/HVS): Quarterly Vacancy and Homeownership Rates by State and MSA," last modified April 26, 2016, https://www.census.gov/housing/hvs/data/rates.html.

20. One might protest that homeownership rates today are not that far below homeownership rates of the early 1990s. But, adjusted for age demographics, homeownership rates *are* much lower. Additionally, many homeowners are grandfathered into their homes. Either they have already paid most or all of their mortgage, or they are continuing to pay down a mortgage that they would not be able to qualify for in today's market. The number of first-time homebuyers has been very low since the crisis. Demand is much lower than the homeownership rate would imply.

21. National Association of Realtors, "Who Really Owns Single-Family Investment Properties?," *Realtor Magazine*, July 21, 2017.

CHAPTER 5

1. It may be that international migration is a significant part of the picture. It could be that when economic growth draws highly skilled workers to the Closed Access cities, it also draws in international migration—either to tap into the lucrative labor markets or to parlay high earnings from elsewhere into nonprimary residences in high-status locations.

If this is the case, the complaints sometimes heard about foreign absentee buyers gutting the cultural flavor of urban neighborhoods has a basis in truth, in the direct sense. If there is demand for living in those cities from domestic buyers, then there should be demand for living there among many types of foreign buyers, too.

There are many articles blaming foreign buyers for pushing up home prices in expensive cities. Here is one example: Patrick Radden Keefe, "The Kleptocrat in Apartment B," *New Yorker*, January 21, 2016.

Yet the source of the problem is still the set of policies that create scarcity. Artificial scarcity creates status. As persistent as these Closed Access policy tendencies are, removing the source of scarcity seems like a much more realistic goal than battling the human desire for status. Note that Texas, Arizona, and Florida all have large international in-migration flows. They have neither relentlessly rising rents nor a tendency for existing housing stock to be taken over by status seekers.

Ironically, if the policy of artificial scarcity itself leads to local housing markets that attract status seekers while creating financial stress that drives away low-income households, then the sense that places like Houston or Phoenix are somehow less trendy or sophisticated might really be a subconscious statement of elitism—a projection of distaste about the places where poor people live—when, in fact, poor households have been driven to those cities by the very policies imposed by the cities that now claim cultural superiority.

In the early 20th century, at Manhattan's population high point, it had many tenements. Hollywood gave Los Angeles its cachet for decades when an expansive housing policy kept costs there reasonable. The connection, at the metropolitan level, between productivity, status, and cost is not strong, historically. This connection is a recent development, created by political scarcity.

2. Fernando Ferreira and Joseph Gyourko, "Anatomy of the Beginning of the Housing Boom: US Neighborhoods and Metropolitan Areas, 1993–2009" (NBER Working Paper No. 17374, National Bureau of Economic Research, Cambridge, MA, August 2011).

3. IRS, "SOI Tax Stats—Migration Data," last modified November 30, 2017, https://www.irs .gov/statistics/soi-tax-stats-migration-data, and author's calculations; US Census Bureau, "Building Permits Survey," last modified May 1, 2018, https://www.census.gov/construction /bps/.

4. Table 4a (Rental Vacancy Rates for the 75 Largest Metropolitan Statistical Areas: 2005 to 2014) and table 5a (Homeowner Vacancy Rates for the 75 Largest Metropolitan Statistical Areas: 2005 to 2014) in US Census Bureau, "Housing Vacancies and Homeownership (CPS/HVS): Quarterly Vacancy and Homeownership Rates by State and MSA," last revised April 26, 2016, https://www.census.gov/housing/hvs/data/rates.html.

5. Ben S. Bernanke, *The Courage to Act* (New York: W. W. Norton, 2015), 503.

6. US Census Bureau, *Population Change in Metropolitan and Micropolitan Statistical Areas: 1990–2003*, September 2005; US Census Bureau, *Population Change in Central and Outlying Counties of Metropolitan Statistical Areas: 2000 to 2007*, June 2009.

7. Also, about one-third of the bottom two quintiles are households over 65 years old, many living in very expensive homes that have no mortgage.

8. Alicia Sasser, "Voting with Their Feet? Local Economic Conditions and Migration Patterns in New England," *Regional Science and Urban Economics* 40, no. 2–3 (May 2010).

9. US Census Bureau, "State-to-State Migration Flows," last revised December 21, 2017, https://www.census.gov/data/tables/time-series/demo/geographic-mobility/state-to-state -migration.html. Population data are from table SA1 (Personal Income, Population, Per Capita Personal Income, Disposable Personal Income, and Per Capita Disposable Personal Income) from Bureau of Economic Analysis, available at https://apps.bea.gov/iTable/index _regional.cfm.

10. US Census Bureau, "State-to-State Migration Flows." Population data are from table CA1 (Personal Income, Population, Per Capita Personal Income) from Bureau of Economic Analysis, available at https://www.bea.gov/iTable/index_regional.cfm.

11. Figure 1 in the White House, *Occupational Licensing: A Framework for Policymakers*, July 2015.

12. For a review of the mobility issue, see David Schleicher, "Stuck! The Law and Economics of Residential Stability," *Yale Law Journal* 127 (January 2017).

13. Contractors State License Board, State of California Dept. of Consumer Affairs, *Reciprocal Classifications List*, accessed March 25, 2016, http://www.cslb.ca.gov/Contractors/Applicants /Reciprocity/Reciprocal_Classifications_List.aspx.

14. *Down-zoning* refers to the political tendency in some cities to create ever more strict rules about what sorts of new housing units are allowed.

15. Information about these surveys, conducted by the US Census Bureau, can be found at US Census Bureau, "American Community Survey (ACS)," https://www.census.gov/programs -surveys/acs, and "American Housing Survey (AHS)," https://www.census.gov/programs -surveys/ahs.html.

16. The survey has only about 76,000 respondents, which is about 1 out of every 1,600 housing units, so the data can be a bit noisy if they are applied to smaller regions. The regions here are large enough, and the patterns regular enough, that we can reach some basic conclusions in terms of broad relative behaviors.

17. The survey is a snapshot in time of all households, and mortgage payments and home prices naturally rise over time with inflation, as households buy homes at higher prices. So it is not surprising that the average home purchase price and mortgage payment have risen over time. But the fact that mortgage payments rose more slowly than prices paid suggests that some combination of lower interest rates and pay-down of principal were dominant factors.

18. In other words, there are two motivations for refinancing a mortgage—to lower payments by negotiating lower rates (tactical) or to access home equity for consumption (cash out). Households with high incomes have the flexibility to be more tactical, and they tend to refinance when rates are low, which is apparent in the graph, as their payments were declining over time. Households with lower incomes are more likely to need cash, which leads them to refinance regardless of interest rates.

19. Atif Mian and Amir Sufi, "House Prices, Home Equity-Based Borrowing, and the US Household Leverage Crisis," *American Economic Review* 101, no. 5 (August 2011).

20. Atif Mian and Amir Sufi, "House Price Gains and US Household Spending from 2002 to 2006" (Fama-Miller Working Paper, University of Chicago Booth School of Business, Chicago, May 2014), 15–16.

21. American Community Survey. Income quintiles are sorted on the basis of national distribution.

22. Atif Mian and Amir Sufi, "House Price Gains," 3–4.

23. Figure 5 in Atif Mian and Amir Sufi, "House Prices," 24.

24. Mian and Sufi. The Closed Access cities dominate their list of cities with an inelastic housing supply.

25. Figure 10 in Christopher L. Foote, Lara Loewenstein, and Paul S. Willen, "Cross-Sectional Patterns of Mortgage Debt during the Housing Boom: Evidence and Implications" (NBER Working Paper No. 22985, National Bureau of Economic Research, Cambridge, MA, December 2016), 46.

26. Table 2 in Yuliya S. Demyanyk, "Quick Exits of Subprime Mortgages," Federal Reserve Bank of St. Louis *Review* 91, no. 2 (March/April 2009): 89.

CHAPTER 6

1. By "free movement of capital to its most-valued use," I mean specifically the freedom to use capital to build homes where there is demand for them.

2. I chose 2005 as the reference year because migration patterns since then have been disrupted by the housing bust, so local housing policies have not been such a definitive cause of the differences in population growth and housing permits since then. The shortage of units has been extended nationwide.

3. Edward L. Glaeser and Joseph Gyourko, "The Impact of Building Restrictions on Housing Affordability," *FRBNY Economic Policy Review* 9, no. 2 (June 2003). For an excellent overview of how this problem is really focused on city cores, where market values are much higher than the cost of new construction, see Issi Romem, "Paying for Dirt: Where Have Home Values Detached from Construction Costs?," *BuildZoom*, October 17, 2017.

4. Stijn Van Nieuwerburgh and Pierre-Olivier Weill, "Why Has House Price Dispersion Gone Up?," *Review of Economic Studies* 77, no. 4 (October 2010).

5. Lena Edlund, Cecila Machado, and Maria Sviatschi, "Bright Minds, Big Rent: Gentrification and the Rising Returns to Skill" (IZA Discussion Paper No. 9502, Institute of Labor Economics, Bonn, Germany, November 2015).

6. Some costs, like the cost of commuting time, are nonmonetary. The monetary costs created by the shortage of urban housing understate the full cost.

7. Peter Ganong and Daniel Shoag, "Why Has Regional Income Convergence in the US Declined?," *Journal of Urban Economics* 102, no. C (November 2017).

8. Alicia Sasser, "Voting with Their Feet? Local Economic Conditions and Migration Patterns in New England," *Regional Science and Urban Economics* 40, no. 2–3 (May 2010).

9. The effect of incomes and employment on international migration would also tend to push housing costs up, so that net domestic migration, in total, should be negatively correlated with local incomes, because higher incomes mean more international in-migration.

10. See US Bureau of Labor Statistics, "Consumer Price Index for All Urban Consumers: Rent of Primary Residence in San Francisco–Oakland–Hayward, CA (CBSA)" (CUUSA422SEHA), retrieved from FRED, Federal Reserve Bank of St. Louis; San Francisco Rent Board annual statistical reports, available at http://sfrb.org/rent-board-annual-statistical-report.

CHAPTER 7

1. Note that this is largely a result of regulation and barriers to entry, not taxes. In fact, a common structural problem in expensive cities is that property taxes on existing property owners are too low, and so funding for public goods falls disproportionately on new units, raising their cost.

2. International Labor Organization, *Global Wage Report 2012/13: Wages and Equitable Growth* (Geneva: International Labor Office, 2013), 41–45.

3. Pundits explicitly acknowledge this effect when they complain that credit spreads and risk premiums are too low after long economic expansions—for example, when they complained about low spreads on mortgage securities during the housing boom. Taken literally, complaining that credit spreads are too low is complaining that capital incomes are too low.

4. In the epilogue to this book, I will outline how the framework of "open access orders" and "limited access orders" created by Douglass C. North, John Joseph Wallis, and Barry R. Weingast describes this governance problem, and presents no easy path to follow for its reform.

5. Normally times when the real estate price/income ratio is low should correspond to periods of high real long-term interest rates.

6. For instance, imagine two households with identical incomes—one in suburban Chicago and one downtown. The family living downtown will very likely live in a much smaller unit than the family living in the suburbs. Income is a major determinant of how much we spend on an item as large as housing, and, on average, households make significant adjustments to their housing consumption to fit their incomes before they tend to accept broad increases in housing budgets.

7. Regional price parity tables released by the Bureau of Economic Analysis estimate non-housing prices for goods and sevices in Closed Access cities to be about 5% to 10% higher than average. Bureau of Economic Analysis, "Regional Data: GDP and Personal Income," accessed June 28, 2018, https://www.bea.gov/iTable/index_regional.cfm.

8. Lawrence H. Summers, "Larry Summers: Corporate Profits Are Near Record Highs. Here's Why That's a Problem," *Wonkblog, Washington Post*, March 30, 2016.

9. Thomas Picketty, *Capital in the Twenty-First Century* (Cambridge, MA: Belknap, 2014).

10. Josh Bivens and Lawrence Mishel, "Understanding the Historic Divergence between Productivity and a Typical Worker's Pay" (Briefing Paper No. 406, Economic Policy Institute, Washington, DC, September 2, 2015).

11. Atif Mian and Amir Sufi, "The Most Important Economic Chart," *House of Debt* blog, March 18, 2014.

12. Matthew Rognlie, "Deciphering the Fall and Rise in the Net Capital Share: Accumulation or Scarcity?," *Brookings Papers on Economic Activity* 46, no. 1 (Spring 2015).

13. Some measures of corporate profit also include profit on foreign operations, which also is not a meaningful factor in domestic income shares.

14. The same is true of corporate profit margins. The ratio of the operating surplus of corporations (which includes both profit and interest expense as the total return to all forms of corporate capital) to corporate value-added fluctuated around a relatively stable average level for many decades. Margins have risen slightly above the long-term range after the financial crisis.

15. Here, the income is the rental value of the home. Instead of benefiting from this income by receiving cash, owner-occupiers benefit by not having to make the rental payment.

16. Total net capital income means income after expenses, depreciation, etc.

17. The Consumer Price Index (CPI) reflects prices related to household spending while the GDP deflator is a broader measure of prices across the economy.

18. James K. Galbraith and Travis J. Hale, "The Evolution of Economic Inequality in the United States, 1969–2007: Evidence from Data on Inter-industrial Earnings and Inter-regional Incomes" (UTIP Working Paper No. 57, UT Inequality Project, Lyndon B. Johnson School of Public Affairs, University of Texas, Austin, February 2009).

19. Jason Furman and Peter Orszag, "A Firm-Level Perspective on the Role of Rents in the Rise in Inequality" (presentation at A Just Society Centennial Event in Honor of Joseph Stiglitz, Columbia University, New York, October 16, 2015).

20. One of the defining characteristics of new-economy firms in sectors like tech, biotech, and finance is that there are substantial reputational and network effects that lead to a sort of winner-takes-all life cycle for firms and competitors. In tech, especially, life cycles can be short.
   This leads to two factors that increase profit margins: (1) Any firm can quickly and unexpectedly be knocked from its competitive perch. This means that, to justify investment in disruptive hardware or software, firms need to be able to earn back invested capital quickly. (2) Many potential competitors will not survive the early fight to be the leaders in their categories, so there is tremendous survivorship bias in the financials of existing firms.
   Risky investments that demand a higher return are dependent on successful early-phase investment and implementation, which means that most of the costs of the eventual leaders will be sunk costs with very high future gross profits, and by the time firms are recording profits, most of the sunk costs of the sector as a whole will have been written off the books of failed competitors. So one set of firms has profit margins that are very high, but the sector-

wide profit margins over the full life cycle of the sector should be bid down closer to normal levels by competitive pressures, or to slightly higher-than-normal levels because of the competitive risks.

Let's say your firm has "won" in its category. Now you have an outsized valuation and outsized profit margins. If you ran a car company 50 years ago, your worry on a year-to-year basis was whether you might gain or lose 2% market share. But if you are Facebook, your worry is whether you become Myspace or Friendster. So, what if locating in Silicon Valley greatly increases your costs (which are very low on a cash basis) but decreases your chance of becoming Friendster by 10% every year? That's a no-brainer. You pick up your operations and you move them to Silicon Valley.

True, there are inefficiencies here, which in academic finance have been well covered, pertaining to firms with large cash holdings or high profit margins. When the risks of inefficient operations or financial management aren't imminent or palpable to a firm because of high margins or a large cash stockpile, it is difficult for the discipline of the marketplace to work sharply. This allows managers in such firms to maintain higher costs than investors would normally stomach. But part of the explanation of the higher costs of these highly profitable Closed Access firms must be the value of tapping into specialized and limited pools of labor.

But what if that market inefficiency was the main factor at work here? What if managers put up with higher costs because their high gross margins insulate them from shareholder discipline? Then we should see established tech companies remaining in high-cost cities while startups move to less expensive cities as they battle over who "wins" the next marketplace development. We don't see that, though. Tech startups also seem to be attracted to the high-cost cities, even when they are burning through cash.

21. Jason Furman, "Barriers to Shared Growth: The Case of Land Use Regulation and Economic Rents" (remarks delivered to the Urban Institute, Washington, DC, November 20, 2015), 2.

22. Elisa Giannone, "Skilled-Biased Technical Change and Regional Convergence" (2017 Meeting Papers 190, presented to the Annual Meeting of the Society for Economic Dynamics, Edinburgh, Scotland, June 2017). See particularly Giannone's figure 24, which shows the increasing returns earned by skill. For all cities, since 1980, income growth has been higher for workers with college degrees than it has been for workers without degrees. This is a reversal from the 1940–1980 period. Giannone concludes that much of the shift in income growth away from convergence has come from skill-biased technological change. Figure 24 suggests that this is the case within cities, but that Closed Access cities are responsible for the lack of high-skilled income convergence across metropolitan statistical areas. Wages for workers without college degrees continue to converge across cities, as they had before 1980. And, while a regression of wages for workers with college degrees across cities now does not show convergence, it appears that this is largely because of the Closed Access cities, where incomes are rising at above-average rates, even though wages were higher to begin with. But the general shape of the relationship across cities still has a downward slope (wages in cities that started low rose more), so it appears that even for college-educated workers, convergence continues for the most part outside the Closed Access cities.

23. Jae Song et al., "Firming Up Inequality" (CEP Discussion Paper No. 1354, Centre for Economic Performance, London School of Economics and Political Science, London, May 2015).

24. Stephen Lake, "Debunking the Myth of Higher Pay in Silicon Valley," *Medium*, December 21, 2016.

25. Keep in mind that Canada has a housing supply problem, too, though Toronto appears to be more similar to Seattle than it is to the Closed Access cities.

26. Lake comes to a similar conclusion for midlevel engineers: he estimates that they earn Can$80,000 gross in Toronto, with Can$23,000 left over after cost of living and taxes. In San Francisco, they earn Can$174,000, with Can$12,000 left over.

27. The entry-level worker paid Can$45,000 in taxes in San Francisco and Can$13,000 in Toronto. The midlevel worker paid Can$59,000 in San Francisco and Can$17,000 in Toronto.

28. Richard Florida, "The Extreme Geographic Inequality of High-Tech Venture Capital," *CityLab*, March 27, 2018.

29. Bureau of Economic Analysis, interactive tables for Regional Price Parities at metropolitan statistical area level, https://www.bea.gov/regional/.

30. Since the product offerings in finance are more stable than in sectors like information technology, it may be easier to see this effect in finance. There has been a significant focus on the problem of a bloated and powerful financial sector, frequently termed "financialization." For one example, see Thomas I. Palley, "Financialization: What It Is and Why It Matters" (Working Paper No. 525, Levy Economics Institute of Bard College, Annandale-on-Hudson, NY, December 2007). Closed Access housing leads to bloat of the financial sector because rising real estate values lead to increased mortgage financing and because rising costs of living in financial centers increase the costs of financial services.

31. Chang-Tai Hsieh and Enrico Moretti, "Why Do Cities Matter? Local Growth and Aggregate Growth" (NBER Working Paper No. 21154, National Bureau of Economic Research, Cambridge, MA, May 2015). For a good, broad overview of the challenges of the current wave of urbanization, see Enrico Moretti, *The New Geography of Jobs* (Boston: Mariner Books, 2013); see also work by Richard Florida, such as Richard Florida, *The New Urban Crisis* (New York: Basic Books, 2017).

32. A rentier collects excess income above the competitive rate by owning an asset that has limited competition.

33. Emily Badger, "There Is No Such Thing as a City That Has Run Out of Room," *Wonkblog*, *Washington Post*, October 6, 2015.

34. Sam Roberts, "Commuters Nearly Double Manhattan's Daytime Population, Census Says," *City Room*, *New York Times*, June 3, 2013.

35. One way that developers are responding to this problem is by converting commercial space to residential. "The Trump International Hotel and Tower was the first conversion of a modern high rise office building to residential use." Stockton Williams, "Solving Two Problems: Converting Unused Office Space to Residential," *Urban Land*, July 22, 2016.

36. How can I refer to the value of Closed Access homes as "intrinsic value" if I claim that prices on those homes would decline sharply if supply were increased? The concept of consumer surplus is important here.

    For homes in Closed Access cities to have very high values, the locations *must have* intrinsic value. Rural Wyoming does not provide intrinsic value for firms in the human-capital-intensive industries that have flocked to the Closed Access cities. So no amount of supply constraints in rural Wyoming will create a market there for a metropolitan area full of million-dollar condos. The fundamental issue of Closed Access isn't whether the real estate has value or not. It does. For the most part, Closed Access doesn't create value, it just transfers it from consumer surplus to economic rents for asset owners, as shown in figure 7-3.

    Adam Smith explained this concept with his paradox of water versus diamonds. Water is much more useful than diamonds are, but diamonds are much more expensive. The reason is that water is abundant while diamonds are scarce.

    If some monopolist firm cornered the market on water, it could charge *very* high prices for water. That is not because the monopolist will have created value. The monopolist will have simply captured for itself the value that is intrinsic to water. Today, water is plentiful, so its value is captured mainly by its consumers.

    One way to think about this transfer between consumers and asset owners is through our measure of real GDP. It is difficult to measure consumer surplus directly, but one way that we do measure it is through real GDP growth. For instance, the market for automobiles is competitive. If the average car sells for $20,000 and a new innovation allows cars to be manufactured for $5,000 less, the price for an equivalent car will decline until it settles around $15,000. That shift will be recorded as deflation, and real incomes will increase, because consumers will have more income left over to purchase other goods and services as a result of the innovation. The average car won't have a lower intrinsic value. It will still be worth $20,000 to the marginal consumer. But now $5,000 more of that value will be captured as consumer surplus, and the growth in real GDP will roughly reflect the value of that newly captured consumer surplus.

Likewise, the prices of homes in Closed Access cities would decline tremendously if those cities allowed supply to expand. The reason home values would decline is that the rental value of those homes would be permanently reduced. The lower rental values would be recorded as deflation, and real incomes would rise, just as they would with the innovation in automobile manufacturing. A home that rents today for $5,000 per month would still have $5,000 of value, even if it only rented for $2,000 in the future, in the same way that a life-giving glass of water has intrinsic value for you today even though its price isn't jacked up by a monopolist.

37. Bill McBride, "Update: Real Estate Agent Boom and Bust," *Calculated Risk*, June 15, 2015.

38. David H. Autor, David Dorn, and Gordon H. Hanson, "The China Shock: Learning from Labor Market Adjustment to Large Changes in Trade," *Annual Review of Economics* 8, no. 1 (February 2016).

39. Nontradable sectors provide goods and services that are difficult to trade across space—for instance, restaurant visits and services pertaining to health, beauty, fitness, etc. These are things that must be delivered or performed where the customer is. Housing and homebuilding are examples.

40. Autor, Dorn, and Hanson, "China Shock," 28–29.

41. For commentary about the difficulties of class and racial legacies that can prevent opportunity from being widely available, even for those living within a growing metropolitan area, see Alana Semuels, "Chicago's Awful Divide," *Atlantic*, March 28, 2018.

42. Autor, Dorn, and Hanson, "China Shock."

43. Frequently, job training and investment in skill development are suggested as solutions to stagnant labor markets. But there are millions of workers with the will and the ability to take jobs in the Closed Access cities. The problem, on the margin, is not a lack of skill or willingness to work. The problem is that they are physically not allowed entry to the market, through strict limits to housing expansion.

Some suggest that workers should not be expected to move to urban areas for employment, and that instead areas with stagnant labor markets should provide more support in the form of jobs programs, social services, etc. The basis for these proposals is that it isn't just people who are struggling. It is places. And depopulating those places will only cause those places to decline further. It's a compelling point of view, and would that it were so.

There are small ghost towns scattered across the Midwest—usually nothing remains but an old sign denoting a town that no longer exists. These towns existed during a period when most Americans required an occasional horse ride to the general store. When travel was difficult, having a small commercial center every few miles was useful. When these commercial centers weren't necessary anymore, the towns' decline was inevitable. The unfortunate death of these towns was surely painful for their residents, yet progress always requires change and dislocation. Programs for rejuvenation and local support should obviously be applied where they can be useful, but they should not be a siren call for a panacea.

On the other hand, consider the families who have been most exposed to the dislocations of today's technological shift. Poor workers are moving into their towns in an effort to trade up to a better life, but these families can't do the same thing by trading up to the Closed Access cities. Is it any wonder that they feel a sense of unfairness about immigration, in practice?

44. Alicia Sasser, "Voting with Their Feet? Local Economic Conditions and Migration Patterns in New England," *Regional Science and Urban Economics* 40, no. 2–3 (May 2010).

45. Autor, Dorn, and Hanson, "China Shock."

46. Autor, Dorn, and Hanson, 38.

47. Autor, Dorn, and Hanson, 30.

48. Neoclassical economic models are traditional models of supply and demand based on the idea that, on the margin, prices and quantities reflect reasonable costs and benefits of various goods and services, and that markets pushed out of equilibrium will resettle at a new

equilibrium that utilizes inputs efficiently. Neoclassical models are less helpful where natural frictions prevent buyers and sellers from matching production and consumption effectively.

49. Autor, Dorn, and Hanson, "China Shock," 26.

50. David H. Autor, David Dorn, and Gordon H. Hanson, "The China Syndrome: Local Labor Market Effects of Import Competition in the United States," *American Economic Review* 103, no. 6 (October 2013): 2159.

51. Autor, Dorn, and Hanson, "China Shock," 38.

52. In other words, their powerful position in the market allows them to sell fewer services at higher prices than they could in a more competitive environment.

53. Board of Governors of the Federal Reserve System, "Nonfinancial Corporate Business; Corporate Equities; Liability, Level" (MVEONWMVBSNNCB), retrieved from FRED, Federal Reserve Bank of St. Louis; Board of Governors of the Federal Reserve System, "Households and Nonprofit Organizations; Real Estate at Market Value, Level" (HNOREMQ027S), retrieved from FRED, Federal Reserve Bank of St. Louis. Deflated with GDPDEF.

54. The White House, *Housing Development Toolkit*, September 2016.

CHAPTER 8

1. "Too Much of a Good Thing," Business in America, *Economist*, March 26, 2016.

2. Some of this is tax arbitrage. US corporate tax rates are high, so corporations are incentivized to report profits abroad. This likely leads to a shift in how operating profit (profit before interest expense) is reported, with interest expense shifted to the US and profit shifted abroad.

3. Ricardo Hausmann and Federico Sturzenegger, "Global Imbalances or Bad Accounting? The Missing Dark Matter in the Wealth of Nations" (CID Working Paper No. 124, Center for International Development at Harvard University, Cambridge, MA, January 2006).

4. Pierre-Olivier Gourinchas and Hélène Rey, "From World Banker to World Venture Capitalist: US External Adjustment and the Exorbitant Privilege" (NBER Working Paper No. 11563, National Bureau of Economic Research, Cambridge, MA, August 2005).

5. I note, however, that this issue appears to be largely an American issue, and doesn't necessarily generalize well across countries with Closed Access housing problems. Work from the Bank for International Settlements suggests that the US is alone in the extreme advantage it has in its foreign private investment returns, and among other major countries, there doesn't seem to be a systematic relationship between high returns on foreign direct investment and Closed Access housing problems. Alexandra Heath, "What Explains the US Net Income Balance?" (BIS Working Paper No. 223, Bank for International Settlements: Monetary and Economic Department, Basel, Switzerland, January 2007).

6. The Federal Reserve targets the nominal short-term rate. The Fed has little systematic effect on long-term real rates. Those low rates were largely a reflection of high demand for low-risk securities.

7. Paul Krugman, quoted in Financial Crisis Inquiry Commission, *The Financial Crisis Inquiry Report: Final Report of the National Commission on the Causes of the Financial and Economic Crisis in the United States*, January 2011, p. 104. Krugman's use of Spain and Ireland as examples is a little bit awkward for my analysis. Spain, for instance, doesn't seem like a great example of an economy that is bathing in high incomes from limited access economic rents. But I think there is a bit of misplaced hindsight bias in Krugman's observation. The characteristic that makes Ireland and Spain noticeable isn't that they had housing bubbles. It's that they had housing busts. Many countries, such as Canada, Australia, the United Kingdom, France, and Sweden, have seen housing appreciation as strong as appreciation in the US,

Spain, and Ireland, yet prices remained high. Capital flows haven't ended and interest rates haven't risen. If global savings caused the housing bubble, it is the countries that didn't have a bust that should provide the best examples. In hindsight, the bust makes Spain and Ireland *seem* like good examples of housing bubbles, but it actually makes them poorer examples of the relationship between housing bubbles, interest rates, and capital flows.

8. Edward L. Glaeser, Joseph Gyourko, and Raven E. Saks estimate that by the year 2000, home prices in the California coastal metropolitan statistical areas were two to four times the cost of construction. Edward L. Glaeser, Joseph Gyourko, and Raven E. Saks, "Why Have Housing Prices Gone Up?," *American Economic Review* 95, no. 2 (May 2005).

9. Complaints about foreign buyers are often heard in Closed Access cities, but the complaints are only loud because Closed Access makes foreign buyers seem disruptive. Foreign buyers do not appear to have a systematic preference for Closed Access real estate. National Association of Realtors, *2017 Profile of International Activity in US Residential Real Estate* (Washington, DC: NAR Research Division, 2017).

10. Ross Kendall and Peter Tulip, "The Effect of Zoning on Housing Prices" (RBA Research Discussion Paper No. 2018-03, Reserve Bank of Australia, March 2018).

11. Populations in cities such as London, Paris, and Toronto appear to be growing at least as quickly as the populations of their host countries, so the constraints on Closed Access population growth in the US may be more severe than they are in some of the other countries that have had high home prices and capital inflows.

12. Qiao Yu, Hanwen Fan, and Xun Wu, "Global Saving Glut, Monetary Policy, and Housing Bubble: Further Evidence" (working paper, School of Public Policy and Management, Tsinghua University, Beijing, May 2015).

13. Thomas Piketty, Emmanuel Saez, and Stefanie Stantcheva, "Optimal Taxation of Top Labor Incomes: A Tale of Three Elasticities," *American Economic Journal: Economic Policy* 6, no. 1 (February 2014).

14. Edward L. Glaeser, presentation at the Conference on Housing Affordability (American Enterprise Institute, Washington, DC, April 7, 2017), available at https://www.aei.org/events/online-event-conference-on-housing-affordability-presented-by-the-american-enterprise-institute-bank-of-israel-board-of-governors-of-the-federal-reserve-system-tel-aviv-university-and-ucla/.

15. See Paul Romer, "Interview on Urbanization, Charter Cities and Growth Theory," *Paul Romer* blog, April 29, 2015.

16. Emily Hamilton and Salim Furth, "California Can Improve Housing and Transit by Preempting Local Ordinances" (Mercatus on Policy, Mercatus Center at George Mason University, Arlington, VA, March 2018).

17. Robin Harding, "Why Tokyo Is the Land of Rising Home Construction but Not Prices," *Financial Times*, August 3, 2016.

CHAPTER 9

1. Kerwin Kofi Charles, Erik Hurst, and Matthew J. Notowidigdo, "Housing Booms, Manufacturing Decline, and Labor Market Outcomes" (NBER Working Paper No. 18949, National Bureau of Economic Research, Cambridge, MA, April 2013, revised April 2017).

2. This tweet seems like a nice under-140-character summary of both the collaborative, ad hoc nature of Silicon Valley (that creates the demand for residential density) and the obstacles to housing expansion (that prevent residential density from comfortably reaching its potential): "You know you are in Silicon Valley when you have fewer co-workers than housemates" (Katy Levinson, @katylevinson, January 6, 2017).

3. IGM Forum Experts Panel, "Factors Contributing to the 2008 Global Financial Crisis," October 17, 2017, http://www.igmchicago.org/surveys-special/factors-contributing-to-the-2008-global-financial-crisis.

4. Certainly, when a bank fails, that bank was, in hindsight, too optimistic. But this determination, in hindsight, is only the result of the bank having found itself with a lack of money, which was the direct cause of its failure. The benefit of hindsight does not serve to establish optimism as the cause of failure. Here, I will just suggest that if home prices had dropped by 5% and there had been sector-wide failures of financial firms, there may be a case for labeling optimism as the cause of the collapse. But even pessimists are likely to fail when home prices nationwide collapse by a quarter or more. And, by the time most bank failures happened, there had been many public policy choices that explicitly chose instability over stability. Or were bankers supposed to have had a scenario in their 2006 models that included a public policy decision to raise the average FICO score on accepted mortgage applications by 40 points?

    Or maybe optimism was to blame, and because of that optimism, once homes had lost 5% of their value, panics, runs, overleverage, and bank failures caused a snowball effect that led to an additional 25% drop in values after the financial sector imploded. But if that was the case, and a maimed and panicked financial sector was the cause of much of the collapse, then why in the world was monetary and credit policy being tightened so harshly in late 2008?

5. One respondent, Richard Portes of the London Business School, did complain that he believed the failure of the Federal Reserve to act as lender of last resort for Lehman Brothers was an important factor.

6. Robert J. Shiller, "The Housing Market Still Isn't Rational," *The Upshot*, *New York Times*, July 24, 2015.

7. Board of Governors of the Federal Reserve System, "FOMC Statement," press release, August 7, 2007.

8. Ben S. Bernanke, "Ben Bernanke: The Courage to Act," interview by Diane Rehm, *Diane Rehm Show*, NPR, October 6, 2015.

9. For instance, see David Dayen, "Elizabeth Warren Asks Newly Chatty FBI Director to Explain Why DOJ Didn't Prosecute Banksters," *Intercept*, September 15, 2016. And, related, see Elizabeth Warren, Senator, letter to the Honorable Michael E. Horowitz, US Inspector General, September 15, 2016. Warren complained that the FBI had "failed to hold the individuals and companies most responsible for the financial crisis and the Great Recession accountable" for alleged misconduct that occurred in 2006 and after. The presumption that lender excesses were the primary cause of high prices before 2006 changes the meaning of that complaint.

10. Ben S. Bernanke, *The Courage to Act* (New York: W. W. Norton, 2015), 125.

11. American Housing Survey (US Census Bureau).

12. Figure 9 in Christopher L. Foote, Kristopher S. Gerardi, and Paul S. Willen, "Why Did So Many People Make So Many Ex Post Bad Decisions? The Causes of the Foreclosure Crisis" (conference paper presented at Rethinking Finance: New Perspectives on the Crisis, the Princeton Club, New York, April 13, 2012), 55.

13. Karl E. Case and Robert J. Shiller, "Is There a Bubble in the Housing Market?" (Cowles Foundation Paper No. 1089, Cowles Foundation for Research in Economics, Yale University, New Haven, CT, 2004), 340–42.

14. See figure 3-6 and its associated text, regarding the earlier decline in homebuying by both first-time buyers and existing owners. And see figure 5-14 for evidence that the early exodus from homeownership happened among well-to-do households, not middle- or low-income households.

    This is another example of the strange perceptions that the moral panic had fomented. There is no reason to treat a frenzy for AAA-rated securities as a sign of recklessness. Investor demand for AAA-rated securities is clearly a sign of fear and risk aversion. Yet the CDO market has universally been treated as if it was a part a of a reckless bubble mania that had somehow been instrumental in creating high home prices. The CDO market only existed because sentiment among homebuyers had become so *sour* already that a stampede for safe assets was flooding out of home equity and into fixed income.

15. Board of Governors of the Federal Reserve System, "FOMC Statement," press release, August 7, 2007.

16. "Bernanke's Bear Market," Review & Outlook, *Wall Street Journal*, August 6, 2007.

17. Gillian Tett, *Fool's Gold: The Inside Story of J. P. Morgan and How Wall St. Greed Corrupted Its Bold Dream and Created a Financial Catastrophe* (New York: Free Press, 2009), 207.

18. George W. Bush, quoted in Tett, 194.

19. Note, however, the many claims that Fed policy should have been tighter in 2003 through 2005 to help keep home prices from rising. If a model of Fed policy calls for that, then surely the same model should have led to loud demands for much looser policy in 2007 and 2008. A strange consensus has developed in which the Federal Reserve is blamed for the housing bubble, and it is claimed that the Fed should have tightened policy more in 2004 and 2005 to keep home prices from rising, but when prices are collapsing, the Fed is supposed to sit idly by, because if the Fed always steps in to stabilize asset prices, then markets will become complacent.

This is quite a common view. See, for example, William C. Dudley, "The 2015 Economic Outlook and the Implications for Monetary Policy" (Remarks at Bernard M. Baruch College, New York City, December 1, 2014).

What a perverse choice of asymmetry. One might argue that the Fed should react to the prices of assets like homes, or one might argue that it shouldn't. But a principled policy norm that the Fed should react only to keep prices from rising but not to keep them from declining is a recipe for crisis. In fact, the connection between the Closed Access problem and the moral panic that developed is clear here. The misplaced blame for high home prices is the source of this asymmetry.

20. We can conceptually divide economic risk into two categories: (1) idiosyncratic risk and (2) systematic risk. Idiosyncratic risk is the result of competition and change. Even though failing firms will be tempted to petition the government for protection when they experience idiosyncratic risk, it is generally best to let them fail, because their failure is likely the result of some other firm's success. It is the result of progress and change.

Systematic risk is the result of the broad ebbs and tides of an economy. The minimization of systematic risk is a public service. Being relieved of systematic risk allows firms to focus on competition and growth. Idiosyncratic risk is at work when a new bagel shop moves in across the street, leading to the failure of the old bagel shop. Systematic risk is at work when both bagel shops close because a sharp drop in money supply suddenly causes both shops to lose their customers.

The problem with "bubble" explanations for economic phenomena is that a bubble allows us to treat systematic risk as if it were idiosyncratic risk. So, instead of seeing stability as a public service, we see both bagel shops going out of business, and we say, "Well, they had it coming." The mass imposition of failure is treated as a prudent form of discipline. And the more failure is imposed, the more discipline it seems was required.

The fact that the bust infected the entire financial sector and the entire housing market should have been taken as a significant clue that this was a systematic episode that needed a systematic response.

21. Bernanke, *Courage to Act*, 162.

22. Board of Governors of the Federal Reserve System, "FOMC Statement," press release, September 18, 2007.

23. Board of Governors of the Federal Reserve System, "Factors Affecting Reserve Balances," H.4.1 statistical release, last modified July 5, 2018, https://www.federalreserve.gov/releases /h41; Bernanke, *Courage to Act*, 237.

24. *Liquidity* is a sort of general term economists use for cash or things like cash that help individuals to complete transactions.

25. "Until this point we had been selling Treasury securities we owned to offset the effect of our lending on reserves (the process called sterilization). But as our lending increased, that stopgap response would at some point no longer be possible because we would run out of Treasuries to sell." Bernanke, *Courage to Act*, 325.

26. Normally, the Federal Reserve buys and sells Treasuries to adjust the money supply. In normal times, when interest rates are above zero, the Fed tends to describe these activities in terms of an interest-rate target, and the quantity of Treasuries the Fed holds only changes by a few billion dollars here and there. But when the short-term interest rate is near zero, investors don't mind holding cash, because it doesn't cost them much when the alternative is earning interest that is nearly zero anyway. *Quantitative easing* is the term used to describe the large quantities of Treasuries that the Fed had to buy to try to inject enough cash into the economy to meet its inflation target after interest rates dropped to near zero.

27. "The Fed Holds," Review & Outlook, *Wall Street Journal*, September 17, 2008.

28. Antonio Weiss and Karen Dynan, "Housing Finance Reform: Access and Affordability in Focus," *Medium*, October 26, 2016.

29. Quantitative easing happened in three phases, usually referred to as QE1, QE2, and QE3. QE1 purchases lasted from December 2008 to March 2010.

30. Federal Reserve Bank of New York, "Quarterly Report on Household Debt and Credit: Historical (Pre-2003) Data," accessed June 30, 2018, https://www.newyorkfed.org/medialibrary/media/research/national_economy/householdcredit/pre2003_data.xlsx.

31. Consider the perverse effects of that tax credit. Regulators were preventing all but the most financially secure households from getting mortgages. Those that could get mortgages were buying homes that were highly discounted. And the federal government targeted a subsidy at them. It does appear, at least, that the subsidy was helping to stabilize prices by partially making up for the gaping lack of buyer demand that was created by tight lending standards, so that temporarily, existing homeowners had some reprieve from collapsing prices.

EPILOGUE

1. Jeanna Smialek, "Home Price Rebound Creeps into Policy Debate of Bubble-Wary Fed," *Bloomberg Brief: Real Estate*, November 23, 2015, 12.

2. Even worse is the idea that the risk premium should be increased. This is usually described in terms of investors "reaching for yield" by taking on too much risk in order to raise investment returns. Kasia Klimasinska, "Fed's Rosengren Says Search for Yield Is a Risk of Low Rates," Bloomberg, November 15, 2015. A risk premium is waste. Lowering risk premiums is a public good. If higher risk premiums really are beneficial, the stock exchanges and title registries should be closed down. Asset prices will be reliably lower.

   Since buyers wouldn't voluntarily assume a risk premium, it is supplemented with an access premium, with the result that now many households can't qualify for a mortgage, but the ones that do receive handsome, above-market returns. And the rest get ever-rising rents.

3. Aleksandrs Rozens, "Introduction: Global Real Estate and the 'B' Word," *Bloomberg Brief: Real Estate*, November 23, 2015.

4. From 2007 to 2016, the national rate of housing permits ranged from about 1:300 to 1:550. By 2016, the US had recovered and had begun to level off at what had previously been the bottom of V-shaped lows. US Census Bureau, "New Private Housing Units Authorized by Building Permits" (PERMIT), retrieved from FRED, Federal Reserve Bank of St. Louis; US Census Bureau, "Total Population: All Ages Including Armed Forces Overseas" (POP), retrieved from FRED, Federal Reserve Bank of St. Louis.

5. Douglas C. North, John Joseph Wallis, and Barry R. Weingast, *Violence and Social Orders: A Conceptual Framework for Interpreting Recorded Human History* (New York: Cambridge University Press, 2009).

6. North, Wallis, and Weingast, 114.

7. Hernando de Soto, *The Mystery of Capital* (New York: Basic Books, 2000).

8. We aren't going to see favelas on the outskirts of San Francisco where informal shanties provide shelter for the underclass. The homelessness problem in San Francisco parallels problems we would see in third-world cities, but if the homeless population gathered together in some abandoned industrial part of town and erected a city of cardboard, plywood, and tin, as similar populations do in third-world countries, the city government would be organized and powerful enough to tear it down.

9. Edward L. Glaeser, Joseph Gyourko, and Raven E. Saks, "Why Have Housing Prices Gone Up?," *American Economic Review* 95, no. 2 (May 2005).

10. J. K. Dineen, "Long Shadows Create Political Hurdle for S.F. Skyscraper Project," *San Francisco Chronicle*, April 28, 2016.

11. The $12 million, if we discount it at 5%, amounts to a perpetual payment to the city of $2,000 for every hour that a shadow is cast on a park. (That assumes that there is never cloud cover or morning fog in San Francisco.)

12. Notice how filtering these political restrictions through putative markets allows the anger and blame to shift to landlords charging market rates. What a strange phrase—"market rate"—to describe the price of the new building, a price that is mostly attributable to fees, kickbacks, taxes, and obstructions. It is interesting how that phrase creates a sort of rhetorical lie that buildings sell for two or three times their cost because of the *market*. The rhetoric encourages us to suppose that to solve the housing problem, we need to protect renters from *landlords*. This is an example where barriers to entry are the overwhelming source of inequity, but a focus on negotiating power is more tantalizing. Policy prescriptions that arise from this error simply add to the problem by imposing further limited access order rules.

13. Dineen, "Long Shadows."

14. I am using a $300 million present value estimate for the $647 million Mello-Roos tax.

15. This might be the case at a very local scale. What an odd time and place this is, in which adding value to a location reduces support for its development.

16. Here is another example of public conversation in a limited access order, from Tim Wu, "Why Are There So Many Shuttered Storefronts in the West Village?," *New Yorker*, May 24, 2015.

    > "High-rent blight" happens when rising property values, usually understood as a sign of prosperity, start to inflict damage on the city economics that Jane Jacobs wrote about. . . .

    > If high-rent blight hurts New York's municipal economy, what, if anything, might be done? Because the problem is tied almost inextricably to the value of New York real estate generally, there are no simple fixes. The #SaveNYC movement and the Small Business Congress NYC advocate the regulation of lease renewal. They support a bill written by the small-business advocate Steve Null that tries to limit rent spikes by making commercial-lease-renewal disputes subject to mandatory mediation and arbitration, like some baseball salaries. Gale Brewer, the Manhattan borough president, supports a different regulation of lease renewals, coupled with zoning rules, that encourages landlords to quit waiting for the jackpot and to start renting. Some, like Moss, want to fine landlords who leave storefronts abandoned, in the hope that they'll then rent to smaller, quirkier companies instead of Chipotle. There may also be other original solutions to the specific problem of high-rent blight, such as, perhaps, finding ways to let pop-up stores use abandoned spaces on a seasonal basis.

    > Waits, the owner of the House of Cards & Curiosities, doesn't endorse any particular solution. . . . But he said, the tax increases passed on by his landlord have pushed individual businesses like his to the "bursting point."

Notice the litany of mandates and impositions cited in the *New Yorker* article. Nowhere is there mention of supply. This is the anatomy of a limited access conversation. The solution— Open Access—has been exorcised from the field of vision. Proposed solutions all involve control and confiscation.

17. Evolution is an example of path-dependent development. It would be very difficult to make a human from scratch. The recipe for humans contains many vestigial adaptations left over from ancient species that have little to do with our own current biological challenges. Some of those patches work well and some cause problems, but the stew of DNA that makes a human is irreversibly bound up with the challenges that some proto-ape was dealing with 10 million years ago. The only way to make a human is to take a particular evolutionary path that begins in the primordial ooze and ends here. Regional economies and industrial sectors are the same.

18. The reaction of households with lower incomes to a healing housing market will be to maintain their real housing consumption but to take advantage of moderating rents to reduce their nominal housing expenditures. Millions of them have been moving out of the Closed Access cities in order to reduce their nominal housing expenditures, and it would be a huge win to stop that migration flow. The benefits of a healing housing market on the low end of the market would mostly come in the form of things that would *stop* happening.

That's a tough rhetorical argument to win, though. "Look! Our new housing expansion programs are working because rich people are moving into new fancy apartments and low-income families are staying in the same apartments they had." It's a losing argument, even though that outcome is a vast improvement over the current state of affairs, in which a high-income family moves into the low-income family's house and the low-income family moves to Las Vegas because it can't afford to stay.

It seems, at first glance, as though the better solution would be to build below-market-rent (BMR) units so the low-income family can move into one of those units instead of moving to Las Vegas. But the main difference between this solution and the market-rate solution is simply that pieces of the puzzle are unseen rather than seen. With new BMR units, unseen in the city somewhere, on the margin, is a low-income family priced out of the housing market as market rates are bid up; and the seen part of the policy is that, on the margin, a low-income family moves into a BMR unit. The family in the BMR unit might have especially affordable rent, but families in the rest of the city will likely have marginally higher rents because supply in market-rate units will be more constrained. This is simply a ratcheting up of the incongruities that define Closed Access polities.

The main goal to make housing more affordable should be an expansion in total units. The composition of the city's population isn't going to change because local leaders insist on building units that are "affordable" instead of "luxury." The reason high-income households are bidding up the housing stock isn't that Closed Access cities are full of magnificent units. It's that those units are located in Closed Access cities.

But the main point I want to make here is that the existence of BMR units and the expectation that they will continue to be part of a city's housing stock is, a priori, a description of a housing problem that won't be solved. Developers forced to build units at below-market prices will only be able to justify projects where they are confident that the rents for their "market rate" units will provide excessive returns. Those excessive returns must come from future political obstructions. There are many cities in this country with functional housing markets, where families spend a normal, comfortable portion of their incomes on rent. For most families, there are a range of options for real housing consumption, and they tend to settle on a level of housing that fits within a comfortable range of spending for a given income level. What characteristics do cities have where this is the case? Universally, they have policies that allow adequate building of market-rate housing, and they don't have BMR units as part of the city housing policy (except for select units that qualify for typical federal rent subsidies and other programs directed at poverty relief).

The way to make housing affordable is to stop piling a bunch of idiosyncratic costs (taxes, fees, logistics, delays, inflated construction costs, etc.) on new units. The city has complete control over allowing "BMR" units simply by refraining from these impositions. If new housing could be built at cost, it would be affordable. At this point, though there are a variety of paths that take many Closed Access constituents to their shared conclusion, it seems that, at bottom, the one thing that they *don't* want is affordable housing, writ large. They all (homeowners, renters, advocacy groups, etc.) want unaffordable housing, and they want to engage in interest-group battles that carve out exceptions that make their personal housing afford-able (property tax limits, rent control, BMR units, etc.). This is understandable. As I outline in this epilogue, once an electorate becomes defined by limited access governance, these sorts of positions are a necessary form of self-defense.

These political battles tend to take on a moral undertone. How much of the motivation for BMR policies comes from a sense of the sanctity of homes and the vulgarity of market prices? This same sense seems to populate opinions about things like education and healthcare, too. While these attitudes come from an understandable motivation, a lack of appreciation for the power of market prices to undergird an affordable and civil economy is leading to policies that are causing these sectors to eat city dwellers alive. Because housing is local, the experi-ences of different cities demonstrate the damage that can be done in the name of sanctity. This sense of markets imposing vulgarity on transactions that have an element of sanctity causes many people to be more comfortable with demand that is routed through a local com-missar, who doles out supply in a fashion that is explicitly sanctified by an organized program of desert and fairness, than with demand that is supplied by uncaring landlords and develop-ers. Where this sense of sanctity has a strong hold on local policy choices, concerns about the vulgarity of markets tend to overwhelmingly be expressed through political opposition to new units, and cities have very low rates of new building. As a result, these cities tend to also be places where vulnerable families are stressed out by high costs and a lack of choices.

Parts of this endnote have been taken from my blog post "Housing: Part 189—Below Market Rate Housing," *Idiosyncratic Whisk*, December 1, 2016.

19. For an extensive review of the history of California housing policy developments, see Kim-Mai Cutler, "How Burrowing Owls Lead to Vomiting Anarchists (or SF's Housing Crisis Explained)," *TechCrunch*, April 14, 2014.

20. Michael C. Munger, "'Euvoluntary' Exchange and the 'Difference Principle'" (paper pre-sented at the Property, Markets, and Morality Symposium, University of North Carolina at Greensboro, Greensboro, NC, March 18–20, 2011).

21. Adam Ozimek, "Sticky Rents and the CPI for Owner-Occupied Housing" (working paper, Econsult Solutions, Philadelphia, January 2014), 10–11.

22. Bruce Yandle and Adam Smith, *Bootleggers and Baptists: How Economic Forces and Moral Persuasion Interact to Shape Regulatory Politics* (Washington, DC: Cato Institute, 2014).

23. As a general rule, presume that widespread problems have a systemic or structural source and specific problems have an idiosyncratic source. The fact that the housing supply prob-lem has developed during the same period of time in several cities (and, in fact, in many cities with similar profiles, internationally) suggests that something structural and specific to our time is at work. The citizens of these cities didn't all decide to be unreasonable at the same time. The breadth of the problem suggests that the development of the different factions engaged with this issue is the product of contemporaneous forces of technology, political norms, etc. If outcomes have become dysfunctional, such as millions of low-income households being forced to move away from economic opportunity, this is a sign of a struc-tural problem. In the end, the solution won't come from one faction overpowering another so much as from changing the political structure that enables these factions.

The same problem exists in the reactions to credit markets. Causation for the housing bubble is frequently assigned to individual choices of bankers and homebuyers—anecdotes about unsophisticated buyers being pushed into homes that were too expensive, flippers greedily and recklessly bidding up prices in a speculative frenzy, bankers unloading increas-ingly toxic mortgage securities. As with the political activities in the local housing disputes, these activities create a disgust response, and their causal import tends to be overstated. This is counterintuitive, but the fact that so many bankers and investors were engaged in similar activity should lead observers to give less weight to the individual choices that they were making.

As with the factions in the local housing supply debates, the sudden rise and fall of these phenomena in credit and investment markets suggests a structural issue. The unfortunate focus on fraudulent lending and irrational speculating detracts from the focus that will provide understanding. (This is not to say that there are no unethical bankers or irrational buyers.) There still remain questions about cause. But the focus should be on the factors that might have pushed prices higher or lower in different contexts rather than on who did what, or how some category of actors *did this to us* and deserved punishment.

This is why the pervasive recent concern about "bubbles" is so dangerous. Conceiving of these trends as "bubbles" creates a subtle rhetorical shift. Now, rhetorically, humans are cast as lemmings, irrationally plunging with one another off the cliff—each individually succumbing to maladapted psychology. Hence, a systematic event is recast as the accumulation of millions of individual irrational errors that are prone to happen together because of a herding instinct. There doesn't seem to be a need to look for systematic causes when the herding explanations are satisfying.

24. Issi Romem, "Can US Cities Compensate for Curbing Sprawl by Growing Denser?," *BuildZoom*, September 14, 2016.

25. Alexander McQuilkin, "The Rise and Fall of Manhattan's Density," Architectural League of New York, *Urban Omnibus*, October 29, 2014.

26. David Neiman, "How Seattle Killed Micro-housing," *Sightline Institute*, September 6, 2016. David Neiman's article, which had the tagline "One bad policy at a time, Seattle outlawed a smart, affordable housing option for thousands of its residents," outlines a series of regulatory hurdles that developed over a period of years, strangling the nascent market in urban dormitory-style housing that had been filling a need for affordable shelter. The comments on that article are a view into the cultural changes that develop in Closed Access cities. There is a highly negative correlation between the frequency and passion of public debates about housing in a city and the number of new homes that are built there. Seattle does not yet have all the characteristics of a Closed Access city, but it is becoming one. Debates and complaints about new housing are visible and ubiquitous in the California cities and New York City.

Sometimes, these conflicts are blamed on the need for new housing in those established cities to be in-fill housing, which upsets the balance of existing neighborhoods. But this is more of a cultural matter than a logistical matter. Consider a new homeowner buying a new tract home at the edge of a development in Phoenix. That homeowner will experience more change, more upheaval in infrastructure and surrounding amenities, than a homeowner in a core Closed Access city could imagine. Freeways will be planned, adjusted, rerouted, and built. Schools will bulge, shift, and redistrict. Retail will fill in, in fits and starts.

The difference between the homeowners in established Closed Access cities, who picket and petition to obstruct new housing, and the homeowners in suburban Phoenix, who generally accept the convulsions of their local environs, is culture and expectations. San Franciscans will fight for years over one condo building going up in their neighborhood. In the same period of time, homeowners on the outskirts of Phoenix will be surrounded by whole new neighborhoods. There is nothing fated about this difference. The young immigrants and hopefuls who have moved to New York City, San Francisco, and LA for decades moved there because these were dynamic places. They should have no more claim or expectation of stability than the homeowners on Phoenix's developed frontier.

27. This includes an unwillingness to accept prices as information. Nonmarket prices destroy information. Nonmarket prices also diminish the availability of alternatives in the market (as discussed earlier regarding euvoluntary exchange). These two effects mean that policy prescriptions that use nonmarket pricing can be very corrosive and damaging, and frequently lead to wasted and underutilized resources and to social unrest.

APPENDIX

1. In other words, yields tend to be close to those on other types of assets with similar risks. This is the price that maintains a relative value with other assets. In the strict sense, this idea applies to assets with very defined substitutability, such as a stock and a derivative based on that stock. In those cases, a no-arbitrage condition is a mathematical absolute. Here, I am using the concept in a looser sense, to mean that, if the housing yield has tended to move

in parallel with the risk-free yield for many years, then the difference between those yields must reflect a general, long-standing set of risk factors that serves as a loose tether on prices. In checking for efficiency, we might first check to see whether the yields diverge from their long-standing relationship. If they do not, this is a good sign that the markets are finding efficient prices. If they do diverge, then this is mathematically expressed as a change in the risk premium, and our challenge is to find the source of that change.

2. Philip Lowe, "National Wealth, Land Values, and Monetary Policy" (speech for the 54th Shann Memorial Lecture, University of Western Australia, Perth, Australia, August 12, 2015); see also Callan Windsor, Jarkko P. Jaaskela, and Richard Finlay, "Housing Wealth Effects: Evidence from an Australian Panel," *Economica* 82, no. 327 (2015).

3. This is similar to income treatment for most financial securities. Lenders book nominal cash payments as interest income, and pay taxes on it, even though the portion of the interest payment that reflects inflation is not income at all, in the real sense.

4. Board of Governors of the Federal Reserve System, "Households; Owners' Equity in Real Estate as a Percentage of Household Real Estate, Level" (HOEREPHRE), retrieved from FRED, Federal Reserve Bank of St. Louis. Leverage spiked in 2006, but this was after prices leveled off and housing starts began to collapse. The spike in leverage was part of the beginning of the bust.

5. Table 7.12 (Imputations in the National Income and Product Accounts) from Bureau of Economic Analysis, available at https://www.bea.gov/iTable/index_nipa.cfm; table B.101 (Households; Owner-Occupied Real Estate Including Vacant Land and Mobile Homes at Market Value) from the Federal Reserve's Financial Accounts of the United States.

6. Here, as I do throughout the book, I use "efficiency" in the financial sense—meaning that predictable excess profits aren't available by trading two assets against one another—rather than in the sense that economists use the term.

7. For a review of the existing literature on estimating housing valuations and testing for market inefficiencies, see Christopher J. Mayer, "Housing Bubbles: A Survey," *Annual Review of Economics* 3 (September 2011).

   Other models that suggest that home prices in 2005 could be generally explained by fundamentals such as expected rent and costs of ownership include Christopher J. Mayer and Todd Sinai, "U.S. House Price Dynamics and Behavioral Economics," in *Policymaking Insights from Behavioral Economics*, ed. Christopher L. Foote, Lorenz Goette, and Stephan Meier (Boston: Federal Reserve Bank of Boston, 2009); Margaret Hwang Smith and Gary Smith, "Bubble, Bubble, Where's the Housing Bubble?" (Brookings Papers on Economic Activity No. 1, Brookings Institution, Washington, DC, Spring 2006).

8. Charles Himmelberg, Christopher Mayer, and Todd Sinai, "Assessing High House Prices: Bubbles, Fundamentals, and Misperceptions," *Journal of Economic Perspectives* 19, no. 4 (Fall 2005).

9. Edward L. Glaeser, Joshua D. Gottlieb, and Joseph Gyourko, "Can Cheap Credit Explain the Housing Boom?" (NBER Working Paper No. 16230, National Bureau of Economic Research, Cambridge, MA, July 2010).

10. On such a stable measure as long-term real interest rates, which tend to shift slowly over time and which we can only estimate until recently, it is difficult to come to firm conclusions about rate sensitivity. In the 1970s, when home yields appear to have declined along with real interest rates, it could be that high inflation had increased the tax and hedging value of homes, which lowered their pretax yields at a time that happened to coincide with low real interest rates. And, in the decade after 2000, the development of persistent rent inflation in several cities lowered home yields again (because total returns now included a growth factor plus the yield of net rent). And, again, this coincided with low real interest rates. So the high correlation of housing yields with rate movements could be spurious. Or, possibly, some causation runs from yields in housing to risk-free long-term real interest rates.

11. I treat cash flow values the same way for owner-occupiers and for renters. Owners do not pay cash income, but, in the aggregate, in an efficient market, the value of the house should

reflect the market rent the home would fetch. I also treat all homes as unleveraged for the sake of valuation in this exercise. Here, I treat net rent to gross rent as a constant ratio. As values on a given property rise above replacement value, net income should be a larger portion of gross rent. This would mean that the future gross rent inflation required to justify high prices would be lower. On the other hand, investors in properties with prices well above replacement value (because of political exclusion) should also demand a higher discount rate for political risk, which would have the opposite effect. The basic relationship I find between rent, rent expectations, and price would not change, though. Only the scale of the relationship would change with major changes in these assumptions. Certainly, as with any model, changing specifications can change the details of the model's results. Here, I think we can regard this at the conceptual level without debating the exact specifications too much, because using this model we can see that there is a strong relationship between rent and price at the metropolitan statistical area level, under any specification. And the relationship itself seems to have been widely written off in debates about the housing market over this period.

12. This model is based on pretax yields. We should expect post-tax yields on housing to include a premium compared to yields on treasuries, but since homes include substantial tax benefits, the pretax premium on housing yields is likely not significant. In the model, the valuation in each city will be calibrated so that valuations in 1995 reflect an expectation of zero rent inflation. This calibration will be created by using a constant multiplier. To the extent that there is a yield premium that doesn't match the discount rate that I have constructed here, it will be reflected in that constant multiplier. In any event, discretionary differences in the discount rate should be minor, and the relative importance of rent as an explanation is not sensitive to the discount rate.

13. Property Tax Estimates, 2005–2007 Avg., from the Tax Foundation, "Property Tax Data by County," accessed July 2, 2018.

14. The Case-Shiller and Bureau of Labor Statistics data I use here are different sources of data than the Zillow rent and price data I use elsewhere, but they tell a similar story.

15. The 2.5% adjustment in the discount rate is the rate that makes $0.4 \times 30\text{-}Year\ TIPS\ Yield(t) + 2.5\%$ equal to the estimated real 30-year treasury rate in 1995. In the model, after 1995, the discount rate applied to home values reflects 40% of subsequent changes in the 30-year real treasury rate. Changing this sensitivity changes the relative valuation of homes in all cities. If we assume 100% sensitivity to long-term real interest rates, homes were undervalued across the country in 2005. If we assume no sensitivity to real long-term interest rates, homes were overvalued across the country. But this specification has little effect on the relationship of rent inflation to prices among the different cities, as described in the following pages.

16. Since owner-occupiers do not pay rent to themselves, they do not experience rent inflation directly. This may also trigger a cognitive bias. In a city where rent is persistently rising faster than prices in general, homeowners will not have a way to mentally benchmark their home prices to their imputed rent. They will naturally benchmark the rising values of their homes to prices in general. This would add to the perception that home prices are disconnected from fundamental values. Where renters might greet rising rents with indignation, owner-occupiers would naturally not tend to notice the rising rental values of their homes. It is difficult to intuit a market price on an asset that we rent to ourselves, when that same rent would seem high and would make us angry if we had to pay it to someone else.

17. On a natural log scale, an increase in the natural log price of 1 is generally associated with an increase in the price/rent ratio of more than 4. In the model, I have associated an increase in price/rent of 4× with a log increase in price of 1, which is roughly an increase of 3× for each doubling in price.

18. Since the model assumes zero growth expectations in 1995, it may be more accurate to say that these are the expected future rent inflation rates relative to the rates expected in 1995. If we were to be more picky about this specification, I suspect that we might assume that New York City still had slightly positive expectations in 1995, so that the model understates its current rent expectations, but that LA and Boston had seen five years of relative rent deflation of 2% annually in 1995, so their current rent expectations might be slightly overstated.

19. The 2005 estimates of expected rent inflation are adjusted for the price/rent effect described in chapter 4. Rent expectations in 2014 are not adjusted for that effect, which, in any event, should be low or negligible for most cities because of the contraction in home prices.

20. In figure A-10, the outlier in the dots that compare 2005 expectations with rent inflation from 2000 to 2005 is San Francisco. Expected rent inflation implied by home prices in 2005 was about 1.2%. In the short period from 2000 to 2005, rent inflation took a brief rest because of the decline in the tech sector. The R^2 value of this regression is above 0.5 without San Francisco. In the other regressions, San Francisco is not an outlier, because rent inflation in San Francisco over longer time periods is higher.

21. Some of what appears, in the model, to be rent inflation expectations could instead be from higher net rental income. As rents move well above the unencumbered replacement value of the property, the value of the home is mostly due to the value of exclusion, which accrues to the land. This value does not depreciate and doesn't require maintenance and upkeep. So, in high-priced Closed Access cities, net rental income might be higher as a proportion of gross rental income. This would mean that expectations of future rent inflation would not have to be as high as the levels implied by the model, since some of the added value is coming from this higher net margin.

22. Giovanni Favara and Jean Imbs, "Credit Supply and the Price of Housing," *American Economic Review* 105, no. 3 (March 2015); Jack Favilukis, Sydney C. Ludvigson, and Stijn Van Nieuwerburgh, "The Macroeconomic Effects of Housing Wealth, Housing Finance, and Limited Risk-Sharing in General Equilibrium," *Journal of Political Economy* 125, no. 1 (February 2017); Gianni La Cava, "Housing Prices, Mortgage Interest Rates, and the Rising Share of Capital Income in the United States" (RBA Research Discussion Paper No. 2016-04, Reserve Bank of Australia, May 2016).

23. Òscar Jordà et al., "The Rate of Return on Everything, 1870–2015" (NBER Working Paper No. 24112, National Bureau of Economic Research, Cambridge, MA, December 2017).

ABOUT THE AUTHOR

Kevin Erdmann was a small business owner for 17 years. In 2010, he sold his business and earned his master's degree in finance from the University of Arizona, which grounded his real-world experience of investing in the rigor of the academy.

In 2013, he began blogging at idiosyncraticwhisk.com to share his contrarian observations about investment strategies and research. He was surprised to uncover evidence that seemed to contradict conventional narrative and common assumptions about the housing bubble and the financial crisis. As the evidence accumulated, he developed a new account of the causes of the housing bubble and financial crisis. That account eventually became a two-book project, *Shut Out* and a follow-up book still in development, both of which synthesize and expand on the housing theories he originally published on his blog.

He lives in Gilbert, Arizona, with his wife and three kids.

ACKNOWLEDGMENTS

This book is a bit of an accident. It only exists because I happened to discover an alternative history that kept getting deeper and broader as I kept probing to confirm it. Pulling together all of the threads of this new history required a long book (two books, as it turns out), which was a task I had neither intended to embark on nor prepared for. I owe its existence to the patience, generosity, and assistance of a number of people.

Michael Kelley has been my research assistant. He gathered and compiled data from the IRS, the American Housing Survey, and the American Community Survey. His assistance was very helpful in determining what those sources could tell us and in compiling it in a way that was informative and useful.

It has been a pleasure to work with Patrick Horan and Ben Klutsey, who have managed the project at Mercatus. This has been true of all the Mercatus staff, including Kate De Lanoy, Thomas Ressler, Bob Ewing, and others too numerous to list.

The project started with a bloated and meandering manuscript that the first, unfortunate reviewers had to slog through. I don't know who those reviewers are, but they probably deserve as large a thanks as anyone. The developmental editor, John Paine, helped tame that beast into what I hope is now a readable and succinct text. It certainly is much better than it was, and it took a significant amount of wholesale restructuring to make it that way.

Corrie Schwab performed some of the final editing, which was made more difficult, I am sure, by my habit of adding multiparagraph endnotes at a point where we should have been addressing the placement of dependent clauses.

Charts and graphs have been instrumental in my discovery of this story, and I believe that they are instrumental in my communication of it. Including more than 100 figures in a book like this is more than a bit unusual, and managing editor Mark Ingebretsen had the unenviable task of managing the figures, on a tight schedule to boot. He and the design team did a great job. I was afraid that many of these figures would not make the transition from their original color format to black and white well, but I think they have turned out nicely.

Garrett Brown, the senior director of publications at Mercatus, has been an invaluable guide to a rookie author. I am indebted to Garrett for having enough faith in the project to work hard at getting as wide a distribution as we could; and to Jon Sisk, the Rowman and Littlefield acquiring editor, for being willing to listen to Garrett and take a chance on a first-time author.

I also need to thank my blog readers, who saw all of this first in a stream-of-consciousness form that only became a coherent paradigm over the course of months and years. When I look back, I see that some of the central themes of the work were posed as challenges and questions from readers before their importance had even dawned on me. Especially, I need to thank Ken Duda, who was reading the series of housing posts back at the very beginning, when the idea of a book was the last thing on my mind and when I would blather on for pages about things like housing tax policies. Once that growing series of posts had coalesced into a big idea, Ken was instrumental in supporting a book project and encouraging me to approach Mercatus. Learning is, by its nature, a disruptive and radical process. Ken recognized that I had happened upon a way of looking at the existing information that would continue to surprise us. I am deeply honored by the trust that was given by Ken, and then by the staff and the scholars at Mercatus, to push ahead with this intellectual pursuit of "creative destruction," not knowing the conclusions it may lead to.

This gratitude extends to the broader online community. I couldn't have begun to do this work without the development of the internet and the democratization of communications that includes public availability of so much data from public sources like the Census Bureau and the Federal Reserve, and private sources like Zillow.com. To a large extent, the insights of my work were made possible because of the generous way Zillow.com handles much of their data.

That democratization has also been made possible by the willingness of scholars to use blogs and online publishing to be accessible to those outside the academy. Several bloggers were willing to address my work based on its merits, and this included Scott Sumner and Tyler Cowen. Long ago, Garrett Peterson invited me to share the work on his podcast, *The Economics Detective*; and more recently, David Beckworth was willing to share the work with his listeners at *Macro Musings*, which helped get the word out while the book was still being finished.

Because I come from outside the academy, there is sometimes an autodidactic element to the mental models I use. This may explain why I, of all people, happen to be the one who saw and developed this evidence in a new way. But it also makes the work more difficult to audit, because my methods may sometimes have subtle differences from textbook approaches. Scott Sumner and Mercatus editor Tracy Miller spent many hours reviewing the economics to help me divine where it was idiosyncratic versus where it was just weak or wrong. There may still remain some weak or wrong elements, but if that is the case, it is due to the generous way in which Scott, Tracy, and the rest of the Mercatus staff have treated the end result as a product of my learning process and my voice. I am grateful for the great pains they have taken to help make it a stronger product while allowing me the freedom to express it on my terms, even where they may not entirely agree with my approach.

I also want to thank my family: my mom and dad, Ruth and Harold Erdmann, for teaching us the value of working hard and doing things the right way, mostly by setting an example. My dad passed away before this project developed, and it saddens me that I can only guess at what he might have thought of it. Also, I am grateful for the faithful support of my mother-in-law, Amy Brady.

Finally, blogging was my wife, Jennifer's, idea. If I hadn't begun to blog, I wouldn't have started to create serialized records of these ideas, and the ideas in this book would have probably remained a scattered set of curiosities uttered over the dinner table rather than a cohesive new point of view. As my thinking expanded into such an extended project, however, my efforts were sometimes diverted away from the more important needs of my family—Jennifer, Adam, Keegan, and Paige. I trust that with the certainty of hindsight, we will look back at this as the beginning of something new. But in the meantime, they have endured too many uncertainties. They have my eternal love and gratitude for all the times they have chosen to support my quixotic efforts, and a plea for forgiveness for the times when they had little choice. Every day, they are a reminder that behind all those scatterplots and line graphs, life is about appreciating the small stuff of our lives—laughing together, loving each other—while muddling through the tough times together.